OPENING UP

JAMES FARRER

OPENING UP

Youth Sex Culture and Market Reform in Shanghai

THE UNIVERSITY OF
CHICAGO PRESS

CHICAGO AND LONDON

James Farrer is assistant professor of sociology at Sophia University in Tokyo and earned a Ph.D. from the University of Chicago in 1998.

The University of Chicago Press, Chicago 60637
The University of Chicago Press, Ltd., London
© 2002 by The University of Chicago
All rights reserved. Published 2002
Printed in the United States of America

11 10 09 08 07 06 05 04 03 02   1 2 3 4 5
ISBN: 0-226-23870-9 (cloth)
ISBN: 0-226-23871-7 (paper)

Library of Congress Cataloging-in-Publication Data

Farrer, James (James C.)
    Opening up : youth sex culture and market reform in Shanghai / James Farrer.
        p.   cm.
        Includes bibliographical references and index.
        ISBN 0-226-23870-9 (cloth : alk. paper) — ISBN 0-226-23871-7 (pbk. : alk. paper)
        1. Youth—China—Shanghai—Sexual behavior. 2. Sex—China—Shanghai—Public
opinion. 3. Man-woman relationships—China—Shanghai—Public opinion. 4. Youth—
China—Shanghai—Social conditions. 5. Shanghai (China)—Social conditions. 6. Public
opinion—China—Shanghai. I. Title.
HQ18.C6   F37   2002
306.7'0835'0951132—dc21

                                                            2001005454

To Gerry Suttles

CONTENTS

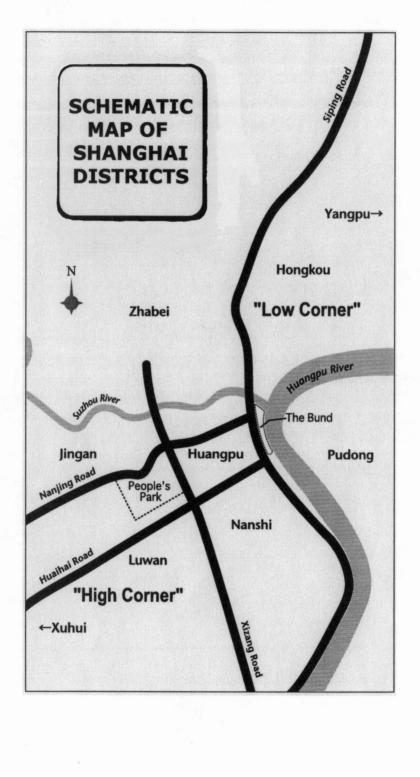

ACKNOWLEDGMENTS

I most want to acknowledge the very many anonymous people in Shanghai who contributed to this study, especially those whose words, ideas, and actions appear in these pages. I must also thank teachers and friends at the University of Chicago who inspired or guided this research, especially Gerry Suttles, William Parish, Wendy Griswold, James Schulman, David Smilde, William Schaeffer, Mary Brinton, Prasenjit Duara, George Chauncey, and the members of the Culture and Society Workshop. Special thanks are due to Xu Anqi, Lu Hanlong, and Zhao Nianguo at the Shanghai Academy of Social Sciences, who supported my work in Shanghai and made my group interviews a success. More recently, my great colleagues at Sophia University have provided incisive critique and support, including David Slater, David Wank, John Clammer, Rich Gardner, Linda Grove, Antoni Ucerler, Angela Yiu, Thierry Robouam, John McCreery, Harold Wippich, and Kate Nakai. Also, two anonymous reviewers from the University of Chicago Press provided key critical advice. Doug Mitchell, Robert Devens, and Erin DeWitt provided generous and deft editorial guidance. Watanabe Yuko created the map of Shanghai. Alan Lepp assiduously edited sections of this manuscript, and Gerry Suttles edited all of it, *several times.* Though the flaws of this book are all mine, its strengths owe much to Gerry, and I dedicate this book to him, a great sociologist and friend without whose aid and inspiration I never would have conceived nor finished this daunting task.

Too many people in Shanghai contributed to this book for me to thank all of them, but I want to especially thank those friends who often went beyond the call of friendship in supporting my work, including Danielle Zhuang, Sun Zhongxin, Shi Mengqian, Wang Xin (Mian Mian), John Uldrich, Chen Zhaoxiang, Fons Tuinstra, Yuan Wanli, Jack Marr, Fritz Hoffman, Ian Johnson,

Zhuang Min, Zhang Chen, Luo Yun, Nakano Tetsu, and, above all, my family in Shanghai—"Mom," "Dad," Fangfang, Wei, and Sensen—who took such good care of me. I also must thank my own parents, James and Billie Farrer, whose years of patient support allowed a boy from Chattanooga, Tennessee, to travel so far and see so many things. Finally, this book would have been completely different without the wit and inspiration of my wife, Gracia, who contributed both spirit and substance. She has guided and aided me from beginning to end.

This research was made possible by an international predissertation research fellowship from the Social Science Research Council with funds from the Ford Foundation and the American Council of Learned Societies and a Fulbright-Hays dissertation research fellowship from the U.S. Department of Education.

INTRODUCTION
Sex and the Market

In the spring of 1989, while China roiled in political protests, I observed the events on the mainland from Taiwan, piecing together a story from media reports and travelers' accounts. One such personal story was told to me by an American teacher at the English-language school where I worked, describing a brief but passionate sexual affair with a young Chinese woman working at his Beijing hotel, beginning with embraces in a park close by the protests in Tiananmen and ending in a night making love in the hotel where she worked. We fellow teachers were taken aback. Such casual sexual affairs seemed increasingly common in Taipei, but we still imagined mainland China to be a society where premarital sex was rare and foreigners kept at arm's length. The young woman could lose her job. She had acted foolhardily; he, irresponsibly. On the other hand, the story as he told it seemed intimately tied to the momentous public events in China: the personal sexual revolution of a young woman encouraged in her quest by a visiting American, a bold act staged against the backdrop of a political revolution led by youth bearing an American-inspired "Goddess of Liberty." Both narratives of rebellion, the political and the sexual, seemed convincing at the time, and we other young male teachers secretly envied the American participant. Probably this was my first personal Chinese sexual story, this romantic allegory of social and sexual revolution.

Many popular accounts of social change in China still present us with this type of romantic tale—a "sexual revolution" in China led by China's urban youth, struggling against oppression, and guided by foreign models. I am not telling that story in this book, rather, I am using it as a starting point—a "representative anecdote"—that reveals not only the romantic logic of a dominant narrative of sexual revolution I once shared, but also how such stories of social

1

change shape social experience, not only for researchers but for participants as well. For the most part, my own romantic notions of sexual and social revolution had soured in my imagination by the time I went to China for my first extended stay. The larger political revolution in China seemingly had failed and faded quickly in the popular imagination. Graduate education—Foucault, feminism, and queer theory—had discredited my naive concept of sexual liberation, without, however, replacing it with a more convincing story. With this peculiar mix of deconstructed romantic sentiments and poststructuralist cultural theory, I began my predissertation field trip in the fall of 1993 in Shanghai, a city I had never even visited but that was supposedly returning to prominence as a cultural leader in China—in other words, a choice grounded in another story of social change, the "reemergence" of Shanghai to its former glory.

At first Shanghai wasn't the site of sexual foment I expected. Compared with American college students, students I met at Shanghai's elite Fudan University were cagey about talking about sexual relationships. Their sexual attitudes seemed conservative, even in comparison with friends in Taipei. In 1993 there was almost nothing of the wild nightlife that seemed a key site of Taipei's ongoing sexual changes. Even Shanghai's winter streets seemed colorless. At the same time, on this first trip in 1993, I fell in love with a Shanghaiese woman, and this intensely passionate experience informed my later project in innumerable and unexpected ways. While living out one personal romantic narrative, I became aware that the stories others were telling around us, and about us, were not romantic stories of "liberation" or of "sexual awakening," but morally ironic stories that cast foreign men less as heroic agents than as convenient vehicles for emigration, and young Chinese women less as romantic heroines than as conniving pragmatists. On the other hand, I heard countervailing stories of romantic passion told by Chinese women, including my girlfriend. Gradually I realized that this dual discourse of material and romantic motives was widely employed by Shanghaiese, not simply to relationships involving foreign men, but as a general rhetoric for expressing and disputing the temptations and compromises of sexual relations in the new market society.

At first I tended to dismiss such stories as clumsy "folk sociology," but I ultimately realized the importance of these sexual stories as everyday media in which the new market society is imagined and critiqued, including stereotypical stories about the generic "others" of the market economy—the "white-collar misses," "little country sisters," "foreigners," and "big moneys" of Shanghai. Such sexual storytelling is a way in which people represent a new market-oriented "modernity" to themselves in China, everyday communicative practices that mediate macrosocial changes.[1] I also became aware of the ability of Shanghai people to collectively fashion stories that transform the conventional meanings of sexual behaviors—including romantic stories that legitimate premarital sexual flings, ironic stories that dismiss failed romances, or jokes and smirks that mark some behavior as "play." My point in this book, then, is not to try to prove the truth of one sexual story over the others—for example, feelings versus pragmatism, free choice versus family pressures, seriousness versus play—but to document Shanghai people's everyday sexual stories and sexual dramas and to understand what they do with them and the social conditions that shape their telling and performance.

The methodological appendix to this book discusses how I did this ethnographic study: finding informants, collecting magazine stories, and conducting focus group interviews. Here I sketch the broad history of this project. In the fall of 1994 I returned to Shanghai to begin systematic fieldwork on the sexual culture of young people in Shanghai. Guided by the inductive orientation of "grounded theory,"[2] I decided that I should let my initial experiences in "the field"—itself an amorphous and idiosyncratic space[3]—guide my data collection. I began with a study of public leisure and entertainment culture, interviewing magazine publishers, writers, "sex experts," and other public figures. While living in local university dorms, I began to visit nightlife spots, including university dance halls, and to conduct group interviews with students at various colleges in Shanghai. This early focus on public culture is most clearly evident in chapter 4 on magazine stories and chapter 9 on dance halls.

As I became more involved in social life in Shanghai outside the university, I focused on the rhetoric of sexuality in everyday social interactions. This sexual rhetoric includes the moralizing discourses of gossip and personal storytelling, on the one hand, and the demonstrative discourses of romancing, flirtation, and sexual play, on the other. Most of the book describes these everyday discursive practices. By 1996 I was married to the girlfriend I had met in 1993 and living in a typical Shanghai housing compound with my in-laws. My social circle now ranged from the white-collar elites and primary school teachers I initially met teaching English in companies and schools, to the factory workers and working-class youth I initially met at local dance clubs. This eclectic group of long-term informants provided the most in-depth information for this study. I also conducted several dozen personal life history interviews and organized a dozen focus group interviews of strangers moderated by Shanghai women. I use these individual and group interview transcripts throughout the book as illustrations of the language Shanghai youth use to talk about sexual matters, and as ways of reconstructing practices in the early reform era. Two follow-up visits of ten weeks each in the spring of 1999 and the summer of 2000 allowed me to revisit long-term informants, conduct new interviews, and observe developments in the fast-changing nightlife and media.

In some ways Shanghai itself is the most important protagonist of the stories I tell. Shanghai in 1993 was at the onset of an economic and building boom on a scale beyond most any in the history of capitalist development. During the 1980s Shanghai had lagged behind southern China in economic development. Former residents returning to the city in the mid-1980s sadly marveled at its dilapidated visage,[4] its famed boulevards and alleyways falling into disrepair. According to popular political folklore, aging Chinese leader Deng Xiaoping's cryptic remarks of "faster, faster" as he crossed a bridge on a 1992 tour of Shanghai signaled a new national focus on developing Shanghai and the Yangtze River basin. Since then the city of 13 million residents (roughly 1 percent of China's population) has experienced spectacular growth, with GDP growth rates over 14 percent in the mid-1990s, outpacing other major Chinese cities.[5] Over $30 billion in foreign investment and $25 billion in basic infrastructure investment have transformed Shanghai's geography. During the 1990s urban Shanghai expanded rapidly into the surrounding countryside, tripling the area of paved roads, doubling residential floor space, and greatly increasing the area of parks and greenery, even in old areas of the city. Shanghai also grew upward. In the mid-1990s fully one-quarter of the world's construction cranes were employed in Shanghai.[6] Buildings over eight stories increased from 959 in 1990 to 4,498 in 1998, while buildings over thirty stories increased from 15 in 1990 to 135 in 1998, including many modern office towers and hotels. The resulting demolition in the inner city meant the forced displacement of hundreds of thousands of residents to new suburbs. At the same time, a vibrant, cosmopolitan consumer culture emerged in Shanghai, driven by a quadrupling of per capita expenses on recreation, clothing, and dining out during the 1990s. Starting from one KFC when I arrived in Shanghai in 1993, dozens of international fast-food restaurants now compete with local chains throughout the city. Hundreds of bars, clubs, and massage parlors[7] now dot the urban nightscape. By the end of the 1990s, former residents who returned to Shanghai found themselves literally lost in an utterly new geography of skyscrapers, urban greenways, subways, elevated highways, Italian boutiques, Japanese *izakaya*, Taiwanese "bubble-tea" shops,[8] and American tequila bars. Simultaneously, there has been a revival of Shanghai's pre-Maoist heritage as a cosmopolitan city. Before 1949 Shanghai was the center of a Chinese sexual modernity, associated with courtesans, starlets, and dance clubs. Something of this earlier sexualized modernity remains embedded in the social geography of the city, its "Occidentalist" boulevard architecture, its penchant for fashion, even its styles of neighborhood gossip.[9] Books on the colonial past are best-sellers in Shanghai.[10] Bars and restaurants deck themselves in 1930s nostalgia. Shanghaiese thus understand their "sexual opening" simultaneously as a con-temporary "foreign influence" as well as the "rekindling of old embers" of Shanghai's own sexual past.[11]

In focusing on Shanghai, I do not suggest that Shanghai is now leading China's cultural development as it did in the 1920s and 1930s.[12] My point is to reproduce a sense of the local texture of sexual culture through a study of a single urban culture, a level of analysis that I feel best represents the complex everyday life worlds, cultural vocabularies, and identities of ordinary Shang-hai people.[13] Methodologically this presents difficulties, of course, since an "ethnography" of an entire city is not possible, and the assembled fragments represent the choices and judgments of one author. This introduction provides what I hope is an orderly outline of the ideas tying together this unruly ethno-graphic project, one whose lapses and digressions are more often evident in the chapters that follow.

Toward a Rhetoric of Sexual Culture

This book describes the sexual culture (xingwenhua)[14] of unmarried heterosexual Shanghai youth (qingnian),[15] concentrating on people from eigh-teen to thirty-five—their dating lives, personal sexual stories, and public nar-ratives—and analyzes how these cultural practices have changed during the market reforms from 1980 to 2000. Most directly, this book contributes to a small but growing ethnographic literature on sex and love in contemporary China.[16] However, in contrast with most studies of Chinese sexual culture that focus on marriage, state policies, and official discourse, this book focuses on sexual behavior before marriage, interactions in daily life, and an unofficial public culture of neighborhood gossip, urban myths, and leisure. It also de-scribes the activities of both men and women, a corrective to approaches that focus only on one gender.[17] Sociologically, this study has two larger purposes. First, I use Shanghai as a case to conceptualize sexual culture not as a narrow set of socially constructed acts, but as a broad symbolic field of stories, per-formances, and metaphors in which conventionalized actors, scenes, instru-mentalities, and purposes are as important as the acts. Second, I use Shanghai as a case for conceptualizing cultural change, in particular how sexual culture is transformed during the transition to a market economy. This is no attempt to construct a general theory of cultural modernization, an idea inimical to my approach, but to provide a grounded theoretical description of one such process of cultural transformation in particular historic circumstances.

Most of what we know about sexuality has been learned from structured interviews. The structured interview is a special kind of discourse that aims to condense and make uniform questions and answers and, usually, takes words for deeds. But there is another kind of discourse about sexuality, that is, the discourse that the speech community itself uses to talk about things "sexual." This discourse is less one of questions and answers than a kind of storytelling—the spinning of narratives with their casts of characters, vocabularies of motives, scenes of action, and instrumentalities.[18] This is the kind of discourse the ethnographer aims for, not only to record it, but to make up a sociological story about it, a story that is hopefully not very far from the in situ discourse itself. That is the aim of this book. Both the raw materials of this study and the analysis of them require a literary sense. Stories are only one form of symbolic action studied here, but they are the paradigmatic form, including exemplary tales that regulate public behavior and personal tales that make public sense out of private behavior. My model of the normative order, then, is less a set of rules analogous to the Mosaic code, than the remainder of the Bible, which consists of exemplary (and often ambiguous) tales, parables, and poems.

I conceive of the practices of sexual culture primarily as "symbolic action," a term I borrow from Kenneth Burke. I also borrow from Burke the methodology of dramatism, the study of symbolic action as drama and as a performance aimed at a particular audience.[19] Throughout this study I simultaneously pursue three analytically separate goals, which I frame through Burke's tripartite division of cultural criticism into a grammar, a rhetoric, and dialectics.[20] My first goal is to describe a dramatistic "grammar" of Shanghai's sexual culture, an ethnographic account of the conventional purposes, socially coded places, socially understood character types, accepted means of action, and conventional acts that make up the basic "story elements" in conversations about sex and sexual feelings in Shanghai. This shared grammar of conventional scenes, actors, agency, purposes, and acts—Burke's "dramatistic pentad" of story elements[21]—gives a loose coherence, structure, and continuity to the diverse conversations that make up Shanghai's public sexual culture. For people involved in these conversations, these conventional narrative elements comprise a shared grammar of motives within which new actions and stories are imagined and plotted. As Burke argues, this grammar of motives is not merely a pattern for describing events. It is the symbolic form through which experience is constituted.[22]

The second goal of this study is a "rhetoric" of this sexual culture—how these cultural elements are employed in stories, conversations, and social interactions, a description of the ways in which youth describe, negotiate, and act out the sometimes contradictory meanings of sexual relations in the new market society. In explaining the rhetoric of sexual culture, I rely on a broad literature of the micropolitics of sexuality that includes such everyday conceptions of communicative practice as storytelling, caricature, play, gossip, dance, cruising, and emotional style.[23] Finally, I discuss the dialectics of this culture, how it changes over time, in this case how youth adapt elements of a preexisting sexual culture to the new situation of a market economy. Within Burke's framework, the dialectic incorporates both changes in grammatical elements (and conventional relations among elements) and changes in rhetorical contexts (changing social institutions).

This approach to sexual culture works within a tradition of social construction and symbolic interaction that explains variations in sexual culture in terms of cultural vocabularies, social organization, and social interaction.[24] My approach is agnostic to the popular claims of evolutionary psychology that sexual drives are biologically programmed for mate selection.[25] As a sociologist, my concern is with sexual *motives* as socially constructed practices, rather than biological *drives* abstracted from social practices and cultural forms. These socially constructed sexual motives are not mere reflections, deflections, or legitimations of biological essences, but essential constituents of personal and social identity. As Burke argues, "Symbolic communication is not a merely external instrument but intrinsic to men as agents. Its motivational properties characterize both 'the human situation' and what men are 'in themselves.'"[26] I take a similar position with regard to social exchange theory and other rational choice perspectives on sexual behavior. While these approaches may be useful in analyzing bargaining in sexual relationships, they are not useful in explaining the cultural vocabularies in which these exchanges are negotiated or changes in the norms that govern them.[27]

Sexuality is imagined in every society as a problem of social and moral order, and my first concern is with how youth make moral distinctions about sexual relations. Most simply, sexual relations are an integral part of the normative and practical order of everyday life,[28] an order partly constituted and maintained by an everyday rhetoric of stories and gossip that justify and critique sexual actions. At the same time, people designate certain practices of eroticism—

often described as "play" by my informants—as external to this everyday moral order.[29] Play entails its own rhetoric, aesthetic as well as ethical. Finally, sexual culture also involves a metonymic moral rhetoric, in which sexual relations work as moral allegories through which the members of a community defend and dispute social boundaries.[30] Chapter 3 in this study describes how Shanghai people use sexualized character types to represent and critique the shifting social boundaries of the emerging market society.

In modern societies generally, sexual storytelling plays a key role in self-identity formation, in which selfhood can be defined as the "capacity to keep a narrative going."[31] While basically agreeing with this narrative identity thesis, I find sexual storytelling (and identity) to be a more contingent and interactive practice than this literature implies, and as much about constructing an image of others, and an image of society, as simply a project of self-identity formation. Even the most personal sexual story is usually a social event, a presentation of the self aimed at a particular audience. The "identities" thus created may be temporary, intentionally misleading, or purposefully ambiguous.[32] People tell sexual stories to justify their actions to others, to criticize the actions of others, and to persuade others to act. In other words, everyday sexual talk can also be understood as rhetoric, and sexual culture as a process of social mapping and social criticism as well as self-presentation and self-identity formation.

The study of rhetoric offers ways of conceptualizing these everyday tactics of persuasion, self-presentation, and social criticism, even nonverbal tactics of walking, dancing, and glancing.[33] Rhetoric is an analysis of language as speech oriented toward the listener and his answer, emphasizing the social imbedding of cultural texts.[34] My sense of rhetoric involves an actor's purposeful use of language, but one whose purposes and strategies are also constructed by the larger language the actor uses. There is no instrumental backstage actor pursuing objectively rational strategies. More than anything, the study of rhetoric is an analysis of observable social interactions that doesn't presume the consistency, sincerity, or internalized values of those who are speaking. As such, rhetoric is more compatible with empirical sociological inquiry than the study of less-observable constructs such as values, attitudes, or cultural orientations. While much contemporary culture theory emphasizes the silences and constraints imposed by culture, rhetoric has been concerned with empowerment through language,[35] emphasizing persuasion, identification, and argumentation. It focuses on the way a speaker manipulates or reshapes the ethical doxa and conventional beliefs of an audience, framing ethical judgments and making actions plausible.[36] Burke argues that rhetoric comes into play when people are potentially free to make choices,[37] an idea with important implications for studying Shanghai's youth sexual culture. With increased freedom of sexual choice and uncertainty about moral rules, Shanghai youth must persuade others to act, persuade others about their own choices and even about the ethical assumptions and beliefs upon which they base these choices. Following Ann Swidler's formulation, in "uncertain times," such as those that Shanghai youth now are experiencing, established cultural strategies and discourses become a "cultural tool kit" for youth constructing and legitimating new tactics of social action.[38]

Storytelling is a key rhetorical tactic in sexual culture.[39] Storytelling configures a social world in terms of ethical value and moral action, including the audience in the narrative through a process of identification,[40] and establishing collectivities around certain values.[41] Narrative tropes such as romance and irony lend themselves to different arguments about moral order and personal choices.[42] In this study I focus on the types of actions made plausible through different narrative tropes, particularly what people try to achieve with ironic or romantic stories.

Although rhetorical theory provides a language for representing everyday cultural practice, it is not an adequate framework for understanding the transformation of sexual culture over time. Burke calls this diachronic study of linguistic and cultural transformation "dialectics."[43] First of all, a cultural grammar of sexuality is grounded in particular social practices established within a particular institutional setting, so that terms take on new meanings in new institutional settings. In my account, changes in social institutions—neighborhoods, magazines, dance halls, dating conventions—create new contexts for sexual communication. As Burke argues, if a change in moral order is achieved, it most usually occurs as the manipulation of existing moral categories rather than through an overt challenge to these categories.[44] I describe how preexisting concepts of romantic feeling (ganqing) are given new meanings in practices of dating, romance, and premarital sex. Recycled elements of old stories are an important part of this dialectic, in which stories are in a dialogue with preexisting stories.[45] To explain the dialectics of sexual storytelling, Ken Plummer argues that what is required sociologically is an account of the social and historical conditions that facilitate the making and hearing of stories, including traditions of storytelling and the social conditions for creating an audience.[46] My account emphasizes young people's uses of friends' stories, as well as materials from a shared popular culture.

The Dialectics of Sexual Culture and Market Reform

The macrosocial narrative that runs through this ethnographic study is how changes in sexual culture in Shanghai relate to China's "market transition" over the past twenty years to a society based more on liberal market principles than on central planning and socialist equality. In focusing on this question, however, several caveats and qualifications are in order. The first qualification is that capitalist labor markets and consumer markets are themselves part of a larger institutional transformation led by the state. My study situates cultural practices in this larger social context of labor, commodity, and culture markets; family authority; and state-controlled institutions. Second is the problem of historical legacies, the rather obvious point that sexual culture is not purely the product of recent transformations. Xin Liu identifies three conventional sources of historical influence on everyday practices in the Shaanxi village he studied: the traditional, revolutionary, and the modern.[47] My study shows that Shanghai's sexual culture represents a layering of multiple historical "modernities," which each contribute distinct elements to Shanghai's contemporary sexual culture: a presocialist colonial modernity, a utopian socialist modernity, and now a transnational, consumer modernity. Finally, this is only a study of Shanghai's urban resident population. China's emergent liberal market regime gives urban residents greater civil rights, labor market freedom, and resources than rural residents and rural migrants to cities.[48] This study should not be taken as representative of China as a whole, or even as a complete picture of Shanghai's sexual culture. For some readers, the most glaring omission may be an extensive discussion of same-sex relationships and of sexuality in marriage (although a Chinese culture of "compulsory heterosexuality"[49] and "compulsory marriage" is central to my account of dating culture). I leave a fuller account of these issues to others.

In general, I link the dialectics of sexual culture in Shanghai to the emergence of institutions and practices aligned with a market economy. In setting up my question in terms of a transition to a market economy, I am privileging the market as a factor in explaining sexual culture in Shanghai. Briefly, I would like to justify my own emphasis on the market transition while suggesting how I plan to account for important issues emphasized in alternative accounts of modern sexuality. One view, associated with the work of Michel Foucault,[50] aligns modern sexuality with the mechanisms of discipline and social control of new medical, educational, and scientific institutions. First of all, while China has an infamously strong state and a growing cadre of semiofficial sex experts,

I do not believe state institutions and expert ideologies so thoroughly dominate everyday life that a continued top-down state-oriented approach to Chinese sexual culture is helpful. Interpreting Foucault more broadly, one might argue that the market itself imposes a new regime of discipline on youth,[51] but I would argue that labor markets, consumer markets, and marriage markets are from the standpoint of youth rather specific social local conditions, posing specific practical problems, for which youth come up with their own definitions and conventional means of approach, which might be considered Foucauldian "disciplines of the self," but which I consider as flexible performative (or rhetorical) competencies that youth develop to their own purposes. In any case, we cannot chart the new structural conditions—or disciplinary mechanisms—of the market society without also seeing how youth evade and appropriate these mechanisms for their own playful, subversive, or simply self-serving purposes.[52] I thus present a grounded study of everyday sexual practices that points out the mechanisms of bureaucratic discipline and market-oriented self-discipline, but emphasizes the practices of youth constructing their own sexual culture and their tactics for evading the disciplines of the new economic and social order (including the "disciplines" of romance and courtship they impose upon one another).

Another prominent view, associated with Anthony Giddens,[53] conceives of sexual modernity primarily as a secular increase in the equality and intimacy of sexual relationships. I see Giddens's approach as missing the social context of this intensified rhetoric of "romance" and "intimacy," specifically young people's cultural accommodations to labor, marriage, and consumer markets. Like Giddens,[54] however, I do not accept deterministic accounts in which the relationship between sexuality and the market is primarily conceived as a "commodification" of sexual desires,[55] or in which sexual desires themselves are the repressive products of capitalism.[56] Rather, I describe cultural practices that represent an adjustment to market conditions but are not simply forms of sexual commodification and sexual consumption. Most importantly, my account emphasizes how young Shanghaiese respond to the less predictable and more competitive social relations of the market society through a more romantically expressive but also more skeptical, more intimate but also more playful sexual culture.

Finally, as the title of this book references, the most popular account of changing sexual culture in China is the story of an "opening up" to a more liberal (or "open") sexual culture from the West and Japan via entertainment, news media, and personal exchanges. Such a story is echoed, though in a more nuanced form, in scholarly accounts of sexual globalization.[57] In my view these popular and scholarly narratives of sexual globalization claim both too much and too little. As many critics have pointed out, accounts of globalization are often too quick to identify foreign influences without considering the local cultural landscapes in which imported concepts are given meaning. On the other hand, observers' accounts of globalization often fail to acknowledge local historical narratives through which foreign influences, invasions, exotic longings, and emigrations have long been imagined.[58] Shanghai, in particular, has its own century-old history of opening up and being opened. In chapter 1, I describe this narrative of opening up as a dominant feature of a local rhetoric of cultural change. In my constructionist account of cultural change, the supposedly objective origins of particular cultural forms are far less important than these local attributions of foreignness, Shanghainess, or non-Shanghai Chineseness (waidi) to people, behaviors, and ideas. What matters most for my account is how these terms are used to mark moral and social boundaries in a newly forming market society.

While the transition to a market economy in China began with the reform of agriculture under the "responsibility system" in the early 1980s, by the 1990s cities were the area of greatest economic dynamism. During this period capital, labor, housing, commodity, and cultural markets moved closer to the liberal model of freer choices, rational markets, and lower transaction costs.[59] Real per capita income doubled twice during the reform era, and the income gap between the richest and poorest rapidly widened.[60] The result is the demise of a culturally homogenous and egalitarian working class of state-enterprise workers with fairly similar expectations and lifestyles. In contrast, the market society creates new winners and losers[61] and new popular conceptions of class divisions.[62] Foreign investment has produced thousands of new white-collar elites and wealthy foreigners living in Shanghai's "high-corner" (west-end) neighborhoods,[63] while rural migrants fill positions in the building and service sectors and sleep in workplace barracks. Freer labor markets mean that Shanghai residents can more easily change jobs, while companies can more easily fire them, destroying the sense of equality and security that defined the old socialist working-class culture. Commercial housing markets allow the wealthy to move at will and purchase a private "oasis,"[64] but leave the poor with fewer housing options and without the safety net of a government housing allocation. The commercialization of leisure and entertainment has vastly increased the quality and variety of consumer culture activities,[65] creating spaces for urban youth subcultures at odds with adult expectations but also differentiated by social class.[66] Finally, the greater liberalization of the media means the proliferation of magazines, books, and television programs dealing with sexuality and romance, giving urban youth many more models of sexual stories than previous generations.[67] At the same time, the liberal economic model has been accompanied by less state monitoring of private life, including sexual behavior, part of a "changing social contract" between the state and citizens in which increased personal freedom and choice entail increased personal responsibility.[68]

All of these institutional changes have created a new social environment for young people engaging in sexual and romantic interaction. In focusing on adaptations to market institutions, I follow Foucault in searching for the "incitements to discourse"[69]—the institutionalized practices and ideologies that make people notice, discuss, and contest some topics rather than others. I argue that Shanghai youth have fashioned a new sexual culture, finding particular "cultural tools" and "strategies of action"[70] that respond to the incitements of the market society—including increased pressure to make personal choices, greater emphasis on money, wider social inequality, and a growing consumer leisure culture. The cultural changes I describe are not simply the functional outcome of market principles. They are historic, localized processes in which youth fashion market-oriented cultural practices out of ideas and practices handed down from the Maoist era and previous eras, or borrowed from abroad—or imagined to be borrowed from abroad. Through conversation, conflict, and negotiation, Shanghai youth create a new sexual culture oriented to the market but not an exclusive product of the market nor represented in language exclusively drawn from the new market culture.

The new social environment of the market society puts contradictory pressures on young people in making and explaining sexual choices. First is the problem of choice itself. The 1953 Marriage Law legally guaranteed free choice of a marriage partner, but familial, community, and institutional restrictions on mixed-sex interaction limited courtship in practice for much of the Maoist era.[71] Only in the reform era has a true peer-governed culture of dating emerged in Shanghai, associated with the new institutional locus of courtship in consumer leisure establishments. At the same time, the criteria of choice have become more problematic. For Shanghai women especially, the choice of partners is assumed to be a difficult balance between "material conditions" and "romantic feelings," a choice made more consequential by increased differences in wealth and income among men and a greater emphasis on the emotional quality (and worries about the fragility) of subsequent marital relationships.[72] The tensions between commitment and choice present a related problem. In general, the less predictable futures of potential partners in capitalist labor markets mean that youth delay commitments to marital choices and are more willing to engage in short-term relationships.[73] Faced with structural uncertainties in the new capitalist labor markets, Shanghai youth now allow one another greater freedom to break off or withhold commitments before marriage, creating more competitive dating practices and more permissive moral codes consistent with the ideal of free choice. With fewer institutional sanctions on sexual behavior, Shanghai youth also allow themselves the choice of more sexual intimacy before marriage, but more intimate sexual relations also heighten the contradictions between the sincerity of love commitments and the uncertain and playful nature of dating relationships. In sum, in order to cope with the contradictions and conflicting goals of this new liberal market environment, Shanghai youth employ a loosely ordered repertoire of compensatory codes that balance one attitude with its opposite. Young women, anxious to be both pragmatic and pure of heart, rhetorically balance "conditions" with "feelings." Young people wishing to engage in premarital sex redefine intercourse as an expression of love. Finally, youth evade the inherent contradictions between romantic commitments and an ideal of free choice through a consumption-oriented discourse of play in which dating relationships can be described as "just for fun." This compensatory rhetoric of sexual motives—balancing pragmatism with romance, lust with love, and seriousness with play—has evolved under the contradictory pressures youth face in the market era.

My discussion of a changing discourse of sexual motives in Shanghai builds on an ethnographic literature that relates a modern culture of romantic love to the structure of capitalist labor markets and consumer markets.[74] For instance, Jane Fishburne Collier describes the romantic discourse of Andalusian youth during a period of transition to a national labor market in Spain. She argues that rural Andalusian men and women talking about courtship in the 1980s adopted a vocabulary of "inner desires" to correspond to participation in labor markets in which all behaviors are interpreted in terms of individual choices and abilities. A discourse of individual desire thus replaced an earlier discourse of "duties" and "honor," which made more sense in an economy based on inherited wealth. According to Collier, this change is largely rhetorical, representing less a change in people's willingness or ability to act out their inner desires than a difference in the concepts and practices people use for managing their perceptions of self and for interpreting the actions of others.[75] Similarly, I argue that a liberal market regime emerging in Shanghai in the past twenty years encourages young people to engage in a rhetoric of individual motives, in which the central terms are "feelings" and "conditions" (or "love" and "money"). However, rather than accepting the everyday Shanghai interpretation of romantic love and material benefit simply as opposed motives, I interpret them as paired rhetorical opposites in which the increased emphasis on one entails the compensatory emphasis on the other, reflecting socially constructed dilemmas of sexual choice and a desire for ethical and practical resolutions to the pressures that youth face in the market economy.

Labor market pressures are highly gender specific. The gendered organization of household and market labor produces a similar dilemma for women in all liberal market societies: maintaining skills and a separate identity compatible with an individualized labor market while relying on a man for financial and emotional support during child rearing.[76] Despite enjoying higher levels of gender equality in education, income, and the division of household labor than in most capitalist countries, newly married Chinese women still must take far more responsibility for child care than men, while they also seek and hold jobs in an increasingly precarious labor market.[77] These contradictory demands on women are increasing in the freer labor markets of reform-era society. Young Chinese women face increased discrimination from employers who prefer not to hire women of childbearing age. Moreover, later in life women can expect to be the first to be laid off in downsizing. Therefore, one need not resort to the teleology of evolutionary psychology to explain Chinese women's desire to "marry up." Women generally look for husbands who will provide the best economic conditions for them and their children. At the same time, women must rely upon husbands as their own emotional refuge from the struggles of the market economy. The institution of dating in Shanghai reflects these contradictory considerations, with Shanghai women expecting to date men better off than themselves, yet still expecting to fall in love. In response to this new sexual marketplace, Shanghai youth work with the terms of a preexisting romantic and moral grammar to create stories about good and bad sexual motives, contriving a new ethics of sexual choice, in which women's motives are the point of greatest contention. For instance, as premarital sex becomes more acceptable for Shanghai youth, women's motives become the decisive moral criterion for their premarital sexual relations. "Purity" becomes purity of motive, sex for feelings rather than for some material end.

Men feel the sexual pressures of the market economy somewhat differently. Young men entering the market economy are expected to provide their wives and families with the housing and economic security once provided by the state under the redistributive socialist economy. If anything, the contrast with the security and equality of the socialist era only increases these pressures. In a 2000 magazine article, Liu Kang, a young single white-collar man from Shanghai, summarizes the change: "In the past you could blame your poverty on the country; now it's only your own fault." In the same article his college sweetheart describes her decision to leave Liu Kang for an older, richer, but less-educated construction contractor:

> I know this is an inferior choice. But the 21st century is a competitive era, and women are fated to be the weakest in this competition. I can't rely on social welfare. I have to find someone to lean on [kaoshan]. I know that Liu Kang is a good man, but the responsibilities of not having money are too great. I know that he will get money one day, but I can't wait.[78]

In the market society emerging in Shanghai, masculinity is tied to "ability" (nengli), a concept that combines economic and sexual potency. A general "crisis of masculinity" pervades Chinese popular culture,[79] particularly in stories of weak or effeminate Shanghai men,[80] evidence of the strong new pressures men face in proving their "ability." Given the identification of masculinity with earnings and career success, men experience tremendous dislocations through the segmentation of the labor market into high-paying and low-paying sectors. Poor and working-class Shanghai men, particularly, express a deep resentment at their low position in the new sexual economy. On the other hand, it is not enough to be rich. A rich man without romantic charms is a laughable "big money" (dakuan), an object of women's mercenary sexual strategies but not a sexual subject in his own right. In addition to economic success, the new man must also know "how to flirt" in the words of Shanghai informants: how to demonstrate a capacity for romantic feeling that proves the moral and transcendental quality of a romantic attachment (destiny/yuanfen).

Along with labor markets, consumer markets are equally important sites for the construction of new youth sex culture. As Eva Illouz argues, the consumer values of freedom of choice and of transient but renewable pleasures radically alter the romantic and sexual sensibility.[81] Seen from a functional perspective, the competition of the market leads to tensions that can only be resolved in a playful way, and for Shanghai youth, consumption, including commercial nightlife, is the chief means of playful escapism. However, play is not merely escape. Sexual play is a way in which youth test out new social roles, including "play forms" of more earnest sexual behaviors,[82] and thus a way in which youth cope with the incongruous choices they face in the "real world."[83] Therefore, not only is there an intensified vocabulary of motives to describe sexual interactions in the market society, but there are more public and institutionalized forms of sexualized play (wan/baixiang),[84] such as dance, flirtation, fashion, or even romance (langman), in which sexual motives may be played out in disingenuous, ambiguous, or disguised forms. Within the framework of play, individuals are judged aesthetically in terms of their performances rather than morally in terms of their motives.[85] Although accompanied by notions of success, failure, and competition, their designation as mere "play" separates these sexual performances from the practical and moral consequences of serious sexual choices.

Finally, the relationship of sexual culture to the market is also one in which sexual stories act as public allegories of social relations in the market society. In Shanghai the discourse of sexual motives features in a slow-burning moral panic over the cultural consequences of the market transition, especially greed and avarice and the weakening of sentimental bonds. In popular culture and in idle talk (xianhua) about society, Shanghai people construct a mythic world of materially and sexually motivated characters, a dramatistic tool kit of "big moneys" and "girls today," who serve as foils for interpreting the actions of real people. These stories reflect a pervasive concern with false motives, expressed in official condemnations of money worship (baijinzhuyi) or cautionary tales of youth blindly pursuing (mangmuzhuiqiu) money and/or sexual passion, a moral language also exemplified in a 2000 magazine article's description of a female university student's sexual lifestyle:

> We live in an open age and a competitive society. Everyone has the right to choose their own way of self-development and personal growth. But, no matter for what reason, no one has the right to choose depravity! She was a female university student, and standing at the crossroads of life, she chose materialism and money worship.[86]

According to the writer, in order to practice her English, the student began to visit dance clubs, where she danced with "foreign types" (waiguolao), some of whom gave her large tips for dancing and drinking with them. If my own dance hall ethnography is a guide, the woman's own account of her dance club experiences probably would sound more playful and less morally dire. In the eyes of outsiders like the writer, however, her choices reflect a general social condition of impure material motives.

The transition to a liberal market society highlights individual motives as a source of moral crisis, especially the motive of seeking wealth. Over the twenty-year course of the market reforms, money has been transformed from a deviant goal to an established one, but one fraught with moral danger. In surveys in the mid-1990s, the vast majority of Chinese reported "getting rich" as their main goal in life, while an increasing number of young people expressed a consciously alternative desire to pursue "their own tastes regardless of wealth or fame."[87] As "getting rich" becomes the established motive, a compensatory rhetoric of romantic individualism has become a dominant language of moral critique, especially in the youth culture. As the active temptation, money, the "god-term" of the market society, is also rhetorically the source of a whole range of new virtues, which rest in the ability to resist the temptation of money.[88] That is, the dominance of money as a motive increases the weight of its opposite ethical sensitivities, including this choice of "pursuing one's own tastes," but also human feelings (renqing) generally[89] and romantic feelings (ganqing) particularly. In the new youth sexual culture, feelings become the supposedly authentic value that counterbalances the money motive. The trope of the young woman weighing true feelings and material conditions thus becomes a persuasive allegory of all moral choice in the market society, and prostitution becomes a general allegory of moral compromise.[90]

Such moralistic melodramas of sex and money, like the story of the college student cited above, are unable to resolve the antinomies of sexual choices in the market economy. Love is never pure enough; even a beautiful romance may be a pretense for lust and greed. In order to cope with these practical incongruities and conflicting moral standards, Shanghai people also resort to more ironic forms of storytelling, stories in which accepted moral standards are shown to be arbitrary, moral heroism is impractical, and only pragmatic "little people" endure. Irony involves not a rejection of moral vocabularies, but an acceptance of their contingency and a chance to explore alternative formulations.[91] In an ironic emplotment of Shanghai's moralistic discourse of sexual motives, a melodramatic world of pure "heroes" and materialistic "villains" can alternatively be seen as a comic world of the "tricked" and the "clever."[92] As a moral leveling, irony allows for a compromise with moral principles and an acceptance of a socially determined fate.

Youth achieve a somewhat different evasion of moral and pragmatic consequences in sexual play. For Shanghai youth, play is what Burke calls the "comic corrective," a dramatistic frame in which both pure and impure motives are dialectically embodied.[93] Play is similar to irony in that it allows conflicting motives to coexist, but play doesn't require critical distance. In play, contradictory motives can be exposed, and also *celebrated*, even reveled in, without long-term consequences, a "comic corrective" to the moral and practical aporia of serious sexual choices. Play represents an aesthetic rather than a practical or ethical resolution to the contradictions between ideals and reality, romance and pragmatism, love and money.[94] Both irony and play represent life as drama,[95] but whereas the ironist observes the drama from a distance that allows for a pragmatic cynicism, the player plunges into the performance and enjoys a momentary release from both moral and practical necessity.[96]

In sum, my account of a changing sexual culture is not a story of sexual liberation, sexual globalization, or rebelling youth, but of youth collectively constructing (and individually coping with) a new culture of sexual choice, publicly articulated through a dramatistic rhetoric of motives. Romantic moralism and ironic pragmatism are the two dominant tropes of this discourse of sexual motives, the earnest nature of which is (temporarily and partially) evaded in sexual and romantic play. While sympathetic to the tactics of youth, I try to avoid the naive political hagiography that pervades many accounts of sexual culture, presenting us with good subalterns struggling to subvert a bad patriarchal order. I highlight the cynicism of individual tactics and the serious class and gender inequities that internally structure youth sexual culture. Finally, for me as for anyone now publicly writing about sexual culture, this project owes a great deal to the questions and politics of queer theory.[97] In contrast to most queer studies, however, this book attempts a deconstruction of Shanghai's heteronormative sexual culture from the "inside," one that doesn't focus explicitly on sexual "outsiders" or "queers," but tries to show the internal fissures and conflicts within the dominant sexual culture by fully displaying it in its own grammatical terms. In the end, I return to Burke for a conception of the critical role of the sociologist of culture. Burke sees the sociologist as an ironist whose aim is to reveal the limits and assumptions of what is taken for granted in culture, doing this through incongruity, by showing the social world from as many vantage points as possible.[98] I hope that my multiplex view of Shanghai's sexual culture works in this way, as a Burkean "comic corrective," an incongruous perspective on sexuality that helps us to better comprehend the cultural and social construction of a sexual culture but also to recognize the folly of all sexual essentialisms, whether of gender, biology, economics, or politics.

The Organization of the Book

Topically, the subsequent chapters fall into two major parts. The first four chapters provide a dramatistic account of Shanghai's public sexual culture, outlining the major "story elements" of scene, character, and plot that structure the sexual culture of Shanghai. The last five chapters provide a more narrow account of Shanghai's youth dating and sexual culture, focusing on personal stories and interactions and the cultural codes around which these practices are organized.

Chapter 1 introduces the reader to the grammar of Shanghai's sexual culture by describing how changes in sexual culture, both macrosocial and personal, are represented through a local grammar of space and character. Continuing this grammar, chapter 2 describes the geography of Shanghai as a historical legacy that shapes Shanghai's contemporary sexual culture. It also introduces two key communities in which I conducted my interviews, an exclusively working-class community situated in an old "shanty district" and a geographically dispersed community of professional white-collar workers. Chapter 3 describes how Shanghaiese use a set of prototypical sexual characters in casual private conversations as well as in public artistic representations. Chapter 4 traces the development of the genre of "true story" magazine articles in the most popular Shanghai youth magazine. It discusses how the social organizations of magazine production and consumption impact the contents of the magazines, thus providing a view of how a state-controlled media culture shapes the production of a popular sexual culture. The central argument about the stories themselves describes a shift from a romantic or utopian view of sexual love and modernization in the early reform era to an ironic view of sex and money in the late reform era.

Chapter 5 describes changes in the meanings and expectations of courtship in the reform era. While marriage remains a compulsory goal, youth have created rules allowing multiple premarital dating relationships increasingly removed from immediate considerations of marriage. Chapter 6 uses group and individual interviews to describe how young people talk about romantic love and how these romantic themes have been influenced by the changing organization of courtship in the late reform era. Chapter 7 focuses on one of the central changes in Shanghai youth sexual culture—the collective deconstruction of a norm of premarital chastity. While girls' virginity retains important symbolic value in Shanghai, most youth no longer expect girls to wait until marriage to engage in sexual intercourse and other forms of sexual behavior. Continuing the discussion of sexual behavior, chapter 8 outlines the new "rules of the game" by which youth attempt to govern premarital sexual interactions. The chapter lays out several "games" that youth play with sex, ranging from "deepening a relationship" to "playing around." It briefly considers how youth cope with the unintended practical consequences of sexual activity: disease and pregnancy. Finally, chapter 9 describes how youth use the spaces of the nightlife to engage in forms of sexual play that are defined as outside the relatively earnest world of courtship. Trying to give the reader a feel for the different social worlds of different types of dance halls, the chapter is organized around six different trips to different dance venues, describing the types of encounters the author experienced.

Each chapter in the study (other than chapter 1) also can be seen to focus on one element of Burke's dramatistic pentad: actors (chapter 2), scenes (chapter 3), purposes (chapters 4 and 6), agency (chapter 5 and 9), and acts (chapters 7 and 8). Or they can be roughly grouped around the three major tropes that I identify in Shanghai's sexual culture: irony (chapters 1, 2, 3, and 4), romance (chapters 5, 6, and 7) and play (chapters 8 and 9). I have therefore declined to formally divide the book into sections. Moreover, each chapter is meant to stand alone for readers interested in only one particular topic.

•

开放

OPENING UP
And Other Stories

Stories of Sexual Change
The AIDS Exhibit

On a dreary December day in the first week of my fieldwork in Shanghai in 1994, I wandered into the commercial center of an outlying residential neighborhood and noticed the AIDS Exhibit. A ten-by-two-foot plastic banner above a narrow alleyway between a public toilet and a furniture store advertised "AIDS Exhibit with information about human sexuality." Below the banner a large canvas poster pictured deformed fetuses and descriptions of two-headed babies, babies with wings, and babies with tails. "AIDS can lead to deformed fetuses," another banner read. I paid two yuan[1] to see the exhibit and walked along the alleyway. The exhibit began with about twenty posters pinned on the alleyway wall. The posters featured textbook drawings of the human reproductive system, photos of genitals ravaged by venereal diseases, and photos of various genetic deformities of the genitalia.

The "sexuality" depicted in the AIDS Exhibit was a phantasmagoric vision of a dangerous invading foreign sex. One poster, titled "The Hotbed of Venereal Disease," featured a half dozen large illustrations—photos of two foreign women kissing, cross-dressing men marching in a U.S. gay rights parade, an early-twentieth-century drawing of women dressed as men, an eighteenth-century European print depicting a man being spanked, a magazine illustration of a man fondling a child—images whose connection to disease seemed to me more metaphorical than biological. Throughout the exhibit most illustrations of sexual depravity and sexual dangers portrayed white Westerners, including a nude couple in bed, a suspicious-looking longhaired man (a hippie or gay) entering Chinese customs, and a Western businessman (a customer of a pros-

22

titute). Inside the shed the illustrations continued, with one poster speculating about possible origins of the AIDS virus, including the possibility that it might come from outer space.

The main attraction, however, was a long U-shaped table displaying about twenty pickled deformed human fetuses in large bottles, some nearly fully formed. They were labeled with rambling texts, vague warnings about bad eugenic practices, and some useful advice not to take too much medicine during pregnancy. Mixed in with utter falsities and practical bits of advice were strict moral admonitions copied from old government publications, mottos of "vigorously enforcing marital monogamy" and "punishing all sorts of sexual deviance," a rhetoric typical of government propaganda a decade or two earlier.

As I was leaving, the voluble manager of the furniture store next door asked me to sit down. He was sitting with the people putting on the exhibit, enabling me to ask them some questions. Half the time the furniture salesman answered for them, since they were shy about talking to a foreigner, like many other poorly educated rural and small-town people I met in Shanghai. The exhibitors said they were from near Changzhou (a town between Shanghai and Nanjing) and that this was a privately owned exhibit. It was "allowed" by the government, but it was a profit-making enterprise. After paying the rent, they could clear about seven to eight thousand yuan a month. "Business is pretty good" were the only words they said with any conviction or interest. I asked if Shanghai people were really interested in the exhibition. The furniture salesman waved dismissively. "If they have never seen it, they will stop and go in once. No one would come in twice." The exhibitors didn't disagree. The exhibit would be there for about six weeks. I heard some people cooking behind the shed housing the exhibit and discovered that was where the five or six people associated with the show were living, sleeping at night on the floor of the shed among the lugubrious, bottled fetuses.

The spectacle is a peculiar entrepreneurial vision of Michel Foucault's "sexual science," a medical rhetoric of deviant types, illnesses, and unhealthy practices, with a peculiar Chinese emphasis on procreation and eugenics. Yet tracing this Chinese sexology is not my point, and others have already done this.[2] Rather, now as then, I see in the traveling AIDS Exhibit more of an unintentional Chinese joke on Foucault, an artless caricature of Foucault's sexual science and its ideal of a "calculated management of life,"[3] from which it literally cuts and pastes, an effect not of an esoteric Chinese taxonomy,[4] but of the careless hands of small-town entrepreneurs out to make a buck. The AIDS Exhibit raises the question of whether an emerging discipline of "sexual science" should be considered the main subplot of the story of Shanghai's changing sexual culture. In my view what holds the AIDS Exhibit together is less its scientific rhetoric than its rhetoric of social change, a graphic portrayal of the "heterotopia" of a globalizing sexual culture invading China, a story of sexual opening (xingkaifang) that is the dominant narrative of sexual change in China. AIDS is the metonymic agent of this invasion; money, the real viral carrier, infecting, reproducing, rapidly mutating into all of these proliferating perversions. The prostitute, the foreigner, and the businessman are the human carriers of both. China "opens up" and is infected by money, AIDS, foreigners, and sexual perversion. A stern vigilance against this foreign sex and money is the only way to protect Chinese homes and wombs. This story of sexual opening is immensely popular in China, a story of social change that justifies the vigilance of state authorities and warns against foreign influence.

Many questions arise from the AIDS Exhibit, but in this chapter I will focus on the stories Shanghai people tell to make sense of their sexual modernity. First, what are the consistent local story elements in the stories of personal and social sexual change in Shanghai? What sexual stories are told in the junky dystopia of the AIDS Exhibit or the pleasurable consumer utopia of Shanghai's boulevards? What is the cultural and social grammar through which these visions are constructed? In this chapter and the next two chapters, I present the basic elements of Shanghai's peculiar sexual culture, including the plots, scenes, and characters that are the building blocks of sexual stories, the dramatistic substance of a grammar of local sexual culture.[5]

In studying these stories of social change, I believe we should shift from a predominant focus on the political and scientific discourse "deployed" by state agents to one on the unofficial communicative practices of ordinary people. Moreover, in describing this everyday rhetoric of sexual culture, we are probably better served by such everyday conceptions of rhetorical practice as storytelling, gossip, play, dance, and cruising,[6] or as de Certeau more colorfully suggests, the "clever tricks" and "hunter's cunning" of everyday cultural practice.[7] On the other hand, the state and its agents also have their "clever tricks" and their own official sexual stories. Individual stories of loving, choosing, seducing, and strolling respond to and are shaped by these loud official voices. The result is a politics of storytelling in which private stories respond to public stories, and individuals create their stories partly out of the materials borrowed from a state-dominated public culture. I will therefore begin with the most popular story Chinese tell about their own changing sexual culture, a story repeated in the AIDS Exhibit and one that echoes throughout Chinese official culture, the story of a sexual "opening up."

Opening Up (Kaifang)

Back then the word "sex" was not talked about like now. Now it is more *open*, and more uncovered. (Yi, married female bookkeeper aged 38)[8]

I think it is wrong that those people in their twenties live together without getting married. Parents don't really criticize them, not really, not like a decade ago when people would have hated them for doing that. The society has *opened up*—a lot of people come back from [working in] Japan. So it is not a strange thing. (Yao, married female quality-control officer aged 38)

[On the question of extramarital affairs] It is acceptable to me as long as it doesn't influence the family. The society has *opened up* now. (Hong, married male driver aged 35)

In the reform and opening period, then sex has also *opened up*. There is everything, karaoke, beauty parlors, discos. The Communist Party closes one eye and opens one eye, though it's not like in other countries where it is completely legal. (Old Wu, married but separated male low-level factory manager aged 50)

Most Shanghaiese agree that sexual norms have changed greatly since political and economic reforms began in the late 1970s. As these casual statements from group and individual interviews illustrate, people often employ the metaphor of "opening" to describe these changes in sexual culture, whether they approve of them or not. What do Shanghai people mean when they say that "sex" or "society" has "opened up"? Does it imply something different from the U.S. metaphor of "sexual revolution"? I am not arguing about the truth of these stories of "opening up." To paraphrase Michel Foucault's questioning of a Western narrative of "sexual liberation," we should ask not whether sex has become more "open" in China, but why the Chinese insist that there has been a "sexual opening" (xingkaifang).

"Opening" is used in China to refer to more than just sex; it also connotes the official politics of economic, social, and cultural liberalization that have governed China since the late 1970s: reform and opening (gaigekaifang). Not only is sexuality opening up, but so are the economy and virtually every other aspect of society. "Opening" thus functions as a kind of folk metanarrative, tying together diverse changes in society and culture. As Beth Bailey writes of the U.S. metaphor of "sexual revolution" in the 1970s: "The metaphor of revolution lent coherence to impulses that were in fact often in tension with one another. . . . In subsuming a diverse set of changes under the term revolution,

Americans conflated changes that had very different origins, intentions and outcomes."[9] While not as evocative as the metaphor of revolution, the metaphor of opening similarly subsumes a set of contradictory tendencies and trends and lends them the coherence of a general story of social change. "Opening up" is a very ambivalent narrative of progress. "Society is opening up," and previously unacceptable behaviors are accepted now. Behaviors that are not accepted now will undoubtedly be accepted in the future. The "open" West is a key figure in this narrative, an "othered modernity" of sexual license, a notion reinforced by years of socialist propaganda that portrayed the West as sexually decadent, now ironically reconfigured as an ambiguous hallmark of progress. In the view of many Shanghaiese, China is indeed becoming as "open" as the West, although too "wide" an opening may not be desirable, a worry one focus group participant expressed in a discussion of chastity.

> In the past feudal society, and even my parents' generation, chastity was more important than life. If you lost your chastity, you go kill yourself! Our generation is much better, and later it will progress more. But it should not be too open. In some countries young people are together to-day and break up tomorrow. It is too thoughtless, and not necessarily good. (Ping, married female bookkeeper aged 38)

In her story, which typically reflects the influence of a socialist education, traditional norms are represented as "feudal morality." "Opening" inevitably will eliminate these feudal ideas, though the narrator expresses hope that such opening will fall short of the quick and easy sexual relations thought to prevail abroad.

While the idea of revolution is at the heart of Western representations of modernization,[10] foreign invasion and foreign influence are central to Chinese representations. "Sexual liberation" or "sexual revolution" in the West implied release from repression, while "sexual opening" in China is a spatial metaphor of invasion, exposure of sex to public view and the exposure of Chinese to foreign ideas. As the patriarch Deng Xiaoping famously said, "When you open the door, a few flies are bound to enter." The most prominent of these "flies," in official propaganda, were these foreign ideas about sexuality. Just as America's sexual revolution rhetorically privileges revolutionaries (Hugh Hefner, Nancy Friday, youth) and counterrevolutionaries (Jerry Falwell, antiporn feminists, parents), China's opening is a narrative that privileges those who "open" (Deng Xiaoping, pimps, girls who "open" themselves) and those who stand guard at the "door" (the Communist Party, teachers, editors). To be a doorkeeper is to keep watch over the health of the national body, not a role easily dismissed when social change is perceived as invasive and chaotic. The stories of sexual opening I heard in China are consequently more ambivalent, authoritarian, and nationalistic than those of sexual revolution in the West. Moreover, while the sexual revolution of the West was perceived by some as a utopian movement that might free sexuality from the pragmatic exchanges of market relations, the Chinese sexual opening is a narrative in which sexual commodification works as a synecdoche of the commodification of everything. To be "open" is to be for sale. Material temptation is the primary motive, followed by sexual temptation, the desire to consume the sexual commodity. In sum, whereas the Western narrative of sexual revolution is a romantic saga of liberated desire, the Chinese narrative of sexual opening is an ironic melodrama of increasing temptation, sexualization of public life, commodification of sexuality, and Westernization of local sexual culture.

Finally, Shanghai people give their own more positive twists to the narrative of sexual opening. For Shanghaiese, "opening" is an ambivalent narrative, representing both the pride and shame of the city. Shanghai before 1949 was both "Paris of the East" and "whore of Asia,"[11] alternately admired and despised for its illicit pleasures and mix of Western and Chinese culture. In contemporary Shanghai, residents frequently proclaim that Shanghai is more "open" than the rest of China, more engaged with the outside world and therefore more modern, including sexual matters some find disgraceful and others simply "normal." One unemployed man of forty used this conception of Shanghai's opening to justify his own visits to commercial sex establishments: "Things have opened up. There are 'little misses' [xiaojie] everywhere, bars, discos, KTV,[12] nightclubs, beauty parlors. If you don't find them, they will find you. It's like foreign countries. It's like America—very normal." The ambivalent narrative of opening is not the only way in which Shanghai people consider social change, but it is a dominant way, one employed by state agents as a legitimation of censorship and social control, but also by citizens articulating their concerns about social change or offering their offhand dismissals of conventional moral standards. Such stories of social change frame events for people, incorporating the basic dramatistic elements of a local sexual culture, including scenes and characters with a local Shanghai flavor. Next I consider an alternative way in which Shanghai people imagine social change. As Kenneth Burke once wrote, sounding a bit like Zhuangzi, "A way of seeing is also a way of not seeing"[13]; there are other sexual stories in Shanghai that allow Shanghaiese to see (and not see) different features of sexual change.

Romantic Revolution

No one narrative is hegemonic to the extent that other possible stories become unimaginable. In Shanghai, as in the rest of China, a strong countervailing story to the dangers of sexual opening is the personal story of romantic heroism, of love and passion that overcome social conventions. While these stories typically focus on the fates of individuals, they also represent personal allegories of social revolution, typically stories of "modern girls" struggling against a background of conservative or "feudal" ideas, narratives strongly influenced by Marxism and liberal romanticism. These are not girls blindly succumbing to the temptations of an invading foreign culture, but young women acting according to deep feelings. As such, they are counternarratives to a story of sexual opening. In this section I discuss contrasting conceptions of romantic heroism in the reform-era popular fiction, seen through the stories of three prominent writers, one from the early reform period and two from the late 1990s. All three of these writers became famous for works more of sociological than purely literary significance, works widely seen as representing the new sexual ideals of their generation.

The first of these writers is Beijinger Zhang Jie, best known for an influential short story called "Love Must Not Be Forgotten," published in a Beijing literary journal in 1979.[14] The story is about the young female narrator's discovery of her deceased mother's diary, on whose title page the mother had written, "Love must not be forgotten." While reading the diary, the woman finds that her mother, a novelist and long a widow, was in love for decades with a married man, a hero of the Communist Revolution who was murdered during the recent Cultural Revolution for standing up to ultra-leftist elements. Their love remained chaste but true, the narrator insists. The narrator defends this secret love, quoting the man whom her mother loved: "You should remember that loving someone is not wrong in itself." As for the mother, "she had truly loved and had no regrets for having done so." The story about her mother is imbedded in the narrator's own polemic against accepting an offer of marriage from a young man with good "conditions" but whom she doesn't love. Not minding that mid-1970s China was a socialist state, the narrator lifts a critique of loveless marriage directly from Friedrich Engels's critique of bourgeois marriage: "In a society where commercial goods still exist, marriage like many other things, can hardly escape the process used in commodity exchange." In a language reminiscent of Engels's Victorian romanticism,[15] she affirms her mother's passionate love as a "force somehow stronger than death." She argues that marriage in China is still stuck in the feudal past, that the "blame [for China's loveless marriages] lies with the old mind-set passed down from earlier times," returning to a theme popular in Shanghai fiction in the early Republican era: true love confronting a feudal ethical code.[16]

In its day Zhang's story was understood as an affirmation of individual romantic passion in the aftermath of the negation of individual human feeling during the Cultural Revolution, but the story also reflects the revolutionary rhetoric of that recent period. Romantic passion is a noble revolutionary principle, worth defending against social pressures and pragmatic considerations. Typical of early reform-era writers, Zhang invokes Engels and Russian authors in support of the morality of romantic passion.[17] Such citations reflect more than an attempt to clothe romantic sentiments in socialist garb, but were, in fact, important sources of inspiration for this post–Cultural Revolution generation. Many middle-aged intellectuals and writers I interviewed mentioned the influence of Engels and Russian novelists. Partly reflecting this legacy of socialist romanticism, romantic feelings (*ganqing*) still are accorded great moral authority in public discussions of sexual relationships, including the 1980 Marriage Law, which stipulates that *ganqing* is the basis of marriage. In "Love Must Not Be Forgotten," the narrator implicitly extends Engels's critique of materialistic marriage to the more radical conclusion that *any* relationship based on affection, even extramarital love, should not be considered immoral, a view that would become increasingly mainstream in China,[18] though meeting with strong official disapproval. Despite the political criticism the story drew from the Maoist left, fiction and magazine stories during the next decade widely echoed the story's portrayal of a new romantic heroism among youth and a new morality of romantic feeling that rhetorically trumps "feudal" norms, parental objections, materialistic concerns, and everyday social inhibitions.

Pleasure Babies

Only twenty years separate "Love Must Not Be Forgotten" from the two young Shanghai women writers Mian Mian and Wei Hui, but the cultural chasm seems much wider. Through their sexually explicit fiction and their outrageous public personae, Mian Mian and Wei Hui have gained fame in China and attention globally.[19] While the popular reception of "Love Must Not Be Forgotten" was largely contained within China, Wei Hui and Mian Mian are products of global cultural markets. Foreign correspondents were easily enamored with their mastery of the global rebellious idioms of drugs, sex, and rock and roll. After appearing in magazines and newspapers including *Time, Newsweek, Der*

Spiegel, the *Asahi Shimbun*, and the *Observer*, the authors gained the attentions of mainland Chinese media and literary critics, a now-familiar process of star making that the Chinese call "reimporting" (*waizhuan neixiao*)—the translation of foreign fame into local status. While the Chinese government has now banned their most famous novels and stopped local media interviews, they maintain their local public personae through a hyped-up rivalry on the Internet, including charges of plagiarism and public nudity, public beer fights in Shanghai bars, threats involving the secret police, and, most reasonably, charges of drumming up controversy for commercial profit.[20] Both novelists now have contracts with prominent U.S. publishers, translating their suppression at home into status abroad, another familiar movement in the transnational circulation of contemporary Chinese culture, which Geremie Barmé calls "packaged dissent."[21]

Mian Mian can claim to be the first young writer to publish a sexually explicit account of underworld youth culture in her short story collection *La La La*, which first appeared in Hong Kong in 1997. Her biography requires no exaggeration. Until the publication of her novel *Candy*, more people read about Mian Mian's life than read her fiction, including her career as a manager in a ritzy Shenzhen brothel, her fight against heroin addiction, and her life as a Shanghai nightlife maven and avant-garde novelist, all achieved before age twenty-five (she was born in 1971). In her dark rude stories, virtually devoid of the everyday trappings of family, work life, and marriage, Mian Mian mordantly dissects her once-ruinous lifestyle. In person, the author is both self-indulgent and self-effacing, off hard drugs but famously hoarse from chain-smoking, sardonically lovelorn, hanging out in bars with a retinue of wanna-be avant-gardists and foreign barflies.[22]

Wei Hui is a year younger than Mian Mian. Described as a nightlife dilettante and a "good girl trying to be a bad girl" by Mian Mian, Wei Hui enjoyed the more respectable upbringing of a student at Shanghai's premier Fudan University and lives at home with her mother, though she portrays herself as a denizen of Shanghai's underground. A notorious show-off, rumors circulated that her book was banned after she revealed her breasts at a press conference in Chengdu.[23] Situated in the same social milieu as Mian Mian's work, Wei Hui's pulp is more approachable and more popular with Shanghai's young readers. Before it was banned, her novel *Shanghai Baby* sold over eighty thousand legal copies and probably several hundred thousand pirated copies. In some ways, both these young women represent a return to the Shanghai-style literature (*haipaiwenxue*) of pre-1949 writers like Liu Na'ou and Mu Shiying, who similarly dwelled in the nightlife, embellished their writing with trendy English phrases, and ostentatiously posed as decadent playboys.[24] Condescendingly labeled "pretty young women writers" by Chinese critics, Mian Mian and Wei Hui have the advantage of looking the part of the femme fatales they portray themselves to be and the disadvantage of being identified personally with the characters they describe.

"La La La" is the title story of Mian Mian's first published collection and the basis of her popular novel *Candy*.[25] Like "Love Must Not Be Forgotten," it is a story of romantic passion, but with a decidedly ironic portrayal of romantic heroism. The story describes the female narrator's sexual love affair with a rock-and-roll star in a depressing milieu of drugs and prostitution, situated in Shenzhen. The details of the narrator's life resemble those of the real-life author, an impoverished childhood, adolescent rebellion, a career in the Shenzhen nightlife world, alcoholism, heroin addiction, and an eventual return to Shanghai to write her story. The boyfriend Saining's profile would have been equally unimaginable in fiction twenty years before: a rock musician, sexually promiscuous, a heroin addict, and a victim of child abuse by a rich father now living abroad. But in other ways he also resembles the improbable romantic heroes of popular Taiwan romance novels: a rock star educated as a classical violinist; a poor student who has nonetheless read Proust and Joyce; a faithless lover but also a hopeless romantic who magically appears at fortuitous moments. Despite these elements of Chinese pop romance, the story begins and ends on a harsh sexual note. An opening passage describes the protagonist's first night with Saining and her first sexual experience:

> The Doors are playing. This dreamlike first time seems kind of violent, and that goes against all my years of sexual fantasies. I can't understand the excitement on this man's face. I can't find that in my own needs. I am a silent, frustrated cat. The thing appearing in front of my eyes seems almost evil, rude, and pressing. Later, out of my body comes something that isn't mine. I walk into the bathroom. The blurred mirror reflects a blurred face. He is a stranger I met in a bar. I don't know who he is.[26]

Despite this disturbing sexual initiation, their sexual passion keeps them together and yet constantly threatens them for the next five years. The narrator explains their romantic attraction in sexual terms: "Saining is the kind of man who gives me that 'dream feeling' when we make love. We both knew that was one of the main reasons we stayed together." However, even this sexual passion can't endure their alcoholism, heroin addiction, suicide attempts, and his sexual affairs with her friends. Finally, he disappears for three years. When she sees him again, their passion has faded. Angry at the wasted years, she pens a vulgar song about him with the constant refrain "He is such a bastard! He is such a bastard!"

Wei Hui's similarly autobiographical novel of a young woman's sexual awakening, *Shanghai Baby*,[27] provides more self-indulgent, explicit, and positive images of a young woman's sexual pleasure and a celebration of Shanghai's consumer leisure culture (more accessible to the reader than the underground rock scene Mian Mian describes). This steamy potboiler follows its protagonist CoCo (named for the fashion designer) through a few months of a tumultuous love affair in Shanghai, simultaneously providing a guided tour of the trendy Shanghai nightlife spots in which the action is situated and a shopping guide to trendy Western brands the protagonist uses. After a disappointing college love affair, CoCo moves in with a heroin-addicted artist boyfriend, Tian Tian, also supported in fine style by a mother living abroad. Unfortunately for CoCo, Tian Tian is impotent. Tiring of her sexless life, CoCo meets a young married German businessman, Mark, with a "sexy foreign smell," a "build like a Nazi," and "a frightfully large member."[28] Explaining her infidelity to her boyfriend, she writes, "From the perspective of many liberated women, finding a man whom you love and another man who can give you orgasms is the best solution for their private lives."[29] Her racially stereotyped German boyfriend serves as an exotic mirror for her self-explorations and a prop for her physical indulgence, a tendency revealed in a comic description of her thoughts while making love:

> We ate the big bowl of sweet Jell-O bite by bite, staring eye to eye. Suddenly we broke out laughing, and he pushed me down on the bed. Like a wild man from an Adriatic sea cave, he began licking my abdomen with his cold, sweetened tongue. "You have the most beautiful private parts," he said. "From Berlin to Shanghai one couldn't find such a fine specimen." I threw my head back and looked up at the ceiling. Physical pleasure robbed me of all my intelligence. "The most beautiful private-parts prize," I thought, that doesn't sound bad to a girl, maybe even better than "best novel of the year."[30]

In the end CoCo fails to keep love separate from sexual passion, falling in love with Mark. But he returns to Germany, Tian Tian dies, and CoCo is left alone.

Shanghai Baby is a celebration of sexual self-indulgence, cut with occasional self-irony. "Self-love is my most beautiful trait," CoCo gloats.[31] Her exuberant masturbatory episodes figure prominently in the sexual descriptions of the novel. While the juxtaposition of the impotent Chinese man and the potent foreigner may read as an unsubtle jab at Chinese manhood, men (Chinese or foreign) are not the focus of the novel, which seldom strays from the feelings of the protagonist herself. Foreign men are but reflexive resources for constructing a new type of Chinese romantic heroine: sexually self-indulgent, morally uncertain, and financially independent.[32] The novel uses a mythologizing "spatial rhetoric" that elides great chunks of the city and exaggerates others, transforming Shanghai into a sexualized archipelago of expatriate parties and nightspots inhabited by voracious white-collar women,[33] artists, foreigners, and prostitutes.[34] Tourists now seek out the real places the novel mentions, such as YY's Disco, where CoCo had sex with her German lover in a toilet stall.[35]

Explicit sexual descriptions and settings in an underground club scene distinguish "La La La" and *Shanghai Baby* from "Love Must Not Be Forgotten" as from all Chinese fiction in the early reform era. In their treatment of romantic love, however, the break is not as absolute. Both celebrate the individual romantic experience as transcending everyday experience and everyday morality. For both writers, romantic passion, not pleasure alone, is the true measure of sexual intensity. In comparison with the romantic idealism of Zhang Jie, however, Wei Hui and Mian Mian express a cynicism about the inherent morality of romantic passion and a pessimism about the stability and reliability of romantic relationships, reflecting an awareness of the fickleness of sexual desire. Their stories of sexual rebellion also represent a decisive break with the modernist Chinese tradition that sees cultural and social proscriptions, especially oppressive "feudal tradition," as the primary obstacle to individual happiness and freedom. Mian Mian, in contrast, describes her characters as "outside of society." Before "La La La" was published, the author told me the line she believed best summarized the story, which appears near the conclusion: "Did we lose control of ourselves because we were seeking freedom, or was our freedom itself just a kind of loss of control?" In this world the obstacle to happiness is freedom itself: the inability of Chinese to cope with bewildering choices, to manage their passions, and to hold on to the things they wish to keep. Wei Hui's story ends on a similar note of moral uncertainty, with the character asking herself, "Who am I?" For both writers, romantic love now unfolds in an ironic and morally uncertain society in which too much choice has become the greater problem, not feudal oppression.[36]

Both writers celebrate romantic passion, but with little conviction of the viability of the relationships and choices they represent. Although superficially more radical than Zhang Jie, the sexual radicalism of these more recent writers provides a weaker rhetorical basis for stories of social and personal sexual awakening than the romantic radicalism of "Love Must Not Be Forgotten." In my view, expressed in greater detail in chapter 4, post-Mao Chinese public sexual culture experienced its most truly radical phase in the romantic heroism of the early reform era. In contrast, the popular fiction of the late 1990s, represented in Mian Mian's and Wei Hui's writing, gives us a more ironic and playful sense of social transformation in which sexual choices are freer, but also more confusing and morally ambivalent. They are not conservative stories, but neither are they revolutionary.

The Politics of Sexual Storytelling in Contemporary Shanghai

Censors first banned Wei Hui's wildly popular *Shanghai Baby* in the spring of 2000, then Mian Mian's *Candy*. State media denounced Wei Hui as "decadent, debauched and a slave of foreign culture," invoking the political mythology of sexual opening in which all forms of sexual deviance originate in an invasive foreign culture (rather than in the romantic and sexual longings of China's youth). State media accused the "pretty women writers" of forgetting the "rich historic and cultural background of Chinese literature."[37] The Party-state will not allow a breast-baring woman writer to celebrate sexual debauchery in Shanghai. According to Ken Plummer, the politics of sexual storytelling works through people sharing sexual stories among like-minded people and building a community around these stories through the mass media.[38] It is the latter public phase of sexual politics that is most difficult in contemporary China. The first fact of public sexual politics in China remains Party censorship. Odd avant-garde pieces, illegal pornography, and academic treatises may slip past the censors, but not a mainstream novel with such popularity among young people as *Shanghai Baby*. All Chinese media are formally controlled by the Party, but the mechanisms of actual control are often more informal. Magazine editors I interviewed frequently mentioned fears of the telephone call from an "old cadre" unhappy at a "daring" sexual article. Hence, editors censor themselves from publishing controversial articles on topics such as homosexuality or even overly positive portrayals of premarital sex.

Even among the community of professional writers, not everyone is happy with the open marketing of sexual stories. Partly this reflects a generation gap. In 1995 I attended a discussion group on "women writers" organized by the Shanghai Academy of Social Sciences and attended by representatives from the Shanghai Women's Federation and Shanghai Writers' Association, now dominated by writers who earned their fame directly after the Cultural Revolution and attained positions of influence in these Party organizations. In a high point of this meeting, one Writers' Association cadre attacked a new group of young female writers for graphically portraying women's sexual experiences in fiction.[39] Afterward Zhu Lin, a Shanghai woman writer who also writes eloquently on sexual themes, decried this criticism as self-serving. "They are attacking us, saying we are displaying women's psychological and physical intimacy for the sake of attracting readers . . . , but in reality their criticism is fake. They are just protecting their own positions [as established writers in the Writers' Association]."

Opposing the permissiveness of the market society, the "old guard" discourages the emergence of any sexual lifestyles outside the heteronormative patterns of (chaste) dating, (monogamous) marriage, and (single) child rearing. The types of sexual stories typically featured in the Chinese media for the past twenty years have, therefore, on the whole been romantic tales leading to marriage or cautionary tales of the dangers of sexual adventures outside of marriage.[40] On the other hand, contemporary consumers are no longer interested in politicized moral tales. Young people want sexual stories that reflect their experiences and fantasies, including stories such as *Shanghai Baby* and *Candy* situated in the new consumer society. The result is a constant tension between the desires of consumers and the strategies of the state for disciplining these desires.

Most Western sociological treatments of sexual storytelling focus on what Plummer calls "modernist" "personal confession" stories of "suffering, surviving and surpassing," stories around which survivor communities are built, sexual subcultures are legitimated, and political movements are formed.[41] Sexual stories in Chinese public culture are seldom so affirming of sexual difference. For instance, volumes of "true life" sexual stories were immensely popular in Shanghai in 1999. The most popular, a national best-seller that prompted many imitators, had the unselfconsciously ironic title *Absolute Secrets*, loudly revealing its "secret" true stories of sexual suffering, betrayal, and revenge to readers all over China. The volume highlights the romantic travails of Beijing's white-collar women, the 1990s version of the sexually independent modern woman. In her preface the author, An Dun, a columnist for the *Beijing Youth Daily*, describes these "true stories" she originally collected for her newspaper column:

> At first I was very alarmed, because of the people I interviewed, I never ran across any who fit the ordinary idea of the "good husband and wife."

> I never recorded a happily married couple with any hope of growing old
> together or a dating couple who was able to be faithful without desiring
> others. All of the stories are tragic and broken, all of their plots even more
> full of life and death than those plays full of life and death, even more
> likely to make you feel like wringing your hands and sighing.[42]

This description would also hold true of many edited volumes and popular magazines I saw on sale in 1999: "true stories" of greed, betrayal, and infidelity in a time of sexual disorder brought on by the opening of society, largely affirming the liberal but conventional family values of the typical urban reader.[43] These melodramatic stories of "big moneys" and "white-collar misses" appeal to urbanites vicariously exploring new urban sexual geography, while avoiding any sexual radicalism that would arouse official condemnation. They are a compromised form of sexual politics, governed by self-censorship that avoids overt moralizing but also skirts any open calls for sexual liberation.

On the other hand, neither state censors nor self-censoring editors can determine the uses readers make of stories. The fact of a story being told *at all* may be more important than its political packaging or even a moralistic denouement.[44] Readers and listeners have the ability to read stories in ways that contravene the meanings intended by producers and censors. Even the melodramatic writings of An Dun reassure young women about the "normalcy" of their own sexual experiences and serve as models for telling their own personal sexual stories. Several of the young women I interviewed in the summer of 2000 mentioned An Dun's work and their desire to have their own story recorded in the same fashion. An Dun also has described people offering to pay her to record their anonymous stories.[45] People use stories in different ways. While some young women find Wei Hui's *Shanghai Baby* "excessive" (*guofen*), echoing official condemnations, others I interviewed found her book an affirmation of female sexuality or a description of the "truth," as one female informant who dated only foreigners told me. Other references are more ambiguous. For instance, one young woman seeking a foreign boyfriend playfully invoked the "Shanghai Baby" in her personal ad in a popular Shanghai English-language magazine:

> **Looking for nice conversation** or great friendship or true love. Plus, I
> won't be your sexy Shanghai Baby. Take care. Apple5151@ . . . .com.[46]

For readers with knowledge of Chinese, her e-mail address adds a humorous ambiguity to her disavowal—5151 reads in Chinese as "I want. I want."

Scenes and Characters

If stories are the way in which people make different senses out of sexual experience, then an analysis of a local sexual culture must pay attention to the conventional story elements that structure these stories. Burke identifies five different elements that comprise a "grammar" of dramatic action: scene, actor, agency, purpose, and act.[47] Further tools of Burke's dramatistic analysis include analyzing the "ratios" of these elements in a story, for instance, the relative importance of scenes versus acts. Below, I focus on the first two elements of Burke's pentad, using ethnographic descriptions to demonstrate how Shanghai's sexual culture is broadly organized around local conceptions of scene and character, representing a local cultural repertoire of modernist sexual imagery.

The Opening Scene: The Sexual Rhetoric of Shanghai's Boulevards

"Opening up" is a story of spatial transformation. Shanghai's contemporary geography is built upon the "skeleton"[48] of the Western-style boulevards that defined the French and International Concessions before 1949. Shanghai's sexual opening is most visibly a reopening, renewal, and reconstruction of these mythologized arteries of leisure, consumption, and sexual spectacle. The contrast with the style and geography of other Chinese cities is still remarkable.[49] Meandering, crowded night markets still dominate public spaces in many inland Chinese cities such as Xian and Kaifeng. The center of Beijing is dominated by the old Imperial Palace and, in concentric rings, by more contemporary monuments to national power, concrete socialist office blocks topped with pagodas and pavilions—unintended architectural parodies of Deng's "socialism with Chinese characteristics." Shanghai's boulevards, in contrast, structure the visual experience of the city around strolling, shopping, and "cruising" the human vistas, each pedestrian scrawling their own "long poems of walking" in the city.[50] The hybrid, layered, and heterogeneous sexual rhetoric of Shanghai's boulevards can be best comprehended with a virtual stroll down Shanghai's most famous boulevards: Nanjing and Huaihai Roads.

A first day's stroll in Shanghai would invariably place you on Shanghai's waterfront, known as the "Bund," staring across the turgid waters of the Huangpu River at the ever-denser knot of office towers in the new financial district of Pudong. Beside these burgeoning, gleaming towers, the first noteworthy sight will be Shanghai's Orient Pearl, Asia's largest TV tower, which was built in the 1990s and is adorned with two huge pink glass balls speared on a concrete spike. The Orient Pearl shocks the architecturally sensitive with its giant pink dance hall glow balls, but the antecedents of its vaguely indecent style can be seen in the Occidentalist beaux arts fantasies of the amusement parks and department stores of Shanghai's colonial century, structures that still line Shanghai's boulevards.[51]

Turning our backs on the river, we head up Shanghai's oldest shopping boulevard, Nanjing Road, a long section of which is now a sanitized pedestrian mall lined with shopping centers. If you are a sophisticated Chinese urbanite, you will undoubtedly dodge past the poorly dressed farmers and workers from outside of Shanghai who flock to this most famous of Shanghai's boulevards. If you are a man, however, you might be approached by the many out-of-town prostitutes who solicit visitors near the waterfront. All along the way, numerous street-side display cases sell condoms and sexual aids, a booming market in the late 1990s.[52] This boulevard is constantly changing. In the early 1990s, before there was a pedestrian mall or sex-aid vendors, not far from the waterfront you would have passed a display case of newspapers for citizens' edification. If you were in a hurry, it is unlikely you would have noticed the men glancing from the newspapers to one another in this busy male-male sexual cruising spot. (This wall has been demolished recently, but in 1999 there was still a gay meeting spot in a small park directly adjacent to a police station a few hundred meters down a side street from the former newspaper wall.) If you were a Westerner and visited in the spring of 1999, you might have paid special attention to a large billboard advertising a Chinese dress shoe brand. In the ad a beautiful blond woman in a black minidress stoops awkwardly to pick up several hundred-dollar bills strewn in front of her, looking up anxiously at the seated man who dropped them. Only the suited legs and black dress shoes of the man are visible. As the sign suggests, Shanghai's Occidentalism is not a simple "worship of the West," but can also be represented through a financially invigorated Chinese masculinity—fetishized as an expensive shoe—dominating the cowering Western woman. As foreigners, however, we also might miss other ironic readings of the sign, such as a remark by my Shanghaiese wife that this provincial Chinese brand of shoes was unlikely to impress anyone from Shanghai.

Just down Tibet Road from the billboard, the Great World is worth a side trip. Built in 1919, it was the largest amusement park in Asia in the early twentieth century and attracted a mass audience including families and women.[53] The Great World featured entertainment and rides but also sexual spectacles with an exotic foreign edge, including nude photo galleries, dancing shows, and "flower contests" among Shanghai's most famous courtesans.[54] In 1995 I visited the Great World, now dwarfed by postmodern office towers and its own neoclassic colonnades cased in neon advertisements for Gillette shaving products. It had lost its chic appeal in Shanghai but remained a popular attraction for rural visitors and migrant workers. While the traditional acrobats, magicians, and singers attracted a smattering of visitors, one room was packed with tanned, wiry migrant workers in cheap Western-style suits, together with a few wives and girlfriends in plain country dress. They were watching a "fashion show" in which bored young women paraded down a runway in swimsuits and sequined gowns slit high up their pale thighs, a scene from old Shanghai, the rough visages of rural China fixed on the milky feminine spectacle of "modern" Shanghai.

While the Great World may have been visited most frequently by migrant laborers, the genre of sexual display in the fashion show had by no means become a low-status or unpopular phenomenon in 1990s Shanghai. Further up Nanjing Road, the Japanese-owned Caesars Club featured model shows popular with Japanese tourists,[55] where for seventy yuan you could view a song-and-dance routine by a troupe of tall, pretty young women in slinky evening wear with a finale in risqué bathing suits. Model shows were popular entertainment in the 1990s, and in 1996 there were thirty-eight troupes of models registered with the Shanghai Ministry of Culture. Further down the street, you could drop into the private Sexual Culture Museum of sociologist Liu Dalin (dubbed "China's Kinsey") housed in the newly rebuilt Sincere Department Store, which contained a notorious dance hall before 1949. The fascinating sex museum displayed antique Chinese sexual toys, pornographic ceramics, erotic scrolls, and a membership card for a Republican-era lesbian club.[56] Or, more conventionally, you could stop to shop for fashions at one of the many new shopping complexes lining Nanjing Road's new pedestrian mall, including the New World, a giant building topped with a multicolored ball of lights evoking its pre-1949 incarnation as a competitor to the Great World.

Nanjing Road's pedestrian mall now ends with a bronze statue of a husband and wife carrying a baby girl and their shopping bags. The new pedestrian mall works as an official spatial narrative of the city's opening up: sanitized, family friendly, oriented to the mass consumer—cosmopolitan and kitschy in a distinctively Shanghai style. On the other hand, the various sexual side trips, erotic diversions, and individual "walking rhetorics" remain a realm of chance sexual discoveries and an opportunity for deviant pleasures. Despite the state's attempt to write its own dominant spatial story for Shanghai through demolition, urban renewal, and the central pedestrian mall, Shanghai's boulevards and adjacent alleyways retain a variety of incommensurable and changeable sexual texts, allowing the casual visitor a chance to write his or her own sexual poem of walking in the city.

You might end your stroll in the late afternoon on the fashionable west end of Huaihai Road at the Sunshine Café, a rather famous exemplar of the Western-style café boom in Shanghai. I met the author Mian Mian in the Sunshine Café for the first time in 1995 and introduced her to her first Western journalist at a bar not far away.[57] The success of such locales, their commercial self-mythologizing, depends on their ability to attract the mythological characters of the city, the "pretty woman writer" or the "fashionable woman" generally. The manager of the Sunshine explained this process to me: "We opened up and didn't have a lot of customers at first. My boss looked at all those beautiful young women walking down the street and said, 'How do I get them in here? If they are in here, then business will be good.' I did it for him." The manager turned the Sunshine into a popular and inexpensive boulevard stop for dating couples and women. Young Shanghai women liked the small intimate tables suitable for chatting, with American-style wall paintings, candles on every table, and Western and Chinese pop music piped out at high decibels. In contrast, the typical Chinese restaurant in the early 1990s was set up mostly for the banquet—a male-dominated ritual staged on large round tables, with bright lights and no music, a space for loud toasts and networking, not romantic conversations or chats with a friend. Next door, the Sunshine's manager also operates a fashionable bar called the Cotton Club, where foreign and Shanghai singles mingle and listen to local rock and jazz bands.

If you've walked as far as the Sunshine Café, you've spent a fairly typical weekend day for a young Shanghai person. Shanghai youth, especially women, consistently described their favorite pastime as "strolling the streets" (guangjie), not necessarily buying anything but enjoying the display of commodities and the anonymous sociability of the sidewalk. These young women strollers are also described in a youth magazine as "the most beautiful and pleasant urban scenery,"[58] a sense coinciding with the reform-era reclaiming of Shanghai's boulevards as places of consumption and leisure, places where fashionable young women are both central actors as consumers and the central "attraction" and "style" that make dull commodities and marketplaces exotic.[59] However, this conventional description of women as "scenery" implies a passivity, which is neither accurate nor always intended. In an interview a Shanghai woman fashion writer described Shanghai's feminine boulevard culture of fashion and flirtation:

Women's sense of feeling [*ganqing*] has much to do with flirtation. This is a very urban sense, an expression of city life. People use this to express a kind of dissatisfaction, but they won't generally go beyond a certain limit. . . . Anyway, this [daring fashion] isn't what people wear all the time. They have to dress quite seriously in other places. Wearing these clothes increases their head-turning ratio [*huitoulu*] and girls like that. . . . Of course, people like people looking at them. This is the basic feminine vanity. She wants others to appreciate [*xinshang*] her.

Different from the nineteenth-century idea of the voyeuristic male *flâneur*, the boulevard *flâneuse* is both voyeur and exhibitionist, aware that she is being watched as well as watching others.[60] The boulevard is a stage for promiscuous flirtations of the eye that last an instant and are probably the most characteristic sex act in urban life and the one most free of consequences.[61] The boulevard entails the improvisational art of the flirtatious glance, which must be distinguished from the sexual gaze of a privileged observer. Not that glances are always flirtatious, friendly, or devoid of judgment; take, for instance, a type of glance I became very familiar with from interviews and my own experience, the glance directed toward a Western man walking with a Chinese woman down a boulevard. Shanghai people, particularly young women, are often very interested in these relationships, and their long glances convey this interest. Almost always the eye falls first on the "foreigner" then drops quickly to his female companion, scanning her from head to toe, judging her the way an audience judges any performer, whether she is cut out for the role, whether she is pretty enough, tall enough, confident enough to play the character she has chosen to play: the ambitious Shanghai girl who has "caught" a foreigner. When asked, their comments reflect their judgments of her performance. For an unattractive woman: "Why do foreigners pick such ugly Chinese girls?" For a young woman with an incongruously unattractive old man: "That's no different from prostitution!" For a performer who fits her role: "Pretty girls all want a foreigner or a rich guy."[62] Such largely unspoken judgments, while not friendly in content, are part of the visual rhetoric of boulevard sociability and seldom have overt social consequences.

Urbanism can be understood as the rhetoric of urban space, the ways in which places are made into scenes for stories and actions. The boulevards and their adjacent spaces of consumer leisure support a relatively free and democratic sociability of flirtation, self-display, and impersonal commentary, alongside a heterogeneous commercial culture of fashions and sexualized spectacles. The sexual rhetoric of the boulevard is thus one of heterogeneity, play, and ca-

sual critique as opposed to the sameness and discipline of the planned socialist utopia or the domesticity and personalized gossip of the residential alleyways described in the next chapter.

The Main Character: The Shanghai Girl

On Huaihai Road (formerly the avenue Joffre), the main street of the
old French Concession and still the most fashionable shopping boulevard in
Shanghai, the local district government erected a peculiar monument to the
main character of Shanghai's stories of sexual opening. Next to a busy subway
entrance, a shapely young woman in a miniskirt and a tight-fitting blouse
grasped a phone as though chatting with a friend or perhaps arranging a date
for the evening, a casual moment of flirtatious possibilities frozen in bronze.
The statue of the girl stood near the gardens of what was once the French Club,
now part of an exclusive Japanese-owned hotel. The statue was both cute and
shocking. Her skirt rose high on her thigh, and you could see the outlines of
her nipples through her blouse, reminding us that Shanghai women have always shocked rustic outsiders with their bold dress.[63] She blended well into her
surroundings. Across the street the Old-New Lingerie Shop advertised its wares
with quaintly painted, buxom, and vaguely East European women lounging
outdoors in underwear. (In 1999 the ads were changed to glossy photos of Chinese models in bright red lingerie for Chinese New Year.) On the other corner,
the Guotai movie house, formerly the famous Cathay Cinema, advertised the
latest Hollywood blockbusters in hand-painted posters. Fashionable young
women, resembling the woman in the statue, jostled past her with their male
companions on arm.[64]

In addition to its physical landscape of boulevards and bungalows, every
city has a cultural landscape of tall tales, personalities, and reputations, including imaginary characters such as the Shanghai girl (Shanghai xiaoguniang) celebrated in the statue on Huaihai Road. According to Gerald Suttles, cities tend to
accrue their reputations during the periods of economic and demographic
growth when they burst into global consciousness as "shock cities" representing the economic and spatial frontiers of new forms of capitalism and urban
organization.[65] Shanghai was the shock city of China, and the most shocking
representative of Shanghai's modernity was the "modern girl."[66] In Shanghai's
stories of social and personal sexual transformations, she plays the dominant
role. She is, to use the language of Burke's dramatism, the "most representative
character, . . . embodying the conclusions of the development as a whole."[67]
Shanghai's Republican-era modern girl was the product of the cultural foment

in Shanghai following the May 4th Movement in 1919 and the influence of Hollywood film and Japanese literary representations. Film, advertising, theater, literature, and magazines promulgated images of a new type of woman who occupied the public spaces of the new urban consumer economy.[68] The prototypical modern girls of pre-Communist Shanghai were the prostitute and the film actress, associated with a free but commodified sexuality and a modern moral sensibility. Shu-Mei Shih writes of the modern girl represented in pre-1949 avant-garde Chinese fiction:

> The modern girl's sexual promiscuity, rather than condemned on patriarchal moral grounds, becomes the mark of her own free will to pursue her own desires. Her materiality, rather than condemned as vulgar and corrupt, becomes the sign of her ability to adapt to the modern world; it is a metonymic extension of the inescapable materiality of modernity. . . . [S]he embodies the speed of modernity that demands pursuit.[69]

In the mass culture of the Republican era, the modern girl was also a metonymic representation of the moral dangers of this market-driven modernity, her changeability, autonomy, and materiality representative of a general confusion of moral standards.

Like the architecture of Shanghai boulevards, the character of the Shanghai girl ties together images of pre-1949 Shanghai with the commercial city reemerging today. In the current imagination of the city, the Shanghai girl's pre-1949 incarnations as Jazz Age prostitute, dance hall girl, and film star shade into the "white-collar miss" and "fashionable girl" of the 1990s.[70] According to a 1996 magazine article, the "fashionable girl" engages in a "completely new type" of autonomous lifestyle based on her new power as a consumer, and now also as a salary earner. Typically a clerical or service worker, she sells her youth and talents, buys her own entertainment, pays for her own living space, and fears commitment, love, and marriage.[71] The new fashionable Shanghai girl subsumes a number of more specific characters (from the "white-collar girl" to the "model" and "hostess") who embody the contradictions of her autonomous (but commodified) sexuality and financially independent (but mercenary) lifestyle. She is young, usually unmarried, and sexually active. Such characters provide a continuity to the episodic public conversations and moral panics about the pleasures and dangers of the market economy and the moral boundaries defined around young women's sexual choices.[72] One celebratory and morbid view of the contemporary Shanghai girl comes from the pen of the avant-garde Shanghai writer Mian Mian:

Shanghai is feminine, like its roses: narcissistic, time-sensitive, snobbish, extremely temperamental, cold, and distancing. Shanghai roses are particularly good at suppressing their yearning for orgasm. They use their sex and gender as a weapon. This is a pretentious city, and expertise in pretentiousness is a necessity for survival in the city's nights. . . . I love all the streets in this city because their tender curving lines suggest loving emotions. But I am only too familiar with the city's potential for cruelty. I enjoy being a Shanghai girl because all the pleasures and pains it brings me are equally special.[73]

Mian Mian's Shanghai girl reserves her sexuality as a weapon and an exchange value, her "roses" evoking the famous "Red Rose, White Rose" of Republican-era woman writer Zhang Ailing. Whereas Zhang's "red" and "white" roses represent the traditional distinction between the pure and fallen woman, Mian Mian drops the standard of chastity and focuses on the contradiction between romantic and pragmatic sex.

According to a 1990 survey, 80 percent of Shanghai men and women still agreed that "a woman's chastity was more important than her life."[74] The Shanghai girl of popular imagination doesn't feel this way. She sees her chastity as something "valuable" surely, maybe something to sell, maybe to give as a token of love, but under her own control and definitely not more important than her life. A major contention of this study is that practical moral conversations aren't usually framed in the rulelike codes of survey questions such as "Is premarital sex permissible?" or "Is chastity more important than life?" Moral discourses are more often represented in flexible conversations about real and imagined people for whom prototypes like the Shanghai girl can be both a model and a foil. For example, at an informal Shanghai house party, the conversation drifted into gossip—as was often the case—in this case a discussion of a mutual acquaintance, a twenty-year-old music student often seen in Shanghai's posh nightclubs. Because she lived alone and had no regular job, her sexual behavior and the sources of her income evoked speculation. Since some of us didn't know her very well, the host of the party, a thirty-two-year-old Shanghai native and avid raconteur, lampooned her younger friend in a dramatic parody:

She is the real Shanghai girl I tell you, not us. When her boyfriend is not here, she goes out every night, every night. When I tell her that she is a bad girl, she always says in this little girl voice, "I'm still little. I don't understand these things." She does this whenever we start talking about sex. She will say, "I'm too young, don't talk about this in front of me." I tell her, "How could you not know? You've been living with your boyfriend for a year." She always does this—when people say something to her that

she already knows, she will always open her mouth and say really innocently [imitating a coquettish voice], "Oh, really, is that so? I didn't know
that," even though she already knows this. People are always being tricked
by her, always! She is really the typical Shanghai girl. When she wants to
go out, she will spend two weeks planning what she will wear, buying the
clothes, choosing everything for the effect, buying a bra that will show off
those big tits of hers. Nothing is accidental with her. She thinks about it
all ahead of time. She is a little vamp [hulijing].

The tone of this discussion was ironic, expressing neither straightforward condemnation nor approval. Although she criticized the younger woman's cunning, the speaker admired her sexual daring and reserved her strongest ridicule
for the men who fell for her tricks. As discussed in the next two chapters, such
ambivalent gossip is where local sexual publics are formed and local sexual cultures articulated and contested. Participants in these conversations use imaginary characters such as the Shanghai girl to represent moral extremes against
which the more pragmatic and ambiguous choices of real people are measured.
Greedy, strong-willed Shanghai girls and stingy, weak Shanghai men are the
foils and protagonists of countless everyday stories. The sexual culture of the
city maintains its coherence and intelligibility through these stereotypic characters (along with other narrative elements, including scenes), all part of the
"cumulative texture of urban culture."[75]

Becoming a Shanghai Girl

I will end this introductory chapter with an example of how this rhetoric of sexual spaces and characters works in everyday social interactions.
Through this ethnographic example, I want to show how lives are to some extent structured by the stories people tell, including characters like the Shanghai
girl and scenes like the boulevard and the alleyway. The example story also
points out that while sexual storytelling is indeed a means of self-invention,[76]
it is never a completely free invention, nor an original one. Rather, it is an outcome of social interactions that rely upon and reinforce gender and class categories, largely represented through these prototypical characters and spatial
categories. This story also brings up many issues that I will take up in later chapters, including definitions of dating relationships and standards for premarital
sexual behavior.

For several spring nights in a row in 1996, I went to a popular discotheque
on Huaihai Road called Touch. Because of ongoing renovations, the managers
decided to let people enter for free after 9 P.M. and the place suddenly swarmed
with Shanghai's impecunious teenagers, producing the largest crowds of teens

I'd ever seen in a Shanghai disco. Hundreds packed the dance floor, teenage girls climbing onto platforms and performing provocative line dances in the skimpy halter tops that had only recently become acceptable in Shanghai. On one of these last free nights at the disco, I met Linda.[77] She was with a group of young people fighting playfully over a promotional Marlboro hat that one of them had been distributing as a part-time job promoting the U.S. cigarette brand. Linda was a tall, pretty young woman with red-tinted hair, a somewhat avant-garde style recently imported from Japan. Her tight white shorts glowed brightly in the black lights, and Linda herself radiated the fresh iridescent charm of a young woman of nineteen who had only initiated herself into the nightlife that summer. When her friends left "on business," she stayed behind and talked to me. She was unusually friendly and confident in replying to my questions. She said she didn't like to dance all that much. "With the boys most of the dance has to do with footwork. With the girls it's all just shaking their butt." I asked her why she didn't leave with her friends. She said her boyfriend was the DJ, and she was waiting for him. I asked her to arrange an interview with the DJ and she agreed.

I met her the next day to find that she had arranged for me to interview a different DJ at a struggling new discotheque called Absolute. Her "boyfriend" wasn't available, and she explained that she didn't see him that often. Linda liked hanging out with the DJs, admiring their long hair, flashy personalities, and fashionable accents that imitated the flat-tongued Mandarin of Hong Kongese. That night she introduced me to Tiger, a DJ from an old family of theater performers in Shanghai, and Johnny, a wanna-be "dance leader" and sometimes hustler.[78] The two guys enjoyed discussing their sexual experiences in front of Linda, whom they described as sexually "naive" (danchun) and bound to "change" (bian) in a few years. When I asked what they meant by "change," they joked that soon she would take up with a "big money or a foreigner." Linda said, "No way, not me," but otherwise listened to these jests without any visible discomfort. She seemed to enjoy the attention. She said that she liked meeting different people in the disco, and when asked about her intentions in meeting guys, she said, "Of course, I'm not looking for a get-married boyfriend at my age."

A few days later I took some friends to a Taiwanese-owned sports bar where Linda worked part-time for six hundred yuan a month. As usual, she wore a tight stomach-revealing T-shirt and her white shorts. My college-educated girlfriend said disparagingly, "She would look better if she didn't wear those stomach-revealing things." Linda seemed interested in my young acquaintance, a Japanese exchange student. She was impressed that he paid four thousand yuan a month in rent. She said she liked his long hair, and they exchanged hair-care details and telephone numbers. They made a date, but things didn't work out. My friend reported that she was an enthusiastic kisser, but that was as far as she would go sexually. (In Tokyo, he said, girls her age often found kissing more intimate than sexual intercourse.) He told her he already had a girlfriend in Japan, and to his dismay, she spent the evening grilling him about his relationship with his girlfriend, his income, and what sort of work his father did. She was too much the conniving Shanghai girl, he believed, looking for some advantage out of a relationship with a foreigner. When I asked her about him, she said, laughing, "He's very bad." Then half complaining, she said, "He has a girlfriend." She added, as a hint of intimate knowledge, that he lied about the shampoo he was using.

I found out that she was completing an education in hotel management at a secondary vocational school, a low-level institution that promised little in the way of employment. She still lived in a tiny room together with her parents and said she wanted to move out, but her parents wouldn't let her. "They are afraid I would have people stay over or something," she said with a giggle. She told me that she had met many businessmen at the sports bar where she worked. She called them "big brothers," a term that some women in Shanghai use to refer to older male friends or patrons. One of them invited her to travel with him to Ningbo, a nearby city. She was very thrilled by the idea because she had never been outside of Shanghai before. I asked her if she liked men of that age (about thirty). She said, "Oh, thirty, that's too old." She declined this first offer (although later she went).

The next time I met her it was at Absolute, together with Johnny, who had finally persuaded the manager to pay him a small salary to dance. She walked out with Johnny, and my girlfriend and I accompanied them down a deserted late-night Nanjing Road. We felt they looked like a romantic young couple, holding hands and chatting quietly. Later that summer I asked Johnny if he liked Linda. He said, "I like her more than a little, but less than totally. . . . She is just bored, so she wants to be with me. We have a lot of time to kill, and she thinks I am good-looking. I am good to her; I accompany her doing this and that. She likes the fact that I hang out with her and will do things with her." He explained that he had another girlfriend and that Linda also knew this. He said, "[Linda] could be only a lover. She couldn't have 'official status' [mingfen]. Also, if she is a virgin, then I won't play with her. I can't bear the burden of responsibility for two virgins at once. That's my belief. You have to be responsible for this." Johnny explained that he was already "responsible" for taking his girlfriend's virginity. "Two virgins would be too much. Some guys don't care. They think sleeping with a virgin doesn't matter at all. But I think God will punish you for this. He will not punish your person, but punish your soul. If a girl isn't a virgin, then there is no burden, no responsibility."[79] Still, for a few weeks he spent more time with Linda than with his girlfriend, frequently walking her home on the long road from the disco, because neither could afford the taxi, sometimes cooking dinner for her and sharing his views on things like sex. Johnny said that Linda would change. "She is very naive, very immature. She has never worked before. Girls are all at first like that when they are just out of school. After they enter society, they change. You can't be hungry and still talk about love."

Later that summer Linda insisted that I visit her home. She met me at a busy intersection in Zhabei, a famous working-class district of dilapidated brick houses and old leaning storefronts. She lived with her mother and father in a twelve-square-meter room in a ramshackle wooden structure. We passed the soot-blackened cavern of the common kitchen as we climbed up the rickety unlit stairway to their apartment, a single room with a window onto a busy commercial street. The only decorations were some clipped magazine photos of a Hong Kong star taped to a wall. "That's my [first] ex-boyfriend," she said. I was puzzled. She explained, "That's not really him, but he looked exactly like [the star], so I cut out the picture. He's very handsome." Her actual boyfriend was a cook in a well-known Cantonese restaurant, she explained. Linda also showed me a picture of herself from her one trip outside Shanghai. It was taken by the "big brother" businessman she had met at the sports bar. He had taken her to accompany him and some friends to Ningbo. Her mother hadn't wanted her to go, she said, but relented at Linda's insistence.

Her mother, a laid-off factory worker, served us dinner. Linda explained that her father was out playing mah-jongg, as he did nearly every night. Her kind and sickly mother apologized for the shabby apartment, explaining that she never had any chance to do better in life because as a youth she was "sent down" to the countryside in the Cultural Revolution. She hoped the neighborhood soon would be torn down so they could move to an apartment where Linda might have her own room. She asked me if I thought her daughter was pretty. Confused, I said, "Yes, she is very pretty." Linda blushed, quite pleased. Her mother said that she didn't think Linda was all that pretty. "When she was smaller, she was really pretty, but now she is too chunky." But maybe she is good-looking enough to marry a man who could take her overseas, her mother suggested, perhaps as a hint that I could help her find someone. Given Linda's poor showing in school, her mother clearly believed her daughter's looks were her best chance for living a better life than what she herself had experienced.

After dinner her mother went outside and Linda and I talked privately about her life. I asked her about her boyfriend, the DJ, whom she almost never mentioned. "In fact, we really went out only two or three times," she explained. He had another "official" girlfriend. Linda described herself as a "third person" in the relationship, with no right to break in. She told me that once when the girlfriend was not in town, she slept over at his house and saw her photo. "She is a model, but she isn't very pretty though." She said that her mother had been angry with her the next day for not coming home, but she was able to make excuses. Linda seemed proud of this illicit romantic adventure, but she said they didn't have sex. That was also the last time they went out. "For a while I really, really missed him. Every day I thought about him, but there was nothing I could do to get in touch with him." He never gave her his telephone number, only his beeper number, and he didn't return her calls.

She also told me that she couldn't be Johnny's girlfriend because he already had a girlfriend, and he would also expect her to have sex with him. Johnny had taught her a lot about sex in their conversations, she said, but she couldn't accept his "open attitude" toward sex nor understand his current girlfriend, "who only comes to him for that thing and for nothing else." Sex was a difficult topic for her. She first told me that she "definitely" would wait until she got married to have sex, but then she equivocated. "Of course, you never know. If that happened, then I would just think, 'What's done is done.' I wouldn't worry about that. . . . When I do that with someone I love, then that will be a very happy feeling." But it was clear that all her "boyfriends" expected sex from her, including Johnny, despite his disavowals. Moreover, she was having great difficulty finding a man who would attach himself to her in a long-term relationship. The attractive well-off men in whom she was most interested—even the DJs—didn't want an "official" girlfriend with such a lowly background and minimal achievements. Her looks could gain their attention, but not their loyalty. Moreover, her friends were not shy of reminding her of her poor circumstances, joking that she would eventually fall for a rich man or a foreigner. With her lack of foreign-language skills and education, that latter option wasn't all that realistic, but with her good looks and cheerful personality, she found it easy to meet older married businessmen like the "big brother" who took her to Ningbo. When I departed, I was surprised that Linda seemed proud to accompany me down the alleyway, where all the neighbors sitting out to "catch the cool" knew her and said hello. Many "respectable" young women avoid the gossip that comes from being seen with a foreigner. Linda, however, seemed to count all attention as a compliment.

In the spring of 1999, I returned to Shanghai and, with some difficulty, found Johnny. I was never able to find Linda, and Johnny said he had lost touch with her. "She changed, changed a lot," he said. She found a Taiwan "boss," and for a while she stayed with the boss, who gave her money. Then, according to Johnny, she found work in a karaoke bar and moved into a rented apartment with another girl. "When you met her first, she was really simple-minded. She just wanted to marry and have a family. Now she's changed," Johnny said, as though narrating a predictable television melodrama. Nor was I surprised. From the first I had trouble imagining Linda in that dreary room, sleeping every night on a mat on the floor beside her parents' bed. I imagined she would take whatever chances she could find. I found that many of my poorest young Shanghai friends, including Johnny, do the same, using fashion (borrowed clothes, for Johnny) and the spaces of the nightlife to create their own modern image, their time there justified with hopes of becoming a dance leader, meeting a foreigner, or finding some other concrete opportunity for a better life. Like the working-class immigrant youth in turn-of-the-century American cities, the heterosocial world of commercial amusements holds a special attraction for these youth,[80] a world in which the pressures and choices of the marketplace now substitute for the moral restrictions and values of the old neighborhood society. Among many people in Linda's new social world, to be seen as attractive and well-off brings more "face" than being considered morally straight (laoshi).

In the summer of 2000, I found Johnny again. He said he hadn't heard from Linda in a long time, but his story had changed—although only its ending, not the moral premises. He said now that she had quit her job at the karaoke bar and rejected the chance to be the mistress of the Taiwanese businessman. She had even sold Amway products for a time. "The problem with her is that she still has fantasies about love. Only rich girls should have fantasies about love. A girl from a poor family like that should sell her love to make money. But she doesn't see that." Johnny's judgments are probably extreme (in their embrace of naked materialism and rejection of romantic values) and his storytelling is unreliable, but the "grammar" of his story is typical. His story incorporates a conventional grammar of motives, in which love and money are the conventional purposes of sexual actions, purposes not easily combined, starkly defining Linda's dilemma. The characters are the conventional Shanghai girl and the Taiwanese big money; the scenes, the conventional poor neighborhood and glamorous discos. This grammar of motives structures the social reality in which Linda and Johnny act. The point is not to reify the melodramatic narrative of the sexually mercenary Shanghai girl. I'm sure, in fact, that Linda's life is not completely contained by that narrative of a naive girl facing the temptations of a sexual opening. But the narrative—and its discourse of motives—certainly shapes her life. It is in terms of the commodity value of her youthful sexual attraction that her life chances are understood both by her mother and her peers. It is in terms of the material temptations of big moneys and foreigners that her old friends confidently predict her change and provide a post hoc analysis of her choices. It is in her guise as a materially motivated Shanghai girl, that the foreign student rejects her and the Taiwan businessman pursues her. Even the spatial story of her escape, from the "nowhere" of her low-corner neighborhood to the "somewhere" of the nearby nightspots, simply retraces the familiar spatial story of Shanghai's commercial opening. For a person with her social background and with her attractive appearance, the narrative of sexual opening provides Linda a precarious model of sexual choice and justifies her sexual adventures, pragmatic choices, even the parameters of her romantic impracticality. It also limits her choices in ways that she didn't seem fully aware of when I met her.

Finally, if we consider the rhetoric of moral judgment in Johnny's discussions of Linda's choices, it is rather forgiving, though laced with irony. This ironic acceptance of other people's "bad options" is common among Shanghai youth. To use Burke's terminology, in Shanghai's contemporary sexual culture, the scene-actor ratio appears strongly tilted in favor of the scene, meaning that actors' choices appear to be made for them by their social backgrounds and the situations in which they find themselves. Even the character types Shanghai people use—the white-collar miss, the big money, the foreigner—are more shorthand descriptions of social statuses than of personality types. Within this ironic, almost sociological, discourse of sexual motives, Shanghai youth sound cynical but also unwilling to pass harsh judgments on the choices of others.

The Grammar of Sexual Culture

Sexual stories are not just descriptions of sexual culture, but are the substance of this sexual culture. The public sexual culture that I begin describing in this chapter is not a tightly organized system of normative rules, nor a hegemonic structure of unquestioned cultural assumptions. Rather, I describe a "thinly coherent" system[81] of conventional goals, socially coded places, and socially understood character types that allow people to produce and share meaningful stories of their sexual experience. Within this loosely organized sexual culture, there are certain conventional stories, such as "sexual opening" and "romantic rebellion," and certain conventional story elements, such as Shanghai's commercial boulevards and modern girls, which (because of their conventionality) serve as practical constraints on what is found to be persuasive.

As Burke argues, cultures do not merely "reflect" material realities; they also constitute realities.[82] Shanghai people experience the emerging market economy through local stories and familiar landscapes, including story elements handed down from previous historic "conversations." For instance, they use the conventional characters of the Shanghai girl and the big money to describe a market society that allows women new sexual freedoms but also subjects their sexual choices to a market logic of "prostitution" and "marrying up." They use the conventional scenes of the boulevard and alleyway to represent and experience the freedom and play of consumption and the constraints of a relatively impoverished home life. This shared sexual grammar therefore also serves as a medium through which Shanghai people represent to one another the moral implications of the market society, with its unequal sexual choices. At the same time, this conventional sexual grammar is subject to the influences of powerful social actors, especially the Communist Party. State agents tell their own stories, such as cautionary tales of foreign influence, and suppress others, such as Wei Hui's sexually aggressive *Shanghai Baby*. They even try to rewrite the multivocal spatial story of Shanghai's Nanjing Road as a sanitized tale of middle-class nuclear-family consumerism. Individuals respond to these official stories with their own stories, not negating these dominant public narratives, but reinscribing them with their own purposes, desires, and judgments, thereby recovering the diversity and disorder of public life.

地理

SCENES
High and Low

Neighborhood Sexual Geographies
"Channel 13":The Sexual Rhetoric of a Neighborhood Park

One day in the summer of 1983, my wife, then a twelve-year-old schoolgirl, walked past her large neighborhood park and saw some boys peering over the wall. Her classmates told her the boys were "watching Channel 13." Television sets had only twelve settings in 1983, and this "thirteenth" channel was the spectacle in the parks of live kissing and petting, something not seen on television at that time. This was the first time she had heard this expression, which was popular for a few years in the early 1980s. By 1995 "Channel 13" was no longer merely a metaphor. The young voyeurs of "Channel 13" grew up to be the viewers of real television spectacles on a growing number of cable television channels—far more than thirteen—which regularly portrayed the illicit sexuality that Maoist surveillance had aimed to repress in the parks as well as the media. "Channel 13" metonymically represents a small but significant "collapse of the 'panoptic' model of sexuality,"[1] but also presages its replacement by a model of controlled, commercial sexual spectacles.

Neighborhood spaces lend themselves to many sexual uses, a local spatial rhetoric of sexuality often ignored in studies of sexual culture.[2] Sexual meanings of spaces are partly carried in preexisting connotations, in this case of our neighborhood park, the romantic connotations of a vista modeled on the famous West Lake of Hangzhou, which made it an ideal spot for courtship. Our neighborhood park is but one example of local spatial rhetoric, uses of spaces in which persistent local publics have no formal authority but are able to take advantage of the oversights and failings of institutional authorities. The police didn't passively accept this new dual use of the park as sexual playground and

53

spectacle. An internal police document from 1983[3] refers to youth making a sport of watching amorous couples in a park—also referred to in the document as "watching Channel 13"—and to it having a "devastating effect on youth morality." According to the police report, 501 couples were caught in Shanghai parks and open spaces from June to September 1983 "touching each other salaciously, making indecent moves or having sexual intercourse." Of the 140 cases uncovered during the month of August, "21.4% were engaging in sexual intercourse." Most of these were young people, the report points out, but many teachers, principals, cadres, and Party members were included. Although the report doesn't describe punishments for these acts, the former policeman who gave me the report said that such violators were detained and reported to their work units. People that police found guilty of "antisocial" behavior, especially prostitution or promiscuous sex, could be held in administrative detention for up to four years with no trial. At my mother-in-law's nearby work unit, for instance, a middle-aged male manager and a young female office worker became involved in an extramarital affair in the early 1980s. Members of a "community policing team"[4] found them embracing in our neighborhood park during work hours and reported them to their work unit. Because both were married, the man was given a large demerit and his salary was reduced, and the woman was demoted from office work to factory work. The police report also mentions several cases of men pretending to be police officers or members of a community policing team detaining couples, separating them, and then raping the woman. The former police officer who had worked with community policing teams in the 1980s told me that actual members of community policing teams were discovered to be raping women they found in parks in Shanghai, and that these incidents led to the curtailment of community policing activities. The bad reputation of local policing teams allowed offended citizens to dispute local police actions, he said, especially when the victims were people with connections to more powerful state institutions.[5]

The park was not the only neighborhood public space reappropriated by local youth. For instance, informants described how they resisted sexual monitoring at the early union-organized dance parties in our neighborhood in the early 1980s. At these dances, monitors kept men and women from dancing too closely, but youth occasionally resisted. "When they came up to watch someone, we would pop them on the back of the head. They wouldn't know who hit them," a now-middle-aged resident told me. Such resistance was only tolerated when official interests were weak, seemingly the case here. Monitoring at dances largely disappeared by the late 1980s, just as it did in the parks. In the spring of 1999 and summer of 2000, my wife and I went jogging daily in the same municipal park. One of the major activities in the park now was social dancing, accepted as healthy exercise for retirees. Nor did anyone concern themselves with the kissing couples we occasionally passed, mostly out-of-town workers and youth who couldn't afford a better place to meet. As the television metaphor suggests, however, formal control of the park's sexual uses never fell into the hands of local people, although they gained free use of the park for some of their own private sexual activities. What changed is that local state agents now were less concerned with surveillance of public places than with extracting profit from them.

In 1999 a large Plexiglas house container was built in the park and filled with 1,222 snakes, including many poisonous ones. Two teenage girls from Guangxi Province lived in the glass house, which contained a bed, a table, a television, and an enclosed toilet. Spectators observed them sitting on their bed watching television, feeding the snakes, napping with two large boa constrictors, or occasionally reaching up to pull a snake off the television. The two young women stayed in the room seventy-two days, establishing a world record for continuously living with snakes. On an adjacent stage, other Guangxi girls in skimpy costumes danced traditional folk dances several times a day, their limbs darkly tanned from constant exposure to the hot Shanghai sun. The municipal park more than doubled its admission price during the snake exhibit, providing income for the park authority as well as the visiting sexual entrepreneurs. The old "Channel 13" was modest in comparison, and cheaper.

This complex cohabitation of sexual entrepreneurs and local state officials was also evident on the outer perimeter of the park, including street-side shop spaces leased out by the park authority. During the summer of 2000, glass display cases on the wall of our park were devoted to an exhibition by the ministry for family planning, describing a large variety of birth control methods, detailed diagrams on how to use condoms, and examples of condom brands now on sale in Shanghai, including foreign brands—apparently an attempt to increase the fashion appeal of these devices. Directly beside the exhibit on land leased out by the park, a hairdressing salon offered illegal opposite-sex massages in addition to shampoos and haircuts. A dozen young women from distant rural areas massaged neighborhood men (and the occasional woman) sprawled on long padded tables, chatting flirtatiously with the male customers, allowing them to embrace their waists, and straddling the men's backs while kneading their shoulders. In many such shops in Shanghai, masseuses are available for further sexual services outside the shop.[6] Further down the same street, and not far from my home, one of several neighborhood sex shops sold vibrators, condoms, and medicinal sex aids packaged to appear like the imported drug Viagra. The manager, a garrulous transplanted northerner, complained that police were shutting down such businesses for selling fake medicines. Since his son was a policeman, he feared less that his own shop would be closed. These activities of local sexual entrepreneurs indicate that the relationship between local state authorities and local sexual license is one of both confrontation and mutual dependence. The state is as implicated in the creation of spaces for sexual entrepreneurship and sexual play as it is in the repression and policing of these spaces.[7] State authorities, however, do not determine all the uses people make of these spaces and facilities.

A Spatial Grammar of Shanghai

Shanghai has been reconstructed several times in the past century, each reconstruction an attempt by the state to shape the meanings conveyed by city spaces. The most dramatic was Mao's attempt to remake Shanghai as a socialist city. Like all utopians, Maoist planners insisted on a spatial unity diametrically opposed to the "heterotopia" of commercial, cosmopolitan Shanghai.[8] The Party spatially implemented its doctrine of the primacy of industrial production by building massive socialist housing estates centered around factories, entailing a form of social organization that one critic describes as "feudalism in a period of industrialization."[9] At the height of socialist mobilization, individuals moved spatially throughout the day from work units, where leaders monitored their behavior, to housing estates, where local neighborhood committees organized political meetings and also monitored personal domestic lives.[10] This spatial containment of everyday life in work units made the work-unit leaders into local patriarchs, a socialist version of the old Chinese lineage structure, which reinforced the traditional family values of Maoist "patriarchal socialism."[11] Neighborhood committees dealt with sexual issues, including birth control and the mediation of marital disputes.[12] Community policing teams monitored nearby public spaces for deviants. Even when people found time to leave their residential compounds, the closing of commercial entertainments such as dance halls and cabarets and the scarcity of commodities left Shanghai's boulevards much quieter than before the Communist takeover.[13]

The latest grand attempt to rebuild Shanghai is a concerted attempt to build back the commercial city that Mao wanted to dismantle. The commercial building boom is the most visible sign of the city's spatial reorganization, but changes in social geography are also dramatic.[14] Since 1979 the panoptical cellular structure of work units has broken down. The work unit, now more often called the "company" (*gongsi*), no longer spatially and socially encapsulates individuals. With the commercialization of housing in the 1990s, workers could purchase and even sell their assigned apartments. People changed jobs and residences more often. Workers more frequently lived far from where they worked and expected "bosses" (no longer "leaders") not to question their private lives. An older spatial rhetoric of leisure and fashion has reemerged on boulevards dominated by commercial activities and strolling crowds.

Yet these changes were taking place within a resilient spatial grammar established by foreign real-estate magnates and Chinese migrants during the population booms of the late nineteenth century.[15] Despite Maoist planning and more recent demolition, 1990s Shanghai remained a city of broad boulevards and dense alleyways. As was the case one hundred years before, the foreign, modern, and frenetic space of the boulevard and the closed, domestic, and familiar space of the alleyway formed basic terms in the spatial grammar of daily life in Shanghai. Similarly, despite Maoist egalitarianism, Shanghai retains a social geography of "high" and "low" areas of the city. "High corner" (*shangzhijiao*) refers to the areas developed as foreign concessions, expanding westward from the original small British settlement centered on the embankment of the Huangpu River known as the Bund. "Low corner" (*xiazhijiao*) refers to the areas of settlement on the northern and eastern edges of these former concessions, originally shantytowns populated by poor rural migrants. Although new types of urban space are now emerging, including the isolated "oases" of the high-rise apartment complexes,[16] these new categories of social space build upon this older grid rather than obliterating it. These residual distinctions also mark a sexual geography of Shanghai, one that reflects Shanghai's cumulative urban culture and the reemergence of a geography of social class based partly along pre-1949 spatial categories.

In the first sections of this chapter, I lay out a very simple grammar of spatial conventions salient in Shanghai's sexual culture. I see the development of this shared spatial grammar as a cumulative and selective process in which some historical meanings of urban space are retained throughout a process of spatial transformation.[17] In the second section, I examine the spatial grammar of two different types of youth sex cultures, discussing how economic and social transformations are represented and experienced as spatial distinctions. The analytical focus is what Burke describes as the "scene-actor ratio," the degree to which the meanings of actions are contained by the physical and social "ground" of these actions.[18] I also emphasize that different types of communities are organized according to different spatial principles, making for different forms of participation in the culture.[19] Finally, I consider the processes by which neighborhood sexual culture is transformed, situating an account of local sexual gossip in a larger ecological context of residential transformations. In understanding change, I work within an ecological understanding of community social forms, recognizing that communities' internal structures are sensitive to larger environmental and ecological influences.[20] Moreover, these economic or ecological changes are recognized and interpreted through an inherited spatial grammar. In sum, changes in Shanghai's sexual geography are the product of local processes of cultural innovation shaped by larger ecological transformations and preexisting spatial categories.

Alleyway and High-Rise

Behind its commercial boulevards, reform-era Shanghai retained a distinctive alleyway architecture redolent of crowded humanity. Shanghai's dense and heterogeneous alleyway communities, many over a century old, supported their own matter-of-fact public sexuality. Glimpses of naked neighbors across hallways and alleyways and frilly lingerie and pajamas casually worn outdoors extended the private sphere of the home into the alleyway and nearby streets. Overheard quarrels and overlooked affairs, late-returning neighbors and early-leaving visitors were all captured in the decades-thick gossamer of alleyway gossip. The residential alleyway, like the boulevard, can thus be understood as a broad band of communication, with its own sexual rhetoric, and not just a place to live or a locus of social control. The transformation of this form of residential life also represents a transformation of Shanghai's sexual culture on a spatial level.

Republican-era alleyway row houses are as emblematic of Shanghai life as its department stores—much like the hutong are considered typical of Beijing, or the bungalow typical of Chicago.[21] Shanghai's long narrow alleyways (linong) abut onto its boulevards through decorative covered arches, often with a name carved in old-style characters and a date beneath. Old-style alleyway dwellings (shikumen) are brick two-story walk-ups, each with a small courtyard, laid out in a grid along deep narrow alleys. Old-style alleyway row houses built before 1920 still lack indoor baths and toilets, while many new-style row houses built in the 1930s and 1940s have running water and indoor baths on each floor. While most Shanghaiese lived in alleyway houses during the early reform era, by 1998 alleyway houses were only 17 percent of housing floor space and by 2010 will be largely gone from the city center except for the few historic blocks slated for preservation and renovation.[22] Finally, 1990s Shanghai still retained tracts of shantytowns (penghuqu), privately owned housing built by poor rural migrants in Republican and early Maoist times, miserable tracts of windowless straw huts fifty years ago,[23] now mostly multistoried brick dwellings, though still lacking indoor toilets. Most shantytowns were also slated for demolition.

Though far less attractive than the old alleyways, newer low-rise housing developments in Shanghai retained the basic design of a single easily-monitored entrance off a main street, with numbered apartment blocks built along a geometric grid of pedestrian alleys, where children played and older residents socialized and observed the goings-on. These newer developments were known as "new villages" (xincun), shorthand for "new workers villages," and larger new villages housed tens of thousands of people in rows of multistory walk-up apartment blocks. Accounting for well over half of all housing area in Shanghai, the low-rise new village or public housing development (gongfang) was considered intermediate in its level of privacy and crowdedness, with less density than the old-style alleyway but more sense of neighborliness and community than the new high-rise developments.

The chief fact of Shanghai residential life has always been crowding.[24] According to the 1990 census, 4.4 million people still lived in the eighty-six square kilometers of the old central city, with per capita living space of 4.5 square meters and a population density of fifty thousand persons per square kilometer, roughly ten times the density of Chicago.[25] In some of the old two- and three-story row houses, densities remained at two square meters per person, a living space roughly the size of a bed.[26] The crowding meant that through the 1990s many Shanghaiese grew up with little privacy, sleeping on their parents' floor until well into their twenties, while two married couples often shared the same room, separated only by a curtain. During the late 1990s, the housing situation improved immensely. The urban area expanded through the building of large apartment complexes on the fringes of the city, more than doubling per capita living space to nearly ten square meters per person, at least in official figures.[27]

On the other hand, density also had an enabling effect on reform-era social life. Crowding imposed an almost physical pressure on Shanghai youth, squeezing young people out into the still-crowded but freer spaces of the boulevards. Density created markets for the small businesses that enlivened local streets. Young women walking alone late at night felt safer simply because they were seldom alone. Crowded living conditions created a familiarity with both physiological and social aspects of sexuality.[28] For example, until recently most Shanghaiese had no baths in their apartments, and only 37 percent had facilities for hot water showers in 1995. Most people bathed in public bath-houses. Unlike many other Chinese regions, these communal bathing practices increased comfort levels with nudity. Crowded living conditions in the alley-way also created thick contexts of gossip, which constrained behavior through their judgments but also were a means through which sexual possibilities were shared among neighbors.

The semipublic life of the old-style alleyway is often contrasted with the more anonymous and private life of the high-rise apartment building, and re-spectively they represent the past and future of Shanghai's residential pattern. In the 1990s more than two thousand buildings over eight stories were con-structed in the city, mostly mixed residential and office blocks.[29] These high-rise apartments now have become the second most common living arrange-ment, after low-rise new village apartment complexes. This rapid transition from the alleyway to the high-rise also is transforming the nature of commu-nity life in Shanghai. In *The Uses of Disorder*, Richard Sennett points out that dense and heterogeneous neighborhoods (like the Shanghai alleyway) force residents to deal collectively and personally with a wide range of people and a wide range of discomfiting social problems, producing a direct understanding of and participation in community life.[30] Sennett also argues that this urban dis-order is uncomfortable for residents, who at the first opportunity flee to more socially segregated, orderly, and private suburbs. True to form, most residents of Shanghai's old-style alleyways and shanty districts sought the relative order and privacy of high-rise developments on the fringe of the city, often described in advertising as green "parks" and "gardens" walled off from urban noise, crowding, and pollution.[31] Following Sennett, I would argue that the move from alleyway to high-rise not only meant an increase in wealth, freedom, and privacy, but also a loss of complexity of social interaction, albeit a loss most Shanghai people seemed eager to achieve.

For the most part, residents of new high-rise neighborhoods lacked the long-term social ties that existed in most Shanghai neighborhoods before 1990. Next-door neighbors might not even know one another and lacked communal spaces in which face-to-face communities could arise. As a one-year resident of a large luxury complex said to me, "I don't know what kind of people live here. I see them walking about, but I don't know what they are up to." The ubiquitous steel antiburglar grilles that families installed on the doorways physically protected the family space and symbolically excluded the outside world. Neighbors were much less able to observe one another's comings and goings and less able to share gossip, diminishing its function as a means of

communication. Luxury apartment complexes, in particular, were vertical suburbs, or "oases,"[32] in which residents could escape the social heterogeneity and
gossip of old neighborhoods. Even in a lower-cost high-rise community, however, there was less need to tolerate difficult, down-and-out, and troubled
people than was necessary in an alleyway community in which families knew
one another over generations. Moreover, with the end of assigned work-unit
housing in 1999, neighbors increasingly had no common workplace or social
affiliations. Among my young informants who bought their own apartments,
new friends were likely to be chosen according to common interests and other
affiliations rather than proximity,[33] and troublesome old friends were easily
avoided. New bonds may be emerging in these communities, but the spatial
rhetoric of the high-rise is one of private, contained lives. The alleyways and
shanty districts, in contrast, provided a socially mixed cast of characters whose
troublesome behavior must be accepted.

High Corner and Low Corner

"High corner" and "low corner" were colloquial terms of spatial
grammar almost all Shanghai people knew, but like many potentially derogatory social distinctions, they were the kind of social "dirty laundry" seldom
mentioned to foreigners. They were part of a discourse of social class and ethnicity disguised as local geography and containing subtle, but for this study important, sexual connotations. In this chapter I focus on the sexual meanings of
low-corner Shanghai, where I lived the greater part of my time in Shanghai and
conducted much of my research.

Republican-era Shanghaiese saw low corner as an area inhabited by social
undesirables, particularly migrants from northern Jiangsu Province (*jiangbeiren*
or *subeiren*), who formerly engaged in low-status service occupations.[34] The low-
corner people discussed below all lived in old areas of the Zhabei, Hongkou,
and Yangpu Districts of Shanghai.[35] Zhabei is the most famous of Shanghai's
low-corner districts, an expanse of low-rise housing and shanties built in areas
decimated by the Japanese during World War II. Yangpu is a vast district of factories and working-class residential areas that has continued to grow since
1949 and now houses one-quarter of Shanghai's population. Hongkou is more
mixed, including both slums and mansions built for foreigners. Many shanty-
town areas also remain in low-corner Shanghai, and the continued reputation
of these districts as "low class" references this fact.

Shanghai's new consumer culture identifies low corner's denigrated status
with a lack of culture and fashion, the cultural opposite of Shanghai's high-

corner boulevards and villa districts. Low corner remains an area of factories, cheaper housing developments, and low-grade shopping. A dance hall operator who described herself as a "high-corner person doing business in low corner," said of the surrounding Yangpu neighborhood (near my home):

> This part of town is special because most of the people here are working people. They don't have a lot of money like people uptown. They make only a few hundred a month, so they could at most afford to spend one hundred in an evening going out. If they just take a taxi into town and back, they will spend the whole hundred. So they can come here and just spend a little.
>
> People here are really backward. If I go down to Huaihai Lu or some other high-corner place and wear a name brand, people will look at it now and say, "Oh, I know that brand." People here will just look and say, "Name brand, what name brand?" Also they are really dirty. We opened up with this pretty blue carpet and they come in here spitting on the floor and dropping their cigarettes on the carpet when they get up to dance.

Her denigration of low-corner residents focuses on their inferior understanding of new consumer lifestyles. Other dance hall owners argued that it was impossible to develop a high-class dance hall in low corner, perceiving this as an indelible distinction in Shanghai's social geography. Although there were exceptions to these patterns, high corner and low corner retained their class meanings.

"Low corner" also included a sense of sexual and social disorder, but one usually disguised in a language of consumer taste and "civilized" (*wenming*) behavior. In one focus group conversation on premarital sex, however, this reputation for sexual deviance came up explicitly:

> Qing: When we were in school, "going to bed" was still not included. Today's high school students seem to have included "going to bed."
> Shen: I know there is a [school] district that is particularly chaotic [*luan*].
> Moderator: Which one? [All laughed, seeming to know it.]
> Shen: Hongkou District [a large low-corner district].
> Moderator: So Hongkou District has a lot of students playing around [*baixiang*]?
> Zen: That place is pretty chaotic. . . . It is not about feeling. [That type of student] has this thing whenever men and women are in the same room. They don't think they need love, but just a man.
>
> (unmarried women in their early twenties, college educated)

Such stereotypes about low-corner Shanghai youth were widely shared, though usually expressed less directly and extremely. Naturally any type of denigrating typification is liable to produce a counterdiscourse, and many residents of working-class low-corner districts displayed a defensive pride in their own tough neighborhoods. Friends who grew up in low-corner shanty communities in the 1970s described a more adventurous but also mercenary attitude toward sexuality that dated at least back to the Mao era. In their view the shanty area was different from other neighborhoods: chaotic but tough, the home of streetwise, pragmatic people. Bragging about his youthful sexual exploits, one low-corner informant said, "Back then [early 1980s] we went uptown to pick up girls because they were so innocent. The girls in our neighborhood, they were already pretty wise. They weren't so easy to trick."

Two Sexual Geographies

Below I introduce two different informants and two contrasting geographies of sexual cultures. First, this ethnographic exploration shows how people live within and make use of the broad grammatical terms of the social geography described above. A second point is that sexual cultures have local histories. For instance, while Shanghai's recent explosion of boulevard consumer sexual culture is more widely known, idle youth in low-corner neighborhoods created an active youth sex culture that preceded this 1990s consumer revolution. Finally, I describe how sexual geographies are organized along different grammatical principles. The first geography described below is extremely local and pedestrian; the second involves a grammar of fashionable consumer locales that reaches beyond Shanghai to embrace elements of a global consumer culture.

A Sexual Geography for Little Bai

Little Bai, one of my closest confidants in Shanghai, lived in an infamous low-corner shanty district called Riverside Alley, located not far from the new village where I lived with my in-laws. Riverside Alley was the backdrop of a 1980s TV series called Qiongjie (Poor street) about undisciplined but goodhearted students in a poor Shanghai neighborhood. In the 1940s the area was fields and graves, Bai told me. A man from a town near Yangzhou (northern Jiangsu) parceled off the land with bamboo stakes and sold it off to people from his home county, including Bai's family, who bought their house for ninety yuan in the early 1950s. Little Bai still had the nickname of Ox Turd because when he was a kid he helped shoveled cow manure on the farm where he lived with his uncle in his home county. Ninety percent of his neighbors were from this one Subei county, Bai said, and the neighborhood patois remained the language of that county. Material life in Riverside Alley greatly improved in the forty years of its existence. Winding dirt paths were cemented over and equipped with an underground drainage. Shanties became three-story constructs of reinforced concrete, enlarged to accommodate the families of grown children, but still lacking toilets. The public toilets at the end of the alleyway were filthy, a condition that Bai and his friends blamed on the out-of-towners (*waidiren*) who worked in the vegetable market. Bai's own house was three stories high. On the second floor over the kitchen, he built his own "bachelor's room," where he sang karaoke and watched video discs, including occasional pirated pornographic discs provided by a married "girlfriend." His mother slept in the adjacent room, which he had to pass through to reach his own. His brother, sister-in-law, and their child lived above.

Bai and his family described the neighborhood as a tight community. Friends dropped in unannounced, not even bothering to knock. "Here people are very warmhearted, very easygoing," Bai told me. "Apartment block [*gongfang*] people are different. They don't even know their neighbors. If you go to someone's home in an apartment block, they have a defensive attitude. They think, 'What are you doing here?'" Nonetheless, in my view, an atmosphere of mistrust clouded the close relations in Riverside Alley. Bai never introduced a male neighbor without warning me vaguely to "be careful around" him. "They might cause you trouble," he would say about others, sometimes referring to criminal histories of theft and swindling. Lanky and bookwormish with thick-rimmed glasses, Bai himself was known as a poor fighter, but Riverside Alley was famous for fierce youth gangs who fought running street battles during and after the Cultural Revolution. The crime rate was still high in the 1990s, according to residents. Several of Bai's neighbors had done time in prison. Bai proudly described the reputation of the neighborhood when he grew up, "High-corner people looked down on us, and we didn't like them either. If they came around here, we would beat them up. They were afraid to come down here. Most people in Shanghai, when they heard the name of Riverside Alley, they were afraid of us." He said that outsiders feared getting lost in the expanse of winding alleyways. When I visited in the late 1990s, high-corner people were still reluctant to enter the neighborhood, but there was much less chance of getting lost now that demolition had shrunk the patch of private housing to an area of about one city block. All around Bai's alleyway, tracts of self-built houses were being demolished and replaced with new apartment blocks. In the new century, Bai's neighborhood is slated to become a new city park ("I guess the neighborhood is too infamous [to build housing]," Bai joked). Most residents, all of whom were moving out in 2000, were accepting free replacement housing far on the outskirts of town (mostly in Pudong). Still, most were happy for the move. In 2000 Bai had already located a secondhand apartment across the nearby Huangpu River in an old area of Pudong. He hoped that by moving into an apartment with an indoor bathroom, he would improve his chances of getting a wife.[36]

According to his own description, Bai was a good student when he was in high school in the early 1980s, but his parents didn't encourage his studies. "Our parents didn't have any education. They didn't think anything about this; they thought if they just give you food, that's enough. When I was a kid, we just played. In the summer we went swimming in the Huangpu River. Every year kids would drown in that river." Only one child from their neighborhood had ever gone to university, Bai said, and he left Shanghai for Japan. Bai worked in a beer factory, a decent job for a local man, but factory jobs were disappearing daily and unemployment in the community (estimated by Bai at about 40 percent) was far higher than the city norm. Like many other men I met from Riverside Alley, he had tried his hand at private business and failed. In his social relationships, Bai couldn't shed the neighborhood's bad reputation. After a minor altercation, a longtime friend of Bai complained to me about Bai's character:

> I don't like Little Bai anymore. He has changed. Growing up in that neighborhood, you can't help but be influenced by that kind of person around you. Everyone there is too poor. I really believe he has changed. I think he cares too much about money, and the kind of money they care about there, that is just a piddling amount of money. I look down on those people.

Although he was thirty-six, Bai was unmarried. It's hard for a factory worker from Riverside Alley to get a wife, others said. Few women wanted to move into the infamous alleyway. Men married late and often married women from small towns outside of Shanghai, a big step down the social ladder from marrying a Shanghai woman. Another single low-corner man with a similar background to Bai described local men's worries about country brides: "I can't find a wife. There aren't many girls in Shanghai. The only girls I can meet are little country sisters, and I don't want a little country sister."

I asked him, "Why not?"

He answered, "I can't afford one. They are lazy. They don't work. They just want to stay at home and take care of the baby. . . . And they are too much trouble. After they come, then their relatives will start coming one after another to stay with you. And where are you going to put all those people? Are you going to have them sleeping all over the floor?"

One of Bai's neighbors, a wizened ex-convict in his mid-forties called Old Zheng, recently married an impish twenty-three-year-old woman from a rural Shanghai county. She appeared to spend most of the day lounging about in her pajamas watching television and scolding their child, while her husband earned their meager living as a salesman. Both she and her husband seemed to believe they had married down. He visited prostitutes and older women he met in dance halls, and she slyly flirted with the young men who visited their home.

Bai also met many women in the dance halls he frequented. Younger women were too picky, he said. Almost all the women he slept with were older married women he disparaged as "old cabbage leaves" (*laocaipi*), though he became emotionally involved with some of them. He said he didn't like to take women back to his place for sex:

> In the alleyway everyone would see it and talk. Only if it is very late at night will I take someone back, and then we will leave early in the morning before anyone gets up. Most of the time I go to a friend's house who lives alone. This friend's got a room to himself after his parents were allocated another room by their work unit. He doesn't work; he just takes money from an old cabbage leaf who works in a textile factory. I give him thirty yuan and he goes dancing. By the time he gets back, we are already finished.

According to descriptions by older residents, the sexual norms in Riverside Alley were always looser, more pragmatic, and more mercenary than in many other neighborhoods. Old Zheng described the neighborhood youth sexual culture in the late 1970s:

> We would find someone who had a bigger house than most, then we would get one of these little bitty radios. We would bring a few girls together and a few boys together, and if they liked each other, they would just dance together. It was very casual. We would dance and then we would turn off the lights and people would dance together in the dark. This was called a "lights-out dance party," and it started here the earliest of all. Yangpu was famous for its dancing then. This started in 1975, before old Mao had even died. Back then if you were caught dancing, the police would arrest you. . . .

Back then it was not like today. At night after dinner, most girls didn't have anything to do at all, and they would just go out walking around the neighborhood. We would go out walking around, and then we would find girls and ask them if they wanted to go play with us. Sometimes they would just ignore us, but sometimes they would come along. This was really common then. There was no commercial entertainment then, nothing else to do.

I asked how the girls' families reacted.

Back then these girls had no education, and families didn't pay much attention to what they did. If they had a good time with us, they wouldn't want to go home. They would lie to their parents. They would tell them they were out staying at another girl's house or out studying with another girl. Sometimes their parents would beat them, but it didn't do any good. The more they beat them, the more they would go out. . . . Back then, families tried to control us kids, but they couldn't.

I asked if they had sexual relations.

Back then girls would sleep with you, but we had no idea what we were doing. We just did what we felt like. We would do something to get them to stay with us. Sometimes we just wouldn't let them go home, and they would just go along with it. Girls back then were really naive. They would do what you wanted. . . . We would do everything secretively then. We would take them back to the house in the middle of the night and then quietly "do it" and then leave. We couldn't let our parents know. . . . If girls got pregnant, they would try to keep it secret from their parents. They would go to a hospital where they knew someone and have an abortion.

Neighborhood opinion still exerted an influence on youth in those days, however. Old Zheng explained, "We wouldn't fool with the girls in the alleyway because that might cause conflict among the families. When we were young, we boys would go out together and meet girls from other neighborhoods."

A woman who grew up in the alleyway, and described by Little Bai as a "good girl," said she started dancing in 1984 and 1985, when she and her friends were about eighteen years old. She described herself and her girlfriends as shy and naive and, compared to girls today, not very good dancers either: "When we went out, we did it secretively, a group of girls, not letting the family know, not letting the people in the alleyway know. The people in the alleyway would talk. . . . It was really very different then than from now. We matured very late, not like kids today."

I asked if they met boyfriends in the dance hall. She said:

> Of course we did that. They would make a date with you to go dance or make a date to go out to eat. But you wouldn't let people know it back in the alleyway because they would think you were no good, or they would think you girls in that alleyway are not respectable. Now people accept it. They *should* accept it. Young people should be like that. Back then we were really cowardly; we didn't dare go out and play very much.

I asked if people had sex.

> If they had strong feelings, of course, some of them did this, but they did this really secretively. They didn't tell anyone. If they were not successful [didn't get married], then they would be laughed at by everyone. This was something they did when they thought they were settled on someone. If people knew about this, they would think you were not respectable.

These descriptions would not sound very remarkable to Shanghai people today, but they describe very permissive norms for a "respectable girl" in that period, including dating with boys she met in dance halls. Other girls were more daring and engaged in sexual relations. Old Zheng described gangs of neighborhood youth who fought together, played together, danced, and also had sexual relations, almost all within the limited boundaries of Riverside Alley and surrounding low-corner neighborhoods. With many local youth ending their education after junior high school, and with very high rates of youth unemployment (*daiyeqingnian*) in the early 1980s, these low-corner youth had far less to lose by such activities than children from better-off families. Neither local schools nor parents offered many positive inducements for acting respectable outside the immediate community. Although concerned about family and community reputations, low-corner parents in the early reform era seem to have had less control over young people than wealthier and better-connected parents. Moreover, low-status parents without high-profile positions to defend also had less to lose from their children's deviant behavior. This "low-corner sexual revolution," however, does not seem to have had a guiding ideology of sexual liberation. Informants from that generation usually emphasized that they had "no idea" of what they were doing when they engaged in sexual intercourse. Unlike many respectable Shanghai youth in the 1990s (or American middle-class youth in the 1950s and '60s[37]), these were not romantic revolutionaries proclaiming the moral authority of love to legitimate premarital sex. The retrospective accounts of participants indicate a lack of shared meanings for premarital sex (other than an often unrealistic promise of marriage). A romantic revolution in Chinese public sexual culture was beginning in the early 1980s, particularly in literature, but it had yet to embrace casual dating, commercial leisure, or premarital sex. In the early 1980s "respectable" Shanghai youth still expected their peers to wait until marriage for sex.

The Riverside Alley youth who practiced these vaguely permissive sexual codes saw themselves as culturally and geographically outside the respectable mainstream of Shanghai society; however, theirs cannot be entirely understood as a deviant youth subculture vis-à-vis their own local culture. Even in the early reform era, low-corner parents and other adults also allowed for pragmatic sexual arrangements that violated their superficially conservative sexual principles. For instance, Old Du, a forty-seven-year-old man from a low-corner neighborhood near Riverside Alley, told me about an illicit affair he engaged in as a married man with an unmarried woman during the early reform era. In the 1970s he had a good factory job and relatively good family conditions, and in 1979 he met a female coworker who met the approval of his family and factory superiors. Although he didn't have strong feelings for her, he says now, they quickly married. In 1981 he started his own seafood company, making good money for that time. Then, in 1983 he met his lover (qingren) through business friends. She was twenty-four, the same age as his wife. "She was a very attractive girl, a textile worker, smarter and more capable than my wife. But her family was very poor." She also had a boyfriend, whom she kept seeing throughout her relationship with Du. Du said:

> I had money and ability and that attracted her to me. She was very, very daring for the time. This was very dangerous then. We were very secretive. The social attitude [about sexual affairs] was very critical. If a girl got pregnant then, she would be severely criticized. Society wasn't open then, not like today. Back then you couldn't just go out and find a girl selling sex like today. . . . Not many people had the daring to go out and pursue their own happiness. With her, I felt a real pleasure in the heart, an unmatchable happiness. . . . It was really too bad that I hadn't divorced already. I really wanted to marry her.

Du said his wife knew about his relationship with the girl but refused to divorce him until after the young woman had married her boyfriend.

Despite his insistence on the secretiveness of their affair, it actually required the cooperation of many people in Du's immediate environment, including the antagonistic but silent cooperation of his wife. There were no hotels where lovers could meet, and living conditions were crowded. So, he said, they went to his lover's house to have sex. Her brother and father both knew they were having a sexual relationship but never said anything because he gave them expensive presents of frozen seafood. Even her boyfriend allowed this "friendship" with a well-off man, although he supposedly did not know about the sex. Her family's mercenary pragmatism seems representative of the distinctive sexual culture that emerged in low-corner Shanghai in the early 1980s. According to discussions with other informants, many low-corner families with few resources were quick to accept these nonmarital, but mutually beneficial sexual relationships. This pragmatic or mercenary attitude represents an important strain in Shanghai's youth sexual culture as it developed during the reform era, a nonromantic, mercenary ethos still most prominent among working-class, low-corner youth.

The materialism of the low-corner working-class community, as I experienced it in the 1990s, had an exaggerated and fantastic quality. I heard many half-joking conversations about fantasies of marrying rich men or success in improbable business schemes. Many parents showed through their behavior that they would rather let their children be exposed to the dangers and temptations of the market than miss its opportunities. As a result, some disadvantaged young women settled for "eating spring rice," enjoying temporary relationships with older, usually married men who offered good times and expensive gifts. Parents usually discouraged such shortsighted behavior on the surface, but some turned a blind eye, especially when the man generously bestowed gifts upon the family. Parents still disapproved of premarital sex abstractly, but neighborhood gossip was full of off-color sexual stories with fortuitous outcomes. In these stories a mixed pragmatic and moral rhetoric of money, feelings, and filial piety excused many pragmatic sexual arrangements.

Rather than seeing the transformation of sexual culture as a global process that spreads outward from cosmopolitan centers to gradually infiltrate backward localities like Riverside Alley, it is important to recognize local developments within larger processes of social transformation. Youth in Riverside Alley produced an ambiguously permissive youth sexual culture in a process that is probably similar to other cities in China, but also a process that is influenced by a peculiar social geography of concentrated poverty, low-education, and denigrated ethnic status. This also was a culture that early on displayed the materialistic ethos that came to characterize reform-era Chinese culture, a permissive code of material compensations for moral compromises that perhaps developed among low-corner Shanghai people long before the reform era. Included in this ethos is a pragmatic recognition that young women can achieve comfort and status through nonmarital sexual arrangements, which if not exactly moral are often "understandable" (keyilijie) and sometimes "smart" (congming). The denigrated reputation of low corner, its popular dance hall culture, and its mercenary sexual ethics continued to influence the lives of youth who grew up there in the 1990s. However, with the demolition of low-corner shanty areas like Riverside Alley and the removal of their residents to largely working-class satellite communities, the close-knit neighborhood culture that was carried by these older spaces was disappearing. What kinds of working-class cultures or working-class communities will emerge in these new satellite settlements is an open question.[38]

A Sexual Geography for Bei

The spatial grammar of Riverside Alley's early youth sex culture was one of denigrated neighborhoods, youth gangs, and local dance halls. The spatial grammar of a later elite phase of Shanghai's sexual opening was one of disjointed places of consumption, life, and leisure, a shifting archipelago of fashionable places linked by taxi rides, eliding local neighborhoods, though almost exclusively situated in high-corner Shanghai. This was an attractive new sexual landscape for many high-income youth, who were being drawn out of the domestic and institutional spaces of neighborhoods and schools into this disconnected geography of high-rises, clubs, and shopping centers. While low-corner youth in Riverside Alley began visiting commercial leisure establishments earlier than the children of more respectable Shanghai families, economically well-off youth in the late 1990s participated in a much larger-scale leisure culture with no neighborhood or even national boundaries. These glamorous nightspots (described in books like Shanghai Baby, popular magazines, and by word of mouth) benefited from direct connections with distant metropolitan centers of fashion, lending the sexual culture of these places a positive cosmopolitan aura that the local low-corner dance hall never had.

I will describe this fragmented spatial grammar of sexualized leisure spots through the story of one young woman, how she moved through these spaces, and how they provided opportunity for but also gave legitimate meanings to sexual behaviors that a few years earlier might never have become part of the biography of a respectable and successful young woman. When I met Bei in 1995, she was twenty-one years old. She was not a sexual revolutionary. She spoke with me frankly about her fears and anxieties about sex before marriage. These included her worries that sex would be painful, that it would be difficult to "get rid of" a man with whom she had casual sex, that men would discuss their experiences with one another, and most of all that a future husband would be disappointed that she was not a virgin (see chapter 7 for more of her story). She described herself and her classmates as "open in thinking, but not in behavior":

> In other words, I can accept my friends doing this. I can accept that some of them live together. I can even accept that some of them live with foreigners. But I don't want to live with a man. I am more old-fashioned. I don't want to have sex before marriage. Many of my friends are like that. But many other friends have had sex, and they like to talk about that, and I will tell them not to talk about it [laughing with her hands over her ears]. This should be more of a responsible thing. I think sex is like candy, once you start eating, you can't stop. You will have a first time, then a second, then a third, and so on [laughing more].

Her conservative stance against premarital sex was more indecisive than this speech might suggest. Shanghai women had a range of cautionary tales to keep sexual temptation in check, but as I discuss in chapter 7, these stories were also ambiguous "survivor tales" through which young women imagined various premarital sexual possibilities.

Later on the same evening, I joined Bei and several of her friends for drinks at Judy's, one of Shanghai's first Western bars and underground dance clubs. As on most nights, half the customers were Westerners and half the couples were foreign men with Chinese women (the others mostly Chinese). We ate simple Italian food on red-and-white checkered tables and drank beer until 10 P.M., when our table was moved to make room for dancers. The music was the latest U.S. and European dance music, and the dancing was sweaty, close, and amusingly obscene. In 1995 the bar seemed a world away from Shanghai's usual discos playing canned disco pop. That night a German man in our group was trying to seduce Bei, asking her to dance repeatedly. After he abandoned his efforts and left, she said she wasn't interested because he was too old. She confided to me that she had kissed a younger German acquaintance on the dance floor earlier that month. After the dancing and beers, she added a dreamy-eyed, romantic commentary on her sexual aspirations:

> Now I am more mature though. So I figure that by the time I am twenty-four, I will have already done this [had sex]. I am very contradictory. I am tempted. I want a tall man, and then I could lean on him. I like the feeling of my small hand in his hand. I have never met a person I really liked. If I did, then I think I wouldn't refuse him anything [haowubaoliude]. I like to give people things.

Bei's attitudes were more conservative than many women I interviewed but more open-minded than many others, not unusual, including the note of romantic and sexual fantasy. What I want to consider is how her sexual lifestyle was structured by the spaces and situations through which she moved as part of her larger lifestyle as a businesswoman and modern girl.

In most respects, Bei was a typical young woman from a privileged background, both a university student and a white-collar worker. Her major difference was an extraordinary knack for business, at which she was very successful, even while she was still in university. This business orientation drew her interests away from dating, but also provided her with autonomy and resources most other youth lacked. By age twenty-one she already lived the life of the "modern woman" in the magazines. She had her own apartment, her own marketing company, her own spaces and resources for romantic adventures. In this world her social and moral referents were her university classmates, her coworkers, and characters on television and magazines, not the youth of her old neighborhood. Although she feared the surveillance of her building elevator operator, who knew her father, she had few local restraints on her behavior.

Her life revolved around business and leisure, which when she was twenty-one were sometimes but not always related. In her broad social group, to which I belonged, going out to the most fashionable bars and dance halls was an expected part of a modern lifestyle. Even as a teenager in high school, she had visited the famous JJ's Disco near her home in central Shanghai. As she grew older, she visited the bars and dance clubs frequented by foreigners and the local business elite. To some degree, this lifestyle directly conflicted with her relatively conservative sexual mores. She came into contact with numerous men, dated some for a few weeks at a time, and engaged in casual sexual intimacies with many others. Her leisure activities made sexual experimentation far more likely, easy, and legitimate. As a tourist (a popular activity for young educated women), she traveled to southern China with a man and slept in the same bed, engaging in sexual touching, but not including intercourse. She had male friends spend the night at her flat, though chastely, she maintained. Dancing, in particular, aroused her sexual passion, she said. She sometimes found herself kissing men she just met while dancing. She also said that drinking reduced her sexual inhibitions. Social alcohol consumption, a traditional masculine practice (toasts with Chinese spirits), was given fashionable, feminized forms (Corona and lime, cocktails) in Western-style bars and clubs. The foreign friends she made at bars often tried to persuade her that she should "enjoy life," meaning having sex, she explained, more joking than complaining, and some of her casual dancing and kissing partners were from this circle. By the time she was twenty-two, her sexual activities included sexual contact up to and including oral sex, but not intercourse. Perhaps she was more nervous about intercourse than many women, and her behavior in this regard may be atypical. On the other hand, she wasn't unhappy with the gradual development of her sexual experiences, and she did wait (she claims) until she was twenty-four to have sexual intercourse, and then with a serious boyfriend whom she later married.[39]

The spatial grammar of Bei's biography explains more of her casual sexual experiences than a narrative of personal sexual rebellion, or even a conventional sociological story of subcultural involvement. Bei didn't describe herself as a sexual rebel, nor did she reject traditional family values, but, rather, invoked them in novel ways. For instance, even after Bei began living with her boyfriend in their own apartment, they stayed alternately with each set of parents on the weekends in order to stay close to their families. Bei's leisure consumption involved mostly a vigorous pursuit of fashion (*shimao*), not strong commitments to new ideas and new people. A new geography of leisure locales and personal travel provided fashionable scenes for her young biography. This new Shanghai geography of leisure involved a revival of old high-corner nightlife districts (Huaihai Road and its environs), transplanted institutions of a global expatriate culture (Irish pubs, Indian restaurants, nightclubs), and local interpretations of cosmopolitan glamour (disco, bowling, and karaoke). These scenes provided new meanings to sexualized activities that might have seemed "low class" (*xialiu*) ten years before, but now could be described as fashionable ways of "enjoying life." The moral rhetoric of this new spatial grammar was dismissive (sexual activities as "play") and aestheticizing (play as "fashion"). As mere play, Bei's sexual flirtations were not serious actions, but became amusing adventures that could be shared with intimate friends as tokens of glamorous experience, decorative footnotes in a private but occasionally shared sexual biography.

The Dialectics of Neighborhood Sexual Culture
Gossip in a New Village Community

Sexual cultures, whether based in neighborhoods, such as Riverside Alley, or spatially dispersed, such as Bei's consumer leisure culture, are produced and maintained through specific means of communication. Locating the means and forms of communication among participants, but also among interested observers, is critical to understanding how sexual cultures are constituted and changed. While Bei's consumer leisure culture is partly defined through formal media of communication such as magazines, most local cultures rely upon informal means of communication, particularly conversations about what other people are doing, that is, gossip.

I suggest that gossip is a primary medium through which local community norms are negotiated and articulated. Gossip is special kind of moral rhetoric, pragmatically, flexibly, and concretely defining otherwise rather abstract principles of morality.[40] Although gossip tends to support conventional moral codes, its humor dulls its harsh judgments, and gossipers' wide exposure to different stories makes them more "realistic" about human nature, even if not overtly tolerant.[41] Gossip is a particularly disorderly form of communication, allowing multiple voices and free participation with no established hierarchies of control.[42] Finally, gossip does, in certain circumstances, serve as a mechanism of social change. Gossip allows participants to understand their own situations in a comparative context and gain empathy for the predicaments of others, through which they can begin to revise their moral views.[43] Neighborhood gossip, as I experienced it in 1990s Shanghai, is morally reactionary, but it is a flexible and creative reaction to local events, as well as being a very efficient means for communicating information about the novel sexual strategies of local people.[44]

For nearly two years I lived with my Shanghai in-laws in what was in the 1990s the most typical living arrangement in Shanghai, a new workers village in an area of low-corner Shanghai.[45] This new village (xincun) consisted of about fifteen five-story walk-up apartment buildings in a complex that retained the gridlike structure of Shanghai's old-style alleyways (linong). Built in the mid-1980s as company housing for several large work units, it was not an aesthetically pleasing environment, lacking the ornamentation and styling characteristic of both pre-1949 structures and housing built in the 1990s. The poorly constructed brick-and-cement apartment blocks were once painted but were now barren rain-stained concrete, uninsulated, and unheated in the cold wet winter. In the late 1990s the neighborhood was far more socially heterogeneous than either the low-corner shanty district of Riverside or the luxury high-rise communities inhabited by Bei and her friends, housing a mix of people who wouldn't be living together in most American communities: workers, managers, unemployed and wealthy, college-educated and illiterate, people who were finding very different "levels" in the "sea" of the market economy. This ironic conjuncture of Maoist work-unit housing and Dengist reforms created very dense and heterogeneous neighborhoods in many new villages in the 1990s.

Neighbors could hear and observe a great deal of one another's activities in my new village neighborhood. The narrow alleyways between buildings were neither public nor private. People slept outside their doorways on hot summer days and walked about in their pajamas in the narrow spaces between buildings. An outsider entering the alleyway intruded into a semiprivate space. People paid close attention to the activities of both neighbors and strangers. As an unusual character myself, a foreigner, entering the alleyway also meant becoming part of the web of gossip. Being such a conspicuous outsider, I was at first appalled by the omnipresent formal and informal surveillance. But gradually I realized that gossip could be enabling or legitimating for new forms of behavior, even as it restrained such behavior in some ways. As neighbors' sexual affairs and other peccadilloes become shared knowledge and these same neighbors came and went in their daily lives, enduring unscathed the scrutiny of neighbors and local officials, gossip about these cases gradually built up as a vast reservoir of secondhand experience from which people could pick and chose references, excuses, or foils for their own self-characterization. Quite literally, people in such diverse Shanghai communities quickly wised up in the ways of the world, meaning the world of the people living around them. This was an especially rich source of information in my neighborhood because of the density and heterogeneity of the people living there.[46]

Living with my in-laws, I was privy to the neighborhood gossip passed on to me by my mother-in-law while she cooked lunch for me and my wife's three-year-old nephew, who spent his afternoons with us. "Mom" had recently retired from the large state enterprise that built the complex where we lived and for which about a third of the residents worked or once worked, including my wife's father. I didn't directly interview in the complex, thus I can report only what my mother-in-law could tell me after living in the complex for ten years and spending about half an hour a day chatting with neighbors. In the course of a year, my hand-me-down gossip included a large cast of characters in my building. Obviously, these stories don't represent the building statistically, nor do they necessarily represent the lives of actual people; rather, they should be thought of as rhetorical narrative forms conveying locally relevant information and attitudes. I present only thumbnail sketches of what were sometimes rather elaborate narratives, to give readers a sense of the substance of neighborhood gossip, especially in the area of sexual strategies:

- The "girl"[47] downstairs who went to Shenzhen, the special economic zone abutting Hong Kong: Her family liked to show off the expensive gifts she bought them, such as a leather coat for her father. Mom said, "I don't know how she makes her money, but another neighbor said, 'Well, that's easy money, all you have to do is loosen your pants.'" Mom was embarrassed when she repeated that line to me and covered her mouth while she laughed.

- The girl who married a Japanese man: She ran her own business in Japan and lived in a different city from her husband. Her elderly parents raised her son in the building, and he grew up speaking no Japanese, although I heard other children call him "Japanese," almost an insult in Shanghai. These grandparents reported to my mother-in-law all the gifts their daughter gave them. After my wife and I moved to Japan, they made sure to compare incomes and housing arrangements.

- The girl who worked as a hostess in a karaoke club: Her mother bragged that she could make several hundred RMB a night in tips. "How could a mother be so stupid as to brag about that?" Mom commented.

- The girl who disapproved of her father's remarriage: She had moved out, but she insisted on her right to her old room in the apartment, where she stored old belongings and denied her father access. The family was Christian, and someone in the family had posted a sticker on the door saying in Chinese "Jesus will forgive those who sin." We assumed that sticker was just another of the insults exchanged within the family.

- The girl who married a handicapped man and whose parents wouldn't speak to her for a long time thereafter: Her parents bitterly opposed the marriage and forgave her only after the handicapped husband started pulling in good money driving a small three-wheeled taxi reserved for handicapped drivers.

- The star student who now worked in a major bank: She married a few months before I married my wife (also a famous top student in the building). A very proper woman, she told my mother-in-law that she never went out to dance halls and bars. "These places are too chaotic," she said. Now that she is a bank executive with an uptown apartment, she gives her mother a thousand yuan a month and expensive traditional medicines. "The daughter comes back and everyone treats her like a VIP," Mom said. "Her mother says, 'With a daughter like this one, who needs a son?' But I think her son and daughter-in-law aren't happy to hear her talk like that."

These were largely negative examples in my mother-in-law's framing (though given the circumstances, the valences of the stories could shift from positive to negative as did this last one about the good student who became too "uppity"). I also heard more positively framed stories:

- The son who went to England and got a Ph.D.: His father visited him and came back bragging what a nice clean city London was.
- The daughter who went to the United States, became a medical doctor, and married a Chinese American lawyer: They had just recently bought a house on Long Island. This was almost an ideal case in the eyes of a Shanghai mother.
- The airline stewardess who flew to America every other week: She had a boyfriend who was a driver and parked his car in our neighborhood, driving her anywhere she needed to go. (She had a coworker who was arrested for prostitution, just one example of third- and fourth-hand gossip that my mother-in-law passed along.)

Then there were simply funny stories:

- The nice old Subei (northern Jiangsu) lady from down the hall: She always brings back a live chicken for my mother-in-law when she returns from the countryside. Occasionally she comes over to watch TV. While watching a TV program about love and romance, she told Mom, "What is this love and romance stuff? I don't understand it. If my old man dies, he dies. So what?"
- The father of the model student who works in a bank: "He is a retired soldier but acts like a little old lady," Mom said. "He comes complaining to me to get his wife to cook better food for the family. I told him, 'That is your family's business. How can I tell your wife what to do?'" More recently, rumors were spreading that he was flirting with the old women in the building.
- The neighbor's daughter, who is thirty-one and divorced with a small child: She went to Eastern Europe doing private business and now parks a big Toyota Land Cruiser in the narrow alley in front of our building. By late 1999 the daughter suddenly had a new apartment, and the mother took Mom and several other neighbors to see the apartment. As they entered, they noticed a man's shoes, cigarettes, and other signs that the woman wasn't living alone. Later the couple married, and it turns out that her husband is a wealthy northern businessman.
- Of course, there was also the good student (my wife) who married the foreigner (me) with no money: Obviously, we were the object of some gossip, the contents of which we can't be sure. My mother-in-law reported only the neighbors' questions, which included their musings about why an American would live in a Chinese apartment (something

they thought impossible), whether I could tolerate the food, speak Chinese, or use chopsticks. Some wanted to know whether my parents were wealthy, what they did for a living, or how much we earn in Japan.

Neighborhood sexual gossip is a flexible and multivocal community reaction to the changing sexual strategies of residents. Gossip stories, rather than arguments over abstract principles, are the form for articulating standards of normalcy around issues of work, money, sex, and marriage. These stories seldom are told with a purely judgmental tone, but rather as a form of entertainment, including humor, news that also puts oneself in a good light through contrast, comparison, association, or just simply because one is privy to a new and interesting tidbit. Gossip constrains people's actions through the threat of censure and laughter, but its ambiguity and multivalence offer the possibility of alternative interpretations. The actual meanings individuals attach to stories depend on their own circumstances. My mother-in-law collected an elaborate set of stories about young women marrying foreigners and living in Japan, fodder for her own discussions and understandings of her daughter's life. Yet even the mother who bragged about how much money her daughter made as a hostess would have a host of positive references as well. The alleyway society placed great value on the "face" gained through the gifts of the generous daughter, affirming the two highest virtues of low-corner Shanghai culture (and in Chinese society generally)—wealth and filial piety—which partly negated the shamefulness of how the money was made.

Although gossip was considered a women's activity in China,[48] retirees of both sexes contributed stories in their daily meetings in our neighborhood alleyway, where they tended grandchildren. Women dominated my mother-in-law's circle. Although young women didn't usually participate in this talk (because they were busy working), they were the most popular topics of older women's talk.[49] Young women were seen as having chances denied to all previous generations of women. Older women in the alleyway weren't trying to tie their daughters to the alleyway home but hoped that they would become educated modern women living in a comfortable "suburban" apartment with a husband and a child, better yet in an American suburban home with an American degree and a highly paid professional husband (Japan was a distant second). This vision of the materially affluent family life was the most positive statement of the materialistic conception of sexuality in Shanghai. Inasmuch as the strategies of youth conformed to these ideals, they could be bragged about. Inasmuch as they deviated, they could be jokingly dismissed or scorned. Of course, the stories children tell about themselves profess other compensatory values to this materialistic vision, such as feelings, romance, or passion, but these were not the concerns of their mothers. No mother would brag about her daughter's "romantic" orientation.

Even though gossip within a small closed community was likely to lead to judgments that were conservative and conventional, gossip could also subvert conventional morality when it provided access to information and models that defied conventional norms.[50] As Maryann Ayim writes about women's gossip, "The line between talk that sustains and talk that subverts oppressive norms is an easy one to cross for those who are heavily penalized by such norms."[51] I will give an example of how this subversive use of gossip worked in a conversation with a woman from a nearby low-corner neighborhood. She was in her mid-thirties, married, but separated from her husband, living with her father, and involved in a sexual affair with a married man. She framed her affair within the alternative normative context of neighborhood gossip and against the patriarchal values of her father:

> My father was against it [my affair]. He said that I hadn't gotten a divorce and shouldn't be doing that. I didn't listen to him. I think he is really full of it [luosuo]. My father is conservative because he is over seventy. Younger parents in their fifties and sixties are much more liberal. I think, "Why should I be alone?" I want to go out; there is nothing wrong with it. I know that my neighbors are doing the same thing. On the surface they have a really good relationship, but people have seen the man out with other women, and the woman out with another man. If even a couple who gets along well like that has these kinds of relationships, then why shouldn't I? . . . The man told me he has a girlfriend outside. She [his wife] turns a blind eye. . . . As for the wife, she also has a man. In name he is her mother's godson. She calls him "elder brother." But in the market I saw them holding hands, and he always brings her home on his motorcycle. I don't think any real brother is that good to a sister. . . . Anyway, this is all just idle talk, but [neighbors] also saw him [the husband] at the dance hall with his girlfriend.

Although this woman had herself complained earlier about the idle talk of her neighbors, the repertoire of neighborhood gossip formed a rhetorical casuistry for her own affairs. Her neighbors' "bad" behavior provided an alternative to her father's sexual standards, an alternative moral universe of sexual possibilities in which her own affair was normal. Interesting stories of neighbor's sexual peccadilloes thus became normalizing tales in which she could embed her own insecure narrative of self-fulfillment.

I suggest that sharing gossip is a central process in the dialectics of local sexual culture. Echoing Sennett's argument about the virtues of "disorderly" neighborhoods, Lorraine Code writes, "An adequate civil society depends on disorderly and disorganized activities such as gossip and play."[52] Neighborhood gossip is a disorderly medium of communication and a creative reaction to the sexual strategies of local youth. It forms a local semipublic sphere in which neighborhood people share information across class and status lines about real people whose life circumstances they understand, and without the censorship imposed on public media. Despite its apparent conservative bent, this local semipublic sphere of neighborhood gossip is more uninhibited, and probably more subversive (or flexible in its responses to situations), than the public print and electronic media, which receive the bulk of scholarly attention.

Ecological Transformations and Neighborhood Sexual Cultures

The local dialectics of sexual culture are also subject to larger ecological processes of urban change. Changes in the sexual subcultures of Riverside Alley, of the new village in which I lived, and of the more spatially dispersed consumer culture of Bei were all tied up in a larger ecological and political transformation of the city. Most simply, these vignettes can be read together as a single narrative of Shanghai's neighborhood life: past, present, and future. By the time this book is printed, Riverside Alley will have been completely demolished, ending a tightly knit and very localized youth sex culture of a type unlikely to develop again in Shanghai. The new villages continue to house a heterogeneous and rather tightly knit population, even if maintained only through the ties between older people who once belonged to the same work units, but they too are becoming increasingly class segregated as wealthier residents move to better housing. The "vertical suburbs" in which Bei and her husband live represent the future for those with the money to leave behind them the gossip and trouble of the alleyway or old work-unit housing.

The spatial grammar of subcultural creativity also seems to have changed within this larger ecological transformation. In Riverside Alley in the earliest years of the reform era, youth were largely free from the influences of a wider consumer culture in creating their leisure and sexual cultures. The chaotic years of the late 1970s offered no commercial nightlife or public sexual culture. The only controls were ineffective official prohibitions and traditional community norms. This was a youth culture with few resources but with a great deal of local autonomy. In contrast to Riverside Alley, the spatially dispersed leisure culture experienced by Bei is one in which youth consume a globalized media culture, whose production is now dispersed among transnational media organizations, local entrepreneurs, and increasingly professionalized local fashion leaders. Finally, the "civil society" of sexual gossip in the new village that I described remains an especially productive discursive space because of the density of ties and the heterogeneity of neighborhood stories. The cultural creativity of this local gossip, however, might be diminished in the less dense and heterogeneous communities that seem to be emerging in the newer areas of Shanghai.

Shanghai is changing shape. A new city of high-rises emerges literally in the dust of the old alleys, a city of consumers with increasingly private lives, a process that involves conscious state planning and the choices of people moving within the city. Nostalgia for the alleyways increases as they are demolished, receding into the myth of warm, homogenous communities; forgotten are the adultery, fights, and betrayals that constitute the heterogeneous material of real neighborhood gossip. While the more spatially dispersed social networks of the high-rise-dwelling "suburbanites" may be liberating in a negative sense, the new community structure may limit the communication between social classes that characterized the new village. Suburbanized urbanites will know of adultery and promiscuity, but more often filtered through the selective lens of the media rather than experienced through the troublesome and less-predictable lives of neighbors.

This chapter has laid out conventional spatial terms and local geographies that form the scenes for communicating sexual meanings in Shanghai. These conventional scenes are only one element of Burke's pentad of dramatistic elements. The next chapter deals with the conventional characters that are equally constitutive of the neighborhood gossip and other forms of sexual rhetoric this book describes.

3 人物

CHARACTERS
Big and Small

Shanghai's Sexual Characters
Shanghai Women / Shanghai Men

In 1997 I e-mailed a friend who grew up in the interior of China to ask her what she thought of Shanghai people now that she was working in a Shanghai company. The twenty-three-year-old young woman, who had recently graduated from a prestigious Shanghai university, immediately shot off a reply in excellent English, describing her opinions about the men and women of Shanghai:

> Women here have much stronger personalities than men. Here, let me put it this way: If this [Shanghai] were a theater, actresses are at center stage, always in the spotlight, while actors seem to be in a supporting role. However, behind the scenes there is a male director or a male producer. . . . Shanghai women are strong-willed in every way: fashion, education, communication, occupation, family connection, probably even prostitution. They want to control things even if they don't have the ability to control anything at all. They are materially oriented, both the older and younger generation. Young women want to catch up with the modern world; old women want to make up for the losses they suffered during the Cultural Revolution.
>
> About Shanghai men, what should a man be like? Everyone has different ideas. For me there are a lot of should-not-be's for men. They should not quarrel over an unintentional stamp [on their foot] for half an hour; should not struggle for a seat with women on public transportation; should not be led around by a woman; shouldn't write on their faces announcing, "I'm making shit loads of money; I am a *dakuan* [big money]!" Shanghai men do all of these things.

This chapter continues my dramatistic grammar of Shanghai sexual culture. While the previous chapter focused on the rhetoric of space, this chapter focuses on the rhetoric of characters: gendered and sexualized prototypes from Shanghai's public culture and the representative anecdotes in which these imaginary actors are plotted. Authors develop more sophisticated versions of these characters in fictional works, but ordinary people employ simple versions in comments like the one above.

Urban life is much like theater, a constant performance in front of a group of judgmental strangers.[1] In these performances, people play up to the expectations of the strangers surrounding them with the knowledge that they may be judged in terms of a cast of stock characters associated with their gender, age, and other background features. In conversations, people use these sexed and gendered characters as prototypes for ascribing sexual motives to actors around them. Stock characters, such as the "Shanghai girl" and the "big money," are key elements in this dramatistic grammar of urban culture. In describing the rhetoric of these stereotypical characters in Shanghai, I draw broadly from dramatic works, focus group transcripts, and ethnographic observations. Taken as a whole, these characters represent a moral economy of sexuality specific to the conditions of reform-era Shanghai, in which money is privileged as a morally corrupting god-term, sex is a commodity, and sexual relations are a field of combat between men and women. In this ironic discourse of motives, romantic love is only a weak attraction. In romantic reversals of this discourse, romantic feelings become the one authentic value that morally compensates for pragmatic choices.

Shanghaiese employ character prototypes of varying levels of generality. Most generally, as is well represented in my friend's e-mail, Shanghai is the city of strong, mercenary women and weak, small-minded men, a bit of a national disgrace.[2] Shanghai's young women take center stage. A popular Chinese expression goes, "Beijing people dare say anything, Guangzhou people dare eat anything, and Shanghai people dare wear anything." In this saying only Shanghai is defined by a largely feminine proclivity—provocative clothing. Republican-era Shanghai, "the Paris of the East," was known both for both its prostitution and its fashion.[3] Older women tell me that even during the Cultural Revolution, Shanghai girls found ways to dress better than women in other cities, with a more stylish cut of the trousers, sharper haircuts, and nice white socks. In addition to fashion consciousness, Shanghai women are widely reputed to be more fickle, craftier (jingming), and sexually open than other Chinese women, and stronger and more talented than local Shanghai men. The imagined Shanghai girl employs all the tricks and weapons of conventional femininity. As one Shanghai informant said, "Shanghai girls know how to pout [*sajiao*], and how to bitch [*zuopofu*]." While discussing his dating relationship with a Shanghai woman, a college student from Anhui casually outlined his stereotypic fears of the Shanghai girl:

> Girls are really different in Shanghai. Girls here are much more open. This is my first Shanghaiese girlfriend, and I used to have prejudices against Shanghai girls. Girls here aren't very reliable. Maybe they will just play around with you and when they don't like you, they will just leave you. Maybe they will just spend your money or something. Girls from where I'm from are very reliable. If they become your girlfriend, it is because they want to marry you.

The Shanghai man is largely a negative prototype, usually described as clever and educated, but short on virility, particularly short on generosity toward friends (generosity being a highly valued masculine virtue in China). The domesticated Shanghai-style husband (*haipaizhangfu*) goes far beyond the more widespread Chinese stereotypical "bronchitis" (*qiguanyan*, a pun on "my wife controls me strictly") of the Chinese henpecked husband to a reputation for an active role in household labor represented by the expression "*madasao*," Shanghaiese for "shopping, washing, cooking"—all domestic activities that Shanghai-style husbands are reputed to engage in more than other men.[4] Defending this stereotype, Shanghaiese sometimes told me that Shanghai men were widely valued as husbands, not only in China but in nearby Asian countries. Long Yintai, a well-known Taiwanese author, even published a popular paean to the domestic virtues of the Shanghai husband:

> The Shanghai man is so loveable. He can shop, cook and mop the floor without feeling he is lowering himself. He can wash women's clothes and not feel despicable. He can talk to a woman in a quiet soft voice and not feel he has lost his masculinity. . . . He can appreciate his wife's success without feeling he has failed himself.[5]

She argues that the Shanghai man is the one "liberated women have been dreaming of" and is dismayed that Shanghai girls dismiss him as lacking "masculinity." Among other Chinese, condemnations of the Shanghai husband are more common. In a trip across the Yangtze River into North China, I heard frequent denunciations of Shanghai men, that they were "stingy" (*xiaoqi*) "small-minded" (*xiaojiaziqi*), and "effeminate" (*meiyounanziqigai*). Many Chinese joke that the biggest compliment you can pay to a Shanghai man is "You don't seem like a Shanghaiese." Even Shanghaiese employed this rhetoric in their descriptions of their romantic traits and choices. For instance, in a magazine article a young Shanghai woman describes her Shanghai boyfriend as atypical for Shanghai: "His family is from the North, so he doesn't have any of that 'small-mindedness' of Shanghai men."[6]

This discourse of gendered strengths and weaknesses implies an imbalanced sexual economy. On a trip to Guangzhou, a male Cantonese railway worker declared to me that Shanghai men aren't real men because "they let their wives sleep with other men." In this discourse of gendered sexual "strength," weak masculinity implies a surplus of female sexuality, a situation more denigrating to men than women. Intellectuals and journalists seriously lament the "masculinization of women and feminization of men" in Shanghai[7] or that "the yin is strong and the yang is weak," meaning the women are stronger, more conspicuous, more outstanding than the men, a state of disorder inimical to a Chinese ideal of harmony between opposite but presumably complementary male and female identities.[8] These stereotypes represent gender relations in Shanghai as a conflict with no clear outcome: "a battle between men and women."[9]

Toward a Rhetoric of Sexual Characters

Since Robert Park, sociologists have been aware that the city possesses, in Park's words, "a moral as well as physical organization."[10] Sexual character types are an overlooked element of urban moral discourse, imagined prototypes associated with the city and through whom people dispute the moral boundaries of local sexual cultures. This chapter reconstructs the inhabitants of this imagined metropolis of Shanghai from popular discourse and public cultural productions—the "big money," the "strong woman," the "Shanghai baby," the "playboy," the "little country sister," and others—showing how people use these characters to represent, critique, and display sexual motives.

In general, constructionist paradigms of sexuality have been far too normative and deterministic.[11] Following Burke's conception of a dramatistic grammar of motives, I want to move from an idea of moral order as rules and proscriptions toward a focus on prototypes as collective representations, which are both more empirical and more representative of the contested nature of moral discourse.[12] Alisdair MacIntyre describes how stock characters—like the nineteenth-century headmaster and minister and the twentieth-century therapist and manager—function as the dramatis personae of an imagined moral or-

der, the "moral representatives of their culture."[13] From my observations, however, the prototypes most prominently associated with Shanghai's public sexual culture generally represent vices rather than virtues, excess or inadequacy
like the strength of the "Shanghai woman" or the weakness of the "Shanghai
man." Such characters are the imaginary agents in a rhetoric of motives that is
usually ironic or "negative."[14] Such rhetorical "negativity" is a typical feature
of the everyday moral discourse of gossip (see chapter 2) and of the genre of
irony in which these characters often appear (see chapter 4). The classical Greek
source for the rhetoric of caricature is Theophrastus, who compiled a catalogue
of negative character types useful for humorous and ironic comparisons with
real people in casual conversations.[15] The conception of characters employed
here allows us to reflect upon the negative and open-ended nature of public moral discourse. Normatively, these characters are the inverse of Talcott
Parsons's roles and more like Foucault's "outcasts," who negatively define
the characteristics of ordinary people. These characters are intelligibility constructs[16] rather than action constructs;[17] that is, they are a means by which
people represent the moral order of society, not models of how to live. They are
made into overt role models only when people decide to be heterodox, for instance, to play the femme fatale or the playboy, as discussed below. For most
people at most times, they are cautionary foils in a negative rhetoric of motives
representing a sexual society dominated by money values.

A work that intriguingly parallels my endeavor is Keith McMahon's discussion of character types in Qing fiction and the sexual and social dilemmas articulated through them.[18] According to McMahon, the fundamental dilemma
in Qing fiction is that of the polygynous male managing a household of women
and children who dissipate his resources, both sexual and financial, and disrupt
the order of the household through jealousy. In this dual financial and sexual economy, sexual disorder—in the form of male weakness and female
strength—represents a wider social disorder. The echoes of this particular trope
are clear in the representations of weak Shanghai men and strong Shanghai
women discussed in this chapter. However, despite the traditional origins of
some of the character types, the social configurations in which they are now
employed are different, as well as the sexual economy (and its disruptions) that
they are used to represent. The analogous sexual and moral dilemma faced by
the contemporary Shanghai man and woman is the formation and mainte-
nance not of a large polygynous household, but of the "small" conjugal family
(xiaojiating) in the face of the increasing pressures and temptations of the liberal
market economy. The notion of "smallness" has a peculiar resonance for Shang-

hai people, often described as "little city people" (xiaoshimin) aspiring to the "small comforts" (xiaokang) of a comfortable middle-class life.[19] The aspirations of the negative characters associated with Shanghai's public sexual culture are, in contrast, overly large. The negative types populating the sexual imagination of Shanghai, like the big money and femme fatale, represent overreaching greed and sensuousness that would disrupt the conjugal ideal of a "small couple" (xiaoliangkou) starting out their "small family life" (xiaojiating shenghuo). The types of stories these characters most easily lend themselves to are melodramas of sexual transgression that negatively reaffirm the sexual orthodoxy of marriage, child rearing, and modest material aspirations. Through these stories, rapid social mobility of any type is imagined as sexual corruption.

Finally, I am not arguing for or against the truth of these characters as representatives of an underlying "social reality." Rather, I treat them as part of what Northrop Frye calls the "mythological universe" of narrative, play, and ritual,[20] which is not as clearly distinguishable from the "real worlds" of social life as Frye's formulation implies. These characters are everyday literary devices people use to construct meaningful dramas out of the material of everyday social life. They are dramatic foils and masks for positioning selves and others within a "Shanghai-style" sexual modernity, which is as much mythological construct as social reality.

Haipai (the Shanghai Style): Representative Anecdotes of Shanghai Culture

Before considering the literary and everyday rhetoric of these characters, it helps to consider several common myths of Shanghai cultural origins with which they are traditionally associated. As in the discussion of spatial categories in the last chapter, this discussion of the representative anecdotes of Shanghai culture builds on Gerald Suttles's conception of the "cumulative texture of urban culture," the selective accumulation of icons and memories retained within a public understanding of the identity of the city.[21] By retaining elements of Shanghai's semicolonial heritage, these stereotypic narratives project historic urban myths onto the everyday tools of symbolic interaction. There are no Horatio Alger stories in this cultural tool kit. These are rather anecdotes of transgression taken as metonymic of Shanghai's hybrid (or mongrel) modernity. The first is the transgression of Westernization, represented through the Shanghai girl's dalliance with foreigners. Then there is the transgression of migration represented by the out-of-town big money who buys women and by the little country sister who sells herself in the city. And most centrally perhaps, there is the transgression of prostitution represented in the mercenary sexual-

ity of the Shanghai girl and the wastrel playboy. The market society that Shanghaiese thus represent to themselves is not a materialist utopia but an ironic
world of material temptations and sexual dangers.

In popular media and conversations, characters like the Shanghai girl are often explained in terms of a Shanghai style (*haipai*) of culture. Shanghai's peculiar cultural style developed along with its historical emergence as a treaty port,
migrant city, and commercial center. "*Haipai*" originated in the late nineteenth
century as a term describing populist trends in theater and painting, extending
gradually to styles in literature, architecture, and eventually everyday lifestyles
associated with the more commercialized, Westernized, and individualized
culture of the city.[22] Shanghai represents what Robert Redfield and Milton
Singer describe as the city of the "heterogenetic" order, foreign and commercial violator of the unifying national and traditional order, often represented
through Beijing.[23] In this contrastive discourse, *haipai* represents an almost sac-
rilegious cultural mixing, "less Chinese" than the Beijing style, or *jingpai*.[24]
"Shanghai" means the "[city] on the sea." "*Haipai*," then, literally translates as
the "oceanic style." The term "*hai*" in contemporary discourse connotes both
the openness to the West (Western people are still called "oceanic peoples"—
yangren) and the openness and instability of the market economy (leaving state
employment and entering the market economy is referred to as "jumping into
the sea"—*xiahai*[25]). The Shanghai style thus connotes the cultural instability and
openness of Shanghai's position as China's major port and major commercial
center.

Haipai, or Shanghai more generally, should not be taken as a complete or
even primary identity for Shanghai people. Shanghai people easily slip between
Shanghai and China as the framework for cultural identification. A Shanghai
man may identify himself as Chinese, Shanghaiese, Ningbo (a native-place distinction), or a man from a particular district of Shanghai, depending on what
he is defending or claiming. The Shanghai style almost always plays on Chinese
identity. Without the ever-present Chinese context, it makes no sense to talk of
being Shanghaiese. Also, the valuations of these identities change as people play
on their positive and negative connotations. "Feminine" Shanghai men can defend themselves as "modern" and "feminist." Or "masculine" Beijing can be
dismissed as "backward" and "official." The Shanghai miss may be morally suspect, but she may also be deemed more desirable and clever than other girls.
The Shanghai-style husband (*haipaizhangfu*) in his pajamas carrying a basket to
the vegetable market in the morning enacts a character within the imagination
of the city and gains legitimacy. He may be laughable, but he also can see him-

self as more liberal and sophisticated than either the Taiwan bumpkin (*taibazi*) or the northeastern tough guy (*dongbeihan*). Despite their overt negative connotations, the archetypes described in this chapter also work, in Suttles's language, as "defended typifications," negative stereotypes that are embraced by the denizens of a city to define and defend the culture of the city.[26]

Symbolic interaction thus gains historical and geographic referents in these stories. Through their connections with the narratives of Westernization, migration, and prostitution, characters such as the playboy and bold girl bridge a divide between the macrosocial domain of history and the microsocial domain of social interaction. Such prototypical characters provide a larger interpretive context, which actors may or may not desire. When a Shanghai husband shops in the market, this larger context subtly comes into play. When a Shanghai woman meets a foreign businessman in a Shanghai bar, the historical narratives virtually shout out their (cynical) interpretations.

Westernization

When asked about the origins of Shanghai's local culture, natives and non-natives almost always mention that Shanghai is influenced very much by its occupation by foreign powers from 1841 to 1945. From its beginnings as a treaty port, Chinese observers condemned Shanghai as a mongrel non-Chinese city within China. The openness of Shanghai people to foreign things is taken as evidence of their cultural Westernization (*xihua*) and worship of the West (*chongyangmeiwai*). Take, for instance, the culturally central practice of eating. By the late nineteenth century, Chinese were sampling Western food in Shanghai's Western restaurants,[27] practices that survived the Cultural Revolution. Even in the early 1980s, the daily deliveries of the milkman, lines at the bakery for morning bread, "Russian soup" for dinner, and Sunday lunches with the children at a neighborhood Western restaurant marked off ordinary Shanghaiese from the culinary orthodox residents of less Westernized cities in China.

Another association of worship of the West is the reputed willingness of Shanghaiese to go abroad: "There's no money a Cantonese won't dare earn, nothing a Beijingese won't dare say, nothing [dangerous] a Manchurian won't dare to do, and no foreign country a Shanghaiese won't dare go." Shanghai, in fact, leads all other cities and provinces in the number of its people who have gone abroad for work and study.[28] In the popular imagination, the most likely paths abroad are graduate study in North America, laboring in Japan, or—especially for women—marriage to a Westerner, overseas Chinese, or Japanese. The narrative of Westernization shapes the characters associated with the city, especially the fashionable Shanghai girl, but even the Shanghai husband with his Western ideas of gender equality.

Migration

Educated Shanghaiese proudly argue that Shanghai is a city of immigrants and thus has much in common with the United States, a country of immigrants. Shanghai's population swelled with waves of refugees beginning with the Taiping Rebellion in the 1860s and continuing through World War II. By 1930 the Chinese population grew to around 3 million, nearly three-fourths of whom were not native-born. Immigration also impacted the development of Shanghai culture. Migrants lacked family in Shanghai and were freer to patronize the commercial leisure establishments that sprang up in the city.[29] With a male-to-female ratio of 142 to 100, prostitutes never lacked clients.[30] Migrants and sojourners—including 150,000 foreigners—created an atmosphere of cultural diversity in the city, while the everyday deaths of refugees and beggars in the streets established Shanghai's reputation as a coldhearted and materialistic city.

Migration returned to Shanghai in the 1990s, generating a pool of over 3 million migrant workers. In the 1990s out-of-towners (*waidiren*) in Shanghai fell into two culturally prominent groups. First, and by far the most numerous, were the migrant workers (*mingong*), a socially denigrated group that included thousands of little country sisters (*wailaimei*), young female service workers perceived by Shanghaiese as sexually available, conniving, and very low status. Second, there were the big moneys (*dakuan*) who came into Shanghai frequently on business. While not all rich businessmen were outsiders, a socially prominent group was. Taiwanese and Hong Kongers as well as men from many other Chinese areas came to Shanghai to make their fortunes. Shanghaiese caricatured the big moneys from these areas as wealthy but lacking culture (e.g., *taibazi*, the "Taiwan bumpkin")—the same reputation Shanghai's merchant migrants had in the 1930s. In the reform era, big moneys represent the seemingly illegitimate rise to wealth and social status of men with no educational credentials, a common phenomenon in the early market reform era.

The migrant remains a salient figure in Shanghai's sexual culture. The little country sister reputedly comes to the city to engage in morally dubious service occupations and to find a Shanghai lover. The big money tries to buy himself a local woman (or many women) in the city. In the "hypergamous" local sexual economy, little country sisters are perceived as unfair competition for Shanghai women, big moneys as unfair competition for ordinary Shanghai men. Shanghai girls, in turn, can practice their seductive tricks on the unsophisticated big moneys and guileless foreigners who come to the city on business. The narrative of migration is thus a tale of mobility that is also a morally suspect crossing of boundaries, in which the characters of the big money and the little country sister are seen as overly zealous in pursuit of their material and sexual goals. As such, they are a threat to the local sexual economy, tempting Shanghai women and men away from the security of the "small family life."

Prostitution

More than perhaps any other city, Shanghai has been represented through the metaphor of prostitution. In reform-era China, the prostitute symbolizes a crisis of morality that emerges with foreign influence and market reform,[31] while many female occupations, such as the little secretary (xiaomi), the public relations girl (gongguanxiaojie), and even the high-status white-collar miss (bailing xiaojie), are occasionally described in the language of prostitution. The Shanghai woman's Westernization and migration also carry with them this notion of her sexual openness—her sexual commodification through her exposure to foreign ideas. For her to be Westernized (e.g., a white-collar miss), an emigrant (e.g., working in Japan), or a migrant (e.g., a little country sister) is to become a "free" sexual commodity. Using Burke's term, prostitution thus serves as the most "representative anecdote" of Shanghai's sexual culture, a metonym for the money orientation of Shanghai culture.[32]

This urban myth of prostitution builds on historical narratives. Once called the "whore of Asia" by Western adventurers, Shanghai by one count had more prostitutes (and more gambling and opium consumption) per capita than any city in the world before 1949. In 1930 the prostitution industry was the largest employer of female labor in the city, and approximately one in thirty residents sold sex for a living.[33] Contemporary Shanghai women don't escape this legacy. For instance, one man on the train to Guangzhou said to me, "Look, before Liberation [1949] there were so many thousands of prostitutes in that city. These are their daughters." The female characters associated with the city have thus always displayed a love of consumption and a mercenary attitude toward sex.[34] The male characters of the city, especially the playboy and the big money, also participate in this commercialization of sex, the first as swindlers and hustlers and the second as targets for the tricks of the prostitute and the dance hall "fishing girl" (diaomazi).

The cultural prominence of certain sexual narratives over others allows us to place Shanghai's stories in a broader comparative context. Beth Bailey dis-

cusses the mid-twentieth-century U.S. obsession with college students' premarital sexual behavior, forming a representative sexual anecdote of that era's
"sexual revolution."[35] Arguably, public narratives of adultery stole this position
in the 1990s U.S. sexual culture.[36] Prostitution as a representative anecdote of
sexual culture also has U.S. precedents. According to Sharon Ullman, prostitution was the dominant sexual narrative of the Progressive era in the United
States, becoming "the trope through which the heterosexual desire was articulated both by reformers and by the producers of popular culture in 'a public
vision of access and desire.'"[37] Without pushing the comparisons too far, it
seems prostitution lends itself as a likely metaphor for the moral and gender
confusion of market transitions, including the advent of national consumer
markets in the U.S. Progressive era as well as the rather different market transitions in former socialist states.[38]

As a representative anecdote for Shanghai's sexual culture, prostitution
defines money or material gain as a primary motive for sexual interactions, becoming a default cynical reading of others' actions. More broadly, it reflects and
reinforces the status of money as a "god-term," in Burke's language, "a techni-
cal substitute for God," an "overall public motive mediating among the endless
diversity of occupational and private motives."[39] Ironically perhaps, this notion
of money as god-term is recognized in the current official campaigns in China
against money worship (baijinzhuyi). As a privileged public motive in sexual and
other actions, the motive of money also gives weight to opposite ethical sensitivities, a whole range of new virtues, including romantic love, which rest on
the ability to resist the temptation of money. In the ironic moral universe ruled
by this immoral "god," money gives men sexual potency and women a temptation to sell their sex. To have no money or to make no money is to be excluded
from this sexual economy altogether, to be degendered and desexed. Complaining about corruption and inequality in the market economy, a factory
worker I met in my neighborhood park told me, "There's a saying, 'Beautiful
girls rely on the boss. Capable men don't work factory jobs. Those who work
the swing shift are neither men or women.'"[40] The context of the joke is a
gendered sexual economy in which money gives men sexual potency and
women's sexual attractiveness makes them money, so that incapable and unsexy
factory workers, "those who work the swing shift," have no sex or gender at all.

A Grammar and Rhetoric of Shanghai's Sexual Characters

In the following sections I combine a grammar and a rhetoric of
Shanghai's sexual characters, that is, in each section I introduce various char-

acters and their contexts of use. Because of space, I focus on only the most common and conventional characters. Across these various rhetorical contexts, I describe how Shanghai people use these characters to define the moral boundaries of their sexual culture. In theatrical productions these stock characters are
spectacles that represent the moral extremes of action in the market society. In
casual conversations they are flexible cultural schema people use to pass quick
and easy moral judgments on others, lending themselves as metaphors for a
continually changing population of noteworthy people. In games of hustling
and seduction, they can be the masks people don to create illusions of depth.
The contents and origins of these characters do not determine their uses.
People use these stock characters and even create new ones to legitimate moral
transgressions and make people notice them. Finally, in conversation, as in fiction, the number of such prototypical characters is unlimited. Speakers make
endless creative refinements along geographic, occupational, and other lines.[41]

American Wives and Shanghai Husbands: Stock Characters in Shanghai Spoken Drama

Shanghai journalists are fond of writing about "the great theatrical
stage of the market economy" (shichangjingji de dawutai), a pregnant metaphor, I
suggest, because it describes the new market society as both an arena in which
people participate as actors and a spectacle they find morally engaging even
when not directly participating. I begin this exposition of Shanghai's sexualized characters with a discussion of two actual dramatic plays that represent
gender relations in the new market era, employing many of the stock characters associated with the city. I saw the two plays in Shanghai in 1995 and 1996
and interviewed their playwrights. Written nearly a decade apart, the plays reveal a general shift in the characterization of Shanghai's sexual culture during
the reform era.

Both plays explore conflicts of love and material ambitions through the
character of the Westernized Shanghai woman. The first play, The Accompanying
Wife (Peidufuren), explores the experiences of a Shanghai wife who accompanies
her husband to America to study. The action takes place in the home of an American businessman and his wife in California, where the Chinese couple live in
return for providing child care for the American family. The story centers on
the wife's difficult adjustment to American sexual culture. Two stereotypical
women characters dominate the play: the reticent, virtuous, and strong-willed
"accompanying wife" and the loud, demanding, and materialistic American
woman. The male characters represent the equally common stereotypes of the

studious but timid Shanghai husband and the charming but lascivious American man.

The Accompanying Wife, according to its Shanghai playwright Wang Zhoushen, conveys the shocking encounter of post-Mao Chinese with Western consumer culture through the protagonist's conflicts with the American housewife. The Chinese wife is a simple (pusu) but honest (laoshi) woman, concerned primarily with her family's well-being, but the American housewife gradually makes her life intolerable through her selfish demands. The Chinese wife quarrels with her husband because of his timidity and lack of support for her in her conflicts with the American housewife. In the midst of her crisis with the American housewife, the American husband approaches her with a sexual proposition. She reveals a reciprocal interest but firmly rejects his advances. In the end she wins the respect of the American family and of the audience by speaking her mind and showing herself a "strong" Chinese woman.

Written during the early years of the Chinese opening to the West in the 1980s, the play represents a Shanghai family from a "simpler time," the author told me. Nonetheless, the play foreshadows an incipient gender crisis—much clearer in the next play—in the woman's alienation from her husband as she alone confronts the material and sexual confusions of the new open society, while her husband remains absorbed in his studies. Even in this rather conservative story, women, not men, take up the challenge of Western consumer values.

The subdued gender conflicts of The Accompanying Wife contrast starkly with a play on similar themes written ten years later in the 1990s. "If China will be saved, first Chinese women will save themselves," Shanghai novelist Tang Yin said when explaining the meaning of the play The Wife from America (Meiguo laide qizi). Her husband, Zhang Xian, rewrote her novel as a play and produced and directed it. Set in Shanghai, The Wife from America deals not with the American wife of a Shanghai man, as the title would suggest, but with a Shanghai wife who has gone abroad and returns Americanized and asks for a divorce from her Shanghai husband. The development of these two main characters draws deeply on the culture of Shanghai and the sensibilities of its residents. The husband is a prototypical Shanghai husband, content with a small life of books and domesticity; the woman is a prototypical Shanghai woman, adventurous and aggressive, willing to try anything new, to do anything to get ahead, but never satisfied. As an independent businesswoman, she also fits the stock character of the strong woman (nuuqiangren), economically and sexually autonomous, unable to comfort men and be a virtuous wife and good mother. A common suspicion of the strong woman is that she exploits her sex to make her way in life, a view exemplified in the popular Chinese expression: "Behind every successful man there is a woman, but behind every successful woman there are many men." The "wife from America" actually works as a prostitute when she starts her life in America (selling herself to "black men"). Her business acumen and cleverness are the strong woman's positive traits, and the husband bitterly admires these marketable values in his wife, while unable to achieve them himself. At the same time, he condemns his wife for being "the most selfish women he has ever seen." He condemns her for destroying their marriage and tearing him away from his child just so that she can pursue her "self-development" in America. Fatalistically, he recognizes that he has no alternative to her values of self-development: "In this world there are only two types of people," he says in self-condemnation, "those who are smart enough to do something for themselves and those who are too stupid." While his wife has developed a career and a business, he has gone nowhere. When she tells him to discard all the old junk lying around his apartment, he responds by asking, "And I am just a bit of junk thrown away by you?" His wife, in return, condemns his passivity and cowardice. In his acquiescence to failure and despair, she argues, he is just as selfish as she in pursuit of success, and thus must bear responsibility for their breakup.

The two other main characters in the play are also familiar figures in the local grammar of sexual characters: the wife's younger sister, the modern girl who will go to bed with a man at the drop of a hat while always keeping one eye open for an even better man, and her nouveau riche, country bumpkin boyfriend from outside Shanghai, a country big money. The younger sister works in the hotel where her older sister is staying. Together with her coworkers in the hotel, this young sister represents a female type as materialistic and manipulative as the independent strong woman, but shortsighted, frivolous, and crafty in her reliance on men. The strong woman and the materialistic modern girl represent two female strategies for material success in the market economy—making money oneself or finding a rich man. The non-Shanghaiese boyfriend is another stock type from Shanghai popular culture—hick (bazi) but also big money (dakuan)—a nouveau riche who hates the Shanghaiese but loves living in Shanghai. The embodiment of the materialistic culture of 1990s China, he admires wealth even more blatantly than the Shanghaiese do.

The Wife from America expresses a much more profound moral crisis than The Accompanying Wife. The Accompanying Wife finds American sexual and consumer values strange and shocking, and implies a traditional Chinese answer: "Keep Chinese values while embracing Western learning" (zhongweiti, xiweiyong). In The Wife from America, we see the cultural frontiers decisively shifting: no longer between

China and the West, but within China itself, between husbands and wives, market failures and market successes. People pursue love but are incapable of finding it in a society dominated by money values. They face a new society of deformed characters: women who act like foreigners (the wife from America), men who are not like men (the Shanghai husband), and girls who want only sex (the short-term girlfriend of the husband). Yet they cannot return to traditional choices. The husband talks about the difficulty of finding a new partner and establishing a family relationship. Older women are too mechanical and pragmatic, he says, dismissing the "good wife and virtuous mother" type, but the new modern girls avoid commitment, seek wealth, and demand pleasure. Sex with them becomes "a burden and a pressure."

The play's rhetorical focus is a fierce but sympathetic critique of the Shanghai husband. At one point the male protagonist stands up and soliloquizes about how "Chinese men have become completely useless." The future of China, he says, lies in its women who are going abroad and marrying foreigners.[42] The failure of Chinese men is most evident in the masculine arena of politics. In a politically daring reference to the failure of Chinese men to react to the June 4th massacre in Tiananmen Square, the main character says, "People are killing people and we only dare to sit in our living rooms and get angry. If we have children, we don't even dare to get angry there." While men have "become useless" through their political failure, women find power and possibilities in the global consumer economy represented by America. The American wife thus represents a gendered allegory of an emasculated civil society and a prostituted consumer society. The masculine civil society has withered since the June 4th movement, while the feminized consumer society is flourishing but morally debased. Seen from another angle, women are adjusting to the market society, while men (especially the traditional intellectual elites) are failing, except for those amoral tricksters like the nouveau riche bumpkin, who embrace the greed of the market even more than the Westerners themselves.

Tang Yin said she wrote her novel to represent Shanghai women's adaptation to the values of the market economy. Pragmatism in sexual relationships is a particularly strong trait among Shanghai women, she said, and has become stronger in the market economy:

> The female character especially represents a Shanghai type. Northern women are more romantic, more likely to marry a man such as an artist or a writer because she finds him interesting and loves him. She won't care if they don't have so much money. A Shanghai woman wouldn't be like that. . . . Shanghai women use marriage to change their fate, especially the smart women, what we would call the "urbanites" [shimin]. . . .

Tang argued that the new consumer culture with its doctrine of self-development is more compelling to women intellectuals, who can more easily accept the failure of civil society represented by the repression of June 4th. For male intellectuals, the failure of June 4th is their own failure, a theme her husband makes more prominent in his play script. Women see this failure as beyond their responsibility, Tang argued. On the other hand, the ideologies of the market economy—consumerism, Westernization, and self-development—especially benefit women, offering possibilities for fulfillment and fantasy outside the limited roles provided for women in the traditional socialist economy of production and reproduction. From this perspective, ordinary Chinese men see less to gain from these changes and feel more threatened by a life of increasing competition for status, jobs, and the loyalty of women. Ironically, this sense of loss of male position produces a "crisis of masculinity"[43] that pervades Shanghai's popular culture (including this play) at a time when women's socioeconomic status is objectively more threatened through layoffs and employment discrimination.

The stock characters of both these plays are familiar figures in the dramatistic grammar of Shanghai's sexual culture. As a whole, they represent the moral dilemmas of free choice—including sexual choice—in a society increasingly dominated by money values. As the authors Tang and Zhang suggest, the consumer society invites different moral accommodations to dilemmas of free choice. The accompanying wife opts for the traditional role of virtuous wife and good mother. The characters in The Wife from America represent the extreme choices of people who fail to find a balance between material and emotional values: wives becoming "strong" through prostitution, young women throwing themselves at rich men, rich country men trying to "buy" a city girlfriend, country maidens becoming voracious city girls, and Chinese women tempted by foreign men. Through the trope of mercenary sexual choices, mobility in the market economy, especially for women, is described as a moral transgression in pursuit of a profane money god, a trickster who swaps the warmth of the small family life for the cold comforts of wealth and status.

Big Moneys and Shanghai Girls: Sexual Characters in Casual Conversation

The characters of the plays above captured my attention through their similarity to less-developed prototypes that my friends and informants batted about in casual conversations. In these casual conversations, speakers use these conventional characters as a rhetorical shorthand to make quick characterizations of real people or casual generalizations about the anonymous metropolitan society (*shehui*) of Shanghai. Most of the examples that follow are taken from focus group interviews conducted in Shanghai in the spring of 1996.[44] The conversations covered a wide range of topics, and participants brought in many examples from everyday life, also frequently referencing the various character types I have been discussing.

In focus group conversations, by far the most prominent and clearly defined of these characters was the big money, the usually vulgar, often married, nouveau riche boss out to buy women. In conversations about love and marriage, young people often employ the figure of the big money to describe the sexual strategies of young women:

> Guan: These girls all want to latch on to a big money.
> Moderator: What do the big moneys look like to them?
> Guan: Around thirty and able to meet these girls' material and financial
> requirements. Men of this age don't necessarily get rich from their
> own efforts, but through speculation and money given by parents.
> (unmarried female office worker aged 23)

Or speakers may invoke the big money in a direct criticism of the sexual strategies of rich men:

> He: I think we should not be like all these big moneys. Even though he
> has a wife, but because he has money, he has to find a lover to show
> his status. It isn't necessary.
> (unmarried male office worker aged 22)

In these comments, speakers use the foil of the big money to stake a claim as decent "little" people in an ironic society dominated by money values. Conversely, speakers may also use the character of the big money defensively to justify some types of sexual behavior as "normal" given tendencies in society. For instance, the following man argued half jokingly for the rights of rich women to keep young male lovers:

> Xiao: It's normal. . . . It's the tendency of social development. . . . It is
> normal even when a woman has two or three [lovers], as the super
> big moneys nowadays do, keeping two or three [women].[45]
> (married male editor aged 36)

The type most frequently associated with the big money is the modern Shanghai miss (*Shanghai xiaojie*) often named through general terms as "girls today," "girls in society," or "pretty girls," sometimes named through more particular terms such as the white collar or little miss ("*xiaojie*" is used as a euphemism for a karaoke hostess or casual prostitute). In their casual conversations about Shanghai society, youth most often attribute the association of the Shanghai girl with the big money to her vanity or love of "face":

> Ni: This [magazine article] is pretty typical for Shanghai girls. These girls are vain and feel they have face in front of their friends if they have a big money friend. . . .
>
> (unmarried male office worker aged 20)

Young women may also use this character contrastively to paint themselves in a positive light:

> Chen: Those girls who look for rich guys, when they get bored with one kind of guy, will just change to another. Shanghai is just too lenient toward this. It makes me sad. Guys from other parts of China ask me, "Why can't other Shanghai misses be like you?" Other people don't have a healthy opinion of Shanghai misses.
>
> (unmarried female office worker aged 25)

Older women characterize the materialistic Shanghai girl who "eats big money" (lives off the favors of rich men) as sacrificing family life, autonomy, and personal happiness for the sake of material comforts:

> Ping: There are a lot of girls now who "eat big money." It's not worth it, being caged up all her life.
> Nong: No freedom.
> Shi: Like Japanese women.
> Nong: A lot of these big moneys now have two wives.
> Ping: Financially comfortable, but no freedom.
> Shi: No freedom, there is no spiritual freedom either.
> Ping: Not like other people who can go back home and enjoy family life.
> Xiang: They are not happy.
>
> (married working-class women)

The newest incarnation of the Shanghai girl is the white-collar miss, a figure who arouses particularly strong public interest in Shanghai. In the popular imagination, she works in the Shanghai branch office of a foreign firm, earns a high salary, speaks English, enjoys the nightlife, marries late, is sexually active, and even dates foreigners and married men while engaging in a difficult search for a husband with even higher status and earnings than herself.[46] A generation gap emerges in comments about these educated young women. Men and women who grew up in the more egalitarian 1970s and 1980s sometimes express dismay at the sexual attitudes of white-collar girls who have unreasonably high expectations of marriage partners but lack traditional feminine virtues:

> Wang: These white-collar girls are picky about boyfriends. They want not only want rich ones; they want somebody who really loves them.
> Zhao: This type of girl exists for sure. I had a classmate who felt she had a very "high price." She had incredibly high expectations, and that there was no man in the world good enough. She had too romantic an idea and couldn't realize it in reality.
> Qian and Sun together: These girls won't even give you a chance to talk to them!
> Zhao: They think they are surrounded by petty urbanites [xiaoshimin].
> > (men in their late twenties and early thirties)

In these sarcastic remarks about "high-priced girls" (a common term among those who grew up in the early reform era, uncommon among youth now), these young men position themselves among an older generation of petty urbanites (literally "little city people") who won't even be given the slightest attention by these girls. Especially for working-class men and women, this world of white-collar girls and big moneys is beyond the horizon of their own lives. For these little city people, educated urban women have inflated material expectations, romantic fantasies, and estimations of their own value.

Not surprisingly, young women in these focus groups (including many office workers) more closely identify with the characters of the white-collar girl or more generally the city girl. In their conversations they try to develop these characters more fully and sympathetically to account for the dilemmas young urban women face in dating: aspiring for romance, equality, and autonomy while hoping to marry a man who earns much more than themselves.

> Shang: Today's city girls, especially pretty women, have a high requirement for material goods and high expectations [for a husband]. Their lives so far have been very easy and uneventful, and they work in some company or office and make good money. They can't accept people who make less than themselves. Still, I think a good woman has to know how to change a man instead of being changed by some man's property and staying at home enjoying a life with easy money. You should use your ability to change a guy and make him become a person who possesses material wealth.
> Xi: Now there are a lot of girls chasing after big moneys. I have read a

book written by Su Su [a popular Shanghai essayist]. She said: "To-day's girls only want to find successful people in their thirties, but how can they know that men in their twenties will never become successful?" Of course there will be successful ones. The most important thing is that the boy has a strong motivation in pursuing his career.

Meng: I think they [Shang and Xi] have the right idea—not finding a ready-made big money but finding one who will become a big money later. [All laughed.] This kind of girl is really lucky. On the other hand, there are also girls who don't really want to get married and just find a big money for some time, then later they don't want to be with these men anymore.

(unmarried women in their early twenties)

These three women, themselves facing the marriage market, refuse to condemn these city girls and big moneys outright, but invoke these characters as foils against which they stake out a compromise position. Marking off a moral extreme—the materialistic young woman being kept by a big money—allows them to position themselves as autonomous pragmatists who hope to "change" (guide and influence) a "young man with promise" rather than themselves being "changed" (be bought and made dependent) by a ready-made big money. In the sexual culture represented through these characters, pragmatic young women must negotiate this moral middle ground between selling out and staying poor.

Other Shanghai characters also appear in these conversations, most notably the strong woman, the career woman with money, power, and autonomy. As a comic figure in these conversations, the strong woman violates normative expectations by promising a male lover a life of ease.

Moderator: So, if you meet a strong woman in real life, and she is nice to you, what will you do?

Feng: We can get to know each other.

Moderator: Will you refuse her and think she is too strong?

Feng: If I think she is too strong, I can stay away from her and break up.

Han: Otherwise give up your self-respect and go home and do the housework. Let her feed you. [They all laughed.]

(unmarried men in their early twenties)

A similar comic reference plays on the strength of the Shanghai woman's personality relative to the weak-willed Shanghai man:

Xiao: In the Shanghai area, in eight out of ten couples the woman is
stronger. Shanghai men are suffering. . . . People from outside of
Shanghai all think Shanghai women are too strong. . . .

(married male editor aged 36)

Speakers also refer to the sexual unreliability of Shanghai women. Shanghai
wives are characterized as strong women who control their husbands or mess
around with other men if their poor husbands go abroad to make money by
performing menial work.

Jiang: Men go to Japan to "sweep in money" [pafen], and women stay at
home messing around. . . .
Quan: Social moral standards are different now.
Jiang: In the countryside, when the men go out "sweeping in money,"
women stay at home loyally. . . . In Shanghai, men go out, and the
women stay home messing around [with other men].

(married men in their late thirties)

Despite their comic potential as violators of gender expectations, uses of these
characters of the strong woman and the Shanghai husband are not always denigrating. Many men joke fondly of their status as a Shanghai husband, oblique
homage to the pleasures of domesticity. Both men and women jokingly praise
someone as a strong women, also a nod to her talents. For instance, on a popular 1999 television matchmaking program called *Saturday Date*,[47] a young
woman praised a young man's avowed skills at household chores. (He had expressed his wish for a date.) Her father continued her compliments: "I myself
am a Shanghai-style husband. I believe he [the date prospect] also will be a
Shanghai-style husband. I believe he has real feelings for our daughter. He will
take care of her." Similarly, the media portrays strong Shanghai women as especially capable of taking on foreign competition in the new global marketplace. For instance, the 1995 television series *Chinese Misses in Foreign Firms* depicted a strong woman manager and two younger white collars, all dealing
successfully with the sexual and career challenges of working in foreign firms.
Such characters serve as "defended typifications" of the city's culture and of the
attitudes of individuals who identify with the city.

As in the plays described above, these characters also represent the geographic boundaries of Shanghai's sexual culture. For instance, an ethnic version
of the big money refers to rich men from the south—typically Taiwan or Hong
Kong—who have girlfriends in Shanghai.

Deng: Money. We had that too in the past, but not as serious as now.
Now, it doesn't matter whether you are a pox-face or crippled, so
far as you have money, you will have a very pretty girl beside you.
Cantonese men, so short and so dark-skinned, all have beautiful
women beside them. What for? Money!

(married male factory worker aged 39)

Speakers often lump foreigners together with big moneys when discussing the
sexual strategies of Shanghai girls.

Qian: Pretty women on the streets are always either with old men or
with foreigners.
Altogether: This is just a business deal.

(men in their late twenties and early thirties)

Another boundary-transgressing character is the little country sister
(wailaimei) who comes to Shanghai to work and ends up a prostitute, a masseuse,
or in a pragmatic marriage. To Shanghai women, she represents the extremes of
materialism in sexual strategies.

Nong: Now even little country sisters are running wild [with big mon-
eys].
Si: Little country sisters run wild most easily. They are not used to it here
at the very beginning, but once they get used to it [life in Shang-
hai], a lot changes.
Ping: Even Shanghai girls are more self-controlled [anfen] than them.

(married working-class women in their thirties)

Unlike the character of the Shanghai girl, whose mercenary sexual strategies
Shanghai men and women often mention more sympathetically, rhetorical uses
of the little country sister are more exclusively negative. For instance, I asked
some out-of-work youth in a local disco if they dated the little country sisters
who sometimes visited there. One of them replied: "We don't date little country sisters [wailaimei]. They are really different from Shanghai girls." I asked how.
"They lack class [qizhi], lack upbringing [xiuyang]. If you were seen on the street
with one of them, you would feel it was a loss of face. So we don't touch them."
These low-status young men were particularly sensitive to questions of "face."
They use their denigration of the little country sister to distance themselves
from the even lower-status migrants. The same youth jokingly asked me to introduce them to white collars, who they imagined might be willing to spend

money on them. Taking money from a rich Shanghai woman only reinforced their self-image as playboys.

In my experience the casual banter in the focus group resembles chatter among strangers at a wedding banquet or a discussion among friends about a play or movie. Interlocutors typically take positions that exclude themselves from the sexually mercenary society they describe. Except for the socially daring, most participants identify with the petty urbanite, salaried people, or simply "people like us," in contrast with the glamorous but deformed society of big moneys, white-collar girls and strong women, or the socially inferior world of the little country sister. Many young people newly entering society, on the other hand, assume a more ambiguous position vis-à-vis characters like the white-collar girl and the big money. They identify with the market orientation represented through these characters and stake out a compromise position that assumes a morally ambiguous mix of material and sexual opportunism.

Playboys and Bold Girls: The Sexual Economy of Fishing, Vamping, and Seducing

So far we have looked at how types are used to characterize acquaintances or to caricature people in general, in society. These rhetorical uses are typically self-righteous or at least self-serving, the negative connotations of the characters directed at others. But we can also find dramatic uses of these characters in social interactions, games of seduction, and sexual one-upmanship. Because of the negativity of such characters as identities, these sexual games are highly stylized, ironic, and conflictive, a gamble involving claiming their deviant sexual meanings for oneself.

One such game is played professionally by female dance hall hustlers called "fishing girls" (diaomazi), young women who hang out in expensive discotheques and bars and ask men to buy them drinks or simply give them money for sitting with them. This is not simple prostitution, but more of a face game, a manipulation of and commodification of social roles. One evening in a fashionable Shanghai discotheque, I watched a professional fishing girl I knew work an out-of-town big money (waidi dakuan) for tips in exchange for her attentions. After she left him, I sat at his table. He told me he was a successful painter of Chinese paintings sold to foreign tourists at a major hotel. I asked him why he didn't try to meet women who wanted no money for their sexual companionship. He said, "If you don't give girls money, they won't respect you. . . . Look at me. I am ugly. If they want me, they want me for my money.

They love me for my money." He then switched to bragging to me about how much money he was spending on the girls—several hundred dollars in a week. I asked him if he had sex with them, and he replied indignantly, "I don't want to have sex with them," then in English, "My dick belongs to me." He bragged that he had no sexual desire for them at all. In these brief games, the social masks of the big money and the fishing girl are important. The fishing girl pretends to be impressed by the painter's status as a big money. He pretends to find her alluring and glamorous; her real social status, even her average looks, is erased. The content of the game is a sexual economy in which money makes the spender potent. The point of playing the game for him is the face and sexual power he gets from being considered a big money. By saving his "dick" for himself, he retains his potency, an extreme form of sexual miserliness that is not typical, but understandable within the sexual economy of these characters.

The roles of the big money and the fishing girl are far too emotionally flat for sustained interactions. Shanghai youth who want to flirt, seduce, and vamp play characters within the same sexual economy but with more emotional depth, most typically the playboy and the bold girl. The playboy (baixiangren) is the urban romantic antihero. The typical playboy of the 1920s imagination was the wastrel son of a banker or an official, the dandy (xiaokai, kaizi, xiao K—"little gentleman"), a term revived by contemporary youth. To this day the character of the playboy or dandy is associated with gambling as much as with womanizing (as scores of Hong Kong movies featuring gambling playboys attest). For the playboy, money and women satisfy related and nearly interchangeable passions for winning in games of chance. There is no specific Shanghai term for the playgirl, but a special type of feminine play is associated with the words "bold" (dadan) and "bad" (huai). Shanghai women describe wearing a sexy styles of dress that expose their bodies as "dadan." Boldness is an amoral character ideal. It covers behavior ranging from wearing sexy clothes to criminal activity. To be bold means to endanger men through one's own disregard for reputation, safety, and social norms. The other term women like to use is "bad girl," often a sexual taunt. Thus the feminine version of the Shanghai playboy is the bold and bad girl: the Shanghai femme fatale. "Good women like bad men; good men like bad women" is an oft-repeated adage. In the mythology of urban romance, everyone will meet their femme/homme fatale and perhaps be cheated. It is the tricky nature of the city that forms the mythic backdrop of otherwise straightforward love affairs.

The sexual games of the playboy and femme fatale rely upon emotional withdrawal. Unwilling or unable to give themselves emotionally to those who

desire them, the "cool" Shanghai playboys and bad girls represent a less extreme and more typical form of the sexual continence of the big money and the
fishing girl. The standard line of the romantic playboy is "No one understands
me," that of the bad girl, "I am dangerous." The playboy is emotionally
wounded by past loves and thus cold (see chapter 7). The femme fatale is dangerous because of past hurts and her indifference to being hurt in the future.
"Playing deepness" (*wanshenchen*) is the term Chinese youth used to describe this
melodramatic, self-absorbed sexual play, apparent on the karaoke video tracks
of many pop love songs. It is the depth of their wounded self-absorption and,
above all, their ability to draw others into it that makes the playboys and bad
girls successful at seduction. The playboy and the femme fatale thus embody a
peculiar Shanghai style of "cool," representing both sexual openness but emotional distance, an emotional rhetoric that works well within the competitive
new dating culture of the market society. Coolness is, after all, a social bargaining stance, a way of demanding a high price, refusing to pay out, or equivo-
cating on one's basic conditions. The cool playboy and the bold girl don't give
away their hearts easily.

One acquaintance, Little Yang, a nineteen-year-old unemployed "singer"
and sometimes prostitute, consciously played the bold and bad girl in her interactions with men she wanted to impress. For an arranged interview with me,
she wore a white silk designer dress cut high up her thigh and insisted on meeting me at a fashionable bar frequented by foreign businessmen. "I am proud
[of myself], because I am very daring [*Wo danzi da*]," she said at the beginning
of our conversation. I asked her what she meant by daring. She said dramatically, "I don't have work, so where is my money from? I don't love a man, but
I dare to go all the way [*fazhan xiaqu*]." By this she meant that she dared to engage in prostitution, the ultimate "bold" act. She took great pleasure in the
irony that one of her new sugar daddies (*dage*, meaning "big brother") was a
cadre, who she called "the Communist." "He's really ridiculous," she said. "He
even introduced me to his daughter and told her to call me 'big sister.' I felt,
'Isn't that ironic [*fengci*]?'" She proudly showed me her necklace and watch, indicating they were gifts from the cadre. I asked her if she and "the Communist"
were lovers. "He really wants me to bring this [sex] up myself; he won't bring
it up by himself. This guy is a Communist Party cadre, so he thinks that way.
That's fine with me. I want to keep leading him along and let him give me more
and more." She bragged that she used the money she received from men to exercise her own sexual power over men she liked, an irony she consciously embraced. After drinks she invited me and a handsome young male singer for a

"night snack" at a popular Sichuan restaurant, where we sat in the middle of the dining room. When we finished, she ostentatiously paid for our meal out of a thick wad of cash she pulled from her purse, suddenly making herself the big money.

The bad girl, like the playboy, is a gambler, manipulating improper sexual gestures to her own advantage, often reversing normative gendered positions. A typical reversal is the practice of mistresses of wealthy men treating their secret male lovers to dinner when their regular boyfriends aren't around. Not only enjoying an illicit affair by cheating on their lover, they are making a bold claim to sexual power. In Shanghai, as in the rest of China, men are supposed to treat women. A woman who takes a man out is a "payback girl" (daotieguniang) and the man, a "little white face" (xiaobailian). But bold girls can treat men as a way of playing with men, not only being played with. The playboy is also willing to play with the assumptions of masculinity in order to gain advantage. One young acquaintance named Xu, who described himself as a dandy (kaizi), bragged to his friends at a local disco, "If I had a rich girl right now, I would take her money and spend it. I wouldn't care what she looks like." He said he had done this several times in the past. Upsetting gender roles is a form of sexual chicanery in which both playboys and bold girls engage, but this play still derives from a sexual economy that equates money with sexual power.

The sexual economy is not always kept in such perfect equilibrium in the games of playboys and femme fatales. When the games are not going well, they can be disrupted in purposefully destructive acts, a prototypical display of the sexual power of the bold girl. For instance, there is Mei, a tall, beautiful former swimmer who for two years had been the mistress of a Taiwan businessman working in Shanghai. Over drinks with a close female friend, she told me their story. During this relationship, which was several years before our conversation, she was constantly angry because of her lover's refusal to leave his wife. She refused to be "kept" indefinitely, and she admitted that she enjoyed "torturing" the older Taiwanese:

> Once I got so angry I climbed up on the table in the restaurant in front of everyone, in front of all his friends. The little Taiwanese guy begged me to come down. He said "Pretty"—he always called me "Pretty" in English— "Pretty, please come down." I said to him, "There's no Pretty here. There's only the Bitch [pofu]."

She and her friend both laughed hysterically as she retold the story for my benefit, a story the friend had heard many times before. "She is really bold when she loses her temper," her friend said. The term "*pofu*" is the extreme form of the bold femme fatale. It is old Chinese slang. In his study of sexual characters in Qing fiction, McMahon translates this term as the "shrew" and argues that it connotes both the "splashing" of anger and profligate wasting of wealth by the uncontrolled jealous woman.[48] Mei also bragged about wasting this Taiwanese man's money after she decided that he wouldn't divorce his wife.

These characters, and the sexual games in which they are performed, are morally transgressive but still within the same sexual economy broadly defined by the big money, the Shanghai girl, and the Shanghai husband. They are heterodox, but not outside the doxa of a sexual economy in which money is an immoral god-term, sex is fungible capital, and "those who work the swing shift are neither men or women." These games played with sex, money, and gender represent an ironic play on a deeply entrenched Chinese orthodoxy of compulsory heterosexuality and marriage. Every young man and woman is expected to marry. Women "marry up," bargaining their naturalized sex and gender attributes for a man with the best possible economic conditions. In the market economy, these bargains become more complex, tendentious, and negotiable, hence the possibility of new sexual games and the apparent moral crisis of sex and money represented ironically through these mercenary characters and their unorthodox bargains.

Shanghai Babies and Extraterrestrials: Transcending the Doxa

Recognizing this heteronormative doxa of gendered sexual exchange allows us to think about sexual characters who violate this doxa by transcending its equation of cash and sexual power. Such alternative characters are evident in Shanghai's public sexual culture. People are constantly inventing new narrative possibilities for themselves and others. For these iconoclasts, the challenge is whether the characters they invent are persuasive and whether they can avoid capture by more dominant public narratives.

I turn first to the iconoclastic authors Mian Mian and Wei Hui described in the first chapter, and then to one member of Mian Mian's circle, the singer Coco. If anyone in Shanghai personally and artistically represents the fatalistic moral doxa of sex and money, it is Mian Mian, who writes and talks as though everyone in Shanghai were a whore, a pimp, a john, or a cop, a vision she developed in years working as a hostess-club "mama." As she said to me about Shanghai's nightlife scene: "It doesn't matter where you go—what level of place—these places are full of girls trying to cheat these older guys out of their money. Then they go back and let these young guys cheat them out of their money. It's pretty disgusting, but that's the way Shanghai is." On the other hand, Mian Mian sees herself as attempting to transcend this cultural dystopia. Like her nemesis Wei Hui, Mian Mian[49] uses the term "Shanghai babies" to describe the everyday heroes and heroines who manage to avoid the cultural and sexual prostitution she finds everywhere in Shanghai. In an article she wrote for the U.S. magazine *Time*, she describes her musician and artist friends in Shanghai as her own Shanghai babies:

> These people symbolize the future of Shanghai. They are Shanghai's treasure babies, who are growing up along with the supermarkets in the city. They take their steps forward in secret. They are fascinated by Western music technology, not because it originates in the West, but because they believe they are pioneers of mankind. . . . Shanghai babies are forced to come up with peculiar methods in order to lay their hands on desired new stuff. And they find ways. Someday when these Shanghai babies are free to go out in the world, they will be the coolest the world has ever seen.[50]

Characterized by their sly consumer artistry, these babies achieve an aesthetic and technological domination over both their material worlds and "cooled" emotions. By being "babies," they lose their sex and gender and avoid the crude sexual objectification and ownership that Mian Mian elaborately describes in her writing. By projecting a hopeful world of "treasure babies," Mian Mian is imagining a postgender utopia of cool, happy, innocent kids—escaping from the closed circulation of sex and money, not by escaping from the market, but by achieving mastery of its cultural forms.

If I were to take Mian Mian's side, Wei Hui's famous book simply ruined the image of the Shanghai baby by turning it into an eponym for the female groupies of Shanghai's foreign businessmen, simply another type of prostitute in the eyes of most Shanghaiese. Wei Hui's actual writing, however, seems intent on achieving the same goal as Mian Mian's "treasure baby" discourse, discovering an infantile sexual identity that avoids the doxa of compulsory marriage and compulsory heterosexuality. Wei Hui's protagonist CoCo is erotically polymorphous, inclined to both men and women, and healthily obsessed with her own pleasure. In some respects, CoCo represents an autonomous, self-indulgent sexuality for the economically independent white-collar woman, a scary vision for many Shanghai men. In her guise as Shanghai baby, the white collar is no longer the sexless and therefore forlorn high-priced girl of the 1980s, but the indulgent masturbator and confident sexual consumer. In other respects, however, the novelist, perhaps self-consciously, undermines this sexual heroism. In one scene

CoCo steals money she doesn't need from her German lover, simply to prove to herself that she doesn't love him by treating their relationship as an exchange. In another, the sexual self-promotion of Shanghai's white-collar women is likened to prostitution.[51] In the end effect, Mian Mian is probably right. Most Shanghai people, including government censors, seem eager to read *Shanghai Baby* as a simple example of sexual self-commodification. *Shanghai Baby* is too easily captured by a dominant narrative of opening up in which the Westernized woman writer becomes a whore serving a Western audience and corrupting local youth.

Coco (not to be confused with Wei Hui's CoCo) is one of Mian Mian's favorite "babies," though he is not from Shanghai, having moved there from the interior of China to attend the Music Conservatory. As a nightlife entrepreneur, he creates imaginary characters who transcend the prototypes of Shanghai's heteronormative sexual doxa in novel ways. His public persona Coco is a gay nightclub singer who croons Billie Holiday songs and Chinese pop tunes to appreciative audiences in Shanghai. With his new fame, Coco is long past the hard days when he crashed with Mian Mian in a borrowed one-room apartment, but he still struggles to create coherent public and private identities.

In the affluent and transnational gay subculture he described to me as his local social world, positions are defined less according to the economy of sex and money that defines heterosexual Shanghai culture and more by an economy of race and desires, in which each position receives its own joking name. As Coco told me in a mix of Chinese and English, "potato queens" are Asian guys who like white guys; "rice queens" are white guys who like Asian guys; "mashed potato queens" are white guys who like white guys; and "sticky rice queens" are Asian guys who like Asian guys. Though he finds the terms amusing, he doesn't like his own relationships with foreign men to be pigeonholed in this way:[52]

> If you go out and see a Western man together with a Chinese man, people almost always will think that the Western guy is the masculine type, and the Chinese guy is the feminine type. I don't think that way. My own boyfriend is very young and very feminine, but people always ask me, "What are you doing with him? He is too feminine." It's like, if I want to date a foreigner, I should be with an older and more masculine guy.

In his private life Coco's problem is falling into the gendered role expectations predominant in the particular gay subculture in which he socializes. In his public life his additional problem is constructing a public persona that is sensuous and sexual but not so overtly homosexual as to offend his largely straight audiences and the Chinese authorities. A further problem Coco faces with his audiences is the tendency of Chinese to imagine any gay performer in the role of transvestite, a category with a great deal of historical as well as contemporary resonance.[53] Given the views of the larger society and of the particular gay subculture in which Coco socializes, it is not surprising that he tries to create a public persona that transcends these gendered categories.

He performed one such persona at a pay-to-enter party he held at a nightclub in Shanghai in the spring of 1999. It was called the "Extraterrestrial Party" and Coco was the extraterrestrial host. Many of the youth attending the party knew Coco personally, and many others knew his sexual orientation. As Coco said himself, young Shanghaiese are increasingly accepting and curious about his gay identity. He is able to commercially exploit this appreciation and curiosity in organizing events such as this party. The music at this unremarkable nightclub was super-fast all-electric techno, laid on by a young Japanese DJ who played mostly to a crowd of even younger Japanese and Shanghai dancers frenetically shouting and waving their arms in front of the DJ's stage. At midnight the dance music stopped and Coco emerged out of an artificial fog, in silvery extraterrestrial armor with a pointed headdress that resembled the garb of a Tang-dynasty Buddha. For a few moments he glided around like a confused space probe, or emotionless mime, pretending not to comprehend the friendly waves of the young girls who crowded in front of him. He then launched into an unremarkable Chinese pop song, but one that his elegant voice made pleasant. His image was sensual and sexy, neither effeminate nor masculine, vaguely Chinese but high modern.

The sensuous, androgynous persona of the extraterrestrial seemed to appeal to these young, mostly straight Shanghaiese, jaded by images of sexy girls and cool playboys. The androgyny of the extraterrestrial challenges the sexual games of youth without flatly challenging their heteronormativity, which might have been "too much" for many people. The extraterrestrial is not the "real" Coco, certainly not the "gay" Coco, who has a very sexualized persona among closer friends, gay or straight. The performance might be a one-time event, but it is a playful artistic break from the usual gendered economy, a break both by performer and audience that gently expands the heteronormative frame of gendered sexual identities.

Perhaps the Shanghai babies and extraterrestrials represent little more than ephemeral attempts at cultural problem solving, but they do show how artistic Shanghai youth challenge a gendered economy of money and sex through the projection of new types of sexual characters. Shanghai's growing nightlife scene is one area in which such imaginative transgressions are possible, though as the previous section shows, it is also an arena in which the ironic doxa of money and sex is most virulently articulated by other heterodox characters, such as the fishing girl and the big money.

The Specters of Capitalism and the Dialectics of Shanghai's Sexual Culture

There is a specter haunting Shanghai, the specter of capitalism. The spectral quality of Shanghai's emerging capitalism is most evident in its rhetorical scapegoats,[54] these characters who, like medieval vices, parade across the stage of contemporary Shanghai culture: the big money, the strong woman, the foreigner, the fishing girl, the playboy, the little country sister, the bold girl, and the white collar. These are the sexualized specters of Shanghai's market transition, all morally and sexually compromised through their economic success (the big money and the strong woman) or failure (the Shanghai husband and the old cabbage leaf[55]). The rhetoric of these characters reads, to a large extent, as a moral critique of the market society, not decisive rejections, but nagging accommodations and nitpicking critiques through which groups and individuals negatively define a new image of the good life. More rarely, they try to negotiate a new order altogether through new types of characters or comic readings of these conventional ones.

But whose specters are these? The simplest and, I think, most correct answer is that they represent the anxieties of reform-era Shanghai's dominant status group, popularly called the "salaried class" (gongxin jieceng), a vaguely defined majority of Shanghaiese who dominated the reform era demographically and culturally if not politically. The salaried class is the successor of Mao's "working class," a term both overly political and quaint in contemporary Shanghai. The shared identity of the salaried class relates to a middling income and family-centered consumption patterns, not a position in production.[56] Though the term "salaried class" seems to have become popular only in the 1990s, the identification reflects widespread experience under socialism of secure state employment, relative income equality, and shared family ideals. More than perhaps any other Chinese city, Shanghai, with its wealth of large state enterprises and relatively high wages, became the city of China's salaried class, which includes anyone on a state-enterprise salary, including social benefits such as housing and medical care. Despite the economic and social changes that threaten stable employment in Shanghai, the salaried-class ideal of a small family life still resonates with contemporary Shanghai youth, who largely grew up in such families. This ideal encompasses a companionate, preferably neo-local marriage, dual and roughly equal incomes, shared housework, and multigenerational interdependence.[57] This model is not merely fantasy but represents the achievements of socialist policies in which economic competition was minimal, men and women earned roughly equal pay, socialized child care was widely available, and household labor was shared by both parents to an extent not known in most capitalist societies.[58] It is a lifestyle that youth both loathe and long for—longing for its mutuality and security, loathing its perceived lack of money, excitement, romance, and mobility. There is, in other words, a second specter haunting the imagination of contemporary Shanghai youth, the specter of a socialist good life (meaning, above all, economic and domestic stability and equality), which is increasingly nostalgic rather than real.[59]

This salaried class is literally a ghost of its former self. In other words, just as it becomes aware of itself as a class for itself in the 1990s—at least in popular consumer culture—this salaried class is ceasing to be a class in itself, fraying at the top and bottom. Only barely included in the ranks of the salaried class to begin with, the people of Riverside Alley are falling out of it through unemployment and substandard incomes. Beneath them (more "outside" Shanghai society than at its "bottom"), the floating population of migrants, such as the little country sisters, forms a socially isolated underclass estimated at nearly 3 million in Shanghai.[60] Low-corner friends on the verge of falling into the ranks of these street peddlers and casual laborers feel threatened by their competition and disparage the little country sisters and outsiders in general. At the top of Shanghai society, high-earning big moneys and white collars now have world-class incomes that place them in another type of floating population, those who can freely leave and enter China, buy homes where they wish, and convey themselves freely through the city in taxis and private cars. People in the middle of society see this top rising and floating away and seek to defend their own lifestyles against this new money worship.

The spatial grammar and the character grammar described in these two chapters form the basis for the literary and everyday imagination of these changes as shifting spaces and mobile characters, and as a moral crisis of the market economy in which money values threaten the cohesion and status of the small family life. As Sonya Rose points out, such strident moral discourse intensifies when people perceive a threat to social unity, sometimes exploiting the same moral themes in an episodic fashion over long historic periods.[61] Shanghai people rhetorically defend their threatened family values through a sexual grammar of morally coded spaces and prototypical sexual characters, for which the cumulative texture of Shanghai's urban culture provides rich historic sources. On the other hand, it also provides materials for positively imagining sexual and economic possibilities. As a flexible grammar, these conventional sexual spaces and characters allow people to claim and dispute individual and collective identities in the new market society. Young people discuss their strategies and positions in the market economy within this conventional grammar, occasionally disputing its rules and adding new terms. This cumulative sexual culture thus provides tools for contesting social boundaries as well as for maintaining them.

真人真事

TRUE STORIES
From Romance to Irony

"A Pretty Woman's Difficulties"

Throughout the reform era, "true life" stories of the love affairs of young men and women have been a popular genre in magazines and books.[1] Titled "A Pretty Woman's Difficulties," the following story appeared in the April 1996 edition of the Shanghai monthly *Young Generation*, the leading Shanghai magazine aimed at youth. (As with other stories, I provide a paraphrased digest rather than a full translation):

> The narrator, a woman journalist, meets a pretty woman, Liu Feng, in a fashionable Shanghai beauty salon frequented by white-collar women and the mistresses of rich men. A refined woman from a cadre family, Liu worked for an ad agency and was pursued by many men, and she carefully chose her present husband, a Chinese American, from among her many suitors. "He isn't big and strong," she explains to the narrator, "but he is tender and understanding." He is also wealthy, the narrator emphasizes. After her marriage, she quits her job and stays in a condo in a fashionable district of Shanghai enjoying an idle life.
>
> When her husband returns to America for business, she stays in Shanghai to take care of an ailing mother. Separated from her husband, she meets a Shanghai man just back from ten years in Japan. He admires her beauty and her filial devotion to her mother. Now a Japanese citizen, he is handsome and full of life. On their first date, she fails to tell him she is married. "I couldn't say it. He was so cute, so charming, how could I refuse that kind of man?" she tells the journalist.
>
> Soon they are sexually involved. At first she wants to divorce her husband. She writes him a letter, but he replies that he can forgive her. She

can't make up her mind and continues seeing both men, both of whom now know about one another.

However, when she becomes pregnant with her husband's baby, she is met with indifference by both men. Her husband wants to divorce her. She decides to have an abortion, but afterward the Japanese citizen is no longer interested in marriage either. Feeling cheated by both men, she asks the journalist to place an ad looking for another rich overseas man.

Stylistically, this article is typical of magazine narratives during the reform era. Running two full pages of text, the story exhibits many elements of melodrama: exaggerated emotion, conflict, plot twists, and a moralizing narrator. Although written as a "true story," it includes many literary embellishments, such as the brown color of the sky when the couple first makes illicit love in the car. The scenes of action are the most fashionable sites of consumption in 1990s Shanghai: beauty salons, a fancy suburban condo, an ad agency, coffee shops, a private car, a bar. The protagonist is also typical of the 1990s, the fashionable white-collar woman. Two accompanying photos highlight these elements: a fashionable model in a beauty salon and another in a bar.

The white-collar protagonist has all the advantages of modern life: a good family background, education, upbringing, and beauty. She is described many times as "elegant and beautiful." "Who could imagine," the narrator gushes, "such a materially well-off, well-spoken, and beautiful woman also has troubles!" The moral rhetoric is ironic. A woman with every advantage attains a good education, makes careful choices in marriage, gains a comfortable life, follows her heart in love, but ends up in a mess. The narrator guides us along emotionally with her own sympathy for the woman's plight. The woman made mistakes, but she was, after all, contrite and honest with her husband after her affair. It was her husband who argued against divorce. Unlike the relatively clear moral judgments contained in such stories ten years earlier, this narrator finds it difficult to affix blame for what has befallen the protagonist, certainly impossible to condemn her outright. Seen in the context of twenty years of reform and opening, her difficulties are themselves ironic. She enjoys freedoms and material comforts that Chinese people at the end of the Cultural Revolution could scarcely dream of, and yet she is messing it all up. What are we, as readers, to make of her plight?

Romantic Irony in Media Sexual Culture

In a mass-mediated society such as Shanghai in the 1990s, a study of sexuality would be incomplete without a study of representations of sex in the media. In this chapter I analyze stories in popular youth and family magazines. I chose magazines because old magazine editions are still available for study, and because in the reform era, magazines have been the most constantly effusive medium discussing marriage, love, and sex. Methodologically, I understand the sexual politics represented in these magazines as a social interaction involving the contents of magazines, the organizations that produce them, and the people who read them.[2] Both a highly competitive retail industry and a Party-controlled propaganda apparatus, magazines are a site where the contradictions of the socialist market economy are clearly evident, where the cautious sexual politics of the Party-state meet the moral centrifuge of the market.

Magazine editors claim a central role in starting public discussions of sex and love in the post-Mao period. Xia Hua, the first editor of *Young Generation*, the most popular youth magazine in the 1980s, said in an interview in 1996:

> The most important thing we did was in the early 1980s we broke the prohibition against talking about love and marriage. In the [Cultural Revolution] "model operas," there were no husbands and wives, no love, no feeling between men and women. We were the first magazine to dare talk about marriage and love. [In 1979] we had this article about the love life of the Shanghai ballet stars. This was the first one.[3]

This chapter describes changes in stories about love and sex in several popular youth and family magazines from 1979 to 2000. The number of magazines published in Shanghai increased from 42 in 1978 to 591 in 1998. Most of these magazines are in the category of "general culture" magazines, including youth and family magazines.[4]

Scholarly discussions of popular Western magazines aimed at women and girls focus on the contradictions between a liberal sexual ideology and anxiety-provoking "advice" and imagery: magazines advise women to be sexually attractive yet teach them to be afraid and anxious about their attractiveness and sexual performance.[5] In Chinese mass media aimed at women, there is considerable evidence of a similar dynamic,[6] and Western debates about this medium are easily transferred to China. Western journalists' reports of "sexual revolution" in Chinese popular culture[7] meet Western feminist skepticism of this revolution.[8] These discussions reflect a liberal discourse that underlies most Western discussions of Chinese popular culture, asking whether Chinese media have created a space for freer expression or only another space in which free expression is stifled by old political pressures and a new consumerism. Indeed, Chinese magazine articles about sexuality in the reform era do include many discussions that we can construe as "liberalization": debates over the pros and cons of controversial behaviors, such as extramarital affairs; defense of legal rights, such as the right to divorce; and promotion of individual autonomy, such as choosing a marriage partner without parental interference. There are also many "reactionary" trends in these articles, including vicious criticisms of all forms of nonmarital sexual behavior. Yet a closer examination of changes in magazine content over the past twenty years shows that these classical liberal questions fail to capture these melodramatic magazine stories' moral rhetoric, which must be explored in its own terms. Nor do the standard critiques of cultural "commodification" capture the dialects of cultural change reflected in these articles, including organizational changes, market dynamics, and changes in moral frames.

Take, for example, "A Pretty Woman's Difficulties." As the U.S. literature on women's magazines would suggest, the story plays on women's anxieties about sexual choices, but unlike stories a decade earlier in China, this story isn't about clear choices between right and wrong. Rather, the problem is the moral and practical difficulty of being faced with *too many* contradictory choices and opportunities. Neither is the story a simple critique of female autonomy. If anything the protagonist is condemned for a lack of autonomy. The narrator leaves her with the explicit advice that relying on men isn't the way to achieve true happiness. The story, like many of the stories in these popular magazines, can be generally described as melodrama. Melodrama, as Peter Brooks argues, is a statement about moral order,[9] in this case an ironic melodrama, in which the prevailing moral order is confused and contradictory. My question is what notions of moral order are represented by the melodramatic stories in these magazines and how does this moral rhetoric change over time. In particular, to understand the moral rhetoric of 1990s Chinese magazine stories, we must make sense of these ironic narratives in which sincere romantic choices turn out badly and money is both a good and an evil. Liberalism and consumerism are relevant, but in an ironic sense, because the positive values of free choice and material affluence are often turned on their heads through ironic outcomes. As Xu Xiaoqun suggests, such stories represent a "collective anxiety" about the difficulties of achieving a balanced heterosexual relationship in the "open" society of 1990s China.[10]

The narrator is key to decoding the melodramatic irony, or "romantic irony," of these 1990s magazine stories. Burke defines "romantic irony" as an inferior genre of irony in which the narrator uses the ironic characters as foils to express a morally superior attitude toward a philistine society.[11] In this story the journalist-narrator represents the ordinary woman, who isn't beautiful, perfect, or lucky enough to marry a wealthy man. Ironically, by being ordinary, she—and by extension ordinary readers who identify with her authoritative and sympathetic voice—is able to steer clear of the problems brought about by too much good fortune and too many seductive opportunities in a morally confused market society. As with the conversational irony discussed in the previous chapter, such romantic irony generally reinforces the conventional ideals of the small family life (xiaojiating shenghuo). Through this humorless, romantic irony, the "smallness" of the domestic ideal is contrasted favorably with the "bigness" and ambition of the big moneys, the strong women, and the beautiful white collars like Liu Feng. In the moral universe of irony, the practical, unheroic "small" life endures, while overreaching "big" ambitions lead to failure and chaos.[12]

Most magazines stories interweave individual narratives with a narrative about society, educating readers about society through a personal moral example. Since 1979 Chinese magazines stories about love and sex have been centrally concerned with the collective pursuit of an erotic and material "good life" in the context of a changing society. Concerned as they are with the pursuit of individual development in a new social order, these magazine stories run counter to the Maoist utopia of collective political and economic salvation. In their materialism, however, they remain true to Mao's vision of a wealthy and prosperous China, representing a transition from a materialist utopianism to a materialist hedonism.[13] They displace the collective romantic passions of Maoist politics with a privatized heterosexual eroticism of romantic love,[14] formerly a sign of bourgeois individualism, now a sign of a new drive for modernization. In tracing the moral rhetoric in these stories during the twenty-one years from 1979 to 2000, I find an increasingly ironic vision of this materialistic and romantic modernity, a transition from a romance of love and modernization to the ironies of sex and money.

Young Generation and Its Competition

This chapter focuses on the Shanghai magazine Young Generation (Qingnianyidai). Not only a market leader but a political leader, Young Generation was the most influential Chinese youth magazine in the early reform era, reaching a circulation of over 5 million in 1985, then, under competitive pressures, declining to below 500,000 by the late 1990s.[15] As an early market leader, Young Generation typifies the developmental phases of Chinese magazines, from the tentative period of "opening up" (1979 and early 1980s), through the middle period of social activism (late 1980s), to the present period of commercialization and competitive pressures (late 1990s, 2000). It represents the contradictory political and commercial influences on magazine editors, and in its contents and style typifies many aspects of Shanghai magazine culture. Although magazines published in other cities have made big inroads into the Shanghai market, locally published magazines have advantages in distribution, local connections, and local content. International magazines, such as Elle and Marie Claire, are limited to a few joint ventures.[16] In other words, the magazines read and produced in Shanghai still have a strong Shanghai flavor, including Young Generation. Former editor Xia Hua explained Young Generation's Shanghai bias as a civilizing mission—an explicit reversal of Maoist exhortations for Shanghai urbanites to learn from rural China:

> Yes, we wrote more about Shanghai because Shanghai represents the most modern progressive tendencies in society. Why should we write about life in the rural villages when that is really backward? We should let the people in the village understand the modern world, to see that the people in the cities are already facing this kind of problem and this is how they are dealing with it, to see new things and new problems. We didn't want to reflect the backward life of the rural area, but to reflect the modern life, not the old-fashioned and discarded.[17]

Although I focus on Young Generation in this chapter, I also studied other magazines in this research. In addition to Young Generation (YG), I sampled stories from three other monthly magazines with long publication histories, long-term popularity in Shanghai, and persistent attention to love and sex: Culture and Life (CL), also published in Shanghai, and Family (F) and Golden Age (GA), both published in Guangzhou in Guangdong Province. In the early 1980s, the two Shanghai magazines led this branch of magazine publishing, but during the late 1980s the more stylish and colorful magazines published in Guangzhou surpassed both Shanghai magazines nationally. Because of recent shifts in the market, I also sampled a fifth magazine, Girlfriend (G), from 1995–96 to represent a more contemporary publishing success. I visited the offices and interviewed editors from all these magazines. (See methodological appendix for more detail.)

By the 1990s all youth, family, and general culture magazines used a smiling young woman's face as the dominant element in cover design, replacing the less sexual and less gender-specific images of the early 1980s. China still stood out, however, for the relative lack of strict gender segregation in this family/relationship segment of the magazine market. None of these magazines positioned themselves strictly as women's magazines. *Girlfriend*, the magazine with a format most nearly resembling a Western girls' magazine, had a motto of "Girlfriend—woman's friend and man's friend," which defined itself as a female-gendered magazine that welcomed male readership. Sixty percent of *Young Generation*'s readers were female, generally in their twenties. Most readers were urban or small-town dwellers. Rural villagers still accounted for only a small portion of all magazine sales in China.[18] Finally, most of the stories in the magazines described the activities of urban youth, although more rural stories did appear in the Guangdong magazines, often melodramatic stories of bizarre crimes culled from police reports.

By far the most common genre of magazine article describing love and sex was the "true story" article, my term for articles claiming to describe real stories of real people. It is difficult to separate fact from fiction in some of these stories, which are frequently embellished with details and interior monologue that the writer would have had difficulty knowing about from an interview. Yet participants in focus group interviews seldom doubted the factual veracity of these stories. Readers' quarrels, if any, were with their typicality—how representative stories were of ordinary people. I asked editors about the veracity of these stories, and they said that some were based on interviews, some based on the personal experience of the author, while some were tales heard secondhand by the author. This "real life" story form apparently appeals to a wide range of magazine readers. As a junior editor at *Young Generation* said, "Because our readers are not always that highly educated—often only a junior high education—they prefer more simple, everyday [*tongsu*] articles. They like stories."

From Romance to Irony: The Changing Moral Rhetoric of Magazine Stories

While "serious" literature is usually morally complex, magazine stories tend toward the moral simplicity of melodrama. In this chapter I attempt to characterize broad changes in the moral assumptions that govern action in magazine stories. For this purpose, Northrop Frye's narrative cycle of romance, comedy, tragedy, and irony turns out to be a useful heuristic to describe the changing moral rhetoric of these magazine stories. Frye categorizes narratives according to four ideal plots or myths: comedy, romance, tragedy, and irony.[19] Each of these myths includes a romantic quest that takes place within the context of a moral universe ranging from the ordered, moral universe of romance to the chaotic moral universe of irony. The myths form a cycle. Comedy begins in irony, but the hero's marriage typically affirms the harmonious moral order of romance. Tragedy begins in the harmonious moral universe of romance, but the hero typically expires in the moral dystopia of irony. In irony, all heroic action is futile, and only unheroic and ordinary people survive disaster.[20]

Frye's narrative cycle is based on a simple cycle of desire and disillusion, which, though trite, seems nearly universal in application. There is, as Frye points out, a human tendency to generate a romantic narrative in each new epoch—a quest for an idealized object—and then to become disillusioned with this quest over time—a descent into irony. In political economic terms, the cyclic trope of romance and disillusion describes the descent from the grand romances of nationalist modernization—those collective quests for a materialist utopia—to the ironic narratives of market economics—in which the more you get of something the less you want it, and utopia, if it exists at all, is but a momentary point of equilibrium between desire and ennui.

As Hayden White argues, different emplotments of social change lend themselves to different political causes.[21] Following White's paradigm, different narrative conceptions of moral order seem to enable different types of sexual politics in magazine stories. In general, as White suggests, romantic plots such as those that fill these magazine stories lend themselves to anarchist causes, a persistent source of moral instability in the popular sexual culture of the reform era, throughout which romantic passion figures as a positive moral value and a focus of striving and discontent. However, the dominant narrative codes framing and containing these unruly passions change throughout this era. Comic romances, of the type popular at the very beginning of the reform era, have a conservative bent, lending themselves to a defense of the current social order with a meliorist political message. Tragic romances, more prominent in the late 1980s, lend themselves to radical political purposes, including calls for social justice. Finally, ironic emplotments of the type that become popular in the late 1990s lend themselves to liberal causes, because they relativize incompatible values and argue for tolerance.[22] This shift in narrative codes also represents a changing discourse of motives. In short, I perceive a transition from a comic conception of a harmony of motives (work, love, and study); to a tragic discourse of conflicting motives (freedom versus repression, romantic passion versus family responsibility); and finally to an ironic discourse of incompatible motives (the ironies of sex, love, and money). Over this period of twenty-one years, a tragic world of romantic "heroes" and "villains" (a rhetoric of romantic tragedy) thus becomes an ironic world of the "tricked" and the "clever" (a rhetoric of romantic irony).[23]

This sketch is based on a qualitative interpretation of many stories. A quantitative shift is implied, but the basis of the analysis remains interpretive. While romantic comedies and romantic tragedies were more common in 1980, and ironic stories more common in 1996, what I describe is less a quantitative shift in the proportions of specific genres of stories, than a shift in the societal vision represented by stories in a particular era. Simply put, comic narratives in 1996 no longer have the same assumptions about society as comic narratives did in 1980. The method employed is thus comparative rather than quantitative, showing how similar themes are treated differently over time in changing representations of social and moral order.

Two Stories from *Young Generation*

I begin the discussion of changing moral rhetoric by presenting summaries of two stories on a very similar theme—love between a young woman and an army serviceman—both from *Young Generation*[24] but separated by sixteen years. Although both are melodramatic in tone and details, they show a considerable change in story elements and moral outlook and typify the change I am emphasizing in this chapter.

"The Sixty-Seventh Love Letter" (1980)

Slender and beautiful Yan Fei, a twenty-one-year-old textile worker, walked pensively along the Bund in Shanghai, thinking of her love, Little Lu, who was away in the army. They were neighbors and classmates since childhood, and the year before, they fell in love. Just as they were in the heat of falling in love, Little Lu entered the army. As he departed, she gave him a sweater she knitted, some candies, and a box of stamps, making him promise to write her a letter every day.

After happily receiving sixty-six letters, she found the letters suddenly stopped. Yan Fei kept writing but began to fear her love had a change of heart. Finally she boarded a train to his base near the city of Yixing to solve this riddle.

Upon arrival at the base, his drill instructor hands her the sixty-seventh letter. In this letter Little Lu outlines what his instructor told him after discovering his letter writing: "We don't oppose young people courting, but you have to be clear about your priorities. You are still young, and should concentrate on your work and study."

Lu's letter continues, describing his drill instructor's helpful advice on love matters through the examples of Marx and Pushkin. He writes that his love for Yan Fei hasn't diminished at all but now must take second place to his love for his unit and his work. He writes, "If you really love me, you will accept my challenge, and we can see which of us can make a bigger contribution to the 'Four Modernizations.'"

As she finishes the letter, she hears the tune in the background:

For the Four Modernizations, what can we do?

The PLA Soldier has an answer for you!

Suddenly the door bangs open. She sees Little Lu standing in front of her: tanned, tall, and strong. "'You look at me, I look at you.' / Happily they smile. They smile so sweetly!"

"Why Does the Flower of Love Wither?" (1996)

Seven years ago as a military secretary in a famous military unit, I was given a job replying to letters the unit received from the public. One day I received a letter from a high school girl named Xia Yan:

Dear PLA Uncle,

I don't know why, but every time on television when I see the noble silhouettes and strong, sharp marching of the soldiers, I feel so very moved. Every day after school, I walk an extra mile just so I can pass by the military base. . . . I often think if I could walk into that world, all green, the color of life, what a beautiful and harmonious picture that would be.

Moved by her romantic descriptions of the "green" world of the army, I immediately replied to her letter. Soon we had a regular correspondence. She mailed me a photograph and asked my advice. When she took the college entrance exams, she listed a university near my base as her first and only choice.

On our first meeting, I gave her a bouquet of green leaves, symbol of the army we both so admired. We had a photo made with the big green bouquet that she put on her windowsill. By her third year in university, we were a couple and had begun planning a home near the base.

She visited the base frequently, but she began to change. She began to ask herself, "Why am I not so entranced with green any longer?" She frequently asked me to change into civilian clothes, saying, "Always the same color, isn't that too monotonous?"

We fought. Two weeks later, when I visited her dorm, I found a young man placing some yellow flowers in a vase. She introduced him, "This is A-Xian of the economics department."

We argued again. I said she no longer valued the "green of the leaves." "Without the leaves there would be no flowers," I said [meaning, without the army there would be no economic flowering].

She said, "Everyone loves colorful flowers." [Then changing metaphors] she said, "All rivers are flowing into the sea. The economy of the south is booming. You stay closed off in the army base, not noticing what is going on in the world."

Taking her advice, I tried my hand at business but failed, receiving only a serious warning from the army for mishandling the negotiations. Even the roses I planted to give Xia Yan were destroyed in a storm. "All that was left was green leaves."

After graduation she decided to head south to look for a job. At the airport to see her off, I offered her the green leaves from my rosebush, but A-Xian the economics student suddenly arrived with a bouquet of flowers. Happily she grabbed the flowers and her bags and rushed through the boarding gate. Accompanying me, I still had that undelivered bouquet of emerald green leaves.

The differences between the two stories should be clear. In the first, a politicized romantic comedy, we are made to believe that all youth need to do is study hard and patiently serve the country and the humanistic goals of love and marriage, personal career advancement, and nationalist modernity all will be served. Aside from its political context, the story also represents a strong affirmation of the power of love and leaves no doubt about the unwavering devotion of the young people to one another. The second story reads almost as a 1990s parody of the first. The values of the nation (represented by the army) are no longer the values of the people (pursuing wealth). An ambiguously sexual love fails to be permanent and ennobling. Study and hard work sometimes lead nowhere, even when patiently pursued. The market society neither rewards nor values romantic heroism, a situation accepted fatalistically by the ironic antihero of the military officer. I argue that such historical contrasts in magazine contents reflect an important shift in the moral rhetoric of popular sexual culture, a shift I will endeavor to explain below through a discussion of additional magazine stories, their editors, and their readers.

The Romance of Love and Modernization

"In every age the ruling social or intellectual class tends to project its ideals in some form of romance, where the virtuous heroes and virtual heroines represent the ideals and the villains the threats to their existence."[25] In

1979 Deng's China was a new age in need of new heroes and a new romantic narrative. China had embarked on its quest for social modernization known as the "Four Modernizations" (education, science, economics, and defense). Love stories of the period were consciously subsumed into this larger romance of modernization. The first stories about love in these magazines represent romantic dreams for the new heroes and heroines of Deng's China: the students who will lead China in its quest for the secular grail of "modernization." Intellectual youth are represented as a vanguard. Uneducated workers and rural readers are encouraged to imitate educated youth through academic study. Often new college graduates themselves and aspirants to knowledge, magazine editors espouse a narrative that includes themselves as romantic heroes and the anti-intellectual "Gang of Four" as villains. In contrast with Cultural Revolution narratives, youth without clear political colors supplant obvious political figures—the soldiers, workers, Red Guards of the Cultural Revolution era—as the protagonists of these stories. The helpful Party cadre, especially the youth league cadre, plays an important supporting role in stories from this period. The CCP itself establishes and defines the holy grail of modernization, while the Gang of Four is a residual demonic influence blamed for an astonishing array of social disorders, ranging from "hooliganism" to "materialism."

Comic Romance: 1979–83

Freed from the chaos and inhumanity of the Cultural Revolution, youth set off on an idealized and romanticized quest for individual careers and a modern family life. Fictional lovers jointly pursue modernization through the idealized activity of "study," no longer the study of Mao Zedong thought, but rather the study of science and the classics of Western and Soviet literature, which are frequent tropes for the pursuit of both practical and "spiritual" knowledge.[26] The interest in science and literature reflect the "study fever" (xuexire) that accompanied the reopening of the universities after their closure during the Cultural Revolution. Individual goals of self-development and romantic love harmonize with the collective goal of modernization. There is little sense of the confusing conflicts of career and money, social responsibility and profit, love and sex, and self and family that would surface in later stories. Self-development through study and devotion to work contributes to success in love as well as in career. Lovers come to appreciate one another for the same qualities that make them good workers. The stories encourage young people to focus on self-improvement and follow their own high ideals in love rather than the narrow pragmatic standards of their parents. Narrow economic calculation in love is portrayed as a "feudalistic" attitude of backward parents or—like most negative social tendencies—a legacy of the Cultural Revolution, blamed on the Gang of Four.

This ideal harmonization of work and love is represented in romantic stories from these early years. For instance, in "An Unforgettable Love" (*YG* 1979, no. 3), a young woman narrator who was sent down to the countryside in the Cultural Revolution describes her love for a man she met on the farm. Although she returns to Shanghai, as most rusticated urban youth were trying to do, he decides to stay on the farm to work for the Four Modernizations. Now back in Shanghai, she admires him for his idealism and decides to write to renew the relationship. True love based on common ideals surpasses even the attractions of the city. Another example of the inspirational love story is "Engels's Love Life" (*YG* 1979, no. 4). In this "true story," Engels, though from a business family, doesn't choose a bourgeois wife but loves an Irish worker because of her enthusiasm for helping workers. Engels is the most important positive reference for Chinese scholars of the family in this period. His writings on the family are frequently cited to support free choice in love without concern for material values, and his personal love story is sometimes used as a metonym for his ideas. Exemplary moral stories of ordinary people are also typical of this period. In "My Family" (*CL* 1983, no. 1), for instance, a mother praises her children for choosing mates on the basis of their responsible attitudes toward work, despite their less than ideal looks, family backgrounds, and even an accident that left one husband nearly blind. Resembling the idealistic slogans of Maoist social movements, a language of "common interests and ideals" inspires youth to pursue the "noble love" they were denied in the politicized labor teams they worked in during the Cultural Revolution.[27]

Society isn't perfect, but its imperfections are unambiguous. As Frye writes, the apocalyptic vision of social harmony in high romance implies an equally demonic vision of social disorder. This is the case with articles in this early period. Like Dante climbing down the legs of Satan, we see ourselves climbing out of the inhumane hell of the Cultural Revolution up toward the paradise of a new humanistic modern society. The hell of the Cultural Revolution is often evoked through mention of the Gang of Four, whose demonic influence still lurks in society. Some people don't make the climb up, or they fall back into disorder. "The Most Dangerous Age" (*YG* 1980, no. 6) describes 202 girls in labor reeducation camps for "sexual mistakes." The girls are described as "fallen" and "polluted." A small drawing shows two angelic girls, emitting visible rays of purity and rectitude, floating over a girl with her head hung in shame, clearly a fallen angel. Parents are warned of urban juvenile delinquents whose polluted moral standards are also blamed on the chaos of the Cultural Revolution. In this early period, the West is also described as part of this sexual moral dystopia. In the same issue that contains the uplifting tale of Engels's romance with the factory worker, the reader is presented with a vision of Rita Hayworth's descent from movie star to madwoman in "An American Movie Queen's Miserable Old Age" (YG 1979, no. 4).

Looking at these articles in the 1990s, young Shanghai friends found them bombastic and simplistic. Harsh articles like "The Most Dangerous Age" reminded them of the demonizing rhetoric of Maoist thought. That hundreds of young girls could be put into reeducation camps for vague "sexual mistakes" is astonishing in today's more liberal climate. As editors explained in defense of these early articles, just talking about love was considered a great liberalization at that time. "We were walking a tightrope," Xia told me. "Going too far too fast would have meant closing down after a few months."

As Harriet Evans notes, early reform-era stories seem to represent a revival of pre–Cultural Revolution notions of love based on shared social and political commitment, but soon deviated from this simplistic model. Overly didactic stories based on the "common interests" of study, work, and social ideals lacked narrative complexity, and their readability suffered. As editors found their footing, narratives became more complex. The class language and emphasis on political and social commitment virtually disappeared by the late 1980s. A more private and erotic kind of love became legitimate.[28] Throughout this early period, however, blind love—love that doesn't take into account social norms and practical considerations—is called into question. Girls who pursue love blindly are invariably tricked by cads. Love must be incorporated thoughtfully into the good life of career, family, and society. The new modernization of China depends upon individual effort and responsibility.

Even in the idealized world represented in these early magazines, young people face difficulties in their quests for true love and a happy modern life. Still, the world these stories represent is "comic" in the sense that a more perfect modern world emerges through the actions of the heroes and heroines. One typical story problem is parental interference in children's partner choice—in extreme cases described as a violation of the Marriage Law. "A New Matchmaker" (YG 1980, no. 1) is typical of these post–Cultural Revolution comic romances. Two young people stuck in low-status neighborhood enterprise jobs fall in love. The mother of the young woman hopes for a better match for her daughter, but the female youth league activist—supported by her reading of the popular book *Ideals, Study and Love*—encourages the mother to accept idealistic love without considering material conditions. The egalitarian ideals represented by figures such as the youth league activist, the "new matchmaker," mean to give hope to urban youth in the early reform period, many of whom were returnees from the countryside dependent on such make-work jobs.

In these stories parents frequently represent the materialistic and atavistic tendencies of the old social order that youth must push aside, but the stories also recognize that parents are not the only obstacles to modern ideals of true love. As early as 1980, Shanghai had a popular expression for materially minded men and women: "high-priced girls," women who demanded "thirty-six legs" (of furniture) as a condition for marriage, and "high-priced fellows," men with high requirements for women, usually in terms of looks ("Love and Material Things," *YG* 1980, no. 3). Yet in these stories, this materially minded minority is represented by clownish figures with unbalanced values in need of correction. The "Man Who Never Lost Hope" (*YG* 1980, no. 1) deals with the problem of high-priced girls. In this story a young soldier loses two girlfriends because of his low rank in the army and his family's poor economic situation, but his contribution to the army and a good heart eventually win him a loving wife. Soldiers represented the vanguard of society in the 1960s. In this story ordinary soldiers are relegated to the lower echelons in the new marriage market, but not without "hope" if they also pursue their careers. We have left the egalitarian Maoist social order behind, but the heroes of the old social order are still viable, if they study and work like everyone else.

In the modernizing China of early "true life" stories, youth are on a quest for modernity and wealth, with young educated Party members at the vanguard. Heterosexual love is not only compatible with this quest but highly valued in this humanistic new social order. Even the Communist Party cadre is playing the helpful role of matchmaker. As readers foreign to this culture, we should not allow the political language of these early reform-era magazine stories to obscure their profoundly positive valuation of romantic love. Although dangerous if not approached with the proper attitude, romantic love is portrayed as a positive, even revolutionary force, which will allow youth to overcome the chaos and dehumanization of the Cultural Revolution and the "feudal attitudes" of their parents and local community.

Tragic Romance 1983–88

Tragic romances and comic romances can be found in all years, but in general the moral rhetoric of magazine romance can be read as shifting from comic to tragic during the 1980s. By this I don't mean the mere presence of a tragic ending. The earliest tragic stories are little more than crude cautionary tales aimed at supposedly naive women readers, and not representatives of a tragic social order. An early example, "Girl Be Careful" (YG 1980, no. 4), offers three cautionary tales all ending tragically for the girls involved. In "Fooled Love," a vain girl who likes to dress well is raped by a man pursuing her. In "Poisonous Bait," a girl reads pornographic hand-copied novels, starts hanging out with delinquents, and is also raped. In "When Maltreated," a girl who was abused by her parents runs away with a lover who also abuses her. Such stories describe young women who are naive, vain, or unwise in dealing with love choices. Their bad judgment and the delinquents who take advantage of them are condemned, but the larger society isn't questioned. The stories may be tragic in their denouement, but are comic in terms of their facile affirmation of the moral order of practical and careful marriage choices, work, and study.

In the stories I collected from 1988 magazines, in contrast, a great many stories question the assumption of a positive social development. Some are heroic social tragedies, stories in which individuals are unjustly punished by social institutions, including the court system, that are supposed to protect and help them. This genre emerges gradually out of the "cautionary tale" melodramas described above. "Chastity tragedies" are the earliest examples of tragic stories in which protagonists are mistreated by parents and social institutions because of their sexual behavior. In many of these stories, the feudalism of parents and society is blamed for a young woman's suicide. An important pathbreaking example, "Love and Prejudice" (YG 1980, no. 1), describes a love affair between a morally suspect woman and the youth league representative assigned to help her. Eventually the romance fails because parents and Party cadres don't approve of the young man dating a "nonprogressive" woman. The woman's flaw, according to the story, is suffering two attempted rapes by an unidentified man. She is assumed to be partly responsible. We are thus still within the realm of the cautionary tale in which a woman is held responsible for relaxing her vigilance against men. The moral order represented in the story is ambiguous, however. The sincerity and rectitude of the helpful Communist youth league activist isn't questioned, but "social prejudice" prevalent in the work unit is. It is as much cautionary as social-critical, but it is groundbreaking in attacking the work-unit system for unfairness in its governance of sexual matters. Blame for a tragic outcome is shared between the young woman and the work unit.

At the height of its popularity and influence in the mid-1980s, Young Generation published a series of articles that directly attack injustices in society. Politically, this was much more difficult than attacking parents' views of chastity. Criticism of social injustice invariably reflected poorly on the Communist Party. A tragic moral order is described in which good people who make a mistake are unjustly punished by a cruel system. "Returning to a Memory" (*YG* 1988, no. 2) describes a case in which a young woman's marriage is ruined by the work unit's involvement in her private life. She gets pregnant before marriage, and the youth league representative goes to her house to persuade her to have an abortion. Not only this, but after she married, she still suffers discrimination at work for this mistake. What makes this story remarkable is that it is narrated by the interfering youth league worker, who regrets her own involvement in this persecution. The contrast couldn't be greater with the helpful youth league workers described in "A New Matchmaker" and "Love and Prejudice." The Party cadre is revealed as a marriage destroyer who regrets her own actions. In this and other articles like it, agents of the state are revealed as corrupt or immoral. Unlike the cautionary tales of a few years before, these social tragedies describe a world in which justice isn't served by the larger social order.

For instance, in "A Woman without Freedom to Divorce" (*YG* 1988, no. 4), a woman is denied permission by the court to divorce her husband, who is in prison for rape. She meets a man she loves, but when they are found living together, she herself is sentenced to eighteen months in prison for bigamy. A higher court overturns the case, but they are left in a legally ambiguous situation. A character in another story isn't so lucky. Ning falls in love with an American man, and after suffering both harassment and malicious gossip in her work unit, is actually arrested for prostitution and sentenced to eighteen months in prison. The article title condemns this decision as an "Illegal Sentence" (YG 1988, no. 5). These tragic narratives boldly question the justice system, and the moral judgments of the editors and writers are clear and decisive. The tragic moral rhetoric of these stories praises the heroism of people like Ning who ask for justice, and even the repentant youth league worker, who openly regrets her unjust actions. Social injustice may be widespread, but it should be and can be combated.

A different breakdown in the comic vision of romance and material happiness begins by questioning the assumption of a compatibility of love and material ambition. The early comic vision of romance suggested a harmony of economic opportunity and free choice in love. New glossier magazines published in the booming Guangdong Province were the first to seriously question this comic vision of romance and modernization and to explore the corrosive mix of money and sex. Located early in the geographic heart of economic re-form, even the name of the youth magazine *Golden Age* suggests that the "new age" in Guangdong was associated with money. In the 1980s the new culture of sex and money brewing in the deep south was like a hot wind blowing north.

In the early 1980s *Golden Age* published several tragic stories of women who meet disaster in their vain attempts to gain wealth through pragmatic marriages to rich men. "Drinking Hatred" (*GA* 1983, no. 11) represents the cutting-edge sensationalist style *Golden Age* developed. A pretty young hotel worker—a typi-cal protagonist for these stories—desires a high-class husband to match her own good looks. One day she meets a handsome man staying in the VIP room, and they start dating. The man tells her that he has an "influential family back-ground," and she falls into his net, having sex with him and getting pregnant. Unfortunately, he is already married, and when she pressures him to marry her, he hires two thugs to stage a rape and robbery. The thugs kill her, and he is cap-tured by the police. The vain pursuit of material wealth destroys the young woman. The Guangzhou magazine *Family* and Shanghai's struggling *Culture and Life* also published several of these "gold-digger tragedies" in 1988, a genre of cautionary tale that ostensibly supports the values of "true love" as the basis of marriage while—especially in the case of *Golden Age*—casting doubt on the abil-ity of people in society to avoid the temptations of easy money and irrespon-sible sex. The tone of these tragic articles, however, is condemning. The differ-ence between right and wrong is clear, but it is also clear that wrong is often difficult to avoid. We are moving beyond simple cautionary tales to ironic so-cial melodramas.

The Ironies of Sex and Money in the 1990s

The *Ideals, Study and Love* romances, helpful youth league workers, and the demonic visions of sexual deviants of 1979 seem naive, perhaps ridiculous, when contrasted with the social tragedies and muckraking social reports of 1988. By 1988 the helpful guidance of the Communist Party looks much less helpful as Party officials, even judges, are revealed as cruel and unjust. More-over, social reports in these magazines recognize that premarital sex, extramar-ital affairs, and divorce are now widespread among ordinary people, not merely problems of a "fallen" fringe. Despite all predictions and efforts to the contrary, sexual freedom in China leads to the same social problems as in other societies, and some peculiar to China, like the reemergence of concubinage and bigamy among wealthy people.[29]

Similarly, the tragic stories and indignant social critiques of 1988 seem hollow or naive in the late 1990s. The activist editorial vision of the late 1980s—whether liberal or reactionary—aimed to achieve a righteous moral order through social critique and diligence against rampant materialism. But in the magazine articles from 1995–96, we no longer find such an idealistic program or clear moral vision. By the mid-1990s, stories do not assume that cadres will be honest, that women won't marry for money, and that romantic passion can be contained exclusively within marriage. Individual choices in love and career are portrayed as deeply corrupted by the temptations of money and sex. There is no assumption that career, love, sex, and social goals are easily made compatible. There is no assumption that Chinese are any more moral than people elsewhere, perhaps even less. Descriptions of political corruption in magazines in the 1990s lose their attitude of social activism as well. Corrupt cadres are just like other rich men who sometimes abuse their power to satisfy sexual and material desires. The lack of heroism and the resigned recognition that society is neither reasonable nor just is typical of Frye's description of an ironic worldview, not a humorous one, but cynical. Such a large shift in perceptions of social and moral order might seem extreme, but it has been widely noted by Chinese intellectuals and outside observers.[30]

In terms of the morality of nonmarital sexual relationships, sympathetic narratives of extramarital affairs were critical to this change.[31] During the reform era, moral condemnation of adulterers is increasingly muted and sympathy more common. This began innocently enough as a defense of the right to divorce and to a marriage based on "feelings."[32] According to editors, during the 1980s magazines were constrained by a semiofficial ideology that women are usually the victims of male infidelity. Therefore, editors and writers sympathetically exploring the acceptability of extramarital love at first used the safer example of the woman philanderer.[33] In a letter to the editor, for instance, a daughter supports her mother's extramarital affair as an escape from her cruel father (GA 1988, no. 1). Eventually, the sympathy extends to the "feelings" of other parties and to less clear cases of marital failure. Even the disparaged "third person" (typically the young mistress) gets some relief. "She Laughs Bitterly" (YG 1988, no. 3) is told from the perspective of a young woman who doesn't regret her affair with a married man but, as the title indicates, expresses her emotional ambivalence at this experience. Few stories in the 1980s expressed sympathy for male infidelity—although considered much more widespread. By 1995, however, writers begin to call more openly for forgiveness for cheating husbands ("Looking for a Lost Husband," YG 1996, no. 1). Mistresses are treated sympathetically when they consider a good wife's virtues and leave a married man in a timely fashion ("I Saw Buddha's Halo," *YG* 1996, no. 5) or simply ("Love in Silence," *GA* 1996, no. 1). In one letter a wife goes so far as to write that her husband's lover helped her save her marriage ("A Letter I Received from the 'Third Person,'" *F* 1995, no. 10). In my reading of magazine stories from 1999 and 2000, the "third person" has a larger presence than ever as the center of a national discussion on whether to use legal means to control the rising divorce rate and limit the practice of keeping mistresses by wealthy entrepreneurs. The end result of all this ambivalent sympathy for lovers and for extramarital affairs is that romantic feeling (*ganqing*), the moral touchstone of post–Cultural Revolution romantic rhetoric (and the basis of the Marriage Law), is recognized as ephemeral, changeable, and imperfect, an irrepressible but unruly human desire. Infidelity becomes an ironic but routine outcome for people with too much money or too many opportunities for romantic and sexual encounters.

Such representations of infidelity and fickleness also influenced understandings of premarital romance, previously considered a relatively pure and innocent experience. In "A Fairy Tale of 9,999 Roses" (*GA* 1996, no. 1), a young woman uses her beauty to attract a wealthy boyfriend, who expresses his love through expensive gifts, including the title's 9,999 roses. This is an expression of true romantic feelings, she thinks. When she walks in on her boyfriend in bed with another woman, however, she simply accepts her situation. She marries the young man anyway, and they go abroad together. "That was all she wanted," the writer concludes. There is no tragedy or comedy in the story, only a practical realism, which the narrator portrays as ironic given the usual assumptions that a beautiful woman would be able to keep her boyfriend faithful (and would be able to leave him if he wasn't).

Nor will doing all the right things inevitably lead to a good result. The article "No Dream Tonight" (*YG* 1996, no. 7) illustrates how far we have come from the romantic optimism of the *Ideals, Study and Love* years. A young woman, Lizi, has trouble balancing love and career. She is devoted to her work at an advertising company and often too busy to spend time with her boyfriend, even missing his birthday. Finally, he calls her one day at work and says that they aren't suitable for each other. He tells her he wants a more family-oriented woman, while she is career-oriented. Hanging up, she reminisces about the sweetness of their first date and cries. This story flies in the face of all the admonitions to pursue career through study and hard work, or the idea that one will be loved for the same characteristics of loyalty, diligence, and idealism that make one a good worker. However, the story does not condemn her career orientation, recognizing that young women are caught in an ironic choice between love and career, for which the narrator offers no solutions. "Feeling like a speck of dust not knowing where she will land" but also defiantly sure that she "is not willing to be 'a little woman,'" "that she loves her career and must control her own destiny," Lizi has no easy choices. The article concludes, "The night is darker and darker, she calms her heart. In front of her she sees a discotheque and marches toward it. After all, she thinks to herself, tonight there will be no dreams."

From bravely marching toward the Four Modernizations, to contemptuously marching into a discotheque, Chinese career women have stepped into an ironic world in the 1990s. It is no less ironic for many Chinese men. In "Why Did the Flower of Love Wither?" (YG 1996, no. 4, summarized above) even the PLA officer must accept that women are no longer satisfied with the boring "green" of army life but prefer the "colorful" life of the modern consumer society. A fatalistic acceptance of social complexity and individual imperfections pervades the stories of the 1990s. People are no longer expected to make heroic choices. The soldier's perseverance is not always rewarded with a happy ending, nor do tragic endings always await those who compromise in love, career, and social responsibility (e.g., the heroine of "9,999 Roses"). Rather, competing life goals and means of achieving them are morally relative and often incompatible. The old quests for work, study, and free-choice marriage lead confusingly into the quandaries of competitive careers and competitive dating. The romances of love and modernization dissolve into the ironies of sex and money.

In an ironic world, the ordinary person who keeps his head down is the survivor. In the ironic magazine melodrama, those with moderate ambitions, like Lizi and the PLA officer, will survive though they may suffer broken hearts along the way. For those who wildly pursue the modern fantasies of free love and easy money, however, disaster assumes ever more sensational forms. The title of "Pregnant Virgin" (GA 1996, no. 4) says it all. In this story a woman is found to be pregnant on her wedding night and accuses her boss of rape. Her husband almost beats the man to death, despite his claims of innocence. In their investigation the police find the boss did attempt a rape, but failed and couldn't have impregnated the women. They discover the woman is having a sexual affair with a married woman friend and has been impregnated with the semen of her friend's male lover transmitted through vaginal contact. In the end her husband is thrown in prison, and the "pregnant virgin" kills herself by jumping into a river.[34]

Such melodramatic stories, while not typical of mainstream magazines such as *Young Generation*, catch readers' attention, attesting to the increasingly tabloidesque quality of some journals, especially *Golden Age*. On the other hand, these are no longer the cautionary tales of fifteen years before. The average reader isn't expected to identify with these characters or be educated by their bizarre difficulties, merely reassure herself that in this ironic world, her ordinary life is preferable. Too much freedom and wealth lead to bad, even bizarre results. This is the essence of the ironic moral rhetoric of tabloid melodrama, to reassure the "little people" about being "little" (perhaps speaking to the typically "middling" social status of their readers). At the same time, the range of sexual freedoms that ordinary people enjoy is broadened through these gradually expanding public explorations of taboo areas. While the tabloid story affirms the values of the "small family life," it does so in a prevailing climate of moral relativism in which variations in sexual behaviors are normal features of an "open" society, a society that now includes all these mediated representations of unconventional sexual behavior.

In stories from 1999 and 2000, these trends continue. The once "pure" world of premarital sexual relations also looks morally confusing. For instance, in "Looking for a Respectable Woman" (*YG* 1999, no. 4), the narrator concludes that respectability (*zhengjing*) is now far more ambiguous than before, including in his expanded definition of the "respectable," a divorced woman who still has sexual relations with her ex-husband, a single woman who sleeps with a former classmate in order to gain his aid in saving her factory and the jobs of twenty-eight female coworkers, and a taxi dancer who refuses to work as a prostitute but takes money for lesser sexual intimacies. Even the newly competitive practices of dating and romance involve moral ambiguity. "What Is the Taste of Stolen Love?" (*YG* 2000, no. 9) describes a young woman who steals another woman's boyfriend, first befriending her, then inviting the man to dinner and drinks alone, ending with him in her bed. She immediately tells his girlfriend. Despite his furious response to this betrayal, she pursues him tirelessly, publicly humiliating yet another female rival. Her love for him justifies her stalking and her rude treatment of her rivals, she argues, and in the end he marries her. The narrator concludes, "After hearing this, I didn't quite know what to say. As they say, 'Love is selfish.'" The moral lessons are not clear, only the continued fascination with the "power of love" and the difficulties of making the right choices. Such stories represent a kind of world irony (*Weltironie*),[35] a critique of the social world based on a contradiction between an ideal (romance) and reality (pragmatic materialism), lamenting the end of an epoch, in this case expressing a popular nostalgia for the presumedly simpler, more honest sexual relations of the early reform era.[36]

New Visions: Troubled White-Collar Romance, Consumer Utopias, Sentimental Romantic Memories

In Frye's cycle the end of irony is the beginning of romance, as new romantic heroes begin a new quest for the good life in the chaos of the old order. In magazine stories at the turn of the millennium, the new heroes and heroines are absolutely clear: the urban white collars, the high-earning, free-living leaders of the new market economy. Their romantic quest is far less clear. In comparison with the young heroes of the early reform era, these new romantic heroes are morally compromised: greedier, more Westernized, more sexually promiscuous, and little concerned with larger social ideals. Articles dissect their marriage choices, "What Do Today's White Collars Look for in Partners?" (YG 2000, no. 9); their leisure patterns, "What Are Urban Women Doing in Bars?" (YG 1999, no. 4); their living arrangements, "Opposite Sexes Sharing an Apartment" (Shenjiangfuwudaobao, August 9, 2000); and their attitudes toward love, "'Petit Bourgeois' Women's Love Attitudes" (humorously framed in archaic class jargon, G 2000, no. 7). Less clear are their means for achieving their ambitious and incompatible goals: professional careers, warm family life, first-world consumer lifestyles, passionate romance, and personal independence. For instance, the thoughtful article "In the 21st Century, Will We Marry?" (YG 2000, no. 1) describes the hesitation of new white-collar youth to marry. "In the 21st century, facing the information explosion, a daily increase in competition, and the ever-increasing middle-aged divorce rate, what is the biggest worry of those entering this new century? It's marriage! . . . Cohabitation is on the increase. This age doesn't lack love, but it lacks the courage to marry. . . . In the 21st century marriage has become a burdensome intrusion into our personal space." For men, the problem is the pressure of "being prepared" for marriage by getting a good position in the labor market. Men become responsible for providing the economic security and housing once provided by the state. Women fear if they don't marry young, then they won't find a partner and be able to have children, but they also fear the boredom of marriage. "People today can put up with frustrations, but we can't put up with boredom. . . . When we think that after entering marriage we will have to live an ordinary, unchanging life, there are a lot of people who hesitate before crossing that threshold." Young white-collar women aren't willing to face the end of romance in marriage. They don't want their freedom to amuse themselves restricted. They don't want to lose the attention of other men. They don't want the heavy routines of cooking and cleaning. Finally, young women face an ever-greater conflict between career and family. A twenty-eight-year-old woman working in a Korean company says, "The twenty-first-century society is a male-dominated society. Women have clearly become even more disadvantaged. It doesn't matter if you want to admit it or not. If you want to compete with men, then you have to sacrifice getting married. Only then can you throw yourself completely into the competition with no concern for your home life." Citing Marx, she argues that economics is the basis of life, and that base is now individualized. She has lovers, but no thoughts of marriage for now. Her mother has given up pushing her to marry. She says she believes in love but doesn't believe that love can possibly last beyond a few months.

This article and others like it spell out the dilemmas of conflicting choices that these new white-collar heroes and heroines face. Numerous other articles propose solutions, necessarily considering one priority at a time, a holistic solution seemingly impossible. For instance, articles address the competitive labor markets youth face: "White Collars Facing Unemployment" (YG 1999, no. 4). Many other articles describe the new sexual marketplaces associated with this new economy: "How Can Private Entrepreneurs Deal with the Problems of Sexual Passion?" (YG 2000, no. 4). And many stories and articles deal with the problems of finding a partner in the increasingly freer and more fluid urban dating culture. "Not Afraid of Being Single" (G 2000, no. 8) lays out all the good reasons for remaining single instead of entering the "fortress of marriage," including fewer responsibilities, more friends, more access to leisure, more sexual freedom, and more contact with the opposite sex (see appendix for more examples).

Given the dilemmas of conflicting sexual choices, there are no new images of a fully developed modern romantic utopia; instead there are images of fragmented worlds of consumption, romantic nostalgia, professional success, and small pleasures that exist within a larger ironic world. These are not refutations of an ironic moral order, but temporary refuges from it, represented in two new genres of magazine articles that appear in the mid-1990s. The first, the "little woman essay," involves a woman writer's ruminations on some everyday activity such as shopping, reading a book, or sitting at home drinking coffee. These vignettes of consumption and private pleasures are especially popular in Shanghai fashion magazines. One of the most popular writers uses a pseudonym that translates directly as "Huang Loves Things" (Huang Ai Dong Xi). In the little woman essay, sexual romance, with its serious choices, is usually avoided. So are the pragmatic problems of finding a good (i.e., well-off) man. The romantic consumer utopia of the little woman—the not-so ambitious white-collar woman, the office lady—is closed, private, and best enjoyed *alone* or with a female friend, similar to the private utopias of advertising.[37] In fact, many little woman essays read like advertising copy.

While these little woman essays rarely address issues of love and sex, we also find a similar type of idyllic essay about love emerging in the 1990s. These essays involve nostalgic reminiscences about past romances, usually on the college campus, but sometimes high school "first loves." In this nostalgic frame, "pure romance" is only possible in the "innocent" environment of the campus or in momentary encounters protected from the practical calculations of the marriage market. This emphasis on love as a momentary, innocent pleasure contrasts with earlier romantic rhetoric in which love is an earnest and patient prelude to marriage, or otherwise considered a failure. In these new sentimental stories, pure love is but a momentary prelude to the real world of the market economy and serious life choices. For instance, in "A Beautiful Memory Preserved for a Lifetime" (YG 2000, no. 6), a woman treasures her "pure memories" of her first college infatuation, Liu Xuan. She recollects their holding hands, their "spiritual communication," and innocent kisses. "Later when she was working, she met many men, and they were all the same, busy and striving for wealth and fame, but she always wanted to imagine Liu Xuan might have been different." She admits that she doesn't see him because she fears she will destroy the purity of her beautiful memory. Similarly, "Give Me a Chance Again to Confide" (YG 1995, no. 11) takes the form of a letter written to a woman the writer once vaguely loved (paraphrased):

> I saw a woman in a temple who looks like you [my old high school classmate] and started reminiscing about our relationship in the past. You and I both grew up in a low-corner Shanghai neighborhood and met while studying for college exams under the streetlights. We started to write letters to one another and enjoyed a dreamy affection that lasted until the end of high school. I was too poor to go to college but encouraged you to continue your studies. Recently I went back to the old neighborhood, which has now been completely demolished, and found your new address from the Public Security Bureau. You are now married, and I wish you happiness in life, regretting that we grew so far apart because of our different paths in life.

Their "dreamy affection" develops in the egalitarian spaces of high school and the low-corner alleyway, nostalgically represented as vanished enclaves from the market values of the new society. Their "different paths" refer euphemistically to their career trajectories and the fact that a college-educated woman would never consider dating a man without education, a mere low-corner worker.

These two genres—the little woman essay and the school days romantic reminiscence—reflect a popular lamentation among Chinese youth that material well-being and romantic love are no longer mutually compatible goals, no longer achievable within a single romantic narrative. The little woman's idylls of consumption are typically enjoyed alone. The practical negotiations of courtship and marriage, sex and money, are excluded. The school days reminiscence precludes pragmatic material considerations, safe in the past and in the world of innocent childhood. In these romantic fantasies of the market society, the coherent quest of ideals, study, and love is a thing of the past. Love and money are idealized separately in ephemeral spaces of consumption and nostalgia. In the "real world," youth face difficult choices. Ironically, the most consistent magazine advice about these real choices echoes the work-and-study ethos of twenty years before. But this time study is a pursuit of professional credentials, not ideals, and work is a means of independence in an uncertain world. In pursuing these goals, personal selfishness, relational instability, and moral uncertainty are unavoidable.

Stories by Whom and for Whom?

Cultural products like magazines cannot be read as simple reflections of the social climate, but as products of particular markets and institutional environments.[38] The moral rhetoric of magazine stories represents an interaction between editors, writers, political overseers, and readers. In particular, looking at the social space of magazine production and consumption in 1990s China reveals significant institutional constraints on the sexual politics of magazine storytelling.

The Changing Balance between Political Control and Market Pressures

Political control is an important factor in all Chinese media. All magazines are published by government organizations. No independent publications are allowed. *Family* and *Girlfriend* are published under the auspices of provincial women's federations. *Golden Age* is published under the auspices of the provincial youth league, and *Young Generation* and *Culture and Life* are published by large state-owned publishing houses. All are overseen by the Propaganda Ministry, while the sponsoring organizations are responsible for politically vetting content. Publishing house magazines are directly overseen by the publishing house and the Ministry of Publications, doubly layering control of both finances and editorial decisions.

In the 1990s political control was usually less formal than organizational charts imply. Editors complained that there were no clear standards for what could be published on topics such as sexuality and love, only the broad implicit guidelines of "social mores." Editors also complained of the influence of retired but well-connected cadres who wrote complaint letters about articles they didn't like. The power to choose editors was perhaps the strongest form of political control exercised by the governing organizations themselves. Recalcitrant liberal editors such as Xia Hua, the outspoken editor of *Young Generation*, could be removed. Some conservative governing organizations, such as provincial women's federations, appointed political editors with no journalistic backgrounds, stifling creativity, as the chief editor of *Girlfriend* explained: "When the political cadres have a big influence, they will want to stop all discussion of certain issues, such as sex. They can't figure out the right line to take on these issues. So they just won't let you talk about it at all. Some provincial publications are like this." In fact, some big-city publications suffer from this problem as much as provincial ones, some of which are governed very loosely. Magazines published in the politicized atmosphere of Beijing rarely sold as well as the more loosely controlled southern magazines. Even Shanghai magazines suffered from more political controls than Guangzhou magazines, making them less able to follow the tabloid style the southerners developed. In the 1990s, however, market competition exerted pressures on magazines that political leaders sometimes were not able to effectively oppose.[39] Increased competition forced magazine editors to come up with increasingly provocative content. In the 1990s "wilder" magazines from the provinces stole the market from the more conservative market leaders in Shanghai.

Magazines in the 1990s were forced to fend for themselves financially. There were no government subsidies. Conversely, profitable magazines often subsidized local government agencies. Some political entities governing magazines—for instance, provincial women's federation organizations—began to rely on income from women's magazines to finance much of their budgets (*Girlfriend* and *Family* both fall in this category). With large chunks of their budgets at stake, local women's federation and youth league cadres in cities like Guangzhou became loath to interfere with successful magazines. If a magazine failed to attract readers' interest, this income would dry up quickly in the competitive market. This situation undoubtedly influenced the changes in content discussed above. Ironic stories of money and love were entertaining and timely without being offensive to either sophisticated urban readers or conservative Party censors. The countervailing market and political forces thus discouraged both reformist and reactionary political rhetoric.

From Advocates to Businessmen

The first phase of magazine publication was an official cultural movement for mobilizing youth behind the ideas of Deng Xiaoping. Xia explained the decision to publish a new youth magazine in Shanghai in 1979:

> The leadership decided that in order to meet up with the needs of the reform and opening, the youth had to understand new things. Books come out too slowly, so a magazine is necessary to bring things to the youth quickly. The idea was that youth should have hope for the future. Up until then the only magazine was ChineseYouth. This was too serious. The idea of the new magazine was to give youth something more open and more liberated.

In articles from 1979 and 1980, the language of political campaigns was still evident, including the calls to study, the demonization of enemies (the Gang of Four) and the mobilization of youth into the Four Modernizations. While the Chinese people craved the modernity, liberalization, and humanism promised by Deng, the direction of liberalization came from the Party hierarchy itself. The establishment of the magazines was an executive decision, and editors were agents in mobilizing support for reform. In this political climate, the harmonious and hopeful social order described in early magazine articles in which the interests of youth and the Party cadres coincide is thus not difficult to explain. Still, the stories can't be dismissed as mere propaganda, because they also represent the idealistic and romantic aspirations of intellectual youth of the period. In 1980 most junior editors were "sent-down youth," returning from the countryside for some limited schooling before starting work. Enthusiastic about the educational opportunities offered in Deng's Four Modernizations, many of these editors struggled to obtain a university degree. This background explains their emphasis on study in early stories. Many youth of their generation had been forced to labor in the countryside and accepted pragmatic marriages during the Cultural Revolution. They shared the hope that a new political climate would allow urban youth a chance to pursue meaningful careers and free love matches. Moreover, the revolutionary idealism of this Cultural Revolution generation is still evident in their calls for youth to follow their romantic ideals and disregard the feudal mores of their parents and local society.

Few imagined the surge in divorce, premarital sex, extramarital affairs, and a new type of financially motivated pragmatism in marriage that such freedoms would bring. After all, most Chinese of the time accepted the propaganda that such social ills were a symptom of capitalist decadence to which socialist China was socially and culturally immune.

In contrast to this first brief political honeymoon with Dengist reforms, magazines and other media in the mid- and late 1980s featured strong social critiques and political controversy. This phase was pushed by magazine editors themselves, often against the grain of official Party culture. This first generation of editors had experienced the Cultural Revolution (some as victims) and tended to see social issues in highly political narratives. Much of the sense of social tragedy in this period arose from the contradictions editors and writers perceived between Party ideals and social reality. On the other hand, magazines were not pure mouthpieces of reform-minded editors. Magazines also reflected conservative campaigns against liberalism. For instance, in the 1988 article "Why Do They Get Divorced?" divorcing people were criticized for being "under the influence of capitalist money and material worship" (F 1988, no. 5). This is language drawn directly from the antibourgeois liberalization campaign in full swing at that time. Regardless of how much urban Chinese may have valued new personal freedoms, the new social problems of divorce, extramarital affairs, and mercenary sex were certainly very unpopular and became useful targets of campaigns against bourgeois liberalization.[40] Magazines in the mid-1980s therefore should be understood as sites of political conflict and editorial activism, both reformist and reactionary.

Without activist editors as social advocates, magazines wouldn't have published articles critical of Party-state social institutions. Strong magazine editors produced many breakthroughs in liberalizing public sexual culture. Many editors I interviewed pointed to *Young Generation* as an early leader. Though somewhat protected by high-ranking official connections, *Young Generation* editor Xia described his long editorship as a "tightrope walk" between going too far politically and not being daring enough. Occasionally he broke with the Party leadership, he said, refusing to participate in the antispiritual pollution campaign during which he was asked to publish articles against youth sexual culture. *Young Generation* also pioneered popular letter-writing forums in which readers presented different views on divorce and extramarital affairs. The space for social criticism was never unlimited, and after the political repression of 1989, it became even more greatly restricted. After 1989 activist journalism became politically difficult and morally futile, leaving editors and readers disillusioned with the idea of popular political action. The old editor Xia was moved into another less troublesome position in 1995 and replaced with a more conservative and pliable editor.

The third phase in the social environment facing editors thus began in 1989 with the failure of the democracy movement and increased political control of the media. But the more immediate problem that soon emerged was vastly increased competitive market pressure. By the 1990s the newest generation of editors was oriented more toward business than politics, an attitude they shared with many of their young readers who had not even finished high school during the political movements of 1989. By 1995 editors said that market pressures were much greater determinants of what they published than political pressures. The most serious political conflicts with governing organizations involved distribution of revenues rather than issues of content. Ironically, magazines in the 1990s were increasingly "liberal" on sexual issues, but the new impetus toward tolerance was no longer the editors' interest in political reform and human rights but in capturing a market with titillating content already discovered by hordes of illegal tabloid magazines sold through private distribution channels. Headlines like "Pregnant Virgin" in mainstream publications partly were a reaction to this competition. Finally, advertising, while increasingly important, actually accounted for less than half of revenues at all these magazines in 1996. Of the magazines I describe here, *Girlfriend* was the first to make the transition to a full-scale consumer magazine, largely subsidized by advertising and focused on fashion, makeup, and other consumer products. In 2000 it was expanding onto the Internet. The increased reliance on advertising revenue, rather than circulation alone, meant editors focused less on increasing mass circulation and more on capturing a wealthier, urban, white-collar audience, explaining their focus on these new "heroes" and "heroines" of the consumer society.

Old liberal editors, such as Xia Hua of *Young Generation*, were just as out of place in the new publishing world as were old political conservatives. New-style editors, like those at *Girlfriend*, were more interested in finding markets, attracting advertising, and creating an exciting visual style. Chief editors focused increasingly on financial issues, while many junior editors were themselves deeply involved in the market economy as freelance writers or designers. *Girlfriend* pioneered a contract system in which all editors were paid highly, but on a scale based on the amount of materials they produced. Unlike editors under the socialist lifetime contract, they could also be easily removed from their duties if their performance lagged. There was little incentive for social activism in this system.

Finally, stories reflected the changing attitudes of writers, some professional journalists, some part-timers and amateurs. A long-term editor of a love column for *Golden Age* complained he could no longer find writers capable of writing the "soft, misty" romantic stories his column once carried:

> People have lost this simplicity and innocence. Those around twenty-eight or thirty are too old to write about this topic. They are thinking about career and marriage, and this is too distant for them. The younger ones have the passion, but they can't write this kind of thing. They are less and less romantic and more pragmatic. People won't talk about soft love, pure love. They won't talk about sentiments. Now people talk about things objectively, more coldly.

Editors also have personal reasons to be more cynical about the direction of social change. Almost all editors are now college graduates, about half of them Chinese literature majors. In their lifetimes the status of liberal arts majors, especially literature majors, has dropped drastically, giving editors an acute personal sense of the status changes wrought by market forces. With their political idealism shattered in the repression of the student movements of 1989 and increasingly frustrated with their positions in a competitive market economy, young editors in China retain few of the romantic revolutionary sentiments of the early reform era.

From Readers to Consumers

Magazines once had immense moral authority with readers. In the early 1980s readers lined up to buy new copies of *Young Generation* or *Culture and Life* with ration coupons. They not only read every article, but saved the magazines for years or passed them along to friends. According to editors and older informants, they also looked to magazines for guidance. In the 1990s large and successful magazines such as *Girlfriend, Family,* and *Young Generation* still hosted gatherings of readers and received thousands of reader letters, but they seemed to have lost their moral authority. Editors argued that 1990s readers were far less likely to seek magazines for guidance than readers in the early 1980s. Former *Young Generation* editor Xia Hua said, "Now people feel they already understand society themselves. They don't need you to tell them. They have more sources of information." The increasing tendency of readers to seek magazines for entertainment rather than for guidance was noted by many other editors. Editors at the cutting-edge Xian magazine *Girlfriend* largely dismissed the role of the magazine as a serious educating authority and publish fewer and fewer articles focusing on moral issues. The chief editor of *Girlfriend* said: "Many people don't like you teaching them this thing and that. *Girlfriend* is a friend, not a teacher. We don't educate people from a position of superiority. We only propagate love and warmth. . . . But there is no doubt that in the future we will move to more practical things." The "move to more practical things" presages an increasing emphasis on consumer lifestyles, in particular on women's fashion and grooming, which have more advertising potential. This transition is, however, incomplete. The residual but decaying moral focus of magazines is evident in the changing tone (melodramatic irony) but still morally charged topics (dramas of love and money) of the "true stories" discussed above.

With dense print layouts and uninspiring illustrations (often pirated from foreign sources), magazines in the mid-1990s remained visually unexciting in comparison with U.S. or Taiwan magazines. My focus group interviews in the 1990s showed that youth in Shanghai considered magazines a form of casual entertainment, but still as *reading*, rather than browsing or scanning. College students, in particular, tended to read magazines cover to cover, not missing an article. For many readers, three to five yuan for an issue was still a large expense, a day's income in some poorer cities and towns. This type of readership explains the persistent tendency of magazines to publish long-winded "true story" articles rather than snappier, shorter pieces. By 2000 glossy European magazines like *Elle* costing sixteen yuan an issue were becoming popular among white collars in their twenties, but the text-oriented magazines such as *Young Generation* still had a large audience. As Angela McRobbie points out for British girls, youth magazines are an important cultural resource in the feminine "bedroom culture" of adolescent girls.[41] In Shanghai they seemed to be a significant cultural resource for high school and college students and young office workers. For instance, I found that college dorm roommates (typically eight to a room in the mid-1990s) frequently shared magazines among themselves and discussed the articles. Because of this high pass-along readership and the conversations it allows, magazines in China probably were consumed more socially—or less privately—than in more affluent countries.

Readers in focus groups often related magazines stories to everyday life. They frequently responded to magazine articles by saying, "This type of thing happens often" or "This sort of thing is rare." Magazine stories prompted further storytelling, including stories of neighbors and coworkers. When responding to more traditional or sincere love stories, ironic readings were not uncommon, with some younger participants joking that a romantic young protagonist would soon lose interest in his "one true love" and break up with her. Such reactions pointed out that editors were right to allow a more ironic framing of urban love stories and to doubt the moral authority of their own mediations.

A Tale of Two Tropes

The changing moral rhetoric of magazine stories is most clearly reflected in the changing uses of certain story elements. The helpful youth league cadre of 1980 is easily contrasted with the corrupt big money cadre of 1996. Society is no longer just. The good student who earnestly and successfully combines study and romance in 1980 contrasts starkly with the white-collar woman of the 1990s who must face the contradictions of career and romance. Conventional goals are no longer in harmony in the new market society. The disillusioned officer in "Why Does the Flower of Love Wither?" confronts a much less fair world than the idealistic army recruit of "The Sixty-seventh Love Letter." Individual efforts aren't always rewarded in the market society. In sum, what I am describing is a transition in the public moral rhetoric of sexual motives, at least in magazines: a movement from a forced romantic idealism about love and modernization to an ironic appreciation of the problems of free sexual and labor markets. As Lizi discovers in "No Dream Tonight," irony is a necessary attitude for survival in a market society that encompasses both the selling of one's labor and the selling of the self in the sexual marketplace. Aware of the ironies of living the life of the modern woman, Lizi marches off to the disco, a place where authentic feelings and serious choices are irrelevant.

I conclude by suggesting that romance and irony are not only two historic moments (1980 and 2000), but two important strands (complementary rhetorical tropes) in the dialectics of Chinese public sexual culture, played out in a social space defined by media producers, consumers, and censors (magazines being but one such space, though a typical one). The beginning moment of this post–Cultural Revolution cultural dialectics, and the stronger of these two moral voices, is the humanistic defense of romantic feelings against both political suppression and crass materialism. The high value put on individual feelings allowed editors, writers, and presumably readers as well to consider a wide range of sexual behaviors as heroic breaks with feudal tradition and backward thinking. Romantic feelings, translated as a basic socialist and humanistic ideal, provide a persuasive moral and political justification for individual choices in the face of severe opposition.[42]

Irony is no less an important strand in the public sexual culture in urban China, and a counterargument to politicized romanticism. Irony, as described here, is a pragmatic response to the aporia of moral choices, a cultivated disinterest and skepticism, not unrelated to the "cool" cultivated by urban youth in response to the performance demands of romance. Irony, as expressed in these magazines, is not merely a disillusionment with romantic idealism, but an increasingly wide tolerance for difference, for deviation, and for the failure to live up to moral expectations, a tolerance that the romantic idealism of the early reform era didn't display. The romantic irony of state-controlled popular culture is not very deep, however, often reflecting an underlying moral self-righteousness and a grudging acceptance of a morally imperfect world. As discussions in later chapters will show, individuals also employ both tropes of romance and irony in their own personal stories, using them freely to justify some actions and distance themselves from others. Some, especially elites, also employ the self-righteous rhetoric of romantic irony, a thinly disguised disparaging of others for failing to live up to ones own high ideals, perhaps another fading legacy of the moral high-mindedness of socialist education and culture.

5 谈朋友

TALKING FRIENDS
For Love and for Fun

The New Dating Culture in Shanghai
Saturday Date

One of the most popular Shanghai television programs in 1999 and 2000 was a half-hour dating game called *Saturday Date* (Xiangyuexingqiliu), which aired Saturday evenings on Shanghai Television. In each show five men faced five women, aiming to pair up by the end of the program. Producers matched the ages and social backgrounds of contestants for each weekly installment, but overwhelmingly invited white-collar professionals and office workers, an attractive advertising market and a group whose busy schedules and demanding "conditions" for a partner purportedly created difficulties finding a spouse.[1] In a distinctive modification of the Western dating-game format, each contestant brought along a large support team (houyuantuan) of family members, friends, and coworkers who praised their candidate and participated in his or her choices, creating occasional humorous disagreements. On the one hand, the program blatantly emphasized the conventional external conditions (waizaitiaojian) of participants: age, occupation, height, education, and secondary talents such as foreign languages and music. Viewers (including my extended family with whom I usually watched the program) enjoyed commenting on the appearance of contestants, especially women. Countering this typical Shanghaiese pragmatism was a typical Shanghaiese schmaltz. Participants on the program were required to engage in personalized romantic performances aimed to convince other contestants of a deeper attraction. Women displayed culinary skills, a dance, or a self-made personal gift, signs of a caring domesticity. Men improvised poems, sang flowery songs, and otherwise wooed the women with displays of emotional depth and personalized interest.

The program also played up cross-gender suspicions and intragender competition in the search for a spouse. Men and women cross-examined one another with difficult questions about dating and marriage. (Woman to man: "Would you be able to accept your girlfriend going abroad to study?" Woman to man: "What would you do if your wife wanted to buy the house in her name?" Man to woman: "How would you help me if I had a failure in my career?") Gendered expectations of marriage didn't always seem well matched. Men typically sought a wife to take care of them. Women, while also seeking domesticity, seemed to crave autonomy in marriage. *Saturday Date* also set men against one another in competition for the approval of a particularly popular woman contestant (often popular for her looks, sometimes for her "foreign" experience or other glamorous trait). She, in turn, had to choose between these conventionally smitten suitors. Silly interactive games, such as sack races and dance contests, provided levity and mild sexual titillation. Viewers I spoke with found the program amusing, though they doubted any of the matches would lead to marriage and suspected most participants were looking for free prizes and public recognition.

The humor of the program lay in its ability to articulate and poke fun at the cross-gender tensions, intragender competition, and the emotional performance demands that structure the new Shanghai dating culture. The primary dilemma or constraint in this new dating culture was a persistently strong social and familial pressure (or desire) to marry and have children. Friends, coworkers, and family still acted as informal matchmakers (like the support teams on *Saturday Date*), but young people largely assumed the responsibility for choosing their own spouses and dating partners. However, youth faced their choice of a marriage partner in a context of greater uncertainty than youth a generation earlier. First of all, young people faced greater difficulties in judging their own economic futures and those of partners in the fast-changing labor market. Dating, or "talking friends" (*tanpengyou*) in Shanghai patois, became not only a way of choosing and testing a partner, but of postponing a decision until economic prospects were clearer.[2] Second, with nearly half as many people in Shanghai divorcing as marrying each year[3] and the extramarital affairs of wealthy men a national preoccupation, marital relationships also seemed far less stable. Women sought signs of male romantic infatuation and an emotionally close dating relationship as evidence of male commitment. Men sought women who would support them and stay with them in times of career difficulties. With their economic futures tied to a husband whom they hoped would earn considerably more than themselves, young women now individu-

ally embodied the conventional generational conflict between pragmatic parental calculations and unruly romantic feelings. As previous chapters have discussed, their individualized motives became the focus of public moral discourse, including *Saturday Date.* Courtship thus became the institutional setting
in which young men and young women negotiated this culturally constructed
contradiction between women's pragmatic material choices and romantic feelings, sometimes harmoniously through a dating game that allowed pragmatic
purposes (conditions) and moral purposes (feelings) to coincide, sometimes
conflictually in spiteful stories of cheating or betrayal.

"Girlfriend Version 6.0"

Less bound to upbeat cheerfulness than television, print media occasionally present a more ironic view of the youth dating culture. One collection
of snippy reports in a popular weekly paper describes the "dating customs
of the new humanity" in Shanghai,[4] including a vignette of a young office
worker's cultural clash with a recalcitrant old Party cadre:

> There is new gossip around the office about Little Bug, who is in charge
> of design. As he put it, "'Girlfriend Version 5.0' has now been updated to
> 'Girlfriend Version 6.0.'" When someone in the office asked about his
> sixth girlfriend, "When are you going to the marriage altar?" Little Bug
> just scowled at her and mumbled, "Stupid question." Not in step with
> current fashion, one of the old "comrades" in this esteemed office spoke
> out, "If this were years before, you just might be singled out for a deca-
> dent lifestyle." Little Bug looked at him with wide eyes and walked out
> with a forced smile on his face.

"The new humanity is the me generation," the bemused narrator exclaims.
"[For the new generation], love is not necessarily for marriage. Therefore, they
can love and love again. They can see love as one experience after another for
their enjoyment. . . . Love has become a kind of consumption, and a one-time
form of consumption at that. . . . For many of the 'new humanity,' talking about
eternal love is too far removed from real life, an unrealistic and dubious ideal.
It is better to just grab something real for the here and now." Dating someone
who already has a boyfriend or girlfriend is now fair competition, citing a popular maxim: "With love it doesn't matter who arrived earlier or later." Even
married people are fair game when romantic feelings arise, citing yet another
proverb: "There is no point in reasoning about the morality of love."

The humor of this column, like the *Saturday Date* game show, plays on the incongruities of the new courtship culture, in this case conflicting generational expectations of earnestness and playfulness, free choice and loyalty. Dating several partners before marriage was becoming increasingly common in Shanghai, and young men and women were expected to deal with the emotional distress of failed love (shilian). Older Shanghaiese derided these practices of casual dating, but youth found them a way of establishing intimacy and testing relationships without a hasty commitment to marriage.

"Going Out to Play"

The early-twentieth-century United States saw dramatic changes in the social geography of courtship, from domestically oriented practices of "calling" to consumption-oriented practices of "going out" and "dating." With this move into a public, commercial, and peer-oriented social geography, the sexual norms, emotional vocabulary, and normative expectations of premarital relationships changed. Dating relationships retained their conventional purpose as a search for a spouse, but also became a new type of relationship with its own values and internal rewards, incorporating consumption and leisure into play forms of marriage.[5] Within a new geography of commercial leisure activities, reform-era Shanghai youth similarly have reconstructed courtship practices around "going out to play."[6]

Shanghai youth always dated outside the home to some extent, even before and during the Cultural Revolution. According to informants who dated in the late 1970s and early 1980s, however, dating couples typically engaged in noncommercial activities such as meetings at home, letter writing, and walking in the park. Although courtship practices generally occurred outside the home, they resembled earlier U.S. practices of "calling" in terms of their noncommercial contexts (or minimal expense), the influence of family members (who often arranged dates), and the clear intent to find a spouse. When a relationship was "decided," the couple began calling on each other's families, signifying a commitment to marry. Most people had few dating experiences and few dating partners before marriage. Most working-class Shanghai informants who dated in the early 1980s described their courtship as a practical search for an "honest and reliable" partner, while more highly educated informants emphasized shared intellectual interests and activities such as letter writing.

By the 1990s youth expected to "go out and play" on dates, which typically involved spending considerable time and money on commercial leisure activities, such as dining, dancing, shopping, and travel.[7] A 1996 survey of Shanghai married couples found that two-thirds of those under age thirty reported

Table 5.1. Frequency Shanghai husbands reported visiting commercial leisure venues during courtship with current spouse by husband's age in 1996.

	under 30 (%)	31–41 (%)	41–50 (%)	50–65 (%)
Often	8.9	1.2	0	.6
Sometimes	17.9	6.7	4.7	2.2
Occasionally	39.3	16.6	4.7	2.2
Never	33.9	75.5	90.7	95.0

Data from 1996 survey, "A Study of Marital Satisfaction in China," conducted by Xu Anqi (Shanghai Academy of Social Sciences); 1,600 husband-and-wife pairs were interviewed.

visiting "commercial entertainment places" while dating their current spouses. Only small minorities of married couples above thirty reported such dating behavior (see table 5.1). People were also dating earlier. According to my youngest informants, dating came to be considered normal among high school students during the 1990s despite attempts by teachers and parents to keep students' attention focused on college entrance exams. Even high school dating couples expected to engage in physical intimacy such as kissing and petting.[8]

An unstable feature of these new practices of courtship is the conflict between the conventional goal of dating (marriage) and the conventional means of expression (leisure play). As in the U.S. experience, dating is part of a consumer culture of fun and excitement that separates romance from marriage by emphasizing "special experiences" and often expensive forms of consumption, acts of symbolic "excess" that set off the romantic experience from everyday life.[9] In its most playful forms, dating has the qualities of the dance hall play described in chapter 9, temporary sexual excitement with no long-term goals or consequences. For parents this dating as an "end in itself" seems wasteful and sexually decadent; for youth it brings emotional comfort, romantic experiences, and sexual and material gratification. Economically disadvantaged youth, in particular, may use dating as a substitute for longer-term commitments. But consumption is only one element of this dating culture. The consumer market offers no guidelines for how youth are to organize their dating practices, even for who should pick up the check. In allowing for competition and choice in dating, young men and women must negotiate their own new gendered grammar of goals, means, and rules of dating. The moral rhetoric surrounding these love relationships (*ganqing*) and practices of talking friends (*tanpengyou*) employs competing principles of loyalty and autonomy, honor and equity, domesticity and play. Finally, the dialectics of this culture of dating and romance depend upon larger institutional changes, including the rise of consumer leisure institutions, but also changes and continuities in traditional institutions of socialization, especially schools and families.

A Grammar of Dating Culture
Courtship in the Early Reform Era

While some Shanghaiese reported going out on dates even during the Cultural Revolution, most of these dates in the pre–reform era involved modest amounts of consumption such as sharing an ice cream, going to a movie, or taking a walk in the park.[10] The following focus group interview transcript shows the way that women factory workers talk about dating in the late 1970s and early 1980s and their views of youth in the mid-1990s. I present this lively conversation among middle-aged women factory workers at length. In comparison with younger men and women, women in their late thirties seemed especially comfortable sharing ideas about dating experiences in a group interview. Unlike younger people, they could assume great similarities in two important areas: income levels (almost identical in the period of their youth) and conservative attitudes about sex (in comparison with "youth today"). The initial topic of this conversation was "love letters":

Ping: At that time we were introduced to somebody by a middleman to see if we could match. If we could get along with each other, then everything was set, if not, then. . . . We didn't aim at anybody by our own choice. This kind of opportunity was rare. . . .

Sang: I met mine myself. Did I need to write love letters because we did it on our own? Not necessarily.

Nong: Now [people] have more tricks [hua]. There was no such thing before.

Ping: [We] were straight [laoshi] then and didn't start dating until we were twenty-five or twenty-six. Dating was not allowed during three years of apprenticeship. Back then so many people were sent to the countryside. We who stayed in Shanghai had to cherish our "rice bowl." We dared not [date]. And there was no sex education then—"close the bedroom door and reeducate"—how could we know what life was like outside [the factory]? When we were over twenty, we didn't know as much as junior high school students do now. My son is in his first year of junior high, and he has physical health class, learning all about men and women. We didn't know anything when we graduated from high school. We started dating at twenty-three or twenty-four, to meet the government's requirement of marrying late, and married at twenty-seven and twenty-eight. Men didn't marry until about thirty. [A lot of support from the crowd for her speech.]

Ming: Now people play tricks [hua]. Love letters et cetera!

Nong: Today's playboys [xiaochilao] play tricks. Love letters. . . . Nothing like that before. Now they are seventeen and eighteen years old and already dating. . . . [A lot of response from the crowd. All agree.]

Ping: Back then, after three years of being an apprentice, we were all twenty-one or twenty-two, but were so dumb, we didn't know anything. From the factory to home, and from home to the factory, we only thought of being a good worker for Chairman Mao and trying to get into the youth league or the Party and progress politically.

Moderator: What did you do when dating?

Ping: Watched movies.

Sui: There were only movies, and parks on weekends. It wasn't like now, coffee shops. . . . There weren't things like this.

Altogether: Before, there were only movie theaters, and now they all go to coffeehouses.

Ping: Nowadays young people go to coffeehouses, dance halls, karaoke. The atmosphere is not the same. It is "manufactured" now. We didn't have anything like this when we were dating.

Moderator: Did you go to parks?

Sui, Dong: Parks, yes. On the weekends we went to the Bund [Shanghai's riverfront].

Altogether: Where else could you go?

Ping: We had very innocent ideas. When other people introduced somebody, we didn't think as girls nowadays do and want a big house and a lot of money. We only thought of getting an honest one. . . .

Altogether: Straight ones. We didn't want crafty ones. We didn't even want businesspeople.

Ping: In the past parents always told you not to take anything from other people.

Si: When I got into the work unit, the human resources leader sent me to the workshop and told me in three years of apprenticeship I couldn't date.

Sui: We didn't date even when we were engaged.

Moderator: Did men pay for the bills if you went out together? Did they buy you gifts?

Sui: Small things, and small snacks.

Ping: Parents all said: "Don't use other's things and eat other's food. If you use them up, he won't have any savings when you get married. And it is worse if you don't get married, then you will have used other people."

Sui: When spending, we spent both people's money on some snacks. [We were] not like people now who go to restaurants.

Nong: A snack shop [*dianxindian*] was a treat already.

Moderator: Did they give gifts as big as clothes?

Altogether: No way. No money! Before everybody made thirty-six RMB.

Ping: As an apprentice, we only made eighteen and later made thirty-six.
When we got married, we made forty-eight.

Xiang: RMB 17.84. I remember very clearly.

Ping: Everybody had this salary.

(married women in their late thirties)

Interviews with men and women who came of age in the late 1970s and early 1980s emphasize the much greater equality of income in those days and the vast material and cultural gulf that separates them from youth today. Eighteen RMB would barely buy a meal for two at McDonald's in the 1990s. A generational gulf also often emerged between the young women moderators and the women participants. For instance, one of the moderators, herself a very high-earning white collar, casually asked what men in those days would do if a date was interested in a piece of clothing costing several hundred yuan. First shocked, then laughing, the women said, "There was no clothing that cost that much then. Who could have made so much money?"

But expense was only one aspect of the changes in dating practices. First of all, there was the element of social control. As these women point out, work units in the late 1970s imposed age restrictions on dating. Women and men often started courting only when they were ready for marriage, usually involving formal introductions of a marriage partner with little chance to meet and date various partners or become very intimately involved. The women specifically mention their lack of sexual knowledge and the near impossibility of sexual experience before marriage. Second, there was the change in the nature of dating interactions. They specifically reject as "tricks" the flirtations and romantic behaviors that youth now take for granted. Third, they agree that in their day, even though it was the norm for men to pay more for a date, it was questionable for a woman to let a man spend money on her just for the experience of dating. In general, parents discouraged young women from being taken on dates in the 1980s unless that man was certainly going to be a marriage partner. One woman said that otherwise this would be "tricking the man." Finally, for these women, as for other focus group participants from their age group, courtship was clearly about finding a husband or wife. "Playing around" and "deception about feelings" (*pianganqing*) were condemned.

All of these expectations showed signs of drastic change in the 1990s. Work-unit and parental involvement in dating decreased. Norms of dating expenditure changed from modest expenses or none at all to whatever could be afforded or was necessary to impress a date. Flirtation and seduction in dating were considered normal, and women only complained if men's romantic "tricks" were too "common" and unoriginal. As dating relationships became more fun, more emotionally engaging, and more sexually involving, they became more of an end in themselves. All considered, the changes amount to a redefinition of dating practices as complete as that in the United States in the 1920s and with as wide a range of consequences for the relations between young men and women.

"Success":The Changing Goals of Dating

One evening in a local bar with a group of Western friends, I met some female college students celebrating one of their birthdays. Dancing in the center of the dance floor, drinking more beer than they were accustomed to, and flirting with the foreign strangers, they presented themselves as liberated, cosmopolitan, and modern young women. These young women described going to a bar and spending considerable money (fifteen yuan for a beer) as a normal (though not common) practice, and they pointedly criticized an out-of-town classmate who left early because she thought the bar was too expensive. I asked one young woman about her plans after college, and she talked of working in the fashion industry in China or the United States, imagining a glamorous life jetting around the globe. Following on this, I asked her if she was planning to get married. Suddenly she said emphatically, "Oh, of course, I must marry. My parents would kill me if I didn't get married." Even among the youngest Shanghaiese, the language of dating still reflects the primacy of the goal of marriage.[11] Among high school students I spoke with, the most frequent criticism of these relationships was not the typical adult criticisms that they were against the rules or would adversely impact academic performance, but rather that such relationships were unlikely to be "successful" (*chenggong*) or have a "result" (*jieguo*) of marriage.

Although the naturalness or inevitability of marriage is increasingly questioned in popular culture, those who seriously wished to remain single reported immense pressure from family and friends to get married. Informants even spoke of leaving the country to avoid such pressure. For women, this pressure was greater because it came earlier in life, but men experienced it, too. Even homosexual men with no desire to marry usually married at least long enough to satisfy family demands, including producing a child. Divorce was less a disgrace than never marrying.[12] One thirty-one-year-old woman, Lan, who had dated several men and was now in a long-term relationship with a married man, described the pressure her mother applied to her as "unbearable":

> My ideal would be to live alone and not to get married, to have a lover but not to have to be married to him. I am no longer twenty-three or twenty-four, when you can just fall in love with a guy and want to marry him out of passion. I think at this age it is impossible to fall in love like that. . . . All the grown girls upstairs and downstairs have already gotten married. My mother is afraid that people will think no one wants her daughter. She even told me, she said, "You know you don't have to worry so much about whether it is the perfect match. If it doesn't work out, then you can get divorced." I couldn't believe my conservative, Communist Party cadre mother was telling me this. But for her it is more important that I get married than anything. . . . But she was also happy when I mentioned that I might go abroad to study. Going abroad means to Shanghai people that you can do whatever you want, at least you have some kind of "result." Just moving out [and staying in Shanghai] won't do.

Her discussion makes explicit the ancient Chinese notion that marriage is a duty to the parents, providing the only satisfactory closure to childhood. However, going abroad (to a rich immigrant country) is a modern alternative, since it also provides a "result" that brings face to the family. When I interviewed her again in 2000, she was pressuring her lover to divorce his wife, a common but difficult struggle among women in such relationships.

The attachment of dating relationships to the goal of marriage was indeed loosening, however. As one working woman casually remarked when I asked her about her plans with her new boyfriend, "It's too early for me to say that. Love now, it comes fast and it goes fast." In her case "failure" in this relationship was already considered a likely possibility, and not particularly regrettable. On the other hand, young women were generally careful not to give the impression that they advocated casual relationships or were flippant about love. Huan, an inexperienced first-year college student, expressed this more liberal but careful attitude:

> Having someone to date would be very good. Finding a marriage partner isn't so important, but a person needs someone to talk to and to help her. There's nothing wrong with it. It is not necessary to think about marriage. In the past there was a saying that people first married and then talked love. Now I think people first talk love and then consider marriage. It is not normal not to have some type of relationship. . . . But I feel love is very sacred, and people shouldn't be too frivolous about it.

Young men were even more likely to describe dating as a casual short-term interaction distinguished from marriage:

> Feng: Dating is just dating. I don't think about it that much.
>
> Ni: Dating is for fun, and getting married is for having a companion and
>   so that human beings don't become extinct.
>
> (unmarried men in their early twenties)

Practical circumstances could also lead men and women to enter a dating or sexual relationship with no thought of marriage. For instance, one twenty-seven-year-old woman informant had dated a man for five years, broken off the relationship, and was now planning to study abroad. After describing her hopes to leave the country, she remarked to her girlfriend that she intended to find a boyfriend to go out with before she left China: "I need to keep in practice; otherwise, I might develop an 'old-virgin syndrome.'" The notion of "keeping in practice," along with the sexual innuendo, might have been shocking to older men and women but could be accepted by younger friends with sexual experience.

While in the past, extensive dating experience might be seen as morally disgraceful, in the 1990s the inability to attract attention from the opposite sex is a much greater loss of face. Ting, a twenty-five-year-old hotel administrator, described her feelings as she began dating in her early twenties:

> All the other girls at work were talking about all the boys chasing
> them. . . . I thought I was an ugly duckling. When I went to work at this
> hotel, I finally felt the power of a girl's charms. Lots of boys were after me.
> Before that no boys chased me. I was very low-spirited and introverted. At
> the hotel I also began to dress very well and smartly. My clothes became
> the topic of conversation on the bus to work. I felt that I was able to feel
> my own self-worth. I felt better about myself and more and more people
> knew me. Many people called out my name at the hotel. Sometimes I
> didn't even know who they were.

Later in the conversation, she spoke of her envy for her friends' romantic sexual experiences and her desire to experience greater sexual intimacy with her boyfriend. Her story reflects the changing pressures on women in Shanghai. In the new market society, being desirable is more important than being sexually coy. While dating retained the purpose of finding a mate, it was also a matter of proving one's desirability, having fun, and enjoying the attentions of the opposite sex before marriage.

Paying the Bill: The Gendered Rhetoric of Face and Respect

From 1980 to 2000, personal incomes increased more than fourfold in Shanghai.[13] Expectations of dating expenses have risen even faster than incomes. Standards changed quickly during Shanghai's economic boom years of the mid-1990s. When I first went to Shanghai in 1993, a dinner at the newly opened Kentucky Fried Chicken was a respectable date. By 1999 Western fast food was a date suitable only for high school students. A respectable date for young adults, including dinner at a restaurant and a movie afterward, could easily cost two hundred yuan, or about a fifth of a factory worker's monthly salary. Although couples with their relationships "nailed down" often began saving money for marriage, a man trying to impress a woman at the beginning of a relationship was expected to spend considerable money on her.[14] Among the white-collar elite in Shanghai, a first date—meant to impress—often involved dining at a hotel restaurant or similar establishment and might cost several hundred yuan.

Young Shanghaiese with less money complained of the importance of money in dating. A male high school student told me: "Girls want people to spend money. They all want something. There is no love (ganqing) without money. You must be able to pay for things. Of course, when you have a deeper relationship it is different, but first you have to spend money." By the 1990s the stigma of accepting treats from men had largely disappeared. A woman gained considerable face from expensive dates, though women would sometimes split the bill with a man whom they wished to discourage. Women expected men to pay for first dates. On the other hand, steady boyfriend-and-girlfriend couples more evenly divided expenses. Young women prefer to emphasize the long-term equalization of expenses:

> Guan: Usually when we go out, I have it in mind of the amount he [the boyfriend] spends, and later when the chance comes, I will be faster and say, "I pay, I pay." I know how much he spends and give him back the money. On a more formal occasion, I will let him pay and give him some face.
> Moderator: He pays more?
> Guan: If he pays too much, I will slip some into his pocket.
> Moderator: Do you sometimes bring out money and let him pay?
> Guan: Yes, sometimes.
> Pu: Yes, but when it is time to pay, it looks like not giving him face if the woman pays. Besides, waiters always go to the man's side.

Moderator: How about if the man was rich?

Da: Then he must pay more. With ordinary salaried people we pay too.

(unmarried women in their early twenties)

Men and women thus enact a norm of proportional equity and a rhetoric of gender display. By "proportional equity," I mean that women and men agree they should both share in expenses, but men normally should be paying more. This norm reflects the expectation that women should date men who make more money than themselves and that their companionship has an intrinsic value that must be "appreciated" by men's generosity. By "gender display," I mean that men gain face from paying a bill and lose face by letting a woman treat him, especially on big occasions. Several women reported giving a boyfriend money so that he would be able to pay out of his pocket and keep his face. Some informants said that the practice of letting women pay was common only in Shanghai, and that more "masculine" northern men would never allow it.

Most men seemed to accept these norms. Among men who made very little or no money, however, the expectation that they should pay was burdensome, as emerged in the following conversation among single young men:

Moderator: Who usually pays when you go out together?

[Silence.]

Han: I feel embarrassed. [He earlier stated that he doesn't have a job or income.]

Moderator: Usually who pays more, you or your girlfriend?

Altogether: Overall, of course, men pay more.

Feng: If the man is chasing after the woman in the first place, he must pay more.

Moderator: How about when women chase after men?

Feng: Not sure. Traditional ideas still exist. In general the man pays more.

Han: When the waiter gives you the check, it is embarrassing to hand it over to the girl.

Feng: Yes, usually men pay.

Han: The waiters suck. They always hand checks to men.

Wan: Yes, they do.

Moderator: If you went window-shopping with a girlfriend and she liked a piece of clothing she saw, would you buy it for her?

Altogether: Of course, you have to.

Moderator: What will you do if it is too expensive?

Han: Even if I only had a little money left in the pocket, and by buying

this clothes I would have nothing left for tomorrow's groceries, I
would still buy it.
Feng: Yes. [Some people had different opinions.]

(unmarried men in their early twenties)

This conversation brings up the common practice of buying gifts for dates, often while strolling (*guangjie*) on weekends. Most middle-class women were reluctant to sound mercenary when discussing the meanings of the gifts they received. Women emphasized the romantic meanings (personal concern and
intimacy) rather than the expense. When speaking of others, however, Shanghaiese emphasized the status women gained from receiving expensive gifts.
Women in dating relationships also pointed out that there were practical limits on such gift giving in a stable relationship, as expressed by Cui: "It is pretty
expensive to buy a piece of clothing, usually about two hundred or three hundred RMB. If he spent money on both clothes and dining out and used up his
salary, I would end up paying for everything."

A theme that emerged in conversations with lower-status women was the
difficult struggle to get poorer men to perform "responsibly": to treat them to
dates and to buy them presents. Some young women even complained that
men invited them to dinner and then left them with the bill. Lower-status
women also complained about the lack of "respect" from wealthier men who
expected a quick sexual return on a date. Poorer men, in return, complained
about women's expectations of being treated to dates and gifts and expressed
their reluctance to be "tricked" by a woman.

This mutual mistrust emerged during a conversation with three friends,
Little Bai, his date Nina, and Little Zhu, in a low-corner restaurant in 1996:

> Little Bai said his old girlfriend used to "pout and whine" to get him
> to spend money, to take her out for dinner, or to get him to buy some-
> thing for her. I asked Nina if she would flirt with men to get them to spend
> money. She said, "Well, maybe I would do that in some circumstances."
> She looked at Bai, as though testing his response.
>
> He said, "I wouldn't let a woman influence me this way."
>
> She nudged Bai and said, "You mean if some girl you are with leans
> on you and pouts and asks you to buy her a little cup [that was just an ex-
> ample], then you would refuse her? I know you wouldn't for fear of los-
> ing face, would you?"
>
> Zhu said he would buy it. Bai laughed and replied that he would try
> to persuade her that the cup wasn't very good.

> She said, "There's no way you would say that. You would want your
> face."

This joking exchange underscores a tension between working-class men and women over the exchange of gifts in dating and the fragility of men's face in these situations. In reality, Bai was a notorious cheapskate with his numerous girlfriends, ignoring their hints (sometimes blatant requests) for expensive gifts. To save face, he seldom directly refused, usually finding an excuse or a way of procrastinating. In the summer of 2000, he put off a girlfriend's request for a mobile phone for two months, finally breaking off the relationship. Increasingly, the norms of dating were suited only to the well-off, while the poor scrambled to find the money to date and worried about the possibility of being cheated or disrespected. Working-class men easily became resentful of expensive dates that failed to achieve some desired result. Poor women easily became vulnerable to the crass exchange of intimacy for treats or the humiliation of not being treated properly.

Finally, money and gifts could compensate for a man's inability to commit himself emotionally and relationally, generally the case with married men. Women who dated married men often expected gifts and monetary recompense for being a "third person" with no "official status" (*mingfen*) and unable (or less able) to pursue a legitimate boyfriend. The compensation is pragmatic and symbolic. The failure of a third person to obtain gifts often meant a loss of face among her peers (women involved in such relations generally have a small group of female friends with similar experience). Yinyin, a twenty-two-year-old administrative assistant dating her married boss, described a conversation with her friend Grace, a Shanghai woman whose foreign lover was unwilling to marry her (similar to the third-person situation):

> My friend Grace will tell me, "Ask him for money, or don't be with him. Take him to the Mei Mei department store [Shanghai's high-fashion emporium] and ask him to buy you something. If he doesn't buy it for you, then just tell him to forget about it, don't stay with him." I don't think I could ever do something like that. And also I think Grace is just talking for talk's sake. She wouldn't do that. She is saying this from the standpoint of a friend. But she wouldn't do that herself.

While this advice may seem extreme, a logic of monetary compensation worked in many dating relationships that were not expected to have a long-term result, itself often a very material conception. More pragmatic than Yinyin described her, Grace persuaded her American lover to give her a hundred thousand yuan simply to stay on with him. Later they married (only formally, Grace said) so that she would be able to emigrate to the United States (see chapter 6). Still, even Grace emphasized the feelings she had for this man who helped her out.

The Unreliable Code of Loyalty

In the early 1980s, breaking up with a dating partner was taken quite seriously. A forty-seven-year-old man from a low-corner alleyway but with relatively good family conditions described his dating experiences in the late 1970s:

> We met each other at the work unit. She had been my apprentice. I didn't like her, but she kept chasing me. She took care of me, and because I was moved by her kindness, I dated her. She was twenty-four. We dated one year. She never gave me a chance to get away from her. I went to work and went home and she kept seeing me. I was a good catch for her. I was the only son, so there weren't many people in my house. We had a big house as well, by people's standards. This was what people really cared about then, housing and the family background. I didn't love her, but I never had a chance to meet other people. Our factory was a very serious work environment, because we were the first joint venture in China, so I didn't have time to fool around, nor have a chance to avoid her. In fact, the atmosphere was such that we were already considered a couple by everyone else, and there was no chance to break up. People would complain if you broke up back then. They would blame you. Even though you weren't a married couple, you were already considered a married couple. She was also good to my mother. And you know that when a girl is good to a future mother-in-law, it is easy to win her [the mother-in-law] over.

Women who dated in the early 1980s said that although breaking up a relationship in its beginning was considered normal, if a partner had been introduced to the parents on both sides ("brought home"), a breakup would have been a loss of face for both families. As one woman who dated around 1980 said, "When I was dating, this kind of thing [a breakup] was rare. If it happened, other people would look down on you. After all, their ideas were feudalist, and they had tight control over girls." For most young people in the early 1980s, a relationship of several months meant marriage was in the offing, while an introduction to the families of both partners was considered an informal engagement.[15] In the 1990s some youth seemed to retain these understanding, while others, probably the majority, had abandoned them.[16] For those youth who took traditional tokens of commitment such as meetings with parents seriously, a breakup could still feel like a breach of promise. Some older, more "traditional" men seemed to have a difficult time coping with the unexpectedly autonomous sexual strategies of younger women. For instance, one thirty-year-old white-collar woman complained to me about a man she dated in the early 1990s:

> One guy I was involved with came over to my house. I just thought, "Fine, if you want to come over, then come over." But he was thinking like an old Shanghaiese, like if you come over to my house, that means that I belong to you, that I have accepted you as my husband. So when I broke up with him soon after, he thought I had cheated him [pian ta].

This woman complained that this man was "foolish" and that most people no longer had such ideas.

Younger people dating in the 1990s usually claimed to value loyalty in relationships, at the same time they perceived the principle of free choice as even more fundamental:

> Qing: Before you are sure of the choice, you can try to date different people. After you are sure of your relationship, you should be one to one.
> Moderator: If you couldn't decide between two people, and you thought they were equally good?
> Qing: You should decide on one relationship as soon as possible.
> Moderator: If you had a stable relationship with someone, but you were introduced to someone with better conditions, what would you do?
> Cui: If I was not married, I could choose again.
> Moderator: If you discovered your boyfriend seeing somebody else, what would you do?
> Cui: Break up immediately. Maybe I would regret it later, but at that moment I would break up with him right away.
> Qing: I wouldn't be able to stand it and would break up with him.
> Luo: If he thought she was important, I think we should break up.
>   (unmarried women in their early twenties, mostly college educated)

Most men and women agreed that a serious dating relationship implied loyalty, but that people retained the right to choose again. Loyalty may be highly valued within the couple but not necessarily by friends, who may encourage each partner to explore other sexual possibilities, as in the frequently invoked proverb: "Don't die hanging on one tree" (Buyao si zaiyikeshushang). In general, the peer culture supported freedom of choice and an ideal of variety that contradict the romantic notion of loyalty, making loyalty an unreliable ideal. Women were as eager, or more eager, to exercise this right of choice as men, especially in the early stages of the relationship. Youth was assumed to be an advantage for women, and there was an implicit understanding that young women will be choosy. Some older men I interviewed stated that even in the early 1980s, women were more likely than men to date several men at once, because they were more intent on choosing a good husband before they got too old. Men were more likely to entertain the fantasy of having more than one steady romantic relationship (in "two different worlds") or engaging in secondary sexual "play" outside of a primary relationship. In opposition to this tendency, women demanded loyalty from steady boyfriends, but a degree of fair romantic "competition" was accepted both by men and women.

"I Was Cheated!"

"Cheating" (pian) or "being cheated" was a common theme among young people talking about dating. The first connotation of the word seems to be sexual. Although this usage had become something of a joke among more sexually experienced youth, Shanghai young people in the 1990s still mentioned the idea of a young woman "being cheated and lied to" (shangdangshoupian) as an expression for losing her virginity or her "heart" (or both) to a charlatan or playboy. An elementary school teacher I interviewed told me a story that illustrates this cautionary meaning of being cheated:

Many women are really very innocent, especially people who are elementary school teachers. This is because they spend all their time with children. They are often cheated by men. . . . I had a friend who went to a teaching college for elementary school teachers. Her parents were divorced and her father married another woman. She seldom saw them. She lived alone and relied completely upon her own small salary. You know, girls like to be pretty. This girl liked to dress up and go out. She went to a dance hall where she met a man. She said it was "love at first sight." Actually, this guy didn't have a real job and wasn't a very responsible person. Soon they started living together because the girl had her own place. The problem came to light when the girl brought home some money [two thousand RMB] that belonged to the school. The guy stole it and left the woman without returning the money. She didn't have enough money of her own to cover the expense, so the school found out about it. Also the woman was now four months pregnant. Not only was she cheated out of her money but also her virginity [ren]. At first the school was thinking about discharging her, but they took into account her difficult family background and just moved her to another school.

Although such cautionary tales seem somewhat quaint now, mothers in the 1990s still vaguely warned their daughters against being cheated by men. With the relaxation of norms against premarital sex, however, young women were less likely to feel cheated simply because they had sex with a man and then broke up. But the idea of being cheated went beyond discussions of virginity and remained in the vocabulary of dating relationships. One recent college graduate told me what she meant by "being cheated": "Being cheated is when, for example, a man puts out (fuchu) but the woman doesn't put out, or the woman puts out but the man doesn't put out. Both of these are bad." Putting out was not purely sexual. It had the connotation of emotional involvement and also of spending time and money. All were considered an investment that if unreciprocated would mean that one had been cheated. Although women were conventionally considered more naive and in greater danger of being cheated, those I interviewed actually seemed less naive than men about their chances of being hurt in love. In the case of an unexpected breakup, young men were more likely to cry foul. Men seemed to assume that women would be the passive partners in their plans and were shocked when women made unpredictable choices. Women could be very cynical about men's self-pitying stances in these cases. The following story was told to me by an educated white-collar Shanghai woman who had recently returned from a long stay in Japan, studying Japanese and working at odd jobs. The events took place in Japan but illustrate the "cheating" rhetoric of Shanghai young people:

When Shanghaiese boyfriends and girlfriends go together to Japan, it is considered common sense that they will live together over there. Here parents couldn't accept this, but over there no one will know. So when I went over there, I lived with him [her Shanghai boyfriend]. He thought this was a matter of course. But for me I thought we should have feelings for each other. Anyway I care a lot about my feelings. I could stand this relationship only for a while. I didn't think it was any good. His personality didn't suit me. So I left him. His reaction was really ridiculous. He thought that I had cheated him [qipian ta]. He thought I was using him. He thought he had suffered a "loss." I can't believe that a man could feel like that. He wasn't really acting like a man. He wasn't mature. I like to make my own decisions in life, but he couldn't ever make up his own mind. When we broke up, he called his friends to come over and act as a referee between us. That was so ridiculous. This added to my sense of repulsion. Another strange thing is that he liked to show me off in front of others. Before I came over, he had told all his friends about me, bragging about me in front of them. He bragged about me to all his friends, so when he lost me, he felt like he had lost face. That's the strangest thing. He felt losing me was a loss of face.

In fact, she understood his claims of a loss of face quite well but was choosing to dismiss them. The discourse of cheating and being cheated in the 1990s reflects an understanding of dating as an exchange that is emotional, sexual, and material. Men are expected to be generous in this exchange (a concept that includes gracious treatment in a breakup) but often aren't. Women are expected to be faithful but often aren't. While men are considered more likely to cheat women sexually and women to cheat men financially, this certainly is not always the way things work out. Men and women of all classes share in this discourse, but working-class people of both genders use the language more vigorously. Poor people feel more vulnerable to cheating and betrayal in a dating system (and larger social system) in which income levels increasingly diverge and romance depends on expensive consumption. On the other hand, what seems like cheating to one partner may simply seem like the pursuit of a free and attractive choice from the perspective of the other. Seen without the normative ideas of "feelings," "loyalty," and "fate" (see chapter 6), cheating is simply a complaint about the normal pragmatic tactics that many people pursue.

"Old Men" and "Old Ladies": The Play Rhetoric of Marriage

As dating relationships became more sexually and emotionally involved, they borrowed from the language of marriage, the only model youth have for a sexually and emotionally intimate relationship. The term young people publicly used to describe newly met boyfriends and girlfriends often was the ambiguous term "friend," which could mean a romantic interest or a nonsexual friendship. But for serious relationships, youth increasingly used the more intimate and playful terms "old lady" (laopo) and "old man" (laogong), terms previously reserved for husband and wife. The terms implied a sexual relationship and showed the increased sexualization of courtship. They did not necessarily imply an intent to marry, however, merely a claim of temporary sexual possession. The terms could also be used as euphemisms for "sexual relations," as in the expression "She has already been my old lady." Young men were particularly quick to use the term "old lady" to lay claim to a girl, though young women sometimes played the same linguistic game (even prostitutes with clients).

Part of this play rhetoric of marriage involved performances of domestic happiness. It is not surprising that many playboys were also good cooks. One twenty-one-year-old hotel clerk described how he seduced girls into sexual relationships through performances of domesticity:

> Sometimes I will ask them to come over and eat at my home. My parents are not at home during the day. First I cook dinner, then we watch a little TV, and then we have activities on the bed. They really like it when I cook for them. They think, "This one can do housework; he really takes care of the family." They like that.

Given his lack of "real life" economic credentials, his youth, and the short-term nature of these relationships, it is not likely his dinner companions took his performances of domesticity as a serious indication of marriageability. Rather, domestic performances and marital role-playing are a common romantic rhetoric that appropriates the comfortable and familiar images of marriage. Young women in particular find this domestic play to be "romantic," and this young man had learned this romantic ploy.

Young women also perform domestic acts as a romantic token. Take, for instance, the following exchange between a woman focus group participant and a young woman moderator:

> Cui: I think romance comes from ordinary life. It is not something you
>   force yourself to do. If you are in love, a gesture and a word are ro-
>   mantic. Sometimes I clean up things for him, and he will think I am
>   good to him, that I am a good girl [guainuuhai].
> Moderator: This reminds me of Tong Ange [a Taiwan pop star]. He fell in
>   love with his girlfriend because she cleaned up his things. He
>   thought it was romantic afterward.
>   (unmarried women in their early twenties, including moderator)

Ironically, this eroticization of domestic work as a display of femininity seemed to have greater appeal among young women than among the young men it was meant to impress. When the moderator mentioned the example of a girl doing her boyfriend's laundry as romantic to a group of young men, they laughed.

> Moderator: I heard that the most romantic thing a girl could do for her
>   boyfriend was washing his socks.
> [All laughing.]
> Feng: That is a feeling only of girls. [Others agree.]
>   (unmarried men in their early twenties)

For most younger men at least, the better expression of romance was more directly erotic (e.g., the head on the shoulder, as discussed in the next chapter). Correspondingly, successful playboys and seductresses mastered the romantic rhetoric that the opposite sex found more appealing.

Borrowing from the language of marriage also meant borrowing from the language of extramarital relationships, including the term "third person." Popularized through media depictions of extramarital affairs, this term refers to the lover of a married person. However, in Shanghai I heard this term used—often by teenagers—to refer to someone who became romantically involved with a person already in a relationship. For instance, Linda, a nineteen-year-old woman who was "dating" a man already living with his girlfriend, said: "If I found out he is seeing other girls than me, then I don't want to be his girlfriend. But I can't expect him not to see his girlfriend, because, in fact, I am the third person breaking into this relationship. So I don't have a right to ask him not to see her." Breaking into (*charu*) a relationship was considered bad form, but there were now rules to deal with it. The third person in dating relations was expected to follow a kind of queuing rule, as was usually the case in extramarital affairs. Most importantly, the third person should not interrupt the primary relationship. This "third-person" rule of dating was observed as much in its breach as in its observation, but it was widely understood. This is not to imply that all girls and women were willing to accept being the third person or having a third person break in. For instance, a sixteen-year-old girl I met at a discotheque jauntily explained that she broke up with her boyfriend because "a third person entered the relationship." She seemed proud to use this adult language to describe her own experience, which goes to show how the adult language of marriage and sexuality was appropriated by youth as a sign of their own maturity. Youth also appropriated the adult language of commodified relationships. Unmarried young men with extra money and time to spend dating several women talked about "keeping a mistress" (*baomi*) in addition to a regular girlfriend. A teenage girl I met at a disco (see chapter 9) described herself as being "kept" (*bao*) by a twenty-one-year-old unmarried man. Teenage and young adult sexuality thus modeled itself upon the larger and more public world of mature adult sexuality, including extramarital and commercial relations.

"Control": The Rhetoric of Autonomy

Being "controlled" (*guan*) by an overpossessive lover was the strongest and probably most frequent complaint I heard from young people, especially women. Women's complaints about control reflect a struggle for autonomy in relationships. First some young women wanted to keep an open door for a new and possibly better relationship (including the freedom to date other men, usually described as "friends") and resented boyfriends' attempts to monopolize their time. Some young men did strive to control their girlfriends' movements. In an extreme case, a boyfriend distributed photos of his girlfriend to friends at the university she was planning to attend so they would be able to tell him if she was dating other men. ("I told him, 'That's not very good,'" she said. "He really cares about me, but his way of doing it isn't good." Later they separated.) Sexual intercourse was taken by many men as a special concession of possession. Some women mentioned fear of male possessiveness as a primary reason for not engaging in casual sexual affairs.

For the women I interviewed, freedom from monitoring or control was a principal criteria for a good relationship, and it was one of the things they said they enjoyed about life when they were not in a steady relationship. Many Shanghai women, however, took pride in the reputation of Shanghai women for independence. For instance, one night I had a conversation with a woman acquaintance in a popular low-corner bar. She said, "I am already twenty-three, so I have to think about getting married. Thirty is really right around the corner. I don't want to end up being thirty and not be able to get married." She put her head on my shoulder in flirtatious mock despair. She already had a boyfriend who was a seaman and frequently away from Shanghai. When he was away, she saw other men, she said. She complained to me that her boyfriend tried to control her when he was in town. "I don't like boys who are always looking to see if some friend of their girlfriend is in the bar with her, worried [about who she is with]." She then laughed, saying, "They are like this because Shanghai girls are really tough [lihai]. You should know that. If their boyfriend goes out with a girl, they won't just sit at home and complain; they will just go out and find someone themselves."

The marriage orientation of dating should not be confused with a yearning for traditional married life. Shanghai youth, in general, valued autonomy from relationships, both men and women sharing an idea that they should leave one another time and space for independent activities and activities with other people. As one young man said in a focus group, "Even after getting married, both sides should have their own social circles. It is not fun always occupying the other person." Most youth felt that traditional Chinese marriages involved too great a sacrifice of personal time and social activities. This attitude was especially prevalent among women. One reason for this might be the widespread perception of marriage as an unromantic and pragmatic arrangement in which women have almost no time for themselves.[17] Many young Shanghaiese were thus wary of dating relations that encroached too much on personal autonomy, career development, and social activities. Both men and women expected to pursue education and employment. And though women described a growing tension between career and marriage choices, dating was not always put in first place.

Subversive Dating Strategies

As in the market economy generally, increased freedom in dating brought increased inequality and increased struggle to change one's position. For some youth, cheating and playing around become alternative, short-term dating strategies, cut off from the conventional search for a marital partner. In contrast with the normative grammar presented above, I want to introduce two relatively low-status men and women who worked the margins of this conventional dating system. As complete examples they are not representative of youth in general, but their moral rhetoric and strategies reflect the constraints and opportunities of the market-oriented dating culture.

Finding a "Refuge" Is Difficult

Gan, a fashionable and attractive nineteen-year-old woman I met in 1996, lived in a shanty house in a low-corner neighborhood not far from that where Linda lived. She is a "returned youth," the offspring of the nearly 1 million Shanghaiese sent to work in distant cities during the 1950s and 1960s. Thousands of such young people live in Shanghai without their parents at their sides. In her case, she was sent back to live with her grandparents, who were themselves usually absent from Shanghai. When I met her, she was living alone with a cousin and a temporary roommate, a Shanghai girlfriend who ran away from home. Gan moved to Shanghai from western China at age twelve and, like many returned youth, was unprepared to compete with native-born Shanghai children in the schools. She worked first at a hotel and then at a private entertainment group in the popular new occupation of public relations girl, a cross between secretary, receptionist, and entertainment hostess. She typed and entertained customers on their many nights and weekends out with her bosses.

During the last year she lived on and off with a boyfriend in his room. She broke up with him a few months before I met her. Five years older than Gan, he had a job adjusting sound in a disco and was unable to develop better career prospects. "He just sat around and thought about things without ever knowing what to do," she said—a criticism of purposeless young men common among young women in Shanghai. Gan said she was now involved in a sexual relationship with a married college teacher who recently returned to Shanghai from Australia. "He doesn't love his wife," she explained in defense of her third-person role.

At my request, she showed me her home, an old courtyard house (shikumen), designed for one family but now divided into numerous one-room apartments. Her male cousin lives in the tiny back room (tingzijian) off the rickety, unlit stairwell, more a ladder than a stair. He didn't look up as we passed him on the stairs, a few inches from his bed, where he lay watching television. "He doesn't bother [guan] me," she explained later. Nor did she concern herself with her neighbors. Her parents, whom she described as "very conservative," were far away. She showed me the tiny attic room she had recently begun sharing with another nineteen-year-old woman who was having unspecified "troubles with her family." Her roommate sat on the bed, the only space available in the tiny room, watching a small TV set. She was also a public relations girl. She was dressed in a DKNY halter top (probably a pirated imprint of the U.S. brand) and black leather shorts, ready for the disco they were planning to visit.

Gan and her roommate illustrate how young women live in the interstices between the poor alleyways and the commercial spaces of the boulevard. For them, work in the booming service sector is easy to find. Frequently they can make more money than their parents, enough to buy the clothes and makeup to create a fashionable and attractive appearance. Their appearance is no casual preoccupation. In service occupations like public relations, waitressing, and hostessing, a girl's looks are an investment, and an easygoing attitude toward sexuality is encouraged. In the extreme case, some public relations girls are expected to provide sexual services to their bosses or clients. These jobs pay fairly well (over a thousand RMB a month) but offer no long-term prospects.

In the sexual marketplace—which for them is not so easily distinguished from the labor market—these young women face the same dilemma of short-term riches and long-term difficulties. "Most girls now want to find a 'refuge' [guisu]," Gan said, meaning a wealthy or successful husband who can provide material security. She admitted that money was more important than love in her choice of a marriage partner, though she insisted it was important that her husband love her. She said that she was also looking for a "refuge." "But sometimes I feel just like playing around," she said, perhaps suggestively. She liked to talk about the rich men she went out with, but she soberly conceded that her various boyfriends were unlikely to provide the secure future she aspired to:

It really isn't that easy to meet someone with good conditions. Most girls end up marrying a pretty ordinary guy. After all, there aren't many guys with really good conditions. Many of them just want to fool around with these girls, but they won't marry them. They will try to find a respectable [zhengjing] girl to marry. They probably think the girls they fool around with aren't reliable.

Gan seemed to be seeing men other than the married college teacher. For low-status but attractive young women, the dating culture offers fun and entertainment with older and married men, but few long-term prospects with young men their own age. Dating becomes a form of "eating spring rice," a series of sexual relationships with men who will probably not commit to a long-term relationships with a low-status and sexually active woman. These temporary exchanges might be condemned by parents, but these young women justify them as fair, mutually rewarding, and superior to the alternative of more socially equal relationships with poor, unmotivated, and unreliable young men like Gan's boyfriend and the young man I will discuss next.

"Girls Are So Vain"

Johnny, introduced in chapter 1, was a handsome and charming young man of twenty when I met him in 1996. He worked on and off as a cook and waiter in restaurants and as a dance leader at discotheques in Shanghai. I interviewed him at a Japanese hamburger chain near Absolute Disco, where he wolfed down a burger and fries, complaining all the time about the taste (he was trained as a cook). He wore a leather vest, ripped jeans, and a tight white T-shirt that revealed his flat stomach. He was a bit thin, but, as his female dance partner pointed out, he was fairly muscular. We started by talking about his experiences with girls in high school. His story provides an understanding of the moral rhetoric of young men who frequent the nightlife world and live at (sometimes beyond) the margins of "respectability." More generally, the way he tells his story illustrates the resentment that impecunious men feel toward a dating culture based on consumption and expense. Unlike most young men, he enjoyed telling his story, a good example of the ironic "victim/player" narrative described in the next chapter. He began with his "first love" (I edited my questions out of this transcript):

[In high school] I saw a girl in the school yard. She really had a feminine air [nuurenwei], but not in that cheap way [qingfu]. Actually I guess you wouldn't say she was really pretty. She was nearsighted and had really little eyes, but I always judge girls just by the feeling they give me and not something else. I just felt that the way she walked was very pretty, very elegant. I never had the chance to talk to her. I had no self-respect. I was quite stupid. I didn't understand what was popular [with girls]. . . .

In order to get close to her, I stole some dollars from my parents. Then I started taking her to eat evening snacks and taking her out to the KFC. She really liked me. She thought I had money. [When my mom found out,] my mom kicked me out of the house [for stealing]. So I couldn't take her out anymore. When the girl found out I had no money, she started going out with another guy. Girls are so vain. They like either the kind of guy who they can play around with, the kind of bad boy who may even hit her. Or they like guys with money.

I decided to get revenge. I would go to dances and ask a girl to dance the two-step. I would feel her up. If she didn't give me a negative reaction, then I would take her out to eat a midnight snack. I would get her drunk, and then go home or go to a hotel or something and have sex. But the problem is that I never really got the feeling of revenge from this. I mean the girls didn't really care. Neither of us loved each other, so no one was hurt.

So finally I met a girl who especially reminded me of my first love. I took all my savings, and in one week, I spent all of my savings on her. I spent four thousand RMB. I spent all of this money on her. She started sleeping over with me. She said she trusted me, that I wouldn't do anything. The second time she slept over, she said, "I really like you." The third time she said, "I really like you, so if you want me, you can have me." That's how it happened. After that we started living with each other. She just went home while her parents weren't at home and took some clothes. Later she left a note saying she was living with a boy she loved, but her parents were working. They didn't know who I was or where she was living. [Linda told me this girl was only sixteen.] We lived together half a year. My father told me not to do it, but he was unable to control me. This was the happiest time of my life. We would go shopping for food in the market together. Then the three of us [including the father] would sit down to dinner together. Then we would play cards awhile, and finally we would go to sleep together. It was very, very sweet. She would wake me up, and then I would go to work.

But I was worried that she was physically very unhealthy and she was making only about six hundred a month at her job at a factory, so I told her to quit work and I would take care of her. At that time I was making three thousand a month [at the hotel restaurant] and thought I could take care of her. I was very happy then, just walking down the street together, we felt really happy. I made a mistake, though, letting her quit work. She stayed at home with nothing to do and got really bored. She took the spending money I gave her and went to the dance hall, these really cheap low-class dance halls. All the people that go to these places are really the dredges of society. She started learning really bad things. She learned to smoke and started cursing. When I complained, she got angry with me. She said I didn't give her her freedom. Finally, she met some people and got a job in a karaoke place as a hostess, actually that is just a kind of prostitute, you know, sitting and talking with people and drinking with them, and letting them touch your face. Finally, you get used to it. She would meet the big bosses, these customers, and her face got really thick [lost her sense of shame]. She got used to it. By then I didn't have any money. I had less and less income. Afterward she started going out more and more with these bosses, just playing around.

I told her at the time, "It is easy to find a rich guy, but difficult to find a guy who really loves you." But she didn't care. After a while she started often not coming home. I knew that meant she was sleeping somewhere else, that she was being unfaithful to me. She was cheating me because this whole time, I didn't go out with other girls. I told her she was just treating my place like a hotel. This was really painful. I really tried to persuade her over and over. Finally, we broke up. I was completely disheartened. At first she really loved me. At first she would threaten to kill herself just if I made a little joke about seeing another girl or something. Later she went bad. She became really vain; she didn't care about anything. I had sold all my clothes and spent all my money just to buy her clothes. She always used to ask me to buy things for her. When she left, she had three suitcases full of clothes, all of which I bought for her.

Now I really no longer believe in love at first sight, just meeting a girl and falling in love with her. I don't want another tragedy. So now I don't believe in this. I believe in just playing around with a girl. That way you don't have to take responsibility. I don't want to be burdened by her, and I don't want to be hurt by her. I was really hurt by this girl.

Two years after he told me this story, I returned to Shanghai and met Johnny again. Still good-looking and fashionably dressed but clearly in low spirits, he was living with another teenage girlfriend who similarly had run away from her family to stay with Johnny and his father. According to Johnny, her parents were pleased that someone else was "taking care of her." Johnny told me that the period shortly after our first interview was the "high point of [his] career."

He worked as a dancer at a nightclub and picked up well-off young women who would give him money to accompany them. Johnny began to see hustling as his primary profession and bragged to me about a twenty-four-year-old Hong Kong woman tourist who paid him three hundred yuan a day to accompany her every night for a week, leaving him a thousand after sleeping with him on her final night in Shanghai.

> Now I have gone downhill in my life. I have reached a low point. I was picking up Hong Kong and Taiwan girls. Then I was doing "golden cage girls" [mistresses of wealthy men]. Then it was K-girls [karaoke hostesses] who were doing well. Then it was K-girls who were not doing so well. Now it is a girl who doesn't do anything, who doesn't work and doesn't let me go out at all. . . . She controls me. My life is terrible. I don't know how I have ended up like this. My family likes her. When she complains to them—my father or grandfather—about me, they help her to control me. . . . She doesn't work. She doesn't want to work. She just wants to stay at home with me. She thinks that if she goes to work, I will go out to make money [by seeing other girls].

After I left him that night, Johnny stayed on in the disco where we were chatting, hoping to meet a woman to hustle. It was a rare chance away from his girlfriend and to try to make some money, he explained. That night his girlfriend called me at my home at 3:30 A.M. Johnny hadn't returned. (When I met him again in 2000, the girlfriend had predictably taken to hostessing herself. Johnny was still trying to hustle well-off women, but his physical charms and social capital were fading. His latest fanciful plan was to go to Japan to work in a Japanese host club or join an underworld gang.)

Johnny plays with and around the moral codes and conventional grammar of the dating culture. His romantic rhetoric is typical of the youth dating culture, although the practices he actually engages in contradict conventional expectations or bend the rules in ways that others would not consider legitimate. In the extreme case, an ethos of sexual and monetary exchange, not uncommon in working-class dating culture, leads him into direct prostitution. Still, his understanding of sexual relationships is highly moralistic. Though they are unevenly and strategically applied, he frequently invokes norms of faithfulness and responsibility, of equity, and of the appropriateness of revenge when this equity is violated. He also practices and espouses the Chinese equivalent of "family values," engaging in a multigenerational model of premarital cohabitation with his father and girlfriend, whom he "wants" to leave but "can't," unless she moves out of her own desire. His narrative exhibits the typical posture of the Shanghai playboy, whose resentment and sexual manipulation of women are justified by the "wounds" that past romantic experiences and low social status have inflicted upon him.

Dating has become part of a consumer culture that values choice, pleasure, play, and the pursuit of fashion. Youth balance these individualistic consumer expectations with relational codes of romanticism, face preservation, respect, domesticity, and loyalty. Despite the norm-governed character of this new culture, the desires it produces are not easily contained within expected patterns. As with the larger Chinese market culture within which it develops, dating is subversive of its own normative goals, "producing its own points of resistance,"[18] allowing poor youth alternative strategies of cheating, hustling, and "eating spring rice" to the dominant strategy of compulsory monogamy. Johnny's and Gan's cases show how some socially marginal youth appropriate the institutions and codes of the youth dating culture to achieve a lifestyle that defies convention. In pursuing their material and sexual fantasies, Johnny and Gan don't reject the standard moral grammar but creatively exploit its ambiguous and contradictory categories to justify their multiple premarital sexual relations, commercial sexual exchanges, and affairs with married people. They explain their behaviors within a rhetoric that combines consumerism with romanticism, domesticity with sexual play, and loyalty with a strong sense of their own wounded dignity. The moral grammar of youth dating culture thus allows a flexible rhetoric of justification that exists alongside a more authoritative rhetoric of moral critique.

The Changing Institutional Context
Work Units and Schools

During the 1980s there was a dramatic reduction in institutional monitoring of premarital sexual behavior in China. Work units moved from discouraging romance among youth to facilitating it through youth league–organized dance parties and other outings, ending prohibitions on dating among factory apprentices. As with the organization of high school and college dances in the United States, Chinese work units were also trying to provide young workers with "orderly" and monitored courtship spaces to keep them out of the "chaotic," unmonitored spaces that were springing up at the same time. By the 1990s even these paternalistic efforts were flagging, and most work units began to consider romance a matter for individuals to resolve. The exceptions included work units that were overwhelmingly male or female and organized activities with work units with an apposite gender ratio. Many youth league cadres completely abandoned the principle that activities be monitored and simply handed out free passes to commercial dance halls. Censure of "immoral activities" by work units was becoming increasingly rare. By 2000 unmarried cohabiting couples could openly discuss their living arrangements in many work environments.[19] Even malicious gossip or harassment by overzealous or sexually aggressive colleagues became less threatening because the free labor market allowed people to change jobs and more easily escape meddling and harassment.

Schools are another matter. Almost no institution in China is more conservative than the national education establishment, a trend strengthened by the political backlash in higher education subsequent to the 1989 student movements. Shanghai high schools and junior high schools still prohibit dating among students (zaolian, or "premature love"), though enforcement varies from school to school. High school homeroom teachers often call in the parents of boys and girls who appear to be dating for talks about their children's behavior. Parents, however, only seem increasingly resentful of such school policies. When one prestigious Shanghai journalist was told his twelve-year-old daughter was "dating," he became involved in such a violent altercation with the homeroom teacher that he had to move his daughter to another school to assure she wouldn't suffer from a vindictive teacher. (The school continued to support the standpoint of the teacher, despite the father's status.) On the other hand, teachers sometimes covered up for students. For instance, one high school student told me that a classmate got pregnant and had an abortion, but "the teachers kept it hidden and she graduated." Such arbitrary enforcement of policies usually favors children with a good relationship to the teacher or other personal connections.

Despite such policies, students I spoke with described dating in Shanghai high schools as common and "normal" (zhengchang)—evoking the flexible new peer-cultural moral touchstone of normalcy. According to other informants, this was a big change from the 1980s, when high school dating was still considered deviant among students (although it did occur). Wei, a recent high school graduate, told me she had a casual boyfriend her last year in high school. Although her mother disapproved, she said, her father (who lived in Europe) told her it was okay to have boyfriends, as long as they weren't too serious. She described the culture of sex and dating in her prestigious Shanghai high school in the 1990s (she graduated in spring 1996): "In our third year in high school, [my mother] found out we were dating. This was because the teacher found out. You should know that high school teachers are especially against this—students dating. She [the homeroom teacher] made a telephone call to my home. She told my parents to watch me. She also called my boyfriend's home."

I asked her if there were many such cases. She laughed at my term "case." "Every [homeroom] class had at least five or six cases that were found out by the teacher. Out of fifty people in my class, about thirty of them dated [tanguo]. The other twenty were either really stupid, really ugly, or bookworms [shudaizi]."

I asked what kinds of students dated. "Boys chase girls and girls chase boys. Both are really daring [danzi hen da]. There are quite a few girls who will straightout chase guys. They will chase these boys who are especially outstanding or especially good-looking. These boys have a really high value. They can go out with a lot of girls. I don't like that kind of guy."

She said she wasn't sure if any of these couples had sex. "Actually they [the girls] never talk about it. At most they will talk about, 'Oh, when I have a husband, it will be so and so.' But they will never talk about this very clearly. This is something they feel much too shy to talk about. Perhaps they will talk about this while joking. In class, people make a lot of sexual jokes. The boy sitting in front of me always made a lot of dirty jokes. That's normal."

I asked if any girls were upset about this joking. She said, "Yes, there were two really conservative girls in our class. They are really very straight. If people start talking about these things, they will just leave. They are really bookworms."

I asked if girls will talk about kissing.

> Yeah, they will talk about this. That's really normal. But girls prefer to sit and talk about all the things that happened with their boyfriend. They will talk about their perspectives and their way of thinking about him. Boys like to talk more about the physical side of things. And you know boys, they really like to watch these "yellow" [pornographic] movies. They've all seen them. I don't want to see this. Boys look at them. . . . I think this is normal. . . . Probably I will see one too one day.
>
> Girls talk about boys, which boy is good-looking. They especially talk about a boy looking like a star. And they talk about stars, movie stars and singers. They especially talk about who is best-looking. Looks come first and then their singing.
>
> Anyway, most high school romances are just people playing around. Very few of them are successful. I don't think they really know what love is. Maybe it is just a kind of good feeling about the other person. Maybe it is just the attraction of the opposite sex.

For this young woman, navigating the sexual strictures of high school in Shanghai was not especially difficult. Other than her one run-in with the homeroom teacher, she was able to enjoy moments of romance without any apparent damage to her emotional well-being or academic performance. Unlike most women a decade earlier, she was entering university with a positive experience of dating, considerable knowledge of sex, and confidence in her ability to deal with sexual relations.

Families

Traditionally, marriage in China was a matter for families to decide. On the other hand, surveys show a long-term transition toward increasing autonomy of partner choice.[20] Men who dated in the early 1980s confirmed reports of a strong parental influence on courtship then:

> Jiang: When we were dating, if the partner's parents thought you were okay, then everything was set. What did we look at back then? Parents being Party members, belonging to a good class. . . . We would look at each other's family background and wanted to get a straight one.
>
> Hong: The girl would want to know everything about you—family situation, personal quality. . . .
>
> Jin: Back then, girls all listened to their parents. Back then in our time, to put it in a nasty way, it was marrying the mother-in-law. Family [opinion] was very important.
>
> (married men in their late thirties)

In the 1990s such concern with a partner's family seemed to be decreasing. Young people also made their own decisions about whom to date. Parents exerted control over adult children's dating practices primarily through curfews intended to curb sexual behavior. As a rule, sons had less strict curfews. Some parents maintained strict curfews for daughters well into their late twenties, while others (probably far fewer) let even their high school daughters date in the evenings. Coresidence inevitably led to parental involvement in children's dating behavior, but could also lead to the co-optation of parental authority by strong-willed children. The most predictable, and stereotypical, form of parental involvement in dating involved disapproval of a particular partner. Such conflicts could escalate into protracted battles between families and between parents and children. In contemporary Shanghai, parents were by no means assured of victory in these battles. Predictably, parents tended to emphasize practical matters, restraining youth from rash decisions. With young people often making higher incomes than their parents, the economic leverage of parents over children had diminished. Most young people expected to live alone with their spouse after marriage and rely upon their own resources, although parents could still be the source of important gifts.

A less widely discussed but seemingly common problem involved the obverse situation, in which parents aggressively supported a relationship. Two young women I interviewed had this experience. Both were attractive graduates of prestigious universities dating men with arguably poorer "conditions" than their own (less prestigious jobs and family backgrounds). In both cases, the parents of the young men encouraged the young women to sleep over in their homes while they were dating (either on weekends or for longer periods), apparently to encourage the deepening of the relationship. In one case, the parents seemed to be achieving success. In the other case, the young woman left the young man despite their having slept together several months in his parents' home. Such practices of cohabitation seemed more likely in the homes of young men, though I also knew of cases of young women's parents allowing a boyfriend to stay in their home, despite the couple not yet being married or formally engaged. (Formal engagement ceremonies are rare in Shanghai, so the category of engagement is ambiguous.)

As a result of these practices (and the tight housing market), many cases of premarital cohabitation I observed in Shanghai involved boyfriends and girlfriends living together with their parents, a pattern that cannot be attributed to the liberal attitudes of the parents involved, but more to their pragmatic recognition that their children were already involved in a sexual relationship and a desire to monitor and guide the relationship. In these cases, cohabitation—as with many other forms of sexual behavior—should not be seen as rebellious in intent, but rather as subversive in outcome. Children were following the conventional norm of earnestly seeking a partner based on feelings. Parents were trying to guide children into a safe and successful domesticity. Outcomes were unpredictable, however. Children could break off these relationships more easily than marriages, and some (like Johnny) could enter into several such relationships sequentially. As a result, a norm of premarital chastity was subverted, as will be discussed in greater detail in chapter 7.

Dancing around the Fortress

"Marriage is like a fortress: all those on the outside want to get in. All those on the inside want to get out."[21] This saying was popular in Shanghai in the 1990s along with similar bromides like "Marriage is the tomb of love" and "Get married early so that at least you will be happy half your life" (after you are divorced). For many young people, marriage meant the end of the romance and leisure of courtship. Hence many young people who participated in my focus groups, especially women, stated they would prefer not marrying. Most agreed, however, that marriage was inevitable. And for women it was often considered a practical economic strategy. Shanghai youth might denigrate marriage, but it continued to define courtship as a goal, as a point of contrast, and as a positive and negative standard for sexual relationships. The new dating culture thus evolved in a tension between a desire for and a wariness of marriage.

First of all, dating remains a search for a marriage partner. In a newer sense, however, Shanghai youth also see dating, and premarital sexual intimacy, as a chance to develop deeper feelings before marriage and reduce the emotional distance with a partner that makes the "fortress" of marriage so formidable to begin with. As dating relationships become more sexual, they borrow from the language of marriage as the only shared model for committed relationships. This playacting makes premarital sexual relations more familiar and more morally acceptable, but they remain less "real" and permanent than marriage. Dating thus has become a "play form" of marital sexuality, including its earnest familial language and deviant variants such as the third person. But it is play wedded to an external goal, marriage, from which it easily deviates, but without which it loses its dominant meaning.[22]

On the other hand, in a change from early Chinese courtship practices, dating relationships are now defined in opposition to the seriousness of marriage. Dating has become a time in which love is pursued for its own pleasure as much as for the purpose of finding a mate, part of the temporary pursuit of fashionable experiences, like wearing sexy clothes and going dancing. Time spent dating is as much "consumption" as "capital investment." Sexual competition through dating is a game of self-affirmation, and dating relationships can be discarded if something better comes along. Even high school students have developed a dating culture, augmented by images from the sexualized popular culture of American movies, Hong Kong pop songs, and Japanese teenage fashion. In sum, dating matches an orthodox goal—finding a partner—with subversive means—having casual fun—so that the result is an unstable mix of earnestness and play.

Finally, dating gives youth the means to play, but it exacerbates social inequalities and gendered positions in the sexual economy. Poorer Shanghai men complain of their inability to pay for dates and their inability to hold on to the women they date. Poorer Shanghai women complain of the inability of poorer men to treat them to dates and the lack of respect richer men accord them. Some such young men and women bend the conventions of the dating culture into alternative strategies—hustling, cheating, and gold digging—that short-circuit the traditional goals of dating and subvert its norms of fidelity, earnestness, and honesty. The consumer culture of dating thus produces winners and losers—and cheaters.

FEELINGS
Good and Memorable

"That's Romantic, Isn't It?"

I met Ailin when I first arrived in Shanghai in 1993. We were standing on the deck of a large ferry to Putuo Island, popular as a weekend escape from Shanghai, and I struck up a conversation. Although we had just met, she soon was telling me about a young man she was dating, frequently interjecting the word "romantic" into an ardent description of their budding relationship. New in Shanghai, but familiar with Chinese courtship from two years in Taiwan, I assumed that such an open proclamation meant they soon would be married. Ailin stood together with a cool and sardonic young woman, who interrupted Ailin's narrative with derisive quips about how her own boyfriend had become a real bore and that such feelings of romance were doomed to be short-lived. As it turned out, Ailin soon broke up with the boyfriend, while I went on to marry this second woman, after a long romance that began on the boat that day. It was nearly three years before I sat down to interview Ailin about the developments in her love life. She could remember the meeting on the boat, but not the man whom she was discussing that day. "That's too long ago," she said. "I must have nixed him. . . . If I decide I don't like them, I nix them pretty fast," she said, laughing.

I interviewed her Saturday afternoon in McDonald's. Now a twenty-five-year-old manager at the Shanghai branch of a foreign bank, she found it hard to fit me into her schedule of work and study for her upcoming exams for U.S. business school. She came casually dressed, but with her lips glowing with bright red lipstick. She was charming, intelligent, attractive, and emotive. Several times during the interview, tears welled up in her eyes as she described memorable events in her past, especially her first love. It was June 1989, she said, the days of the student protests all over China, including Shanghai. She fell in love with a young man who was active in the movement.

"June 4th was a very, very special time. I felt like we were acting a role in a movie. . . . There is this movie called The Song of Youth (Qingchunzhige) about a love affair among students during the May 4th Movement. It was like that. In those circumstances it is easy for your brain to catch fever. That's romantic isn't it?" Several times during our conversation she asked me this rhetorical question. For her, "romance" (langman) seemed to be a powerfully positive and legitimating idea.

She then explained that because the affair happened during her last months in high school, her parents always blamed it for her surprisingly poor scores on the college entrance exams. She had to settle for a two-year college and a career in finance rather than studying medicine at a four-year college. I asked her if she regretted the affair.

> I don't regret it at all. It was a very, very good moment. . . . But there are things I really think about. If it weren't for all of this, I could have had a completely different profession. I could have been a doctor, as I wanted. These events really changed my life. I was not able to get into a good university, and then I lost my boyfriend. Sometimes I can't figure this out. Afterward I became very inward. In high school I was really happy, cheerful, and outgoing.
>
> He came from Harbin. He was a graduate student. Actually this guy was bad. But in one month together, I only saw the good side of him. Later we just wrote letters back and forth. I didn't know his failings.

"My family was very ashamed of this whole business," she said, changing tone.

> My mother was adamantly opposed. My mother didn't like him because he was a non-Shanghaiese [waidiren]. That was it—that was really the main reason. Shanghaiese have a history of being sent down to the countryside in the fifties and sixties and people will do absolutely anything—leave their children, divorce their spouse—to be able to return to Shanghai, so most Shanghaiese just can't understand how you could possibly want to leave Shanghai. Harbin is backward and wild [yeman]. My mother was afraid I would go there. I told her, "Daughters often leave home." She told me if I were going to a foreign country, that is okay, that is a good thing, I would be going somewhere better, but in China, I had better stay in Shanghai. That is the way Shanghaiese think. My mother still feels she was right. She will say, "If I didn't stop you then, you would be in Harbin right

now." . . . My father is himself a non-Shanghaiese. He wasn't opposed to my match with this guy.

She said that she was nineteen when she went to Harbin to visit him. When she got there, she found that her "boyfriend" already had been living with a girl from his village. "This was a terrible shock for a nineteen-year-old," she said, shaking her head as though still in disbelief. "This girl told him that if he left her, she would kill herself. I told him, 'I love you, she also loves you, but because I won't kill myself, doesn't mean I love you less.'"

Nonetheless, the boy responded to the suicide threat and local pressures and stayed with the other girl. Later he thought this was a big mistake, and he tried to leave her. But the girl's family threatened that they would kill him if he left her. Eventually they got married, but they were quickly divorced. Ailin said, "Later he came to Shanghai three or four times begging for forgiveness, but I was unwilling to forgive him. He regrets it more than anything in his life. But it is too late now."

Tears welled up in her eyes when she told me this story. I asked her what she thinks about her affair now. She said, "I don't really think about it. It was fate [mingyun] that determined this."

I asked her if she cared more about her marital prospects or about her career. She said, "I care more about marriage, but I actually spend my energy on career. Now I am a pretty important person in my work unit, an assistant manager. The manager must be sent from the overseas office. So I am already at the highest level [for a local employee]. It isn't that I am really all that desirous of success, but my personality determines that I will always try to succeed, that I will be excellent at whatever I do."

I asked her about her dating since this first tumultuous affair. She said, "I have gone out with many men, dozens, but I nixed [fouding] all of them." She laughed, with a little theatrical bitterness, shaking her head. "That's what I want to ask you," she said looking at me. "It can't be all their problem, can't be all their fault that we don't work out. It must be something to do with my attitude. Do I have an emotional block [xinli zhangai]? Dating seems like a negotiation. Maybe it's a kind of occupational habit, working in finance."

Without waiting for an answer, she continued. She said that she went out with several men for three or four months, but then she just couldn't stand them.

They all have faults. . . . They are all too pragmatic [xianshi]. When they pursue you at first, they will act very sincere and caring, but after a while they will start thinking tit for tat [jingjingjijiao]. They will start thinking of the relationship like it was an investment. They will think of going out with me and spending this time with me as an investment, and they want to be certain of a return on this investment. They want to be certain that I will marry them.

I was confused, and said, "So all of these guys are seeing you a few times and then want to marry?"
She answered:

Well, they are just talking at this point. It's not as though they take out a ring and present it to me. They ask me what I would think about living together, and so forth. They will look at your conditions, your salary, and give you a score. A lot of it with them is vanity. They want to find a very capable girlfriend and show me off to their friends. They like to be with me in social situations. They see me as a badge of their success.

I asked her if she herself placed much emphasis on a man's economic status. "If he isn't much of anything [careerwise], then I can't accept it either. But I think that love should be about people, not about their [material] conditions. Sometimes, of course, these things are all muddled together."
I asked her if she had actually really liked anyone.

Some of them I really liked, but we don't have the opportunity to be together. One flew in from Hong Kong to see me. That's very romantic, right? I really liked him, but he had just gotten a good job in Hong Kong and there was no way he could come work in Shanghai. He wanted me to go live in Shenzhen, but I was unwilling to do that. You know what Shenzhen is like—all these girls [mistresses of Hong Kong men] living there. People would think I was being kept by someone.

There was another guy who came back from Australia, and I met him. We went out really often for three months, and I really liked him. But he had very different ideas from me. I really wanted to be able to finish a [four-year] college degree. That is important for me. But he didn't want anyone like that. He wanted me to go have babies and not study. He said that if he brought back a woman who went to study, people would make fun of him and think that this woman was just using him as a springboard. We went out every day for three months, and he introduced me to all of his friends. His friends said he told them that he really liked me, but he was looking for a wife, not a comrade. I told him, "I don't want to take up any more of your time. It is difficult to find someone." Then he met a girl, and in just one month they were married. She was a nurse—can you believe that?

She paused. "I guess for me, the benefit of meeting a lot of men is to get to know what I like."

When asked if she had sexual relationships with these guys, she said evasively, "Well, in most cases, I haven't yet gotten to this point and they have already been nixed. . . . I guess most of the guys who pursue me are the more honest, straight [laoshizhengtong] types. . . . Some of them know that they aren't qualified [meiyouzige] to even think about this." She laughed.

Finally she said uncertainly and defensively. "This [sex] is a mutual thing. . . . Anyway, don't you think that if a girl hasn't had some experience like this by the time she is twenty-six, that she lacks charm [meili], and that she would have wasted her youth [never having sex],[1] right?"

Warming up to the topic, she said:

> Well, this Hong Kong guy came to see me, and with him things were really good the two times he flew up here, and then I "gave myself in body to him" [yishenxiangxu]. One thing that I do believe is that a sexual relationship doesn't mean that a girl was conquered [beizhengfu]. If people are getting to the point when they are thinking about marriage, then they should have this kind of relationship. But for me, most people have been nixed before we have gotten to this part of the relationship.
>
> The HK man came up here for ten days, and we were together every day. When we were walking through the Mandarin Gardens, he would just turn around and kiss me. It was very romantic. It was very beautiful. But in the end we couldn't stay together. Finally, he wrote to me that we just must separate. I said, "Well, in that case, just separate."
>
> My parents were opposed to this guy, too. They thought he was too old [about forty]. And people here have doubts about Hong Kong people. They think they won't be good husbands. My parents don't like Hong Kong people.

I asked her why she had dated so many men who were not from Shanghai. She said:

> I have no interest in Shanghaiese men. They only care about themselves. On the surface they are really considerate and sweet, but what they really want to do is to trick a woman into marrying them [pian yige laopo]. . . . I don't want just casually to get married because it's time. If I don't find someone I love, I won't get married. Just going out and finding a husband

and jumping into it, I don't dare do this. I really hate the attitude of some men who think they can just buy a wife. They will say, "Oh, I do such and such and make so much money, marry me." I just tell them, "There is no way that I could marry you; don't waste your time on me." All these guys treat dating like business; they need to have a clear written confirmation.

I asked her what dating was like now.

When I was younger, dating just meant going for walks in the park and things like that. Now people will take you out to hotels [for dinner]. We used to go study computers, study together, or practice English together. People change later in life. When we were young, people wrote love letters. Now people will give gifts. No one will write love letters. That seems too silly and immature. Now they will give you gifts.

I asked if gifts really mean anything. She said, "Yes, they will give gifts like perfume or a lipstick, gifts that will make you feel like a woman; these aren't things you would give a man. Or maybe they will give some flowers."

I asked, "So no one writes love letters?"

She said with a smirk, "They don't want to leave any evidence."

Romance and Satire

Anyone who thinks that Chinese lack the vocabulary and inclination for "romance" never met a Shanghai woman like Ailin. On the other hand, anyone who knows (or remembers) Chinese romance as simplistic, chaste, and accepting of fate also has not met a woman with such an ironic view of modern white-collar relationships and a knack for "nixing" men. Ailin's rhetoric of romance gives positive meanings to early dating and sexual experiences, while her satire makes recent failures and frustrations acceptable. This chapter explores these dual uses of romance and satire in conversations about love among young people in Shanghai.

Romantic passion is in evidence in most, perhaps all, societies.[2] However, the way it is expressed, indeed its essential definitions, depend on social structures, local practices, and cultural traditions.[3] According to Charles Lindholm, romantic love most generally represents an attempt to escape from the contradictions and tensions of strategic social relations through the transcendental love of another person.[4] In societies characterized by rigid and strategic family relations, romance is only possible outside of marriage, as was more or less the case in medieval Europe and classical China. On the other hand, in a society characterized by atomistic market relations of mobility, competition, and individuality, the "couple" becomes a refuge against the hostile world of strategic market relations, and romance is sought in courtship and marriage. Therefore, in a shift to a market society such as in reform-era China, we should expect the greater emphasis on the expression of romantic love in ordinary courtship relations, a trend I confirm in this study.

What such structural-functional explanations fail to appreciate, however, is that for women in market societies, love is both a strategic choice and a refuge from market strategies, a contradiction evident in Ailin's conversation.[5] It is not that Shanghai women are more pragmatic (or more romantic) than women were before, but that their individualized choices are more problematic and subject to critique in a liberal market society in which women must seek love in marriage, but also economic support for child rearing. As Jane Collier writes, "Women in market societies find it difficult to attain the standard of pure love set by men. . . . [A] woman's choice of a husband always appears tainted by greed."[6] Men feel these contradictions as well, but less so, since they are more easily able to pursue strategic relations in one realm (career) and emotive relations in another (marriage). One also might argue that women delude themselves by pursuing both material security and emotional transcendence within marriage.[7] The problem with this feminist critique of romance is that it doesn't explain why women in Shanghai, especially high-status women like Ailin, pursue "romance" far more avidly than men. In fact, white-collar Shanghai women's greatest complaint is that men are not romantic enough. It seems that many Shanghai women indeed wish for a transcendental experience of passion, and it is exactly the calculating and conventionally materialistic nature of the Chinese courtship relationship that they wish to transcend or compensate for through a rhetoric of transcendental feelings.

Romance is about making a coherent story out of sexual feelings and actions,[8] but the rhetoric of romance in social interactions is more complex. Even in an interview, the motives of storytellers range from self-aggrandizement to self-accusation, from flirtation to aggression, from aiming to please to solipsistic self-analysis. However, two uses of stories seem basic: making sense and justifying. Intelligibility aside, the rhetoric of romantic feelings is most basically a moral rhetoric, a discourse of justification that operates within a grammar of easily overlooked, everyday moral categories, key elements of which I explore below. But morality is not the whole picture. "Romance" is—as the Western history of the word itself suggests—also a matter of a *good story*. Put simply, the judgment Ailin is asking for, or implicitly making, in her rhetorical question ("That's romantic, isn't it?") is as much aesthetic as moral. She wants to know if this is a good story, one worthy of memory and retelling. A culture of "romance" (as opposed to "romantic feeling" more generally) involves an appreciation of a romance as a dramatic performance, and not only as a self-justification or practical explanation of behavior. In Ailin's storytelling, partly she is articulating a practical strategy for achieving a future relationship based on feelings. However, much of her storytelling, as with most stories I heard, seeks to confirm *past* experiences as "romantic." Romance for Shanghai women and men thus has as much to do with the construction of good memories as of good prospects. "Good" romantic stories, through positive values of "feeling" and "fate," retrospectively validate and memorialize past feelings, experiences, and choices. This is not a trivial exercise, but essential to the construction of personal and social identity.

Finally, romance is only one trope of the emotional rhetoric used for expressing love relationships. Satire is another. In her study of the history of romance in the United States in the twentieth century, Eva Illouz describes how an "ironic structure of feeling" in modern love relationships has replaced a tragic one.[9] The social background to this transition is, first, an increased suspicion of the fictionality or mediated quality of romance and, second, an increased need to justify brief affairs or frequent changes in romantic partners. Through this historic transition, which Illouz calls the "post-modernization of romance," an ironic appreciation of romance allows youth to pursue romantic love while harboring doubts about its reality.[10] I believe that Shanghai youth, such as Ailin, use satire to deal with a similar dilemma to that described by Illouz: expressing a belief in romantic feeling while belittling the romantic performances of others as faked or incompetent. In Shanghai, I will argue, these sensibilities of romance and satire evolved in tandem. A dual emotional rhetoric of romance and satire reflects the requirements of both men and women to "sell themselves" (or find a "refuge") in a more fluid and competitive dating culture and simultaneously to discipline themselves against romantic disappointment. Therefore, I see romance and irony as two complementary tropes in a moral and emotional rhetoric that emerges not as a particularly postmodern condition, but in response to the conditions of sexual life in a liberal market society in which sexuality has been problematized around individual choice and individual identity. They are two culturally available rhetorical strategies for the justification and dismissal of choices, and for shared memorialization and shared forgetting of experiences. Romance and satire thus are best conceptualized not as rigid and restrictive Foucauldian "disciplines of the self," but rather as flexible linguistic/emotional competencies through which youth express their sentiments within the new social environment of a competitive dating culture based on choice.

The Grammar of Romantic Sentiment

Everyday talk about love employs an extraordinarily large vocabulary of affective terms, only the most basic of which I introduce in this section.[11] Shanghaiese employ a local romantic tradition and recently have absorbed, or reabsorbed, many romantic themes from the West and many, many other sources, including Russian novels, Japanese *manga*, Taiwan teen romances, Singaporean and Korean soaps, Mexican *telenovelas*, and Hong Kong pop songs. Ailin's vocabulary of romance borrows from film and fiction, Western, Japanese, and Chinese. However, this is not evidence of an essential Westernization of romance. I find no essential or stable preference for Western, Hong Kong, Taiwanese, or classical Chinese romantic themes among Shanghai youth. Shanghaiese youth occasionally reference the perceived national origins of these terms tactically, typically to establish a Shanghai identity that is self-consciously cosmopolitan *and* Chinese (as in the romantic performances on *Saturday Date* that combine competence in foreign cultures with a handwritten Chinese poem). In most cases, however, terms from Taiwan pop novels, Hollywood movies, Japanese television dramas, and other sources have simply become part of the vocabulary of everyday romantic discourse, loan words whose foreign origins are often irrelevant or are given new meanings in the contemporary context.

Romantic Feelings (Ganqing) versus Conditions (Tiaojian)

More than any other concept, "romantic feelings" (*ganqing*) define the personal narratives of love among Chinese. The deepening of feelings is the conventional purpose of dating, and the absence of feelings signals the unhappy denouement of a failed romance. Feelings are known to be changeable. The most common view is that feelings of infatuation (*milian*), longing (*lianqing*), or love (*aiqing*) in early courtship fade into feelings of familial closeness (*qinqing*) in marriage. Feelings are also a moral touchstone. Feelings (*qing*) have been a key element of Chinese moral discourse for centuries,[12] but the moral valuation of romantic or sexual feelings has transformed over time, its valence shifting with the terms against which it is contrasted. Sexual feeling represented an individualistic rebellion against "feudal values" and a touchstone of personal moral authenticity in the "free love" discourse of the May 4th era,[13] then, because of these bourgeois connotations, were negatively contrasted with societal duty in socialist China. In post–Cultural Revolution China, romantic feeling (*ganqing*) took on the positive connotations of human feeling (*renqing*) opposed to the inhumanity of the Maoist era. Finally, in reform-era China, romantic feeling has come to represent the authentic human value opposed to the worship of money, but also endangered by it. Relationships based on feelings are accorded higher moral worth than those in which money and status are perceived as the motive, even if relationships based purely on feelings are considered impractical or virtually impossible. Romantic feeling (*ganqing*) hence lies at the core of the moral discourse of sexual relationships in contemporary China. Whereas romantic feeling had been rebellious or unorthodox in other eras or social contexts, it is now morally compensatory in an ironic worldview dominated by money or material values. As such "pure feeling" is not a true escape from the money motive but its necessary discursive apposite, in a larger rhetoric of individual sexual motives.[14]

"Money" (*qian*) is not the most colloquial term of opposition Shanghai people use when talking about materialism in courtship. Rather, it is "conditions" (*tiaojian*) or sometimes "external conditions." "Conditions" are the sorts of things a matchmaker or friend would mention when describing a potential partner: income, education level, housing, household registration, foreign connections, and so on. These are not subjective choice criteria, but publicly recognized facts about a potential partner. In Shanghai during the 1970s and 1980s, for instance, a housing shortage made housing the most important of these conditions. As one male focus group participant said of dating in the early 1980s, "Housing was so important. If there was no housing, then half of the chance was gone. A room was half of a wife."[15] In the media and in everyday conversations, there are many popular sociological narratives of the changing conditions important in choosing a spouse. In the most popular story, political conditions such as class background and Party membership gave way in the early reform era to economic conditions such as income and housing and more recently to personal ability or career prospects. In all these discussions of changing conditions, courtship is conceived as a choice among potential partners (*duixiang*) with varying conditions for whom the chooser has varying degrees of feeling. With youth largely making their own decisions now, they must play the pragmatist and the romantic at the same time, so that individual motives become the focus of moral discourse. A tiresome (and often fatuous) argument in the popular discourse of love and marriage centers on which is to come first, feelings or conditions, as in the following exchange among young women in a discussion group:

> Moderator: How about you [other girls]? For example, if you were
> looking for a boyfriend or husband, do you consider economic
> ability as an important condition?
>
> Luo: If he has no economic ability at all, there will be trouble too.
>
> Cui: Usually feeling [ganqing] should come first.
>
> Shen: "Love can't be eaten like bread." [Everybody laughed at this com-
> mon saying.]
>
> Cheng: In our society, economic ability should be considered. Like the
> old saying "Money can't get you everywhere, but without money
> you can't get anywhere."
>
> Zen: That depends. I think feeling should be put in the first place. No
> matter if it is love at first sight, or you have been dating for a while,
> it depends on how much feeling you have toward him, and
> whether you have a basis for this feeling.
>
> (unmarried women in their early twenties)

The availability of numerous clichéd expressions to express the balance between feelings and conditions shows the prevalence of this discourse. The discourse of feelings is imbedded in the Chinese Marriage Law of 1980, which
makes feelings the proper basis for marriage and the rupture of feelings the
standard grounds for divorce. Scholars pointed out to me that this clause is
based on Engels's idealization of feelings as the basis of sexual relations under
socialism. The explicit use of this phrase in the law recognizes (or assumes) that
marriages were usually based on pragmatic considerations in pre-1949 China.
"Feelings" and "conditions" are thus paired terms in a dominant public rhetoric of balancing love with pragmatic concerns.

While "feelings" were attributed a moralizing and humanizing essence in
the popular discourse of marital choice, they also could be used to construct an
anarchic and individualist conception of sexual morality,[16] including the acceptance of premarital and extramarital relationships.[17] In everyday life feelings
were called upon to justify all manner of relationships. I encountered a situation in which one young man struggled to justify to another man how he had
come to sleep with this man's girlfriend, finally saying to his angry counter-
part, "Don't think she is a loose woman [suibian]! We had feelings." Relationships based on feelings are justifiable, but they are not necessarily acceptable according to social morality (shehuidaode), which becomes the lesser standard. The
moral discourse of feelings was ambiguous and thus allowed youth to negotiate changing public conceptions of acceptability or "normalcy."

In addition to a moral category, feelings are a key narrative element through which the object of a relationship is defined and the goal of the romantic quest revealed. The moment "I started having feelings for him/her" is a key turning point in any romantic story, though not always an easy point to define. Some of the simplest stories I heard were on the order of "Our feelings for each other weren't bad, so we got married."[18] Feelings were the basis of all but the most materialistic romantic narrative, but, taken alone, not enough to make such a narrative interesting or persuasive, so other romantic codes were also employed.

Destiny (Yuanfen)

Romantic passion must extend beyond the simple development of changeable and rather commonplace romantic sentiments to become the purpose of a good story or a romantic one. A central grammatical term in everyday Chinese romantic talk is the notion of "karmic destiny" (yuan).[19] Like feelings (qing), destiny (yuan) is a concept deeply rooted in a Chinese literary and philosophical tradition, the best known exemplar of which is probably the Qing novel Dream of the Red Mansions in which karmic destiny is paired with romantic feelings.[20] In the classical Western narrative, "romance" extends a transcendental quality to passion (or feelings) through a quest for merging with the idealized beloved, perhaps a merging that will only be realized in the afterlife.[21] "Yuan" similarly ascribes a transcendental or mystical quality to feelings and relationships, though it seems to be used without much thought of its religious origins in casual conversations. For instance, youth frequently use "yuanfen" (predestination) to positively comment upon a chance meeting that led into a long-term relationship, like my meeting with my wife on the ferry to Putuo Island.

In a culture in which sexual motives are disputed, the most useful characteristic of the discourse of yuan is that choices needn't be explained, that they are predestined. Destiny provides a way of avoiding the practical (or sexual) purposes that bring people together. Like feelings, it is defined negatively in contrast to pragmatic purposes. As such, it is also given a positive moral evaluation. Moreover, destiny makes feelings transcendental, a metaphysical corrective to the inherently fickle nature of feelings. It implies that one shouldn't thoughtlessly discard those with whom one has a fateful encounter and developed feelings. For instance, I asked a woman why she stayed so long in a relationship with a difficult boyfriend, and she replied:

> I believe in predestination [yuanfen]. I sometimes think that in my past life
> I did something that makes me owe something to my boyfriend in this
> life. Maybe with other things it doesn't matter, but feelings certainly de-

pend on destiny. If it weren't for that, then how could I have known him so long and still liked him? I could have easily changed and found another, or another found me. Even under all these different circumstances, I still liked him, still chose him to live together. I think this is certainly a kind of fate; it is predetermined. . . . Destiny is an empty thing. If you want to explain it, you can't, but it is something that exists.

Like romantic feeling, destiny is something difficult to articulate and impossible to predict. It shares the anarchic quality of feelings that made both concepts rebellious or antistructural in classical Chinese culture. In my interviews, I heard "yuan" used to describe extramarital relations as well as third-person dating relationships. It meant that what happened between two people was fated; social standards were irrelevant. Therefore, it also shares the useful ambiguity of feelings without being vacuous from the standpoint of its users.

In contemporary discourse, "yuan" is associated with another common romantic metaphor among Chinese youth: "love at first sight." A young woman described how she met her current boyfriend, a Japanese man. She said she met him three years ago on a long-distance train:

I guess this was predestined [yuanfen], out of all the people who I could have met on that train, I met him. We were the same age. I guess this is a kind of love at first sight [for him, she explained later, not for her]. At first I wasn't really trying to get involved and maybe he misunderstood me. I just felt he was a foreigner, so I should be friendly to him.

Although "yuan" was sometimes used flippantly, many people seriously told me that they "believed in yuanfen" or that they were brought together by yuanfen. For instance, I interviewed a group of young hotel workers, including a boyfriend-girlfriend pair. The young boyfriend told me that they believed in yuanfen. I asked what he meant. "Because like the two of us [pointing to his girlfriend] coming together from different places to this one place here. It is destiny [yuanfen]," he said dramatically.

The young women clapped appreciatively at this open display of romanticism by her boyfriend. "So," I said, "you guys really believe in destiny. I thought that girls now are supposed to be really pragmatic."

He said, "That is different. 'Yuanfen' means that two people are brought together by fate. Sometimes people separate. That means that they had yuan [destiny] but no fen [practical outcome]."

One young woman began talking about a French guy she knew who came to Shanghai and then within two months met a girl and married her. I asked her if she meant that they also had *yuanfen*. She said, "I don't think so. The French guy really loves her, but I'm not sure if this woman really loves him."

"*Yuanfen*" is a very loose concept, but its use reveals some consistent connotations. One was an emphasis on meetings and separations as the critical points in a relationship. Destiny brings two people together for a special meeting. People who break up, on the other hand, are not fated to be together (*you-yuan, meifen*). Second, there was the connection of *yuanfen* to feelings. Without feelings, destiny is meaningless. Third, fate is clearly a concept of external determination, a denial of motives. The chances life provides are critical rather than one's own efforts. Youth, particularly young women, use "destiny" to avoid the cynical discourse of material motives described in previous chapters. "*Yuan*" also allows youth to avoid actions and choices. For instance, one professional woman, Lanping, talked about how she had split up with a boyfriend because he seemed to be unable to forget a previous girlfriend. She said she still missed this man, and I asked why she didn't openly discuss her feelings with him. She responded by saying, "I guess I believe too much in *yuanfen* to do that, so I didn't try to talk to him about it. Instead, I just decided that he would be better off without me." In this conversation, "*yuanfen*" became a rationale for not communicating about a decision. It also allowed her to point out to me a perceived difference between Chinese and Westerners. Chinese accept fate in matters of relationships, she explained. Westerners are too pushy in love, forcing things along that should better be left alone and saying things that should not be said.

The Poetics of Romance

While "feelings" and "destiny/fate" could be described as the basic grammatical terms of youth discourse about love, the appropriate rhetorical or performative style for expressing these terms was more contentious. Some Shanghai informants, like Lanping above, described to me a typical Chinese mode of expression: subtle (*hanxu*) expression of feelings, not pretentious declarations; unstudied and practical actions, relying on "fate" and not "forced." These characterizations of Chinese romance were meaningful because the main point of comparison was well-known (and emphasized by my presence as interlocutor): the Hollywood romance, with its embarrassingly public travails of lovers aggressively pursuing their lover and loudly proclaiming their love. This Western style of romantic expression was not merely used for contrast, however. Many young Shanghaiese women, in particular, seemed to cherish dramatic and unexpected events in their narratives and performances of feelings, which they often described as "romantic" (langman), like Ailin above, who described her tumultuous "student movement" love affair as very "romantic," or Lanping, who described a night of dancing and drinking ending in a "one-night stand" as "romantic." (She quite often violated her expressed ideal of subtlety in expressing love.) While very different, both of these stories involved an element of conflict, danger, or the violation of normal expectations. While older Shanghaiese considered "romance" contrived and foreign, Shanghai youth absorbed the "native" grammar of feelings and destiny into a "foreign" rhetoric of love and romance that was itself influenced as much by Hong Kong, Japanese, and Taiwan models as by Western ones. Melodramatic movies and pop songs were the measure of what counted as romantic and were models for romantic performances. By the 1990s romance seemed to be a normative style of emotional rhetoric among youth in Shanghai, though one whose contents and form were highly contested.

Saying "I Love You" (Wo Ai Ni)

A common perception of the Chinese rhetoric of love is that the open expression of romantic feelings should be avoided, partly out of embarrassment, but more importantly out of a sense that such expressions are too easily false or too forward. Sulamith Potter, for instance, argues that the verbal expression of emotions such as love was unimportant in Chinese relationships, in which caring was expressed through the performance of practical work for the other person and suffering on their behalf.[22] Based on my focus group interviews and other conversations, it seems that verbal expressions of love were indeed looked upon with suspicion by Shanghaiese who grew up in the period before the reform era. When asked if they had ever said or been told "I love you" when they were courting in the early 1980s, some women focus group participants found the notion very nearly absurd.

> All at once: Why bother saying it in front of the person, "You love me, I love you?" What is good about these words? They were not popular [in the early 1980s]. . . .
> Ping: In the past, honesty was required and speechlessness was appreciated. It meant he was reliable and wouldn't be a dandy. Now, a boy not only needs to meet a lot of material conditions, but also needs to know how to flirt [hua]. . . . Honest [laoshi] boys are at disadvantage. [All agree.]

> Moderator: Shanghai people often say "I like you" [rather than "I love you"]. Have you said "I like you"?[23]
> Ming: Who will say it on normal days? For no reason?
> Ping: I would think he had something wrong with his mind.
> > (married women in their late thirties)

Among such middle-aged informants, openly declaring "love" was seen as a contrived expression of sentiment that has little to do with real commitment. As one male focus group participant in his late thirties said, "It is not that we were embarrassed. These kinds of words are stupid and hollow." Another said, "If you said something so blatant [rouma], other people would think you are too tricky [hua]." Many older informants characterized this overt verbal rhetoric of "love" as a recent trend among youth and a Western import unsuited to Chinese. Moreover, focus group participants in this age group have not altered their negative attitudes toward verbalizing love in their contemporary married lives. Most don't say "I love you" or practice "romance" now either.

There seems, however, to have been a great change in attitudes toward the verbal expression of love among people in their twenties, people who have come of dating age in the 1990s. Younger people in focus groups described a much more positive attitude toward saying "I love you" to their boyfriends and girlfriends.

> Pu: I have a boyfriend who likes saying, "I am keen on you" [zhongyi, a Cantonese word].
> Moderator: Shanghaiese use Cantonese too?
> Pu: Yes.
> Moderator: Do you say it yourself?
> Zhung: My boyfriend says it in three language, English, Japanese, and Mandarin.
> > (unmarried women in their early twenties)

> Moderator: Have you said the words "I love you"?
> Liu: Of course.
> Zu: Of course.
> Sun, Li: Of course.
> Qian: My girlfriend has said it, but I haven't.
> Zhao: Not directly, but words like "I like you."
> Moderator: What else do you say that is similar to "I love you"?
> Qian: "Eat you to death," "Love you to death." . . .
> Huang: "Can't eat you up."
> > (men in their late twenties and early thirties)

People who grew up in the 1990s shared the ideal of verbally expressing romantic feelings through the rhetoric of love. However, their use of foreign languages and dialects to express this type of romantic love indicates the appropriation of this discourse from popular media (especially Cantonese, English, and Japanese love songs), the playfulness of these performances, and an embarrassment in talking romantically in the everyday patois of Shanghai. Thus, even young people who believe in romance mark off this rhetoric from ordinary talk through these linguistic switches.

Practicing Romance (Langman)

Among middle-aged Shanghaiese, "romance," like saying "I love you," was perceived as a reform-era innovation. When asked about romance, Shanghaiese in their late thirties who participated in my focus groups claimed it was a new ideal.[24]

> Yuan: Now people are talking about "romance." The nineties! Back then [the early 1980s], there was nothing like this. . . .
> Yan: We just felt two people being together were happy.
> Moderator: You didn't use this word?
> Yuan: I remember when "romance" started. It was in the early 1980s; there was a Hong Kong singer coming to town and performing. He mentioned "French romance," then Shanghai people knew there was something "romantic." For me, nothing could be called romantic, just felt happy. . . .
>
> (married men in their early thirties)

Middle-aged men and women considered romance an imported idea associated with new forms of consumption in courtship ("flowers" and "coffee shops"). Few of them considered romance part of their own experience. Like saying "I love you," this was one of a set of new "tricks" young people must learn to use. I am not arguing that Shanghai young people have actually become better at expressing their "true feelings" (if anything, the opposite), but rather that this type of romantic expressiveness is now expected and seen as more persuasive than a relationship that "just seems to happen." Relationships must have an original romantic story, including elements of melodrama and fate. People now find relationships that lack such romantic narratives generic and hence inauthentic.

Young people shared doubts about romantic sincerity as did older informants, but most men and women in their early twenties also were eager to pursue and relate their own "romantic" experiences. The following discussion among young men in a focus group discussion brings out many of the themes that define Shanghai romance.

> Moderator: What kinds of things are romantic in your point of view?
> Han: Once I borrowed a car and drove to Bai Long Gang with my girl-friend. I made an "I love you" sign with rope on the beach and burnt it. . . . Just like the movie *Feiyuemiqing*.
> Altogether: Sounds pretty romantic. So troublesome. You have to take the trouble to be romantic. . . .
> Wan: The best will be: one day when it is raining, but we don't take an umbrella. . . .
> Ni: Once when I walked down the street, I saw a man and a woman walking in the rain, and the man covering the woman's head with his hand and both of them walking very slowly . . . [imitating].
> Han: There are a lot of romantic scenes: cake, champagne, candles. . . .
> Moderator: You guys all sound like foreign movies.
> Han: I did these things. My life is like a movie.
> Moderator: What you were talking about are romantic things boys did for girls. What kind of things do girls do that will make it romantic?
> Feng: When I sit with her and hold her shoulder, she leans her head on my shoulder, and we talk freely.
> Moderator: It sounds like men have to make a big effort while women only need to lean their heads on the shoulders. . . .
> Feng: The whole purpose of men making such an effort is to let the women lean their heads on their shoulders. [All agree.]
>   (unmarried men in their early twenties)

In this conventional rhetoric of romance, men dramatically display their feelings through performances modeled on films and songs, and woman respond through a display of erotic tenderness. The contrived and exaggerated nature of these performances shows their close relation to ritual and play, including a separation of romance from the routines of everyday life.[25]

These conventions of romantic expression are repeated in discussions among young women, but with a more critical perspective on men's romantic performances. These gender differences were heightened by the focus group interview situation, in which two young women acted as moderators. While the young male focus group participants were anxious to display their romantic experiences and skills to the young female moderators, young women participants were more anxious to display their sophistication and ability to see through male stratagems, confirming the idea that romance was a male act performed for women, but also that women reserved the right to critique these performances.

> Moderator: What do you think your boyfriend should do to make you feel romantic and moved?
>
> Shen: Something out of expectation, something I haven't thought of, and something surprising.
>
> Xuan: I haven't had this experience yet.
>
> Shen: I have thought of a story. I have a friend who one day was sick in bed. She was in bed when her boyfriend came and she didn't know [he had come by]. Later she saw a note on the door saying: "I will come to pick you up for dinner." When she saw him later that night, he gave her a letter and asked her to read it when she went back. She found that it was a love poem; even if it was not written by him, she was still very moved.
>
> Moderator: What do you think? Is it very romantic? If your boyfriend gave you flowers and took you to cafés, would you feel romantic?
>
> Qing: You wouldn't feel anything. Before there were not a lot of people giving flowers, but now there are too many. You wouldn't feel anything.
>
> Zen: I think if I gave him something and he was moved to tears, I would feel it was really romantic.
>
> Moderator: What will have such a big impact?
>
> Zen: Such as some details from life: a record, a picture book, gathering all the bits and pieces from life and binding them into a book. No matter whether I gave it to him or he gave it to me, I would think it was romantic. If we both had the ability to make the other cry, I would think it was romantic. At that time it might only be an emotional experience, but later when we thought back it would be romantic. For example, I saw something I liked but it was sold out. He ran around the city and went to all kinds of places and finally found this. We were supposed to meet somewhere, but he was late. At the beginning I was angry, but after knowing the reason for him being late, I was moved. . . .
>
> Moderator: So romance is a feeling you feel afterward.
>
> Zen: Yes. When somebody stays alone, she will think of the past and the future, and will think actually that period of time is truly romantic.
>
> Moderator: What do you think is the opposite of "romantic"?
>
> Zen: Mechanical repetition. After getting used to it, it won't arouse your excitement.

Qing: I think romantic is something you feel from plain and simple
things. I resent people who read poems to me. [All laughed.]
(unmarried women in their early twenties)

While young women expected romance from a relationship, they were
skeptical of men's staging of romantic events. While one woman mentioned a
love poem, another woman pointedly dismissed love poems as contrived. Their
dismissal of the simpler romantic expressions of the 1980s, such as giving
flowers and chocolates, gives credence to claims that young men now have a
more difficult challenge in the art of romancing. The relationship to consumer
culture is dialectical rather than strictly imitative. Romantic expression has become part of the world of consumer fashions in which flowers and chocolate
are, in the words of one woman in this same group, "too common." Pop cultural media provide models, but good performances require creative variations
on these models. Young women were not averse to expensive gifts and dinners,
but they wanted a more elaborate and personalized expression of love than the
trite token of flowers. While those outside the dating system (older people) or
marginalized by it (poor young men) emphasized the expense involved in romance, young women, and most young men, focused on personal experiences
and feelings as the core meaning of romance. Expense was part of the symbolic
value of romantic expressions, but as a way of expressing the importance
placed on a partner. Women emphasized the effort and thought that young men
must put into such events in order to make them feel romantic. Moreover, effort
alone was not enough, especially an effort that lacked style and originality.
Expressive content and originality were also important. As Illouz argues in the
U.S. case, the proliferation of commodified romantic narratives and symbols
undermines the efficacy of particular romantic tokens, explaining the suspicion of romantic symbols among the very group that most strongly affirms
them.[26]

Both women and men described romantic experiences largely as a man's
performance to win a woman's heart. It is the man who drives to the sea and
burns "I love you" in the sand or runs about the city in search of a special gift.
Yet while women expected men to perform, they weren't merely a passive audience or a "head on the shoulder." Women were active in creating and imagining the romantic experience, whether through the display of gender in domestic role-play or through the display of passion in melodramatic conflict. For
instance, twenty-one-year-old Bei liked to brag to me about her "romantic" ex-

periences. She told me: "I heard that in Europe if you kissed in the street, people would stop and cheer you, so I grabbed [my boyfriend] in the middle of the street and kissed him in front of the traffic. A taxi driver honked and yelled, 'You're crazy' [shenjingbing]. I guess Shanghaiese aren't so romantic." Her romantic adventures, of which she described several, seemed intended to impress me with her daring and passion. But they also reflect the active work some young women did to create moments of sexual tension and drama. Another young woman described to me how she elaborately arranged to meet with her boyfriend on a Shanghai bridge for "one last meeting" so they could break up like couples in the movies. (He didn't show, ruining the memory.) For both men and women in Shanghai, courtship wasn't just choosing a husband or a wife or making an expensive-style statement; it was to be an adventure that required dramatic expressions of feeling, and women were as active as men, if not more active, in directing these performances.

The evocation of romantic feeling is the most important criterion for judging an experience as romantic, not expense. Staging, whether in an expensive restaurant or on a beach or bridge, should support the performance. Such judgments are more aesthetic than moral. A flat performance is boring (wuliao/meijin). An overdone performance is gross (rouma). Romance is a ritualized and aestheticized memorialization of experiences for reminiscence and sharing among peers, much like the love songs, novels, and movies these young people often mentioned. For the youngest especially, the emphasis is on strong feeling, good or bad. Romantically inexperienced women retold the dramatic romantic stories of other women, and the most appreciated narratives were conflictive rather than merely positive, evincing a strong penchant for melodrama. Male tears were especially moving. The following description from a focus group discussion is typical:

> Hu: I heard from a friend that her sister had a boyfriend for three years; later the boyfriend met some problems and was in a bad mood and lost his temper on her. They split up. She got to know another boyfriend, and when the former boyfriend found out about this, he beat this boy up and walked away. He didn't come to look for her for a very long time, and after a very long time, he came to look for her and held her tightly for a long, long time. . . .
> Moderator: You think this story is very romantic?
> Hu: Yes.
>
> (unmarried female office worker aged 25)

For men, romance could be associated with struggle as well, but in a more clear-cut erotic narrative that women would have found lacking in drama and too generically sexual.

> Moderator: Which part of dating is romantic?
> Huang: Kissing.
> Wang: Chatting with plain friends is very romantic too.
> Zu: The two people's world is quite romantic.
> Sun: Before "attacking" a girl, the mental struggle is romantic.
> Liu: The stage when you are chasing after her but haven't got her is very romantic.
>
> (unmarried men in their late twenties)

For these men, achieving sexual intimacy was the best token of romantic feeling. For young women, such erotic images were generally not personalized or interesting enough, while the painful experiences of others did sound romantic because they dramatized the profound consequences of romantic feelings.[27] Many romantically inexperienced young women seemed to crave experiences of deep feeling and romantic conflict. For instance, Huan, an eighteen-year-old woman who had never before had a boyfriend told me a story about how she met a middle-aged man in the public library who made a sexual pass at her:

> I was in the library studying for the college entrance examinations and a man sat in front of me. He wrote me a note on a piece of paper, asking me what I was reading. I didn't have any reaction. I just gave the note back to him. I didn't know what to do. I thought things like that only happened in novels. He then wrote a note saying, "Let's go out and talk."

She told me that she went out with him, and they had some sort of physical intimacy, which she didn't want to describe, but which sounded like kissing and petting. "I am a little bit afraid. The situation between males and females is difficult to judge." I asked how her girlfriends reacted to her story. She said, "They said they really envied me. They said this sort of thing only happens in those Qiong Yao romance novels.[28] They said I was very lucky that I had this experience, that it was very romantic. They feel their own lives are very boring." Her own reaction, tempered by real events, was more confused, though still excited.

Not all images of romance were as melodramatic or sexualized. Many were as gentle as the head on the shoulder or the shared umbrella in a rainstorm, but romantic stories and performances share a basic rhetoric of dramatizing feeling and fate through acting and staging modeled on film and pop literature. Young women and young men still make practical and ethical judgments through these stories, but the "romantic" judgment is aesthetic, not moral or pragmatic. Aestheticized romance doesn't break up or displace the conventional ethical grammar of feelings, fate, and conditions. Rather, it is like a rotation of this grammar into an aesthetic dimension, in which ethical judgments are momentarily suspended and actions and stories appreciated as drama. The aestheticization of romance—that is, regarding a sexual relationship as a beautiful experience and not only as a practical or ethical matter—also entails, to some extent, a more playful relationship to sexual relationships: an enjoyment of the experience of romance as an end in itself.[29] On the other hand, the contents of this new poetics of romance are often derivative from popular culture sources that offer youth limited models of dramatic romantic performances.

Emotional Rhetoric and Narrative Strategies
"I'm Getting Tougher"

A friend introduced me to Grace[30] in the summer of 2000, telling me Grace could help me with an ongoing project on international dating relationships. We agreed to meet for lunch in front of the statue of the Shanghai girl on Huaihai Road. Grace was a fashion consultant, she explained, dressing for that role in a gauzy blouse and tight miniskirt. "Westerners think I am pretty because I have a good figure," she said later in the interview, in the detached self-critical tone with which women in Shanghai often discuss their looks. "Chinese men think I have small eyes and a flat nose. Western men don't care about that." As a child she lived in central China with her mother, who divorced her father (a college professor) because of his extramarital affair. At age eighteen Grace returned to Shanghai for junior college. We talked for four hours in a Japanese teahouse, beginning with a very typical romantic narrative of her first love:

> The first one was really Chinese-style. We never did anything physical. He was my high school classmate, and after I came to Shanghai, I ran into him. I think you could say that was destiny [yuanfen]. We just sat on the street corner one day together, and he said, "Will you be my girlfriend?" Really silly, when I think about, sitting on the street with all the traffic going by. That day he had to go to the hospital and asked me to accompany him. So we walked all the way back from the hospital and sat down there on that curb, and he asked me. I was shocked. Young girls love to read those love stories, like those Qiong Yao novels. I also read a lot of them. Back then, I always thought, "Why haven't I run into love? Maybe

it's just a lack of destiny." But when he asked that question, I was surprised. I didn't have particularly strong feelings for him, but I thought it was okay, I should try it out. It was the summer holiday after my first year in college. He was extremely good to me, extremely good. Now sometimes I regret it, I really regret that I didn't go on with him. . . .

But in the end I rejected him. He wasn't the kind of guy with any ambition, with direction in his career. I think men should do something with their lives, do something great or important, so that I can respect him and admire him. He wasn't like that. His idea was that he would just be good to me, that we would have this small family life, just live a simple life, that this was just fine with him. That's really weird for me. . . . Every weekend I went to my aunt's house, and she would tell me, "What's the point of this relationship? He's an out-of-town boy. In the future you won't be able to be together." Also, when you've been apart for a while, your feelings change, so I wrote him telling him not to write me anymore. Before that he wrote me every day, words like "I love you," that kind of thing. So disgusting [exin]! So gross [rouma] [laughing] . . . ! [After breaking up,] I told him, "If you have something to tell me, you can just call me, and if I have something to tell you, I will call you."

You know when a girl takes this first step, it is like eating a plum. Most plums are dried [and sweetened], but this is like eating a plum that is still green and it has that pungent taste [se]. That is also very precious, something to always be remembered. . . . We were only together a short time, just three months. I have a friend who told me that if your love can't last longer than three months, it is just a kind of game. I thought, "Well, maybe we just didn't have destiny"; we never found that kind of feeling . . . so it just ended like that. . . . Anyway, if a boy is too good to a girl, then she doesn't value him. You can believe me [laughing]. Girls can easily be spoiled. He was really good to me. Back then I didn't have any money, didn't have any work, but every time we went out, he would buy that really expensive ice cream for me. That was pure, pure feeling, really pure. . . . Now I think that by doing that [breaking off with him], I was pretty mean, so I must deserve some kind of retribution [baoying]. When someone is good to you, you should be good to him, but that is just the way things worked out.

Grace's story of a first love, with her own running commentary, employs the conventional grammar of romance discussed above: "pure, pure feelings," "fate," selfless expressions of love within the relationship (framed against her own commentary about her pragmatic reasons for ending it), all referenced to images from romance novels. Her story shows all the rhetorical modes discussed above: the pragmatic rhetoric of conditions, the moral rhetoric of feelings and fate, and the aesthetic rhetoric of romance. Her aunt's concerns about the boyfriend's out-of-town status and her own concerns about his career are a pragmatic commentary framing her story. No listener would disagree with the importance of these familiar practical concerns. On the other hand, her regret over breaking up, her promises of future help, and her discussion of retribution are moral stances, not practical wishes. Grace believes that she wronged this pure-hearted boy, just as her first American boyfriend later wronged her. Finally, the story demonstrates the aesthetic judgments of romance. She laughs at the clumsy performance of her first suitor, while carefully packaging these experiences as a pure and beautiful story of first love for the attentive interviewer.

Such memories have many psychological and social uses. Grace used this story to assure me that she appreciated pure love, but that it wasn't enough for her. Life is too hard to only consider feelings, she said. Her second romance began in the offices of a prestigious American firm, where she was an intern after her second and final year at college. A young American began "chasing" her, a "handsome blond boy," she said, first studying Chinese with her during lunch and eventually calling her dorm to ask her on a date. They made love on the night of their first date:

> That night he took me out, and my "first time" was with him. At the time I felt it was a bit too easy, too fast. But I thought, "I don't care that I am young, and he is young, and he is going back to America. At least I can think that I loved him, and I hope that he loves me." But now I think the fact is I loved him, but he didn't love me. I think this was retribution for the first love. I dumped that guy; now I was dumped by this one. I guess I deserved it. I really fell completely into it. I guess I really didn't understand that love must be something between two people. It can't just be one person. So I loved him, but I don't think he loved me. He was just one of the young "American boys wanting to have sex" [in English], just wanting to play. He didn't really care that I had feelings for him. . . .
>
> We were together for three months, just like the first one. For a long time he never took me out in front of his friends. Finally, when he had a birthday party, he invited me out in front of his friends. I saw all his friends, and I was very proud. I thought, "Well, at least I have that, all his friends know that I am there with him." Now I guess it probably didn't mean anything to him; he probably just thought that this girl suits American tastes, everyone will probably like her.
>
> Two weeks later he invited me over to his house, and he told me,

"Let's break up." I asked why, and he said he already had a girlfriend. [She is crying.] You know what my reaction was? It was strange. I said, "How am I not as good as that girl? Why not give me a chance?" I think at that time I really could have tolerated that he had another girl. I was that big-minded [laughing]. Also, you know how he did that? He asked me to come over to his apartment, and then we had sex, and after we had sex, he said, "Let's break up." I felt like I had just been played with and discarded, really stupid [again crying]. . . . Well, if you want to accomplish anything in life, you have to eat a lot of bitterness. For me, I try to think of that as a kind of life experience. I won't think, "Oh, I had a really rough life." I think, "I'm getting tougher."

Despite the abrupt ending to this second relationship, the party introductions that day changed her life, Grace said. Through more parties and visits to the foreign bar scene with her new friends, she entered a social circle of foreigners (mostly men) and their Chinese friends (mostly girlfriends). Grace's stories continued through a disappointing one-night stand with an Italian and two additional boyfriends, both Americans. "I found a really rich guy, an American guy," she said in blunt English. This American lover, much older than her, agreed to marry her to help her "have a second start" in the United States. Although she enjoys her life with her husband, she still maintains romantic aspirations about the other boyfriend (not described here).

Although space prohibits a detailed discussion, her story reflects several typical features of the contentious cultural framing of international dating among participants in Shanghai: the use of the "other" as a flattering mirror for one's own sexual explorations; the normalization of quick sex through special considerations of "foreign ways"; an initial acceptance of a short-term relationship; emergent hopes for a long-term relationship prompting a breakup; a disillusionment about Western men's sexual conquests but a conviction that international relationships can be particularly romantic; the entry of the woman into a subculture of foreigners and their Chinese friends. The blatant marriage of convenience seems rather atypical, though hopes to go abroad through marriage to a foreigner are not.

Despite the unusual details (foreign boyfriends and marriage of convenience), Grace's story shows a dual use of romantic irony and romantic melodrama typical in the stories of ambitious Shanghai women I interviewed. The larger frame is romantic irony or self-justifying satire.[31] Grace portrays herself as a "survivor," still dreaming of romance (despite her temporary marital status), but unable to live by its ethical demands ("pure love") in a competitive, materialistic, and cruel world. The basic principle of satire is survival. Satire (in her case verging on cynicism) allows moral and pragmatic compromises. On the other hand, Grace absolutely "believes in love," she says. She believes she suffers for a reason. She is certain romance will come to her again. The basic principles of her romantic melodrama are fate and morality.[32] Romance provides moral grounding (feelings and fate), nostalgic pleasure (her first love and a second American boyfriend), and future promise ("freedom, independence and happiness" in America).

Refugees and Survivors

Grace, like Ailin, frames her romantic experiences within an ironic narrative that characterizes her as a romantic survivor in a pragmatic and insufficiently romantic world. Uwe Japp describes this type of irony as "character irony"—a rhetorical trope in which an individual assumes herself in the role of an ironic character, who can work either tragically or comically depending on the context. More generally, it is a form of "practical irony" whereby the narrator describes the world in terms of a contrast between ideal and reality, or between public image and private life.[33] Young women I interviewed commonly employed two types of ironic self-characterizations, one that I call the "refugee" and the other, the "survivor." Though they reflect different positions in the sexual market, both narrative positions were ways of coping with the contradiction between reality and ideals, or between pragmatic social expectations and private romantic aspirations.

The first of these is essentially an antiromantic narrative, an acceptance of the pragmatic world of satire, in which romantic aspirations can only lead to disappointment, and the only residue of romance is the "refuge" of an economically secure man. Less-educated or working-class women often described their frustrating quest for a reliable man through the metaphor of a search for a "guisu" (a "refuge" or "home to return to"). The metaphor signifies a search for safety in the unpredictable and competitive market economy, like a ship finding a harbor, or a wanderer finding a final resting place. For example, Little Chen was a clerk at a trading company. She was twenty-five, but I thought she looked much older. She was plump, dowdy, and poorly dressed, the daughter of two poorly paid factory workers living in an old low-corner housing estate. She had worked in factories and retail since her teenage years and frequented low-corner social dance halls, where she met some of the men she dated. She hoped for romantic experiences, but found them hard to come by and difficult to believe in. She said she once had a serious boyfriend, who was also her first sexual relationship. I asked why she had broken up with him after dating two years, and she replied:

> After you've been with a person awhile, all of their bad points start be-coming obvious. At first you have this really intimate feeling, this feeling of being loved. Later you begin to feel cracks in the relationship. He had more problems [than me]. First of all he played mah-jongg all the time. Second, he didn't keep promises. He would agree to do something for me, like take me out, but then he wouldn't do it. Or he would say that he wouldn't go play mah-jongg that night, but he would still go play.

Little Chen had dated several men in the half year since her breakup but was disappointed in their poor quality and often mendacious romantic perfor-mances:

> Maybe they will say they will take you somewhere, or they are going to buy you some present, give you some jewelry, just something to get your trust, but, in fact, these are just empty words. Once a girl goes [to bed] with him, then he just casts her off. . . . They always give you a lot of promises, lots of pretty florid language. They tell the girl that they have sta-tus or that they have money. Girls are very vain. They feel he has status or money so they go with him. This is the weak point of city girls now, that they are vain. This gives guys an opportunity to use them.

She dated a series of unremarkable local men and was not overly ambitious about the type of man she wished to find. Despite her skepticism and modest goals, she still felt "cheated" in romance. At the time we spoke, she was dating a low-corner friend of mine who met her at a dance hall. He was married, though he hid this fact from her. Still, she knew their relationship was probably going to have no "result." I asked her what she was up to now. She replied glumly, "Now I am looking for a good man. This is like looking for a grain of sand in a bag of rice."

As discussed in chapter 3, Shanghai popular culture is full of stories about "gold-digging" pretty girls, but the apparent focus of these comments—young women from a poor background who date older and richer men—of-ten saw themselves as lacking in choices. Many doubted the veracity of "ro-mantic" experiences, while still hoping that they could have such experiences with men who would "treat them well." Most agreed that finding the refuge of a well-off husband would be a pragmatic process without the intense melo-drama of romance and the pure romanticism of true love. In a largely anti-romantic narrative, they allow themselves only the fatalistic romanticism of the "refuge" or "final resting place." Lili, a hotel clerk, looked like this typical Shanghai girl, with a wavy perm and thick rouged lips, often pursed in a scowl. She was similar to Little Chen in her low-corner working-class background, except that she was conventionally very pretty, slender, and tall. She had worked in a traveling "model team" before the hotel job. Nonetheless, she lacked educational credentials and opportunities for career advancement. Though she was twenty-four, she was sexually inexperienced and had never had a long-term boyfriend. She said her first boyfriend was her age, and they only went out for three months. "I didn't have the feeling for him. He was too immature. He wanted to control everything I did. He wanted to keep me under his watchful eye all the time." Her next boyfriend was an older businessman from Shenzhen, several years her senior. They dated a few times when he came up to Shanghai: "I really liked him. I even felt a little impulsive [chongdong] with him, like things might develop that way [sexually]. But before things developed that far, friends warned that he was married. So I quit seeing him immediately. I have been careful since then, not so impulsive." She then described several uneventful dating experiences with older businessmen she met or promising young men introduced by her rich uncle, but who didn't take to her. I asked her what kind of man she was looking for. "For me, a man's financial foundation is really important. . . . I want a refuge [guisu]." I asked if a refuge could be a young guy like Zhou, a mutual friend. She replied, "Zhou couldn't be a refuge. He isn't stable. I want to be with someone who is already quite steady. A refuge means a steady career and money. . . . He must have a career. He can't be an overnight rich guy. . . . And he must be honest and straightforward." I asked about Zhou because I knew she actually had a brief vacation romance with him and even had specially purchased some expensive lingerie when he asked her out again, apparently believing (according to her girlfriend) that he might be the right one for her "first time" (she was still a virgin). But Zhou unexpectedly canceled the date, and then Lili found out that he had another girlfriend. Her friends knew she was crestfallen, but she never mentioned her disappointment. In this conversation with me, she said several times that she mistrusted men who were not straightforward with her. I asked her about her girlfriends from school and how they had fared. She said, "Some found well-off guys. Some married factory workers, just 'living day to day' [guorizi]. Not many marry for love; very few people have really strong love." I asked if she could marry a worker and just "live day to day." "Maybe I could marry some poor guy I fell in love with, but I don't let myself meet these guys. For the same reason, I don't go out with younger guys at all." The last I heard, she was seeing a Hong Kong businessman who was also her first lover. ("It was nothing special," she told her friend.)

Little Chen and Lili share a disappointment in Shanghaiese men, especially their indecisiveness and unreliability. Both seek a refuge in an older man with maturity and resources who will love them (but whom they would not necessarily love themselves). Working-class women generally seem less committed to the drama and play of romance than more economically secure and higher-status women. Rather, they see men's romantic packaging as often hiding a poor-quality or deceptive product. On the other hand, I see such cynical disclaimers more as a form of self-protection than a complete disavowal of romance. These women valued the romantic expressions and romantic tokens men presented to them, but doubted the reality of the commitments such tokens represented. Both Little Chen and Lili felt they had to protect themselves from romantic feelings at the same time they hoped that men's feelings would be strong enough to bind a man to them.

In contrast to Little Chen and Lili (see also Gan in chapter 5), many college-educated women or women with more economic and social resources used the metaphor of the "refuge" contrastively as a foil to their own status as romantic "survivors." College-educated women often decried men's lack of interest in more romantic and emotionally expressive relationships, complaining less about false advertising than poor artistry and perfunctory performances. Ailin was not the only white-collar woman who expressed disappointment with men's "businesslike" approach to dating. A twenty-five-year-old professional in a prestigious British firm, Lanping was a fashionable dresser with short-cropped hair and delicate features (some men said beautiful), was ambitious in her work (some colleagues said pushy and arrogant), and had a sexy girlish lisp (which some girlfriends thought insipid). Men liked her more than women did, but she often complained about her experiences with men. (My questions were edited out of this transcript.)

> I would like to find a really interesting boyfriend. I really hate this attitude of just finding a partner [zhaoduixiang]. I think this is a waste of life, a waste of feeling. I think a person should have some higher values. My parents believe that I should find a man who will be very responsible to me, who will be very reliable. They want me to be a traditional woman. Their idea is that you pick a man who is reliable, not a man you love. My mother is afraid I will get old and won't find a partner. . . . I don't just want a refuge [guisu]. Some girls just care about money. They just want a guy who can take care of them. . . . And these men want to find a partner, an "old lady." Men don't really care about falling in love. They don't care about whether you have common interests, ideas, and personality. They don't care about the process of getting to know you. They don't think about whether life

together will really be good and harmonious. They don't think about whether your living habits are suitable. . . . I have met many guys. They are all really childish. They will call you on the phone for two years, and then they expect you to just marry them. I really hate this attitude. . . . The fact is, I really care about my own happiness. My mother tells me that I am really selfish, but I don't care. China is a traditional country. So I know that if I don't care about my happiness, no one else will. Maybe people will say that I am selfish, and I admit that, but I believe, anyway, that you have to care about yourself before you can care about others. . . . Guys say it is easy for girls to get a rich boyfriend and easy for us to get a good job. I think they are wrong. Anyway, I will try to be optimistic.

Lanping saw romance as an expression of a profound emotional involvement in a relationship, which she saw men failing to appreciate. "Stingy," "immature," and "indecisive," Shanghai men are just looking for a wife with no interest in a unique romantic experience. Parents and society ignore romantic aspirations. Lesser Shanghai girls ruin the courtship process through their petty materialism. Women like Lanping and Ailin, even Grace, see themselves as romantic survivors, who "try to be optimistic" in this ironic society of deficient characters. Lanping actually dated quite a few men during the two years I kept in touch with her, including a Taiwanese businessmen several years older than herself, but she said they had trouble "trusting each other." She also had at least one brief sexual affair. One day in another conversation, she mentioned a "one-night stand" (in English). I asked her how that happened: "That's a girl's secret," she said coyly in English. Switching to Chinese, she said defiantly, "Many girls have done that. You could ask B [a staid coworker] about that. I'm sure she has done that too. . . . Chinese people do everything but don't like to talk about it. Americans talk about it too much." She paused, then she said:

That was the only time I've done that [had a one-night stand]. I went out with some friends, and I met him dancing. He was a really attractive man, and I really wanted to be with him. He took us out after the dancing, and later I went home with him. It was very romantic and very wonderful. . . . We had been drinking. Maybe if I wasn't drinking, then it wouldn't have happened so quickly. . . . The next morning we got up and went to the market to buy something for breakfast. That was really romantic.

Such short-term "romance" could be disappointing, however. As Lanping explained, this man turned out to be unavailable, and she was sad about the relationship ending so soon. On the other hand, she also had slept with men whom she soon discovered she didn't like, but who had interpreted sex as a commitment on her part. Her problems were typical for sexually active young women whose romantic adventures were often misinterpreted by men as either meaningless sex or as a token of possession.

For the most part, educated and better-off women such as Lanping were able to frame failed love affairs ironically as learning experiences and as a coming-of-age, casting themselves as romantic survivors in an unromantic world. However, in the gossip of peers, who was a romantic survivor and who was a pragmatic schemer was open to reinterpretation. For instance, I interviewed one college senior who critically described to me, one by one, the pragmatic motives of her classmates who had found matches to men with "good conditions," all cadres and businessmen. She then described the beginnings of her own sexual relationship with a foreign boyfriend:

> I was moved by his charisma, charm, and romanticism. I guess partly it was more or less "animal" desire, the desire to do it [make love for the first time]. . . . Anyway, I really like him, but I don't know what will happen in the future. I expect nothing out of the relationship. I don't want to use a man to make my way in life. . . .

In her narrative the pragmatic motives of the women surrounding her were a foil for her description of herself as romantic and independent. Needless to say, many others described her behavior as a pragmatically motivated attempt to snag a foreign husband. She wasn't unaware of these possible interpretations of her behavior, and thus emphasized her own "romantic" claims to a relationships based purely on feelings (and, less conventionally, lust). Seen from this angle, claims to romance are a reaction to an ironic rhetoric of pragmatic motives shared by others. Irony and romance thus can only be comprehended as paired rhetorical strategies in a dualistic rhetoric of motives, in which material interests are assumed and feelings laid claim to. The one term is meaningless without the other.

People tell sexual stories in order to empower themselves,[34] though such rhetorical strategies of empowerment are often neither so noble or fair-minded as many sociologists would prefer them to be. Shanghai women could describe themselves as refugees from—or heroic romantic survivors in—a competitive and pragmatic sexual marketplace. Either stance as survivor or refugee legitimated difficult choices and experiences. Which stance a woman took depended on her subjective appreciation of her choices, which depended, in turn, on her objective circumstances. Educated and higher-status women often assumed the role of the romantic survivor, pursuing a romantic quest for a man who was both materially successful and romantically "interesting," or else pursuing romance, marriage, and career separately. Despite the apparent naïveté of such ambitions, they were often guided by clear perceptions of self-interest, emotional needs, and ideals, as articulated by Lanping. Less-educated women, with dimmer career prospects, often construed themselves as refugees with little alternative but a capable man who could take care of them. While they did not doubt the existence of romance, many feared emotionally tying themselves to a man with poor prospects. Both the survivors and refugees were telling a story about the same culturally constructed dilemma of choice: money versus love. Romantic survivors were worried they would gain the former and lose the latter, or be perceived as pursuing money over love. Refugees were worried they would seek the latter and miss both. Their narrative is a story of pragmatic choices with only a vaguely romantic conclusion (the "refuge" or "final resting place") evoking the ideal of fate or destiny. Both types of romantic irony also were ways of coping with the pragmatic choices of partners, a concern made more real by increased opportunities for choosing again (and being rejected). Women of all social strata worried about men's pragmatic motives with women, treating women merely as trophy wives or merely as sexual conquests. The ironic framing of men's romantic motives thus represents a vulnerability to the choices of partners as well as a defense of one's own.

Victims, Players, and Cool Pragmatists

The increasing fluidity of courtship relations in Shanghai and the increasingly salient dilemmas of sexual choices meant that men also experienced dating as a disenchanted world of increasingly easy intimacies but increasingly weaker moral bonds. Jie, a slightly built but attractive man of thirty-five with a slow-moving career in sales, described his dating experiences and standards for a wife to me. "I have had seven or eight relationships with women, one after another, in a businesslike fashion," he said as a bit of a joke. I asked what he wants in a girl, and he replied:

> Marriage isn't just an emotional and sexual relationship, but also when you have problems, the woman can understand you. A woman should be able to help you and see your potential. The kind of girl who will look at you and say, "You will develop, you have a bright future," these are very few. Most of the girls want to see that you have money right now. . . .

Men often expressed a desire for such "help" and recognition of "potential." Unable to help men substantively in their careers and impatient with unproven potential, Shanghai women often perceived men's calls for help and advice as "indecisiveness" and "lack of initiative." And like men in Western countries, Chinese men became resentful when women failed or refused to take care of them.[35] Men seemed distressed by their dependence on women for emotional support, more than women, who complained instead of men's lack of feelings. Similarly, men expected loyalty. While women seemed more likely to accept a breakup as "fate" or as their own fault, men seemed more likely to perceive women as cruel and coldhearted. One young man told me, "Girls when they have feelings [for you] will only think of these feelings, but when they lose them, there is nothing at all you can do." Another man told his girlfriend when she left him, "You are the cruelest woman in the world." Men seemed to be shocked when women were disloyal, whereas women suffered fewer illusions about men.

Men subsequently had darker tales of abandonment, some joking, some cynical. For instance, one academic researcher told me bitterly that his past three girlfriends had all left him to go abroad or to marry foreigners. In its ironic and bitter tone, however, this story wasn't much different from a motorcycle-taxi driver who complained that his girlfriend had just left him for an independent businessman with more income, or a millionaire's bitter and vengeful narrative about his first girlfriend many years before:

> This was my first love. I was twenty-five years old. We dated eight years. When I was thirty-three we broke up. This was because she went to Singapore and married a rich guy. This was really a terrible blow to me. I had no money, and here she was with an overseas Chinese. From that time until today, I went crazy to work to make money. Now she regrets leaving me. We still keep in touch, so I know this. . . . Her parents gave her pressure to marry this guy. I was a cadre. I had status but no money. Then things changed, and under the "responsibility system," I have been able to make money. She regrets it now. She went over there and thinks their society is really different. She feels her status is lower. Now I have 10 million a year in personal income. So she regrets leaving me. But if she came back begging now, I wouldn't have her.

In these cases, men construed themselves as victims who had learned to keep an emotional distance from women through bitter experience, sometimes to the extent of not being able to trust women enough to fall in love again, as this millionaire claimed.

Men sometimes used the role of the victim to legitimate a life as a playboy, men who move from one casual sexual relationship to another.[36] One small businessman aged thirty-eight talked with me casually about his bitter love affair and current sex life: "I am the kind of guy who makes loves but doesn't get married. There are a lot of people like me. . . . I don't have the feeling of love. I'm just playing around."

I asked if he has feelings for any of these lovers. "No, I never have feelings. I am in love with this one girl, so no matter what other girl I am with, I can't have feelings for her." He explained that this girl is also in Shanghai and that they dated three years, and that she broke up with him because he wasn't the right match.

> I wanted to marry her, but she wasn't willing. . . . But my whole life I will never get her out of my heart. I have been patiently waiting to get her back. . . . One problem is that she is twelve years younger than me. She feels that is too much. . . . In China it isn't so simple. She has her family, her coworkers, her friends, all of these are important to her. They were opposed [to our relationship]. For her, love isn't the only important thing. All these other things are also important.
>
> As for the other girls, I just feel tired, so I go out with them. They know that [I don't have feelings for them]. Even if I told them I did, they would know that I was lying. They don't need to think a man loves them in order to do that [have sex].

Being the "victim" of a failed love affair insulates the player from commitment and dependency in his current sexual relationships. This rhetorical strategy was common among Shanghai playboys, though a less extreme victim/player role often appeared in other men's stories. Note that the source of this man's victimization was the pragmatic choice of his girlfriend, mirroring the anxieties of the women about men's pragmatic motives.

Finally, not all men were romantics or players. Although men liked to complain about women's high material standards for a husband, some men used these material conditions as a way of avoiding the emotional complexities of relationships. These men described marriage as a practical step they would take after establishing themselves in a career, substantiating the complaints of educated women like Ailin and Lanping that men treated relationships in a businesslike fashion. Such men told me they would focus on their careers before they "found an old lady." Some described dating without a clear prospect of marriage as a "waste of time." After they found housing and a good job, marriage would be an easy matter to deal with. This cool pragmatist stance meant displaying a masculine indifference to romance. Despite their opposite impli-

cations for sexual involvement, these ironic stances of men—as the cool pragmatist or as the victim/player—both seem intended to diminish the risks of
emotional involvement with women and the emotional (perhaps also financial) costs of romantic performances.

Men's and women's ironic narratives both were ways of coping with the in-
security of an increasingly free, unequal, and treacherous sexual marketplace.
The weakening of premarital loyalties was experienced by both men and
women as a disenchantment and rationalization of the dating experience, and
youth developed new kinds of emotional strategies to deal with the frustrations
of competition. Illouz describes this ironic distance toward romance in Foucauldian terms as a "discipline of the self."[37] I describe both "romance" and
"satire" as emotional tropes, complementary tactics for expressing feelings and
denying feelings, used both for impressing others and coping with one's own
frustrations, requiring as much artfulness, or style,[38] as discipline. Ailin's pursuit of romance and her ironic descriptions of actual dating experiences show
how these contrasting frames of romance and irony function less as opposites
than as apposite moments in a binary rhetoric of romance and satire. This rhetoric was highly gendered, but allowed more flexibility than these brief discussions can show. Young men could be sentimental. Young women could be
cool.[39] In essence, both men and women were faced with the same structural
dilemma of choice and uncertainty, represented culturally as a crisis of pragmatic motives, projected onto others in romantic irony. Romance and satire
were paired responses to this dilemma, the one affirming truth and beauty, the
other allowing for ugly compromises.

A Shanghai Style of Romance?

In interviews I conducted at Shanghai colleges, students from other
parts of China often accused Shanghai youth of romantic guile and insincerity.
In turn, Shanghai college students made fun of naive and overly earnest small-
town and rural students, seeing their sincerity as unsophisticated or even dangerous (for instance, leading to suicide or severe depression in the case of failed
love). Shanghai youth valued romantic expressiveness but were increasingly
dismissive of particular tokens of romance, especially those they consider trite
or fatuous. Their aestheticization of romance and ironic distancing from it
might explain the common perception among outsiders that Shanghaiese are
insincere, calculating, and fickle. With my limited comparative data, I can conclude nothing about differences with other Chinese or among Chinese regions.
I do argue that the uses of romance and satire among Shanghai youth discussed

in this chapter represent new or enhanced rhetorical strategies, or poetic arts, for expressing feelings in more fluid and uncertain relationships.

This new Shanghai style of romance encompasses two related trends. The first trend is an aestheticization of romantic feelings, the playful and ritualized expression of feelings though romantic performances that celebrate feelings while revealing their fictionality. Commercial media simultaneously promote this rhetoric of romance while undermining its particular expressions. In this cycle of romantic fashions, particular tokens of romance are reduced to impersonal clichés and are supplanted by newer ones. The second and related trend involves the application of "romance" to short-term love affairs and a subsequent skepticism about the ethical promises of romantic love. As Illouz argues, ironic frames of romantic narratives are empowering for men and women because they empower people to choose again. At the same time, an "ironic structure of feeling" becomes a kind of emotional discipline necessary for coping with romantic disappointment.[40] Irony, however, does not supplant romance in Shanghai's new dating culture. Rather, these emotional tropes develop together. Both romance and irony are increasingly useful arts in the tricky sexual marketplace of postsocialist Shanghai, where failure is always possible and success depends on putting on a good show. In the end, the best romances may simply be memories for sharing with friends and intimate strangers, but a life without romance is dull.

At the pricey Luna Café, Shanghai men and women meet at a Valentine's Day party organized by a commercial Internet provider for visitors to an online chat room. On the wall behind them, an ad for the locally produced Shanghai Beer plays on the reputation of the city for sexual adventure. © 2001 Fritz Hoffman.

A Shanghai couple strolls down fashionable Huaihai Road on a Sunday afternoon. Window-shopping on Shanghai's central boulevards was a common dating activity for Shanghai couples.
© 2001 Fritz Hoffman.

A couple in rented wedding regalia is positioned for the requisite wedding photos at one of Shanghai's numerous bridal photo studios. A set of such photos could cost several thousand yuan. © 2001 Fritz Hoffman.

Shanghai businessmen practice their ballroom dancing steps in an informal group class on Shanghai's Bund at 7 A.M. © 2001 Fritz Hoffman.

A textile company in Shanghai previews its spring fashions to a group of buyers and other visitors. Racier fashion shows were popular tourist attractions in Shanghai. © 2001 Fritz Hoffman.

A male stripper plays with a female patron's foot during a performance at the Adam Show Zone, Shanghai's first male strip bar, open only for one month in 1998 before it was closed by the police for violating prohibitions against strip shows by either sex. © 2001 Fritz Hoffman.

As viewed from the top of Tomorrow Square while under construction in 2000, only a handful of the skyscrapers that crowd Shanghai's burgeoning skyline were built before 1990.
© 2001 Fritz Hoffman.

Visitors at a real estate fair view models of new apartment complexes. Beginning in the 1990s, purchasing an apartment became the primary practical concern of young Shanghai couples. © 2001 Fritz Hoffman.

A Western man chats up a Shanghai woman at YY's, the most popular nightclub in Shanghai in the summer of 1998. The bathroom at YY's is featured prominently in the racy novel *Shanghai Baby*. © 2001 Fritz Hoffman.

On Valentine's Day a couple embraces in front of the Opera House on Shanghai's central People's Square. © 2001 Fritz Hoffman.

Three women and three men (not visible) enjoy a Western-style meal on an expensive date at the popular restaurant and nightspot Park 97 (now California). A date at such a restaurant could easily cost 250 yuan ($30) per person. © 2001 Fritz Hoffman.

A Taiwanese businessman meets with his newly introduced Shanghai girlfriend at an Italian ice-cream shop on the pedestrian mall section of Nanjing Road. After a few meetings, he had decided to marry her and take her back to Taiwan. © 2001 Fritz Hoffman.

纯洁

VIRGINITY
Purity of Purpose

Changing Premarital Standards
"I Am Modern, but I Am Pure"

In the July 2000 edition of the Shanghai magazine *Young Generation*, I saw an article with the quaint title "I Am Modern, but I Am Pure" (*Wo xiandai, keshi wo hen chunjie*). Glancing at the title, I anticipated an old-fashioned exemplary story of a girl who manages to be fashionable and romantic without giving in to the temptation of premarital sex. Illustrating the article is a playful clay-doll figurine in trendy tight jeans, platform sandals, and a scant halter top, but also sporting angelic wings and a halo while floating among the clouds. The hip feminine angel represents the protagonist, the "modern, but pure" Shanghai girl. After graduating from university as an English major, the protagonist finds a job with the Korean conglomerate Samsung, where she falls in love with an engineer from rural China, the son of peasants. Despite his above-average job and educational qualifications, her parents oppose the match because he has no money, no house, and is not Shanghaiese. To break up the couple, they send her off to New Zealand to study for an MBA. After three months she decides not only that New Zealand is not as economically promising as Shanghai, but that she would prefer to pursue her true love rather than finish a prestigious foreign MBA. She returns to Shanghai, and she and her boyfriend move into an apartment together. She decides that she will live with him until they are ready to have a child, then they will marry. The narrator concludes, "I think this is a modern girl who has preserved her purity."

This conclusion would not have made sense ten years before. Despite already changing moral standards, "purity" (*chunjie*) in the 1980s was often simply a euphemism for virginity, especially when describing the romances of college-age **223**

women. Though the word has always had other connotations such as selfless-
ness, until recently one couldn't imagine describing a young woman as "pure"
who was in fact living with her boyfriend in a sexual relationship. But that is exactly the situation described in this July 2000 magazine story. What makes her
pure is not her virginity, but rather her pursuit of pure "feeling" as opposed to
all the impure material "conditions" Shanghai girls are conventionally tempted
to pursue: a wealthy husband, a chance to live abroad, a fine house, and social
status (including the Shanghai background). This makes her "pure" in the eyes
of the narrator, and indeed I would argue in the eyes of most Shanghai youth today (though some might also find her foolish, as with most icons of purity, Par-
sifal, Lei Feng, Xu Hu, etc.).[1] Rhetorically, this discourse displaces the referent of
moral purity from acts to purposes. Purity in premarital relations is now purity
of purpose, rather than the purity maintained by not engaging in a sexual act.
The fact that the couple engages in sexual relations is taken for granted given the
depth of their romantic feeling, but sex is not explicitly mentioned.

Conceptualizing Sexual Norms

During the reform era in Shanghai, a quiet revolution occurred in
the discourses and practices surrounding women's virginity. Based on a 1996
survey of married couples, nearly 40 percent of recently married Shanghai
couples had sexual intercourse with their current spouse before marriage, far
more than previous generations and far more than youth in many other parts
of China (see tables 7.1 and 7.2). These results might be read as a conservative
estimate of sexual behavior among current youth. A survey of Shanghai women
applying for a marriage certificate in 1996 found that nearly 70 percent had already experienced intercourse.[2] This behavior defies traditional injunctions
against premarital sexual intercourse that prevailed for "respectable" women as
late as the 1980s in urban China.[3] In my own research in the 1990s, I found

Table 7.1. Report of premarital sexual behaviors for married Shanghai couples by
age of wife in 1996.

	under 30 (%)	31–40 (%)	41–50 (%)	50–65 (%)	All ages (%)
None	1.1	8.1	15.1	43.4	16.1
Just Kissing and Petting	60.8	68.1	72.7	50.6	65.0
Sexual Intercourse	38.1	23.9	12.2	6.0	18.9

Data from 1996 survey, "A Study of Marital Satisfaction in China," conducted by Xu Anqi (Shanghai
Academy of Social Sciences); 1,600 husband-and-wife pairs were interviewed, and if either reported
a behavior, it was counted as a positive incidence.

Table 7.2. Report of premarital sexual behaviors for married couples by Chinese region in 1996.

	Shanghai (urban coastal) (%)	Harbin (urban interior) (%)	Gansu (poor rural interior) (%)	Guangdong (wealthy rural coastal) (%)	All regions (%)
None	16.1	31.5	85.6	45.2	44.6
Just Kissing and Petting	65.0	62.9	13.0	42.0	45.7
Sexual Intercourse	18.9	5.6	1.4	12.8	9.7

Data from 1996 survey, "A Study of Marital Satisfaction in China," conducted by Xu Anqi (Shanghai Academy of Social Sciences). Only these four locations were surveyed in this study; 6,410 husband-and-wife pairs were interviewed, and if either reported a behavior, it was counted as a positive. All age groups are combined.

that many, probably most, Shanghai youth have come to accept sex as a normal part of courtship and love, while others still hold to a norm of premarital chastity.[4] What, then, has happened to the ancient Chinese norm of premarital virginity for women? More to the point, how do Shanghai youth negotiate a new understanding of virginity in a time of social change associated with the market transition?

Sociologists studying a similar transformation of youth sexual culture in the mid-twentieth-century United States created a "universal permissiveness scale" to describe changing rules governing premarital sex.[5] While such positivistic scales may remain useful in survey studies, they cannot convey the local cultural grammars through which youth express sexual norms and values. Nor can they represent the rhetorical practices through which youth make practical, moral, and aesthetic judgments. The conventional continuum of sexual norms from "conservative" to "liberal," still common in much sociological theory, misrepresents this cultural change as a simple "liberation" from social prohibitions. Sexual norms in market societies may be more permissive, but they also require different forms of social and self-regulation from societies where community norms leave less latitude for individual expression.[6] Sexual norms thus involve much more than conforming to, or disobeying, a rule. As described in the previous chapter, the talk of young women and men reveals a complex rhetoric for expressing sexual emotions and hiding them, including not only new forms of discipline but tactics for evading discipline. In sum, a full description of sexual norms involves not only values and rules (expressed in stories as conventional purposes and conventional means of action), but also the expressive arts and rhetorical competencies through which these norms are articulated, manipulated, and contested.

Sociologists studying sexuality have come to realize that concepts such as virginity are best understood not as discrete and stable "attitudes" but as collectively produced stories and situational scripts used by individuals in tactical and inconsistent ways.[7] Stories are useful precisely because they are not clear rules. Sexual stories convey the complex and peculiar situations in which pragmatic sexual choices are made. Ambiguous, elliptical, and complex, sexual stories of real people are "good to think with" for the very many youth who haven't quite made up their minds about premarital sex.

The arts of rhetoric become most important in these situations when people perceive themselves as making important choices.[8] Particularly in times of rapid social change, contradictory sexual standards coexist in the same social spaces. The conventional elements of sexual culture become a "cultural tool kit" for youth finding and legitimating new tactics of social action.[9] With increased freedom of sexual choice and uncertainty about the morality of premarital sex, Shanghai youth must persuade others to act, persuade others about their own choices and even about the ethical assumptions and beliefs upon which they base these choices. The rhetoric of sexual storytelling involves manipulating the terms of the conventional grammar of motives described thus far in this study. Most typical perhaps is the rhetorical displacement seen in the magazines story above, from a focus on the sexual act to a focus on the sexual purpose. In a society in which virginity is still important, focusing on "pure motives" alleviates the still troubling connotations of the physical act.

Changes in this sexual grammar and rhetoric depend most directly on changes in the institutional contexts in which sexual communication takes place. For the culture of premarital sex, the most important of these contexts is courtship. In China, as in the United States, youth in long-term dating relationships are much more likely to engage in premarital sex.[10] The increasing incidence of premarital sex in Shanghai thus is most plausibly linked to the new institutions of dating and expressive romance described in the previous two chapters. Conversely, in comparison to the United States, the newer and less institutionalized dating culture and the later age of dating also explain the relatively later age and lower frequency of premarital sex in Shanghai. More to the point of this chapter, the peer culture is also the site of production of new sexual norms, and if U.S. studies can be a guide, the most important context in which youth discuss standards for premarital sex is the group of close friends.[11] This chapter focuses on the ways in which youth tell sexual stories among themselves and use the sexual stories of their friends, also considering the continuing influence of parents. Finally, youth also live in a changing institutional environment of laws, schools, and media that impacts their sexual behaviors and their ability to share information with one another.

I present the sexual talk of people of different ages, genders, and social classes in order to explore how they discuss virginity and draw selectively upon others' stories to frame their own experience. Rather than the colliding "deployments" of Foucauldian "discourse," or the discrete "attitudes" of standard sociological research, I argue that we should think of the negotiation of sexual meanings as conversations, including conversations with the self, in which the attitudes of others are taken into account in a Meadian process of moral self-definition and other-definition. Sexual talk among Shanghai youth reveals a negotiated learning process among men and women and the gendered tensions that still exist around discussions of women's virginity. Especially for women, these small-scale public spaces enable a limited sexual politics of identity construction, self-justification, and solidarity,[12] allowing sexually active unmarried young women a step toward "intimate citizenship" in a public sexual culture that has always silenced them or spoken for them only in terms of their regrets.

A Gendered Grammar of Virginity

In Shanghai there is no longer a single, shared standard of social morality (shehuidaode) regarding sex between unmarried people. On the issue of virginity, age seems a far more important organizer of opinions than social class or even gender. Shanghaiese who came of age in the early 1980s or earlier described very strong norms against premarital sex when they grew up and a great difference from the attitudes of "youth today." People in their twenties or younger concurred in these descriptions of more tolerant attitudes among their peers, though they may stake out differing individual positions against this assumed trend. Not surprisingly, sexually experienced youth generally seemed more accepting of premarital sex than those with no such experience. Gender is clearly the other major marker of discursive positions. In the "idle talk" of the group discussion, men and women differed in their expressed willingness to engage in premarital sex themselves. For women, admitting an interest or experience in premarital sex in talk with strangers in a group interview seemed uncomfortable (despite the use of female moderators), and women tended to equivocate in their support of these practices. Men showed more straightforward acceptance and enthusiasm. Among both genders, however, sexual naïveté and sexual moralizing were perceived as unsophisticated. Shanghai youth in general felt that sex was a "normal" topic, about which they should be able to speak without overt embarrassment.

The Spectral Husband

Most Shanghaiese who grew up before the 1990s insisted that premarital virginity was an important expectation for women when they were young. They located this expectation in the insistence of husbands upon their right to a virgin and the support that this demand received by families and the larger society. The following discussion among middle-aged working-class women describes the atmosphere on the factory floors where they worked during their early twenties around 1980:

> Moderator: Did men at your age pay a lot of attention to whether their wives were virgins?
>
> Ping: Yes, they did [strongly].
>
> Moderator: Did you think you could do it [have sex], so far as he had a good relationship with you and you would have a future later [get married]?
>
> Ming: That was more men's way of thinking [not women's].
>
> Sui: In our factory there is a woman who wasn't a virgin when she married her husband, so the husband didn't know how a virgin tasted. She then left her "sister" [workmate] together with her husband in a room and let him have a taste of a virgin.
>
> Ping: At our time, this was very important.
>
> Moderator: How about other people? You all felt that people paid a lot of attention to this?
>
> Shi: Of course. Back then, even if you had the marriage certificate but hadn't had a banquet, you couldn't do that.
>
> Ping: It was just so conservative. . . . If other people knew, she would be looked down upon in the work unit.
>
> Moderator: If you knew that she did it, would you look down on her?
>
> Sui: Yes, we would look down on her [emphatically].
>
> Ming: Unless somebody's stomach stuck out, nobody could know. [Everyone laughed.]
>
> Xiang: Now people don't think that way. So far as two people will be together later and aren't just fooling around, [it is okay].
>
> Ping: Thoughts have progressed one more step.
>
> Nong: Different eras.
>
> (married women in their late twenties and thirties,
no college education)

Men of the same age group shared these perceptions of the prior importance of virginity:

Jiang: We are not like foreigners. In China finding a person who has
   slept with other people, it is always . . . [uncomfortable facial ex-
   pression].

Moderator: So actually you still paid a lot of attention to whether or not
   your partner or wife was a virgin?

Jin: Of course. Now you can't understand it at all. You all are too romantic,
   not like before. . . .

Hong: It is the change of centuries. . . .

Jiang: Today's movies . . . Older people can't get used to it.

Jin: In the past if you showed these kind of movies, there would be a
   class struggle.

Jiang: Nowadays young people, if they find a girl, they don't care if she
   has had sex with other people. In the past people like us, if we
   knew that she had slept with somebody else, who would want her?
   Impossible.

Moderator: [To the others] How about you? According to your moral
   concepts? . . .

Quan: This gentleman [Jiang] is pretty realistic. After all, it is a question
   of social moral standards. In the past we were orthodox. Some of it
   was probably traditional and feudalistic, but there was something
   that was our national tradition, something that women did men
   couldn't tolerate. Now, probably the world has changed quite a
   bit . . . social reform and opening. In this particular era, there is no
   such thing as social moral standards. There are moral standards, but
   people ignore them. Now people are talking about "the rules of the
   game," not moral standards. Chinese people now don't have any
   beliefs, nothing.

Moderator: [To the others] Did you pay a lot of attention to your partner's virginity?

Jin: Extremely important, some would have a bloody fight for that.

Quan: That was her value [shenjia].

Altogether: Very important.

Deng: Everyone paid a lot of attention to it. Absolutely important.

Hong: Now everybody can risk that [losing virginity], but before, at
   most one or two.

   (married men in their thirties, mostly not college educated)

Almost all middle-aged Shanghai people I spoke with emphasized the importance attached to women's virginity in the early reform era. Virginity was a
sign of a women's "value" and a prized gift to her husband. Men would feel
"cheated" by not having a virgin; one might be laughed at by one's peers. The

bizarre story about the man who was compensated with a substitute "taste of a virgin" (unintentionally) parodies this sense of entitlement. The norm was constructed less around the idea of *premarital* chastity, than a man's entitlement to his own wife's virginity, that he should be her first (and only) lover. According to informants, some men and women in the early reform era accepted the idea of sex before marriage with the understanding that this was a "promise" of marriage.[13] However, many women informants said this was "more a man's idea." As one older woman said, "Some men would think, you had sex with me, so you will have sex with other men, too." Although some people in the early 1980s did engage in premarital sex, these practices were not part of the mainstream youth culture of the time.

Women attributed their own norm of virginity to men's insistence on a virgin bride. Janet Holland has described this as the surveillance of the "male in the head," a tendency of women to judge women's sexual behavior based on the expectations of men.[14] For Shanghai women who grew up in the 1980s, this expectation was no psychological illusion. Men seem to have truly expected that their wives would be virgins and even tested this expectation in the wedding bed. However, as a norm, the "male" is less "in the head" than in the stories women share among themselves. Although many more young women in Shanghai now are willing to face him down and engage in premarital sexual relations, the specter of an unforgiving future husband remains an important character in the stories of young women growing up in the 1990s in Shanghai. Women's standards for sexual behavior still focus a great deal on how men react to women's sexual experience.

The Telos of "Opening"

In general, married men and women in their late thirties assumed that "young people today" had more "open" attitudes and behaviors, and that social morality had changed, or in the words of one focus group participant, "disappeared." Regardless of their attitudes toward this change, older and younger informants shared a common narrative of "opening." "Feudal/modern," "conservative/open," and "Chinese/foreign" are the shifting binary terms of this narrative in which Shanghai society is moving in the direction of a "foreign," "modern," and "open" sexual culture, though it still contains "feudal," "conservative," or "Chinese" elements. Given the interchangeability of these terms ("feudal" for "Chinese" or "foreign" for "modern"), it was relatively easy for people in Shanghai to express a positive or negative attitude to this opening up of sexual morality.

These labels also serve as temporary rhetorical positions that people adopt in idle talk. To take an easy example, when flirting with foreign men, some young Shanghai women enjoyed taking positions of the "traditional Chinese girl" to rhetorically affirm her virtue, but also offering pleasurable possibilities of corruption and sudden "opening," a form of flattery to the romantic charisma of the foreign man that could easily obscure other purposes. A similar strategy could be used with local men, though not necessarily with the same easy effectiveness. The uses of "Chineseness"—seemingly the most emotionally salient of these identities—was thus polysemous and tactical. Even the presumed deficiency of the "Chinese" identity (its "feudal" connotations when faced with the "modern") was a source of its resilience as a category, allowing speakers sufficient excuses for violating the traditional moral definitions of "Chineseness" (such as premarital chastity) while reassuming this identity when it was more useful or comforting.

Young Women's Permissive Code of Feelings

Shanghai women in their twenties who participated in my focus groups generally found premarital sex acceptable and common among their peers, though this acceptance was not unequivocal or universal. Some focus group participants expressed surprise at the "open" attitudes of other women in focus groups (and other informal group discussions), sometimes changing their own opinions in conversations. (In university discussion groups, more "open" voices tended to be silenced.) I present the following lengthy excerpt from a group interview transcript because it shows the equivocal acceptance of premarital sex among young women. In general, this group was rather "liberal," but various shades of opinion in Shanghai are represented in this conversation. The discussion shows the way in which a permissive code of feelings has come to challenge the traditionalist rhetoric of "Chineseness" and "the male in the head" discussed above.

> Moderator: How about after leaving school? Among people of your age, how do they date? Do these "four steps"—"holding hands, embracing, kissing, and going to bed"—apply?
> Qing: Among the friends I keep in touch with, some have already reached the fourth step, that is the last step. They made a lot of consideration before making the last step.
> Moderator: Do you mean they considered marriage?
> Qing: Yes, and also their feelings [ganqing] and if it is worthwhile. They thought their feelings had reached this point, and they thought they could do it. . . . It is a way of expressing love. . . .

Moderator: Do you think it is good? Will you do it yourself? [No response.] Do you think it is acceptable? . . .

Cui: I think cohabitation is acceptable. If the situation allows, feelings are deep to a certain degree, economic conditions allow, and parents don't object, I think I will probably do it, too.

Moderator: How about other people?

Luo: It's possible.

Xuan: Cohabitation should be on the condition that the feeling is very deep. Because sometimes the conditions are not mature enough to get married [e.g., economic conditions are not mature], I think people can cohabitate first.

Zen: I don't object if other people wanted to cohabitate, but I won't do it myself. I am "feudal," and [I believe] not only women should keep their chastity but men should, too. Besides, my parents' education makes me not able to accept premarital sex. "Three steps" are enough, and the fourth one is not necessary. I think we should preserve the purity of love.

Moderator: If he had this request?

Zen: I could decline. Because my boyfriend should have the same ideas that I have, otherwise I won't choose him. But I have a colleague who is doing this. She thinks that she can't entrust herself to him, and should experiment for a while to see if they are suitable for each other, and wait till all conditions are met. If she can't stand him during this period, she will break up with him.

Moderator: So your colleague measures his suitability to be her husband in this way?

Zen: She had my point of view before she started dating, but she walked that way step by step after beginning this love affair.

Moderator: How about other people? From pubescence to marriage there are over ten years, what will you do about this?

Zen: I think when dating reaches a certain stage, premarital sex is a kind of catalyst to make the relation more intimate. Then it would be [because] I treated him as my future marital partner. This is acceptable if it happened in a particular environment.

Moderator: But he still should be a marital partner?

Zen: I mean under particular conditions. I still object to it in my point of view, but sometimes given the heavenly timing [tianshi], earthly suitability [dili], and environmental factors [renne], and you have reached this emotional point, [then it is possible with a nonmarital partner]. . . .

Moderator: [To the others] What do you think?

Cheng: I think it is acceptable.

Cui: I think it is healthy behavior.

Qing: I don't object. When love is as deep as this, I will do it.

Luo, Xuan: Acceptable.

(unmarried women in their early twenties, mostly college educated)

Based on questionnaires distributed after this conversation, only one of these women (Cui) had actually experienced intercourse, but most of them lived in social worlds where this was possible, socially acceptable, and desirable if it occurred in a loving relationship—or more colloquially a relationship characterized by feelings (ganqing). Although some opposed premarital intercourse, for all of these women, the development of these heterosexual feelings required expression through physical affection. Their standards ranged from petting and kissing as adequate physical expressions of feelings before marriage, to those who thought that premarital sex was a way of expressing feelings, testing feelings, a natural development of feelings, or a "catalyst" to deepen feelings. The concrete standards for judging and expressing these feelings were expressed as "personal," "felt," and situational and hence resistant to the critiques of others. In practice, it seemed, "feelings" could mean anything from a momentary passion to a committed relationship. As with relationships generally, feelings are the moral touchstone for sex, and a usefully ambiguous one. Sex becomes less a loss of virginity than a new way of expressing feelings. This ideal was expressed by a saying trendy among some young women in Shanghai, that "sex is the sublimation [shenghua] of love." This odd reversal of the Freudian paradigm seemed an attempt by young women to "spiritualize" sex. As such, it was an attack on the spirit/body opposition of the older discourse of premarital love.[15] This is not the rhetoric of self-styled cultural iconoclasts, but of self-styled conventional romantics, which doesn't mean, however, that their romanticism doesn't have subversive consequences.

The prospect of marriage was a desirable condition for engaging in sex for many of these young women, but only for a few was a promise of marriage a necessary condition for having a sexual relationship with a man. "Feelings," however, were described as an essential element for nearly all young women. Because the "giving" of one's "first time" was interpreted as a profound token of romantic feeling, an intent to remain with the person "forever" is implied, although this intent is ambiguous and open to multiple interpretations (and post hoc reinterpretations). Take, for instance, the following story told to me by Aihua, a thirty-year-old white-collar employee at a foreign firm in Shanghai and daughter of high-ranking cadres. Eight years earlier, when she was planning to go to Japan to study, she fell in love with a married man from Hong Kong. Her story indicates the contradictory pressures women faced when considering premarital sex in the late 1980s:

> I can say that I have been very unlucky in love. [She had dated a series of married men.] This man was already married. He was eight years older than me, from Hong Kong. I felt like he was my boyfriend, but I couldn't tell anyone about it. If I didn't go to Japan, I would have continued on seeing him. I really loved him, and I had the feeling that we were dating. But he had already been married two years. . . . . I wanted to marry him, a little, but this was a faraway idea. Of course, I would have liked to have the feeling that I was his only love. . . . . Anyway, for a long time we didn't sleep together. I had never done this before. Then right before I went to Japan, I decided that I wanted to do this with him. I loved him, and I felt like if I didn't do this with him, then I would never have another chance and I would be really sorry about it. I was very, very nervous. I was afraid that something would happen—I would get pregnant. I was going to Japan in two months and was worried that if I got pregnant I wouldn't know what to do about it in Japan. . . . . But I was willing to give my feelings [ganqing] to him, and I wanted to give this to him. . . . . All of our education tells you that this is a bad thing. So I was afraid my family would find out, and that other people would find out. But when I did it, I didn't think it was bad myself. I liked him and he liked me, and it was something I wanted to do. It was bad because others would point their finger at you, but I didn't think it was bad.

Her story contradicts the idea that premarital sex is always calculated by Chinese women in terms of the chance to capture a marriage partner. The decision to give a man this first time was framed as a profound token of feelings. For women, these feelings were measured in terms of an idealistic (often ambiguous) longing for a permanent relationship with the partner, but weren't always a practical calculation based on a real possibility of marriage, but an expression of a depth of feeling freely given by the woman. For young women dating in the late 1990s, the considerations were similar, though many seemed more willing to accept from the beginning the short-term nature of dating experiences. Mimi, a working-class women of nineteen, told me about her first time with a coworker at her factory (when she was seventeen): "One night I argued with my parents. I called him and waited for him. And then I cried on his shoulder. That night we did that. You could say that I gave 'that thing' [virginity] to him," she said with a laugh.

I asked what she thinks about that now. "I think it was worth it because he was a person I loved. I think that's all that matters. It's not necessary to get anything in return. The experience was romantic, even if in the end it didn't amount to very much" (they broke up a few months later).

She said that premarital chastity was not important.

It's not like before when if you did that, a guy had to "be responsible" [get married]. Now every girl has done that. Some people still talk about things like "being responsible" but not many. Of course, I am talking about people in the big city. You had better not even think of doing that out in the village. For young people now, what is important is the experience [guocheng], not a result [marriage]. . . . There is an expression that women in love are really stupid. I am like that. It is because you are so happy [xingfu] that you become stupid.

I asked about her experience of sex. "It was very sweet," she said with an affected sigh.

Young Shanghai men and women increasingly shared an understanding that sex no longer constituted grounds for demanding marriage, as it once had. Young Shanghai women saw marriage as a practical decision in which many more important factors were involved than past sexual history. Strong feelings could justify sexual relations when marriage was not practical.

Managing Parental Expectations

Young women did not develop their new moral code with reference to their peers alone. There was still social pressure for women to be virgins, and the strongest source of this pressure was parental expectations. Sometimes they described premarital sexual abstinence as a duty to their parents—not to do anything that would "shame my parents" (duibuqifumu). Although I did meet some girls in open, noisy rebellion against their parents, most described some degree of circumspection to protect the "face" of their parents in the neighborhood. Shanghai youth typically lived at home with their parents, and parents inevitably maintained more than a passing interest in their children's sexual lives, even into adulthood. Few parents approved of premarital sex for their own children, and most young women mentioned their parents' standards as an obstacle to premarital sex. In particular, in discussions of premarital cohabitation, Shanghai women generally agreed that this might be good in principle but parents wouldn't allow it.

However, "approval" and "permission" may not be the appropriate concepts to describe actual familial understandings, which were usually not openly communicated. Women with sexual experience often had a more complex view of parents' standards. For instance, Li, a twenty-seven-year-old secretary who was dating an older divorced man, said of her parents' attitudes toward premarital chastity: "They really care. Usually you will hide this sort of thing from them. Even if they know, you will pretend that they do not know. Even if they know in their hearts, then you will not just openly and clearly state it."

I asked, "Now if you go to stay with your boyfriend, will you hide this from your parents?"

She replied, "No I won't. I won't do that. After all, he is not a twenty-something-year-old who wouldn't know how to take care of you [contraception, etc.]. So they will have their hearts at rest."

In her view, which was very common, respecting her parents' standards meant not forcing them to deal with her sexuality while at the same time reassuring them that she was taking care of herself. Therefore, aside from their own peer-focused moral standards, adult Shanghai women worked to make their parents comfortable with their sexuality while avoiding actual discussions about sex. Parents' concern for their daughters' virginity wasn't perceived as a purely negative constraint by the daughters themselves, but as a naive desire to protect them from the "dangers" of adulthood. I asked Lei, a twenty-five-year-old stockbroker who lived alone and had already had many lovers, if her parents' concern for her virginity was mainly a matter of face for the family:

> Face is really only a small part of how they think about these things. After all, I live in Shanghai, so what I do here won't affect them very much [they live in Tianjin]. What really is more important is that they see a woman as a very precious perfect object. They protect her so much that they are almost not willing to give her away to anyone.

Like many young women, she found her parents' concern comforting and interpreted it as a sign of their caring rather than purely as a matter of control.

Relationships between children and parents were not a simple politics of control or agreement. Young women in particular desired autonomy from parental control, but also emphasized the trust (xinren) their parents placed on them. Even young women who lied to their parents about their sexual activity, or more typically said nothing about these matters, told me they valued the trust of their parents. "Trust" implied parental support for their general character, which seemed more important than following the particular rules parents set down or communicating openly with parents about sexual and dating experiences.

Male Discomfort and Masculine Cool

Unsurprisingly, young men shared a more permissive rhetoric of premarital sex than did young women. But in contrast with what older men say about the "disappearance" of morality, ideals of virginity were not absent among the younger generation, although the meanings of virginity and the strategies for dealing with it had changed. The following focus group transcript shows how the idea of chastity persisted in 1996 even in the permissive talk of educated young Shanghai men.

Moderator: Do you think it is illegal to cohabitate before getting married?

Altogether: No. There isn't any such statement in the law.

Moderator: How about according to your own ideas?

Wan: It is normal.

Peng: I think it doesn't fit conventions [li], but it is legal.

Moderator: What are these conventions?

Wan: They are the conventions formed by old ethics and morals.

Feng: According to my ideas, this is something one should do, and it is acceptable. It fits my conventions. Nothing wrong with it.

Moderator: [To Peng] Your conventions are related to social opinion?

Peng: Yes.

Wan: This kind of old ethics and morals will disappear when we get old.

Moderator: Do you think this is against morals and ethics [lunlidaode]?

Altogether: Not at all. [Peng didn't say.]

Feng: Because first, it is not forced; second, both sides want it. It is not a big deal; it is okay when both sides are willing.

Ni: "You wish and I am willing" [niqingwoyuan].

Moderator: When people talk about this problem, they will think women are at a disadvantage in this kind of relationship. For instance, in the case of a failure in a "marriage experiment." . . .

Feng: It is the leftover influence of feudal morality.

Altogether: [Agree.]

Han: I say, for women, after the first time it no longer matters.

Moderator: How about the first time?

Han: The first time . . .

Ni: [Interrupting] People get divorced after getting married. It doesn't matter.

Moderator: Have you thought of having a virgin to be your life partner, somebody who at least hasn't had this kind of relationship before you?

Altogether: No, I haven't thought about it.

Feng: You may say so, and everybody thinks it doesn't matter. But if she isn't a virgin, you will have a slightly different feeling. No way around it.

Han: What is the difference—you have something with your girlfriend and she ends up being with somebody else, or she has something with other people and ends up being with you?

Feng: Theoretically there is no difference. But I can tell you, if you meet a girl and want to marry her, and before you go to bed with her, you get to know that she has been with somebody else in the bed, you will always feel some . . . [makes an uncomfortable facial expression].

Han: I don't think there should be something.

Feng: Now you can say you don't feel it, but I can tell you . . .

Han: The girls I am seeing now . . . [Some argument going on here.]

Moderator: That is his opinion.

Moderator: [To Feng] What you mean is that you will feel a little uncomfortable [*geleng*, subtle uncomfortableness].

Wan: Nothing uncomfortable.

Moderator: Just not perfect.

Feng: Yes, not perfect. But I won't mind as much as people used to.

Moderator: Before people called it "Once skip, regret all your life."

Altogether: [Laugh at this kind of saying.]

Han: I should emphasize that if the men have desire, the women have it, too.

Moderator: So there is no such thing as disadvantage [*chikui*]? It is just satisfying each other?

Feng, Han: Yes.

Moderator: A lot of people don't encourage premarital sex, then how to solve this problem that both men and women have desire?

Han: Can't solve it by masturbation.

(unmarried men in their early twenties, mostly college educated)

These young men affirmed premarital sex through a vocabulary of free choice, normalcy, and human nature. Sex is a "natural" urge that can't be suppressed (or resolved through masturbation). Naturalization not only makes sex more legitimate, accessible, and modern, but rationalizes the loss of the male prerogative of defloration. Young women also "need" sex. In contrasting their own liberal values of free choice with conservative "social morality and ethics," men also availed themselves of a teleology of sexual opening by identifying virginity with backward feudal values. On the other hand, this liberal vocabulary of choice and nature makes it difficult for men to articulate their concerns, or discomfort, with a woman's previous sexual experience. The way one young man in the focus group described this discomfort was quite typical: a vague imperfection. Others with stronger reservations described a difficult to articulate, almost visceral discomfort with the idea that one's own wife or girlfriend had sexual intercourse with another man, a kind of retrospective sexual jealousy or possessiveness. This conversation shows the continuing relevance of a concept of virginity for some men, but also the incompatibility of virginity with their rhetoric of free choice and the verbal work men do to dismiss or explain away this discomfort or sexual jealousy.

Even in conversations with other men, men employed a code of gender equality that seems to be a legacy of socialist education. Shanghai youth often employed a golden rule that one should not expect of others what one does not expect of oneself, a norm these men invoked against a sexual double standard. As the male focus group participant quoted above said, "What is the difference—you have something with your girlfriend and she ends up being with somebody else, or she has something with other people and ends up being with you?" This golden rule didn't eliminate men's jealousies about their partner's sexual experience with other men, the crux of the virginity issue for most men, but the ethical grammar of equality, nature, and choice meant that men had to do some of the rhetorical work of managing their own feelings. This can be considered a new "feeling rule"[16] or rule of emotional rhetoric among men, which discouraged men from expressing discomfort about a partner's sexual past. Such emotional "coolness" was an essential competency in the new dating culture. Even among Shanghai men with few feminist leanings, a "cool" attitude toward virginity implied sexual experience and sexual confidence, important new markers of masculinity. As a very "cool" nineteen-year-old dance hall playboy said, "Most young men like us, we don't care [about a girlfriend's virginity]. We have a lot of experience. Someone who hasn't had a lot of experience, he will care more." Seen from another angle, to be a Shanghai man was to avoid the appearance of the rigid moralist. This posture was expressed crudely but clearly by an older self-styled playboy, a forty-year-old married salesman who said, "The only men who still insist on virgin brides are these ugly out-of-town boys with no sexual experience." Especially among sexually active young men out "in society" (not in college), the ideal of premarital chastity was dismissed as "hick" (tu). Being a sophisticated Shanghai man meant conveying a sense of sexual worldliness and coolly accepting women's sexual experience.

Male Experience and Female Silence: A New (and Improved?) Double Standard

This new masculine rhetoric of cool acceptance doesn't mean that men and women judged one another's past sexual experience in the same way. Young women might even see sexual experience as a desirable trait in a lover, while many men still found a virgin bride desirable (if no longer a requirement). As one male focus group participant sarcastically said, "No one will brag about how many men his wife has slept with." Sexually inexperienced men, however, might fear they will be laughed at as poor lovers. One young woman jokingly told me she didn't have sex with a boyfriend because, as she explained, "He had no experience. I had no experience. How's that going to work?" Or as a young woman focus group participant said more seriously, "I think he should have experience. He should know more, because women are more passive in this kind of relationship." Women, on the other hand, were enjoined not to talk about their past sexual experiences with their boyfriends, or even with no one at all. Few women I met spoke out against this silencing of women's own sexual experience. Ailin, described in chapter 6, argued that her future husband must be able to accept her past—"all of it"—if he were to understand her. But most other women seemed to accept the idea that women should hide their sexual pasts, at least from their male partners, to help men manage their discomfort with this issue. Many men and women valued male sexual experience positively (or at least neutrally), but both saw little need for women to have a broad experience, or at most, a limited and secret experience. Some younger women said that a woman having various sexual experiences before marriage might lead her to unfavorably compare her husband with her previous lovers. Although alternative views are heard, the shared ideal for women remained the image of the emotionally sensitive and sexually naive young woman, although now also capable of sexual passion with a man she loves.

The Value of Virginity

Although the focus of young people's moral discourse shifted from the act itself to the purposes of sex, women's virginity retained a sexual "exchange value" beyond premarital abstinence. Virginity was still considered a gift of a woman to a man. The value of virginity was expressed in the adjective "perfect" (wanmei) applied to virgin women. The reference was first to the unbroken hymen. Although Chinese magazine articles and middle school hygiene texts emphasized that a broken hymen was not a definitive sign of virginity, breaking the hymen ("splitting the melon" [kaigua] in crude language) was still considered a male privilege, and "seeing the red" (jianhong) a definitive sign of sexual initiation. Focus group participants pointed out that "you can never know with a man" if he had sex before, but with a woman, "you could know." Beyond the hymen, the "value" of virginity hinged on the power of sex to "make a woman,"[17] a notion compatible with the romantic interpretation of sex as a profound expression of feelings. Only women were assumed to undergo a change through the first time that was both physical, psychological, and moral. As Bei said of herself in chapter 2, "I think sex is like candy, once you start eating, you can't stop. You will have a first time, then a second, then a third, and so on." A sexually active man said more or less the same when I asked him if some of his "play" partners were virgins. "No, most girls are very particular about their first time. But after that, then they don't care. One time is the same as a hundred times. It is like a floodgate that once you open, you can never close it." Sex was considered a transformation of a "girl into a woman" that would also ensure she would become a sexual being thereafter. This notion of the momentous "first time" played into the romantic understandings of sex among less experienced women and into the heroic sexual fantasies of men fascinated with the idea of permanently leaving their imprint in a woman's body and consciousness. On the other hand, this romantic idea of first sex was sometimes contradicted in the ironic narratives of more sexually experienced women, who might describe their first sexual experiences as unmemorable or as a mistaken farce, as I will discuss further below.

Even among those who did not take the hymen to be the standard of virginity, the fetish of female virginity remained strong for both men and women. "Having a virgin" was a special honor for a man. Whether a man was "worth giving my first time" was a consideration I heard from young women who were contemplating a first sexual experience. To be "worth it," there should be some reward of feeling, commitment, or material benefit. The idea of a girl being "swindled and cheated" out of her virginity (shangdangshoupian)—giving it up for nothing—was a stock expression in Shanghai (though frequently a joke in the late 1990s rather than an earnest cautionary tale as it had been a decade earlier). A woman still felt pressured not to appear to be foolishly giving her virginity to a man who didn't value his relationship with her. If her close friends approved of the relationship, however, first sex could be a positive, even semipublic rite of initiation. According to the new "rules of the game" current among both young men and women, gullibility rather than sexual experience was the greater failing for a young woman.

The Changing Characters of Respectability

An older double standard in Shanghai was to divide women into "fallen" (*duoluo*) or "bad" girls with whom one could have premarital sex, and "respectable" or "good" girls with whom one couldn't. This standard is not completely dead, but contemporary Shanghai youth now have different distinctions of respectability. In contrast with the article that begins this chapter, this definition is usually negative, that is, framed through the stereotypical characters of sexually deviant women. In the early reform period, Shanghaiese used the term "*lasan*" (trash/slut) to describe socially and sexually deviant girls. The term descends from the presocialist-era slang term "*lajimache*" (literally "trash wagon") for sexually promiscuous women.[18] The *lasan* in the late 1970s was a low-status woman who wore overtly sexual dress and hairstyle, performed poorly in school, and engaged in "lights-out dance parties" and idle flirting with men. A 1980 magazine article uses the term "*lasan*" to describe girls arrested as "hooligans" (*liumang*).[19] The term "*lasan*" marked a social outcast; her opposite was not a "virgin" but the "respectable" girl automatically assumed to be a virgin. Another term used in the early 1980s in Shanghai was "*meibing*" (slag/slut), a pejorative term for prostitutes (literally "coal block").[20] The "coal block" was a woman "penetrated" repeatedly and sullied beyond hope of redemption, like the Shanghai coal blocks that were made of compressed coal dust with holes punched through them. The terms "*lasan*" and "*meibing*" represented women considered debased, dirty, and outside the ethical margins of normal society.[21]

By the 1990s, however, these harsh terms had almost completely fallen into disuse in Shanghai. In their place was a far more ambiguous set of characters on a continuum from the prostitute to the highly esteemed but slightly disreputable office girl. The most salient dimension of "respectability" (or "fallenness") in the 1990s was a distinction of *motives* between sex for feelings (*ganqing*) and sex for material ends. As described in chapter 2, this discourse of motives is most often represented through stereotypical character types associated with particular occupational and social statuses. These material girls comprise a wide range of feminine types, including the "*xiaomi*" ("little secretary," "little honey," or mistress), the "*K-jie*" (karaoke hostess), the "*diaomazi*" ("fishing girl"), the "*gongguanxiaojie*" (public relations girl), the "*jinsiniao*" ("bird in a golden cage," or a kept girl), the "*wailaimei*" (little country sister), or the more ambiguous "xiaojie" (or "little miss," sometimes a term for a commercial sex worker). These were the less respectable girls of 1990s Shanghai, though with the exception of the "ji" (prostitute or literally "chicken"), they were not considered prostitutes. These character types incorporated some of the features of the lasan (crassness and sexual availability) but remained thoroughly within "normal" society. Even the K-jie and ji were often mentioned sympathetically, and their material motives described as "normal" and understandable. "That is just another way of making a living," many people said of the ji. Such characters inhabited the same moral universe as more respectable character types. Even the "white collar" (bailing) and "strong woman" (nuuqiangren) appeared to practice an "open" and mercenary sexuality, different from the ji only in degree.[22] The fallen girls of the 1990s thus existed on a continuum that ranged from the ji, a professional prostitute, to the white-collar miss, an office worker whose sexual autonomy, material ambitions, and contact with foreigners situate her in a world of material and sexual temptations, though otherwise she is respectable, even admirable. Even the worst sort of "fallen woman," the prostitute, is defiled by a money motive that is fully inside the pale of normal aspirations. In fact, the extremely virtuous woman, who cares only about feelings, is now considered rare, even foolish. Purity, in this new sense, is purity of motive, rather than purity of the body, and such purity is a relative and ambiguous, never an absolute, standard.[23]

In a sexual culture dominated by the twin god-terms of "money" and "feelings," women have sex either for real love or the material motive. In contrast, the idea of pointless casual sex, or sex for "fun," was not the focus of public moral discourse, the way it seems to have been in the United States during a similar change in sexual standards. Still, Shanghai people did occasionally talk about the "sexual play" of themselves and others, usually in the context of the nightlife. Such play, by definition with no basis in feelings, was not "respectable," especially for women, though it usually imputed only a temporary or deniable "fallenness." The character of the bad girl or playgirl could be ascribed to others, as in "girls who play" (baixiangdenuuxiaoren), or taken on oneself as a form of rebellious play role as in "I'm a bad girl," said as a joke or come-on ("I'm a good girl" sometimes serving the same purpose by pointing at its opposite possibility). While usually derogatory out of the context of the nightlife world, the adjectival "play" (baixiang) and "bad" (huai) were not insults like the term "lasan." These were situational identities rather than permanent ones. They could apply to both men and women. To be purposefully "bad," as in available for sexual play in the dance hall, was a kind of temporary rebellion

and an off-color stance, but not a permanent exit from normal society. The transition from "bad" back to "respectable" only required a change of scene and
purpose. Sexually active girls in 1990s Shanghai thus had many positions in
which to define their behavior: as the "respectable" true romantic, as the more
or less mercenary little miss, or as the temporarily bad girl just playing around.
These terms were not equally available to everyone. A low-corner, fashionable
girl such as Gan, Lili, Mimi, or Linda had little chance of escaping the label of
the little miss or public relations girl who would have sex for material advantages. When dating these women, men often expected sexual favors. A university foreign-language major, on the other hand, had a far better chance of
pulling off the self-indulgent bad girl who herself played with men, *even* foreign
men. Still, none of these terms carried the deep moral stain of sexual activity as
they did years before. And none were standards that applied only to women,
though women's motives were scrutinized more closely than those of men by
a voyeuristic society that still assumed a woman's sexuality, particularly her virginity, was a thing of greater value and consequence.

The Rhetoric of Women's Sexual Storytelling

Given the danger of looking gullible, cheap, or frivolous, women must
still justify giving their first time to a man outside of marriage. The most typical
form of justification was through sharing stories among friends,[24] though this
was still a precarious practice for young women in Shanghai. Not all friends,
even peers, welcomed sexual stories from unmarried women friends, and based
on my interviews, quite a few women did not talk about sexual experiences with
friends. But most women had at least a few confidantes with whom they shared
stories, a circle that seemed to expand as women enter their mid-twenties and
sexual experience was assumed. Sexual stories come from a variety of sources,
including the media, but when people talk about right and wrong, the most persuasive sources seem to be people they know.[25] Media figures, foreigners, and
other more distant people lack the moral persuasiveness of the classmate, neighbor, coworker, or friend. Despite the small number of confidantes with whom
women shared their own stories, women very often shared friends' stories
across friendship circles. Such friendship and gossip networks were an important medium for the definition of a new youth sexual culture.

Facing Down the Future Husband

Although some Shanghai women professed to be unconcerned about
their future husband's attitude toward their past sexual experience, many more

seemed to be facing a particular "male in the head," the specter of a future dis-
approving husband. Here I describe how some sexually inexperienced young
Shanghai women I interviewed "faced down" the "male in the head" through
the practice of storytelling and sharing stories, using the forms of other
women's experiences to reflect upon their own possibilities. Friends' stories
were not only persuasive because they are "real," but because they allow for
complexity, ambiguity, and indecision, which made them more useful than abstract and general rules. Inexperienced young women used these ambivalent
stories to think through the conditions for having sex and to prepare for several alternative outcomes.

Some uses of these stories were self-cautionary and led women to propose
avoiding sex, though even the most cautionary stories allowed multiple uses.
Take the following story told to me by Bei, a twenty-one-year-old woman described in chapter 2:

> I have this girlfriend. While she was still in college, she started living
> with her boyfriend. Her parents silently put up with it, but their neigh-
> bors gave them funny looks and talked behind their backs. One day, how-
> ever, the boy took another girl back to their place and she found out. She
> asked the boy what was happening. He said that they were already to-
> gether such a long time, and . . . I'm not sure of the details. Anyway, this
> was a very strong girl. She packed her bag and walked out. He begged her
> to come back, but she refused. When I asked her, she didn't regret what
> she had done.
>
> Later she married a manager of a firm. He was Australian Chinese,
> and they went to Hong Kong for their honeymoon. He had never asked
> her before if she was a virgin. He had just assumed that Oriental women
> were more conservative. Afterward he seemed to be a little upset. She then
> told her husband about her past. Later on he gave her a passage in the book
> Forrest Gump, in Chinese, which said something like, "Sometimes men just
> have to face up to facts." And afterward everything was all right, but there
> was this little shadow on their relationship. She didn't realize her husband
> would be so conservative. She figured that after living in Australia so long,
> he would have been influenced by Western ideas.
>
> I guess that for men, the more perfect [wanmei] the better. I have talked
> about this story with my girlfriends. So we really don't know who will
> care about these things. Nor do we know if we will do this. Sometimes we
> talk about these topics, and I think that when I get married, and it isn't
> perfect, there will be a little regret. So for most of us classmates, we are
> open in thinking, but not in behavior.

Many uses of other people's stories showed a complex rhetoric of self-cautioning and self-emboldening. Wei, a nineteen-year-old music student of more bold disposition than Bei, offered these comments when I asked about the possibility of having sex with her new boyfriend:

> If I really love him, and he really loves me, when the time is right, then this thing is possible. But I don't want to be like this girl I know, and because of one bad experience, because of being hurt, just lose balance. She is already working, and she is a few years older than me. She had a first boyfriend and did this with him. She really loved him, but then he broke up with her, and she was really hurt. She felt really bad, and she just couldn't get hold of herself. She just started doing this a lot with a lot of different people. Sometimes she will just go out with a guy with money or with high status, and sometimes because she likes someone. I just don't think she deals with this well at all. But other than this, she is really a good girl. I just think that if your boyfriend drops you, it doesn't mean you should abuse yourself.

Cautionary tales about losing one's virginity could take many forms, but there were two standard cautionary tales in conversation and in popular culture: the woman whose husband couldn't accept that she gave her virginity to someone else, and the young woman who lost her virginity and then lost control of her sexuality. While cautionary, these stories are usually ambivalent and allow multiple readings. The first story represents a fear that women often decide is misplaced, or a danger they are willing to face. The second story represents an ambivalent anxiety and fantasy about the complex and freer sexual choices one must make when no longer a virgin. The examples of Bei and Wei show how young women use these ambivalent stories of others to work through a range of sexual choices and possible outcomes. Even Bei's story shows that a young woman can be "strong" enough to leave a sexual relationship when it no longer suits her, and that the consequences, though disappointing, won't be unbearable. (Bei, in fact, did later begin a sexual relationship with her boyfriend before they were married.) Wei uses her friend's experience not to simply "say no" to sex, but to prepare for the difficulties of leaving a boyfriend for whom she already had ambivalent feelings. (In fact, she did eventually sleep with the boyfriend she was discussing, a jealous and violent professional athlete, but broke up with him after a few months of dating.) Young women consider the decision to have sex in the light of all these imagined outcomes for relationships, augmented by a fear and fantasy that "sex is like candy, once you start eating, you can't stop."

Not all secondhand stories of other women's sexual experience have a cautionary effect. Other women's stories can also be used more directly for building up courage. Ting, a twenty-five-year-old hotel administrator, used her friends' stories to positively frame a decision to have sex with her boyfriend, a Japanese exchange student. When I asked about the extent of her intimacy with her boyfriend, she said:

> We only hug and kiss so far, but I don't know about the future because our feelings are getting deeper and developing. Now I have a really good feeling about him. We used to have fights and difficulty communicating, but now his Chinese is getting better. He is really good to me. When I come home tired, he will massage my shoulders. So maybe we soon will do this [have sex]. . . . Of course, he wants this. I used to think I would wait until I got married, but now my ideas are changing. I used to want to control myself. But then I went to Hong Kong and Thailand traveling, and I came back thinking that China is too conservative. Now I think I could do this. It's not like my old idea of waiting until I get married. I can change. One day when our feelings are good, we can do this. If we feel this passion, then I can accept this. He is a serious partner, and I want to marry him.
>
> Many of my classmates have now had this experience and told me. They talk about it in a positive way. They see it as a part of love. It is something we should all face up to. It isn't like what our teachers said. Boys now can accept that a girl isn't a virgin, my friends say. As one of my classmates told me, "Sex can be the sublimation of feelings." My classmates were all very conservative, but now they have had this experience. Some have even broken up with their boyfriends, but they don't worry about this. They don't worry about virginity. They don't think like, "Oh, what will my husband think about this?" They don't have this idea. Men now have changed the way they think. They only want your loyalty and fidelity. They won't care about your past, about what you did before.

A very careful and conservative person by her own account, Ting employs nearly all the rhetorical tools discussed in this chapter, including the backwardness of Chinese traditions, the new interpretation of sex as the "sublimation of feelings," the depth of her feelings for her boyfriend, the experiences of her peers, and the changes in what men think about virginity. Although her desire to marry her boyfriend is an important justification for having sex, she also has considered the possibility that they might break up. (His back rubs are an effective form of rhetoric I do not discuss.) Most important in her moral reasoning are the stories of her classmates from a conservative women's middle school in Shanghai (an elite academic girls' school, formerly a Catholic school). These are the women with whom she identifies, and their positive experiences are most persuasive in facing the male expectations she still worries about. Even for women of conservative temperament, sexual stories can be emboldening. (She later married this boyfriend and moved to Japan.)

Talking Past the First Time

After first sex, women also have a rhetorical task in explaining their behavior. Especially for women who are not in the normative long-term committed relationship, coping with the first time is even more complex. In the previous chapter, Grace described her first sexual experience with an American boyfriend at age twenty. I asked her more details about her first time, and her story shows the ways the moral grammar of this chapter works in retrospection. First, she justified her behavior in terms of her *feelings*, knowing in hindsight that his feelings were not strong enough:

> I guess it [virginity] was important, but feelings are more important to me than that. . . . But for him, there weren't any feelings. That is to say, when he was doing this, he didn't have any feelings. He was just a guy. . . . Actually, when we did it, he liked to look at himself in the mirror. I thought that was strange. He had this mirror beside his bed, and every time we did it, he would pull down this big mirror and look at himself. I never asked him about it, but I guess that he thought he was really something special when we were doing that. Americans don't like virgins, you know. After that, he asked me if it was my first time, and I said, "Yeah."

(The boyfriend's use of the mirror gives new definition to the "reflexive" uses of sexualized "others" for self-aggrandizement.[26]) Grace then described this experience in terms of *fate*:

> Before we did that, I had this feeling it would happen. The day when he asked me for a date, I was in my university dormitory. I had a job but had not yet graduated. In the dormitory I broke a cup, and I thought to myself, "Today I'm going to lose my virginity" [*shishen*]. Also, right before we broke up, the cup he gave me, I also broke it. So I believe a lot of things are fated.

I asked her if she worried about losing her virginity, and she poked fun at this specter of a future husband I conjured up with my question:

> I thought about it. But I thought that only those really stingy Chinese guys will really care about that. And if they love you, even those men can give

up this idea. Where are they going to find all those virgins? If you really want that, just go the hospital and sew it [the hymen] up. Just find a plastic surgeon! I don't like to lie to people, so if the guy I find ever asks me if it is my first time, I don't think I would sew it up or find some plastic surgeon [she laughed].

After her first time, Grace said she was really worried because she was bleeding, so she called her mother: "I asked her what I should do. You know what my mother did, she scolded me, she said, 'You are really stupid, doing that with a foreigner. Who knows if you might get some disease. How I am supposed to know what you should do?'" Nor were her roommates' reactions very positive: "Are you sure you should have done that?" they asked in surprise. Grace said they were jealous of her relationship with the handsome American, whom several had also met at the firm in which they were interning. At the time she felt very lonely, she said, and her experience made her less trustful and more determined to depend "only on [her]self." In fact, she moved in with another woman who was dating a European man and socializing in the expatriate nightclub scene. This woman provided more moral and practical support than her old classmates. In her story this romantic disillusion was the turning point in her transition to an ironic narrative frame, and the transformation of her character into a tarnished romantic survivor facing a pragmatic materialistic world, a standard narrative strategy described in the previous chapter.

Her classmates may have been jealous and harsh, but they also could appropriate her story for their own purposes. One classmate, Yinyin, told me that Grace's story emboldened her in her pursuit of sexual adventure with a Canadian man whom she described as "only a friend." Ironically, Yinyin said, Grace's first reaction to her own story was negative:

It's strange, maybe it was fate, but my first time was exactly one year after Grace's first time. She called me up that day and asked how I was doing. At that time my mind was very confused, and my body wasn't all that comfortable. So when she called, at first I didn't know what to say, then I told her about this [having sex]. Grace said, "What?" Later she told me that she cried. She thought I shouldn't have done that with this man. "After all, we are both Chinese girls," she told me, "and the first time should be kept for someone you love or someone who loves you." She felt her first time wasn't worth it, and that my first time wasn't worth it. But I felt, "What does it matter?" She told me, "Later you will regret this." Well, I think, up until now I haven't. I have never had that feeling of regret. I think that was a good feeling, and that kind of thing [virginity], what does it matter? It doesn't matter to me.

In Yinyin's narrative, love was not a condition for her first time, and she had fond memories of her sexual friendship with this man, a musician she met at a bar. (Yinyin told me, "You can't say there was love or feeling or anything like that, only an attraction, perhaps sexual attraction or another kind of attraction.") She said that Grace wanted too much from relationships (especially material benefits but also romantic feelings), whereas she was in it more for the experience (*guocheng*). Probably more and more young women were able to perceive the first time as merely an "experience," but they were not supported by the larger romantic ethos that said it must be for love (or, negatively, that it was for money). Eventually young women like Yinyin could draw some support from friends' stories and from telling their own story to a sympathetic ear, but giving your first time for friendship (or experience) and not for love still wasn't an acceptable public narrative for a young woman in 2000. What was required culturally was an ironic narrative of romantic disillusion, and this was what Grace expected of Yinyin.

For women who married their first lovers, romantic narratives of feelings leading to first sex produce few conflicts with the traditional expectation of giving the first time to the husband. However, an increasing number of women were not marrying their first lovers. For these women, simple romantic narratives of love and marriage didn't suffice to explain their sexual experiences. Mei, a recently married twenty-seven-year-old woman, told me she had had three lovers (including her husband). When I mentioned that I knew she had had sex with more men, she said with a laugh, "No matter, I only recognize having three men in my life. I don't recognize the others because they had nothing to do with my life. Only these had an impact on me." She said her first love began when she was seventeen and he was twenty-two: "This love was the kind that doesn't worry about anything else—don't eat, don't sleep, love is all you need. Nothing else mattered. After dating half a year, we had sex the first time."

I asked if she felt guilty.

No, I thought it was really normal. I thought I would certainly marry him, so it was normal. The first time I was a little afraid. It wasn't a beautiful experience, but neither did I feel guilty. I just thought there wasn't anything special about this. "What is the big deal? It isn't really so great." Actually it was quite painful. It was about the third time that I started getting a feeling of enjoyment. . . . I was very afraid the parents would find out about that. My parents never talked about this. My mother would just hint, "A girl should be responsible to herself and love herself" [*zizhongziai*]. After a while she found out, but she didn't say anything, and I didn't say anything.

I asked what happened to this relationship.

I got more and more sick of him. But it took me seven or eight years to break up completely. If I went out with other men, he would be really suspicious. I didn't do anything with them except go out, and he would be really suspicious. He was so jealous. I got more and more sick of this. I would just go to a movie, go to a dance, just go out, go out with some university classmates. But I was loyal to him. This really wasn't a problem of being faithful. I just didn't want to sleep with other men. If I don't like a man, I can't go to bed with him. After a few years we had nothing to say to each other. We could only make love, that was the only thing we did well together. Toward the end I wasn't even jealous, I wanted him to find others.

I asked what she now thought of the first one.

I really look down on him now. He was useless [*wuneng*]. He didn't know how to live. He messed up his life. I really liked him then. He was very considerate. He would cook dinner for me. But a man being considerate isn't enough. He couldn't do business. I tried to help him, but he would say that I didn't understand him. He had no business head at all.

Her story is typical of Shanghai women's ironic stories of failed first love affairs: a relationship beginning in the late teens or early twenties, a love in which "nothing else matters," leading naturally to the first time. After a gradual disillusionment with the partner, often involving his failure at his career, the initial romantic feelings fade and the woman begins to think of ways of abandoning her "useless" first boyfriend. In these stories of sexual coming-of-age, first sexual experiences take on an ironic quality. The irony lies in the fact that feelings that seemed initially so overwhelming later become insignificant, including the feelings of fear, confusion, and shame at first sex. Framed in romantic irony, such stories claimed resilience, depth of feeling, and stubbornness in the face of social pressure. These claims depended on women affirming some of the conventional meanings of virginity, especially first sex as the ultimate romantic gift and expression of feeling, while denying others, especially the commitment to the man. Through these stories women declared that their own feelings, and their own judgments defined their experience rather than something "done to them" sexually, men's judgments of this experience, parental expectations, or even their long-term relationship to a man. Although sex remained a private topic, many women shared these stories with their closest friends, providing a source of cultural support in redefining the first time as a romantic episode framed in retrospective irony, rather than as a permanent tragic loss.

Changing Institutional Contexts
Official Discourse

The retreat of the Party-state from policing private life gave room for youth to develop their own sexual culture, but state institutions such as schools and media continued to influence the formation of this culture. The legal treatment of premarital sexual behavior changed dramatically during the reform era from 1980 to 1995. In the early reform period, youth found to be engaging in premarital sex could be imprisoned for "hooliganism" or placed in "administrative detention" for "antisocial behavior." Although these laws and regulations remained in place in the 1990s, with the deepening of market reforms, police attention increasingly focused on the more narrowly defined exchange of "selling sex" (maiyin). Official and everyday conversations still vaguely questioned the legality of premarital sex through expressions such as "premarital sexual relationships are not protected by the law"[27] or in the common expression "illegal cohabitation" (feifatongjuu).[28] Participants in focus groups, however, generally seemed aware of the legal distinction that premarital sexual relationships were not "against the law" but rather merely "not protected by the law" (e.g., no rights of communal property). By the mid-1990s government officials in Shanghai seemed uninterested in legislating premarital morality—with the important exception of middle school and college administrators.[29]

Media representations of premarital sex also have lost their condemnatory tone. Before the reform era, official representations of premarital sex in the media were highly cautionary, an attitude that continued during the early reform era.[30] With the proliferation of Hollywood films, television serials, and romance novels, during the 1980s and 1990s youth were exposed to a variety of romantic tales involving sexual behavior. At the same time, ironic stories, such as those described in chapter 6, promoted a general moral relativism. Youth consuming materials in the state-dominated media no longer found a unitary moral voice. By the 1990s magazines and other media seem to have accepted premarital sex as a fact of life without it ever being explicitly condoned or discussed in any great depth. As one editor at Golden Age explained, "We aren't allowed to write about this from a positive perspective. We *are* allowed to write about it from a critical perspective. Maybe there are some good aspects of premarital sex, but we couldn't write about them, so we usually avoid this issue." "Real-life stories," such as the one beginning this chapter, did address premarital sex but gave little practical advice about sexual matters.[31]

School Policies

More than any other factor except perhaps for parental restrictions, school controls on dating limited sexual behavior. Middle schools still prohibited dating with varying degrees of effectiveness. Middle schools and colleges prohibited sexual intercourse among students, and both levels of institutions irregularly enforced these rules with severe penalties, including expulsion from colleges or transfer to reform schools for middle school youth. All sources agreed that young men were systematically treated more harshly by school officials because women were generally considered the "victims" in a premarital sexual relationship. Han Ping, a thirty-year-old sales manager, told me about the outcome of her college affair in the mid-1980s, describing the influence of her parents' political connections:

> My mother found out about our relationship and talked to our school [college] officials. My mother has quite a big influence. This behavior [of my parents] gave us a lot of trouble, so we broke up. This whole affair had an even bigger impact on him. Because my mother had so much influence, she blamed the whole affair on him, and in the end he wasn't able to finish his studies. [He was expelled.] He felt this whole relationship left a shadow on his life. Because it was my family who hurt him, I always felt guilty toward him.

Universities still expelled students for flagrant sexual intercourse during the mid-1990s. At one major university, for instance, a student couple was expelled when faculty discovered that the young woman had been sleeping in the young man's bunk for several weeks despite the presence of seven other men in the room. A woman accused of prostitution and a young man with multiple sex partners also were expelled from other Shanghai colleges during the mid-1990s. A high-level administrator and guidance counselor at one of these universities, who also taught a sex education course, told me in an interview:

> We will take action against them if we find out about it. If a girl gets pregnant, the school will kick them [both] out. Now it may be that a girl will get pregnant and go deal with it herself by going and getting an abortion

during the break, but if we find out, then we will kick them out. . . . I always tell my students that we are in China, and we cannot possibly escape from the traditional Chinese morality. It is not something we can decide for ourselves. . . . I tell these students, the sexual morality in China is changing, but there is one thing that will not change and that is the millennia-old norm of chastity. . . . The basic issue is the reputation of the school. The school doesn't want people to think that it has a bad moral climate. Some Shanghai parents come by on Saturday night looking for their girls who haven't come home, and they find that they are not in the dormitory. They see all these couples all over campus in the shadows hugging and kissing, and then they say that the campus moral climate is bad.

Lower-level guidance counselors at the same university told me that, in fact, younger faculty like themselves sometimes "looked the other way," even in cases of pregnancy, clear grounds for expulsion according to university rules. Faculty usually took other factors such as grades and "attitude" into account, and usually applied lesser forms of discipline to the ordinary cases in which students were found to be having sex but in which the woman was not pregnant. A discreet warning to "be careful" was often the first action against students who otherwise had a good relationship with faculty members. Faculty agreed that it was increasingly rare for students, especially local Shanghai students, to be caught, given the new availability of places to meet off campus for sex and the easy access and anonymity of abortion in Shanghai. Because they were unevenly enforced, these regulations also subjected students to the arbitrary exercise of administrative authority by teachers, parents, and counselors. For instance, Chinese women students found out to be dating foreign men were more likely to be called in for "counseling." Several female students I interviewed experienced these interrogations and warnings from school authorities, described by one young woman as "humiliating."

In general, middle schools and universities remained unfriendly, inconvenient, and relatively dangerous places for first sexual experimentation. The discourse of sexuality in the education system remained that of the paternalistic and nationalistic socialist state in which students were enjoined to discipline themselves in accordance with the commonsensical norms of "Chinese morality" (here clearly meaning premarital chastity). By making themselves privileged spokespersons of "Chinese morality," university officials defended their authority against the encroaching values of the external society in which engaging in premarital sex increasingly was viewed as merely another personal choice.

Student Countermeasures

In China there is a saying that "every measure has a countermeasure." Student countermeasures to university policies included meeting off campus, living together off campus, or simply ignoring the rules and having sex on university premises (not always a safe option, even in the late 1990s). University policing also influenced the telling of sexual stories described above. In the 1980s a woman such as Grace (or a man, for that matter) would have been running a grave risk by talking with her roommates about a sexual affair with a foreigner. Even in the 1990s, university administrators gathered information about any kind of deviant behavior (political, sexual, etc.) through vast formal and informal networks of informants. But at least in more liberal universities, some women students nearing graduation seemed to feel they could breach the topic of sexual behavior among friends. One magazine article even describes the six inhabitants of a women's dorm venturing out together to view a pornographic movie (which turned out to be R-rated). The article argues that talk about kissing and other forms of sexual experience in the dorm room is a relatively new and an important source of sexual information for young women.[32]

According to most of my Shanghai informants, unmarried women students in the mid-1990s seldom talked about sexual intercourse in these dorm-room conversations, a topic reserved for best friends, or discussed with no one. The usual topic was love relationships. On the other hand, with greater cultural acceptance and lower punitive risk, some women were confident enough to openly narrate their sexual experiences to classmates and other acquaintances. These acts of storytelling could become a resistant local politics for both the narrators and listeners, even a kind of "sexual evangelism" by women intent on breaking with tradition. One confident twenty-five-year-old woman, a vivacious former fashion model, Gigi, told me about her roommates at a foreign-language training school in Shanghai:

> They were all little girls from the interior with no experience. They were so funny. They were really curious that I didn't come home at night, but they didn't dare to ask me. Finally, when I came back from staying at my boyfriend's one day, they were all very curious, and they asked me where I stayed. They couldn't believe that I admitted to sleeping at my boyfriend's place. Then they asked if we slept in separate beds. They wanted to be lied to, but I told them, "Of course we slept in the same bed." They told me that before this they had argued among themselves about whether I

was a virgin. They are so ignorant, so stupid, it is like teaching a class. They even asked me whether breasts are for a husband or for a child. . . . I opened their eyes, I guess. Later one of them meets this Japanese [guy], and she comes to me and says that I have been a bad influence on her, that she is now thinking about sleeping with him. I can't believe how stupid these girls are.

The story is somewhat atypical in that Gigi was older than her other roommates and less afraid of university sanctions than the typical undergraduate. But the story also illustrates how more experienced women are able to tell younger women a type of sexual story that a previous generation of unmarried Chinese women had seldom told younger women. Even if narrators' voices weren't all that friendly, their stories were an important source of information and an example for inexperienced young women. Other sources were either distant from their own lives (media), silent on sexual matters (parents), or untrustworthy (men). Sexually experienced acquaintances were immediate experts who could offer support and a more differentiated sense of sexual possibilities.

Romance and Cool: The New Emotional Rhetoric of Premarital Sex

Shanghai young people are telling sexual stories and using the sexual stories told by friends to negotiate a new premarital sexual culture structured around the institution of dating. Notions of feelings and fate, a steadily "opening" society, the value of virginity, female emotional sensitivity, male sexual discomfort, and the types of "fallen women" constitute the accumulated grammar of this new sexual culture. To simplify the discussion above, a feminine rhetoric of romance and a masculine rhetoric of coolness allow both men and women to accept new practices of premarital sex, despite a continuing emphasis on the value of virginity (as a gift rather than an interdiction). Women's sense of romance gives them a reason for risking the emotional, physical, and social dangers of premarital sexuality. Young men's coolness serves as a pose to manage their increasingly unsteady claims of exclusive sexual possession. Such coolness seems to contradict the essence of romantic feeling, and occasionally men's and women's definitions of the situation differ. But neither the gendering nor application of these rules is consistent, and they are best seen as working together in a productive tension. To some extent, it is the cool, playful quality of sexual interactions in the dating culture that allows both men and women to manage the fears, jealousies, and other passionate feelings that both experience and expect. Women's ironic tales of failed love affairs are also a form of cool emotional rhetoric, valorizing sexual experience as a coming-of-age rather than as a tragic failure, allowing for the safe expression of passionate feelings without the fear of a permanent loss. And when things don't work out, you need to know, in the words of one young woman, how "to dust off your behind and walk away." Without passion, on the other hand, coolness would neither be necessary nor meaningful. Men also participate fully in the culture of romantic feeling. Even the playboy's posture of masculine coolness depends on convincing the other of a wounded sensitivity within.

The changes in sexual culture I have described encompass both changes in grammatical terms and changes in the contexts of rhetorical practice. Changes in cultural grammar involve new terms of discourse and new weighting among terms. As has been pointed out throughout this book, these changing weightings are systematically related to the transition to a market economy through a general discourse of motives in which a romantic motive is counterposed to the money motive. Women's motives in engaging in premarital sex have become a new relativistic standard of moral purity measured against the mercenary motive. Changes in rhetorical context mainly involve institutional changes. Decreased state policing of premarital sex gives youth the space to develop a premarital sexual culture, though continued state policing of media and schools still shapes this environment. However, the most important institution shaping the sexual culture of young people is the courtship culture of their own construction, a culture based on choice, competition, and play.

8 作爱

MAKING LOVE
And Talking about It

After the First Time

The "first time" is conventionally an expression of deep feelings or love (though reality may take other courses). After first sex, "the floodgates are open," the "candy is eaten," and sex can take on a wider variety of meanings. Lei, a twenty-five-year-old stockbroker originally from Tianjin and living alone in Shanghai, briefly outlined her sexual history over tea in 1996 in a fancy Shanghai shopping mall. I asked her if she felt guilty the first time she had sex. She said:

> I never felt guilty about this. If I love a man, then I think this is very pure, very holy even. For the first time, especially, love is important. Because for the first time for a girl, there is always a sense of sacrifice. You sacrifice yourself to a boy because you love him. This is because for the first time for a girl it can't be pleasurable. It is bound to be quite painful. So the first time there is a strong sense of giving something. [She laughed a bit, as though this were an old memory.]

I asked her how old she had been. She said, "I was eighteen. I think that is about the right time for a girl to begin her sex life."

I said, "Well, later it seems to get more and more casual for women." She said:

> Yes, sometimes it is just like eating, something that you need to do. Of course with someone you love it will be better. . . . With my first boyfriend, I never really had sexual pleasure. If I could have really relaxed, then I might have felt pleasure. But with him for half a year together, I

didn't. It was always quite painful, and it was something I felt I should do for him because I loved him. I felt it was a duty.

Since then she had had several short-term sexual relationships, including Han, her most recent lover, and one long-term boyfriend, Wang, a student at a sports academy. I asked her under what circumstances she would think she should have sex with someone she has just met. She said:

> Sometimes it is a kind of atmosphere that really determines things. It isn't like a physical desire, but a situation in which you think you should naturally just do this. In this situation you will do it, but it won't necessarily be very good. That's the way it was with Han. With us, it was really a case of both of us being lonely, so we made love. So I think that was all there was to that [relationship].
>
> It takes time to relax with a guy. With Wang, at first it wasn't too good, but later when we lived together for a while, then the sex was really good together. This was also when our relationship was at its best. In any relationship in which there isn't love, then the sex can't really be that good.

I asked what sort of men she liked. She answered, "I like more mature men also, but not necessarily older. Wang was two years younger than me, but more mature. At least he always made me feel like he was a big man and I was a little girl."

I asked her about a fight she had had with Han after he suspected her of sleeping with another man.

> Han completely misunderstood my relationship with this guy. I slept with him, but we didn't really have sex, because he was too young and inexperienced. But he really loved me. That doesn't mean that I wouldn't have had sex had I wanted to—just out of some sense of fidelity to Han. I am a person of strong feeling. If I want to do that with a man, I will, even if I am married [to someone else]. But because I actually didn't have sex with this guy, I felt that Han was really debasing me, by accusing me of that. In fact, if he wanted to be jealous, he should have found Wang more of a problem [because occasionally she was still sleeping with him while she was seeing Han].

Lei describes her sex life within a conventional ethical grammar of romantic feeling, but also allows herself to break her rules and occasionally engage in sex that makes no ethical sense, only aesthetic sense. Sex can be something "holy," or an activity "like eating," a "duty" in a committed relationship or an escape from loneliness. She has a strong sense of her entitlement to pleasure as a woman, but also a highly gendered notion of sexual performance—a desire to feel like a "little girl" with a "big man." More than anything, she aspires to be a person of "strong feeling" who follows her own rules, a very anarchic ethical conception, but ethical nonetheless.

Sex is, above all, a symbolic act that conveys emotional, social, ethical, and aesthetic meanings to self, partners, and other "participants" in the drama. Youth beginning sex lives outside the normative conventions of marriage must decide the meanings of premarital sex acts and new conventions for expressing and performing them. For many informants, first sex before marriage meant a post hoc reordering of the rules they lived by. Young women often told me that they had always intended to wait until marriage to have sex. The sometimes unexpected entry into premarital sexual activity meant that women and men had to come up with much more complex rules than the simple "wait until marriage" rule they had been taught by their parents. They had to decide what sexual intercourse meant to them, when and with whom it was acceptable, and how to deal with its consequences. The variety of meanings one woman, Lei, could associate with sex should show that premarital sex, like romantic love generally, was practiced tactically, accessing multiple codes and expressing multiple ambiguous meanings. Moreover, the meanings of terms within this "grammar of sexuality" were subject to redefinition in dialectical relation to other terms within the same roughly coherent system of sexual meanings.[1]

If a change in moral order is achieved, it most usually occurs as a manipulation of previous moral categories rather than through an overt challenge to them.[2] In Shanghai youth use normative terms ("feelings," "respect," "responsibility") that once supported and defined one convention of behavior, that of chastity, to justify and define its near opposite, that of premarital sex. What this means is that instead of seeing cultural and moral change as a process of rebellion and rupture with traditional ideas (the basic idea of a "sexual revolution"), what cultural change usually entails is an appropriation of traditional moral terms in which the behavioral referents of these terms are nudged in new directions, while the terms themselves retain their force for legitimation, justification, and explanation. As a corollary, the central terms that survive in any living normative discourse are those that have acquired strong emotional and moral resonance but with sufficient ambiguity to allow this semantic "nudging" in new directions.[3] Ideas discussed below—"respect," "responsibility," "feelings," and "play"—all have this quality.

In this chapter I will explain some of the new sexual "games," as some people disparagingly called the new conventions of premarital intimacy in Shanghai. The very notion of a "game" implies an arbitrariness and artificiality to the "rules." While most youth wouldn't feel comfortable describing a current love affair as a "game" (for most it is an expression of serious feelings), they often describe others that way, or sometimes their own behavior after the fact. I keep the dismissive metaphor because it points out that premarital sex involves rules, goals, and conventions that are normative but are also somewhat arbitrary and negotiable and, because of their relative newness, often recognized as arbitrary and negotiable by participants. In fact, there is no one generally recognized "game" of sex, unless it is the old one of "finding a partner," but, in practice, sex has become somewhat detached from the game of finding a partner. Few people, however, are willing to commit themselves to meaningless acts, or at the very least, they try to construct meanings around these acts after the fact. Shanghai youth have developed a new set of "language games," ways of establishing a common language of desire (feelings, fate, play, etc.)[4] that allows premarital sex to happen as a meaningful experience without being a promise of marriage. These games poach on the terms and grammar of marriage, committed relationships, and serious courtship, yet often play themselves out in relatively short-term affairs that do not lead to marriage. These new games usually retain the gendered grammar of these traditional terms (men "respect" women; men "conquer" women; and so forth); however, as the actual uses of these terms change, the practical and rhetorical possibilities of these gendered positions also change. Finally, sexual games also have serious potential physical consequences of pregnancy and sickness. I will briefly discuss these practical consequences and the shared understandings that define and obscure them.

The New Rules of the Game
Respect

In the focus group interviews, we asked youth about the new standards for having sex before marriage. Both young men and women mentioned a gendered ideal of "respect," which seemed the most basic of the new "rules of the game." Before premarital sex was accepted by most youth, "respect" for a woman prototypically meant *not* asking for sex. The term retains its positive value, but its uses have changed. Whereas in 1980s magazine articles "respect" meant not engaging in sexual intercourse or not making such requests,[5] among 1990s Shanghai youth it had come to mean respecting her right of refusal.

Moderator: Do you think the fact that he has this request is a kind of dis-
respect?

Da: Having this request doesn't have to do with respect.

Pu: It is a normal physical reaction.

Xi: Only after hearing his girlfriend's response will he show if he respects her or not.

(unmarried women in their early twenties)

Moderator: Do you agree with the idea [from a magazine article] that
"You should not have this kind of request if you respect a girl"?

Hua: No, respect is that if she says no, you don't force her.

Fang: I think it means [I] should respect her opinion and can't use force.

Ji: I think so, too.

He: The same as them.

(unmarried men in their early twenties)

In the new "social morality" of young men and women, mutual consent ("respect") was an uncomplicated minimum standard compatible with both committed and casual relationships. However, mutuality was not the only connotation of "respect," especially for women. The primary meanings of this
term—which, of course, is not confined to sexual relations—include not looking down upon the partner or humiliating him/her in social situations. These
gendered meanings depended on the negotiated definitions of sexual relations.
Commercial sex workers I spoke with, for instance, wanted their customers to
treat them with respect by being polite and friendly regardless of what they really thought of them. Women who expected money from long-term lovers (being "kept") equated "respect" with not being treated like a casual prostitute
(offered money directly after sex). Women who engaged in casual sex for "fun"
(no future relationship) often wanted men to show respect by treating them
afterward as close personal friends (not being distant, but also not expecting to
be lovers). "Respect" for women in committed relationships meant not being
treated like a sexual conquest (no bragging to friends). Minimally, this gendered conception of "respect" implied treating a woman as a person rather than
a sexual object, but more generally involved acting in accordance with the mutually negotiated definition of the sexual relationship, at least when in the presence of the partner.

Not all sex was mutual and consensual, of course. There was violent stranger
rape in Shanghai and other forms of sexual assault. Several women told me of
being pressured into sex by men who felt that they were entitled by virtue of a
previous relationship or by a woman's signs of making herself available. How-

ever, based on my interviews in the 1990s, it seems most sex was consensual and that the verbal standards of consent were relatively clear. In contrast, it seems that standards for sexual consent were far less clear among sexually active youth in the early reform era, at least among the group of working-class low-corner men I knew most thoroughly. Old Lai, a low-corner resident of River-side Alley, told me about meeting women in the early 1980s:

> Girls ten years ago were very, very naive. It was so easy to pick them up. They believed everything you told them. They would do what you told them [tinghua]. I would meet girls at a dance and take them back to my place. Then I would make my move. If they resisted, I said, "Listen, if you yell, no one here will help you, so you had better just do what I say." I would say, "You can run away, but you probably won't be able to find your way out of here." So they would just go along with me.

I asked if girls would be angry or accusatory afterward. He said, "No, they would be very good to you and follow you around [genzheni]. Chinese girls were like that [back then]. Once you had that kind of relationship, they would just want to stick with you. They would be loyal."

Lai lived in a low-corner shanty district and relied upon young women's fear of the people in his neighborhood to intimidate them. The story seemed strange to me, and I asked Zhu, a friend sitting with us, how girls could be so easily intimidated. "Back then you could have taken a girl and sold her off, they were so naive," Zhu said. People were less geographically mobile and inexperienced. In this time and place, before premarital sex became widely accepted, young men assumed that women didn't know what they wanted sexually or were embarrassed to agree to sex, making their "real" desires a matter for the man's own judgment. In these men's accounts, young women were passive and there was no process of mutually defining the sexual situation or the nature of the relationship. Zhu, who described himself to me as a high school playboy, told me about his sexual experiences in the early 1980s in another low-corner neighborhood:

> It was much easier to meet girls back then. They were really naive [danchun] back then, easy to fool [rongyipian]. It was easy to seduce girls back then, just stay with them all the time and they would start liking you. You could just start unbuttoning their pants, and although they would say "no," actually they would go along with you. Physically she wanted it. This is because you had spent a long time with them, go with them everywhere, and they liked being with you.

Finally, yet another Riverside Alley friend of thirty-five, Little Meng, though he didn't report coercive sex, merely described the unplanned nature of these encounters with his first girlfriend (around 1980, when both were seventeen years old).

> The first time we did that, she came over really early that morning all the way from the other side of the city. It was only 10 A.M. My parents weren't at home, and we started hugging and fooling around, and it just happened. If you ask me what I felt, I didn't really feel anything. My brain was just empty. We didn't know what we were doing. We just did it. Neither one of us had done it before; we had only heard about it from some other people. We were like two kids stealing someone's stuff.

This story is typical of the sexual initiations described by these men. Middle-aged low-corner informants consistently told me that they knew nothing about sex in their youth. As these early playboys (or "hooligans") became more confident and knowledgeable, they took advantage of the inexperience and naïveté of women younger than themselves. However, according to these men, talking ten to twenty years after these events, women have changed. Young women they meet now seem to know what they want sexually, or are more willing to say "yes" or "no," so that such coercion (or persuasion, as they still consider it) is no longer necessary. Low-corner women I interviewed substantiated this account of passivity, and sometimes coercion, in dating relationships in that time and place (an example is given in chapter 2).

It seems that neither young men or young women in the early reform era had clear understandings of sexual consent or of any other practical cultural vocabulary for negotiating the meanings of these relationships, which were so far outside the frame of acceptable behavior. Expectations were unclear, other than the often unrealistic expectation that sex was a prelude to marriage. Most youth who engaged in premarital sex were guilt-ridden and afraid. Before the mid-1980s all forms of premarital sex were covered in a vague aura of illegality, which obscured the issue of consent. For instance, I asked another middle-aged man about sex in the early reform period, and he pointed his finger at the back of his neck and made a gunshot sound, laughing and saying that it was an exaggeration, but that's how people thought back then (that they would be executed for rape). These stories of premarital sex in early reform-era low-corner Shanghai describe a situation in which men had no conception of women's sexual rights because men and women had no shared language to negotiate the meanings of their sexual encounters. Rather, premarital sex was shrouded in well-founded fears both for men and women.

In contrast, Shanghai youth I interviewed in the 1990s seemed to assume that mutual consent is an unambiguous standard and that men must respect this standard. The younger low-corner dance hall playboys I met in the 1990s—similar in social status to Lai, Zhu, and Meng—reported no such stories of coercion and seemed to assume that women knew what they wanted sexually. Moreover, there was a much clearer legal distinction between consensual and nonconsensual sex. Young women I interviewed in the 1990s not only were more aware of their legal rights, but also more able to bring their own definitions to sexual relationships. If only through exposure to media representations, they knew much more about sex and love than young women at the beginning of the reform era. They were far less afraid of being publicly exposed in sexual relations and more capable of turning their backs on men they didn't want to be with. Women's demands for respect, while framed in a conventionally gendered moral language, were demands for rights, not only to refuse or assent to sex, but also to participate equally in defining the meanings of sexual encounters.

Responsibility

Other than mutual respect, the other most frequently mentioned norm of premarital sexual relationships was the ideal of responsibility. "Responsibility" entailed more than respect, which was simply the most basic of conditions for sexual relations. Like the idea of respect, the connotations of the word "responsibility" were changing during the 1990s. Just as "respect" for a girl once meant waiting until marriage to have sex, "taking responsibility" for premarital sexual behavior once meant marrying her if premarital sex occurred. But while "respect" had taken on a clear new minimum definition of mutual consent, "responsibility" had become an ambiguous and a vexing concept for both men and women who were sexually active before marriage.

For instance, Little Chen (introduced in chapter 6) told me about her experiences with men she dated, including some she met at the social dance hall. She said there are all kinds of people in the dance hall, including some people "who have bad intentions." I asked what she meant. She said, "These guys talk a good line, but they don't have a sense of responsibility to a girl."

I asked her what she meant. She said, "To have responsibility is to be like a good friend. A good friend will do what he says he will do. He will care about your mental and physical well-being. A false friend will want to play around with you, but won't live up to the values of a friend. A man should have at least a little sense of responsibility and not lie to someone."

I said, "Well, some friends now are really short term."

She said, "Short-term friends are also okay, as long as you get along well and play together well. I just don't like the kind of people who the first time they meet you they want to possess you, or the kind of woman who the first time she meets a man, wants to spend all his money. I don't like the type of man who the first time you meet him is all flowery language and sweet words. He just wants to get to his goal. Of course he has a goal."

I said, "What, to go to bed with you?"

She said, "Of course, what other kind of goals could a man have when he meets a woman? I myself like to meet a guy first to get to know him for a while. I like someone who is very honest and sincere, someone I understand more."

I asked her how long she had to know someone before she could have sex. She said, "I don't necessarily mean that you have to go out with a guy a long time. After one or two times of being together, then sometimes it is also okay. If your feelings match, then you can do this. If the feelings are right and the man has some sense of responsibility, if it isn't a cheating type [qipianxingde] of relationship."

I asked, "Well, what do you really mean by responsibility in a sexual relationship?"

She said:

It means that if he says he will do something for me, then he does it. Sometimes he says he will meet you somewhere, and then he doesn't even show up. If the guy just disappears, then that isn't responsible. Sometimes a guy feels he has already had you, then he feels he has no responsibility at all to you. He just thinks this doesn't matter. The old idea of "one night husband and wife, one hundred days of gratitude" [yirifuqi bairien], they have completely forgotten it. They feel if they have played with you once, then just forget it, like a shirt you've worn once and just throw away. They feel there is no need to be responsible. The main thing is that they should do what they say they will do. Perhaps they say they will take you somewhere to go out, they will say they are going to buy you some present, give you some jewelry, just something to get your trust, but, in fact, these are just words, once a girl goes with him, then he just casts her off.

I asked her if she had run into this kind of situation before. She said, "I have run across one or two. They always give you a lot of promises, lots of fancy talk.

They tell the girl that they have status or that they have money. Girls are very vain. They feel he has status or money so they go with him. . . . As for me, I won't easily believe this kind of language. I want to wait and see his actions."

I asked, "Does that mean you would wait to go to bed with someone?"

She said, "It isn't really a restriction in terms of time. Sometimes feelings are especially compatible. If my heart accepts it, if he brings up this demand, then I am willing to fulfill his wishes. But the problem is now guys are more pragmatic. In the past most guys felt they should be responsible. Now they really don't think it [sex] matters."

The notion of responsibility that she advanced goes beyond the minimal standard of mutuality, but doesn't go so far as marriage or even a long-term commitment. For Little Chen, living up to promises of romantic dating experiences, including dinners and gifts, was an important connotation of responsibility: that a man should be polite and considerate, that he should take her out to dinner, that he should buy her gifts, that the relationship should have some duration beyond a one-night stand. She also implied that he should take care of her physically, meaning that he should take precautions to avoid getting her pregnant and be considerate of her sexual pleasure. All of these were common referents of responsibility, but her complaints also show her struggle to get men to act responsibly.

This notion of responsibility for sex is often related to the idea that sex is something a woman gives to a man, a gift that men should appreciate in their thoughts and actions. Women often described sex with the colloquialism of "giving" themselves to a man, and of the first time as a special "sacrifice." Among economically disadvantaged women, however, this idea of reciprocal giving could devolve into the notion that a man should appreciate a sexual relationship in more material ways, including gifts and dinners.

Men didn't always ignore these norms of responsibility, and some of them took this idea very seriously as a kind of moral obligation, not simply an exchange of material compensation for sex. For instance, Johnny, whose story is partly told in chapters 1 and 5, had a very strong notion of responsibility associated with sex, despite his playboy lifestyle. In the same interview, he described his love life after his second girlfriend left him to become a karaoke hostess, taking all the gifts he had bought for her and leaving him broke:

> I was unshaven and unkempt for days. Finally, there was this nice girl who worked at the hotel. She told me, "You know, there are still people who like you." She told me she liked me. That night we went out and got

drunk. Then she came home to my place, and we had sex. This was her first time. When she woke up in the morning, she was terrified. She yelled and cried and banged her head on the wall. She is from a really strict family, and she always felt she should wait until she got married.

At that time I promised her that she would be my only girlfriend. I promised her that I would never leave her unless she first left me. I then promised her that I would never go out and seduce other girls. Actually, I left myself open the option that other girls could seduce me, but she didn't notice that. She believed me, but I left myself some room. I felt that I should be responsible for her because she was a virgin. She gave me her first love, so I must be responsible. I don't love her, but if I marry anyone, I will marry her. Of course, I may never get married. I really don't want to get married. Unless she leaves me first, I won't leave her. Actually, I hope she finds another. She is the secretary for the sales department at the hotel, so she has the chance to meet many interesting men. I don't care. I don't love her. I only have some feeling for her.

I asked if she fooled around.

No, she is very straight. She is not the kind of girl who will "make you wear a green hat" [cuckold you]. She is very loyal. Anyway, I think she can meet some other prince on a white horse, some businessman. She is very successful. I was only making a thousand [RMB] when I met her. Before we ended up together, she really would look down on me. All these other guys have money. In the future, she said, she may find another. She is only nineteen. But she comes to see me for this thing [sex]. She sees me once a week just for sex. She has this physical need. I really know how to make a girl happy. About 30 percent of this relationship is just sex. I am amazed at how this girl needs sex. If she doesn't get this once a month, she would go crazy. She will get hungry like a wolf. She comes over just for this. I could go a month without this and it wouldn't bother me at all. A man can easily forget about sex, but a woman has stronger needs.

Since he told me he was open to being seduced, I asked if it was easy for him to find other women.

If she isn't a virgin, it is easy. If she doesn't love you, if it is just playing around, if there is no responsibility and she feels this need, then it is easy. If she is a virgin, then this is much slower. Also, if she loves you, then she may try to preserve a sense of mystery and make you wait. Now, I need a woman who doesn't love me. If a girl is a virgin, then there also are problems. She would want me to give up my girlfriend.

I asked about Linda (introduced in chapter 1). He said:

> Yes, with her it is like that. I could only make her a lover. But if she is a virgin, then I won't play with her. She would want public recognition [mingfen] [as my girlfriend], and I couldn't give that to her. I can't bear the burden of responsibility for two virgins at once. That's my belief. You have to be responsible for this. Some guys don't care. They think sleeping with a virgin doesn't matter at all. But I think God will punish you for this. [He is Catholic.] He will not punish your person, but punish your soul. If a girl isn't a virgin, then there is no burden, no responsibility.

The end of this story was predictable, even to the young man. The hotel-worker girlfriend soon left him, like the previous two. (As described in chapter 5, he was living with an even younger woman in 2000.) But he kept up the facade of responsibility, even though he was chasing after other women actively. Talking about his sense of responsibility seemed to make him feel proud of himself, and his use of the rhetoric of responsibility shows how it can give meaning to behavior even when not strictly observed.

Though the number of his sexual partners made him somewhat unusual among Shanghai youth, Johnny's sense of responsibility for taking a girl's virginity was a typical idea among Shanghai youth. He also followed a rule borrowed from the culture of extramarital affairs in which the girlfriend with public status (mingfen) received special consideration. "Public status" was a term that once only applied to couples with a marriage certificate, but that Shanghai youth in the 1990s metaphorically extended to their steady or publicly claimed "old men" and "old ladies." It couldn't apply to more than one person at one time and implied certain responsibilities, including a sense that this person shouldn't be publicly humiliated by openly bringing another lover into social situations involving friends. Johnny also felt responsible for his girlfriend's sexual needs, also a common ideal.

Although not as public or pronounced, women also felt a responsibility toward a man's first time. Little Liu, a twenty-three-year-old elementary schoolteacher and dance instructor, had her own first time with her boyfriend, Hong, who also claimed she was his first lover. She described this sharing of the first time as a special bond to Hong. This made the beginnings of her next relationship all the more painful. She was still living with Hong, though unhappily, when she began seeing a colleague, Wang Lin. He asked her to give him an opportunity to "compete fairly" for her affections, and they had a few dates. Finally, on his birthday, she agreed to accompany him to a hotel room:

He said to me, "It's not that I want to do anything with you. I just want to spend the night with you talking." So after that we got a room at a hotel and sat in there talking. At that time I thought this was wrong; I hadn't broken up with my boyfriend [Hong] and here I was doing this. After that, well, things [sex] happened. It couldn't be helped, just happened [laughing]. But at that time I felt really bad, I felt this was going against my own principles, I felt I shouldn't be doing this. But we still did it. He always told me that he wanted to save his first time for his wife. He had been dating but had never ever done that. He was twenty-seven. At first I thought he was just saying that. I didn't take it seriously. But that night when we did that, I realized that it really was his first time. Really. I felt really guilty. I felt I shouldn't have done that. And so I just left right after we did that.

He is quite a conservative man, saying he wanted to save his first time for his wife. I don't know how it happened that the first time just suddenly happened with me. I feel some responsibility for that. He told me that he had a chance before with his first girlfriend in college. He said they had already gotten to the point that the only thing he hadn't done was take off his own pants, and suddenly he felt that he shouldn't do that. So nothing happened. And he hadn't done it since then. The first time was with me. I felt that was really strange, how can a guy be twenty-seven and it still be his first time? That's really strange.

Little Liu described a bond of responsibility to both men that was partly based on first sexual experiences. Hong was her first lover, and she, his. And she had been Wang Lin's first lover. This sense of responsibility was partly mitigated by Wang Lin's age and Hong's laziness, though it caused her both regret and guilt. (In the end, however, the contradictions in her feelings canceled out her responsibility to both. Although she returned to Hong that night and continued to see Wang Lin for a few weeks, she soon broke up with both, saying she needed time alone.)

Conventionally, men were supposed to take responsibility for sex "given" by women. On the other hand, men also take sex as a token of commitment by women. Jie, the salesman introduced in chapter 6, explained this implication of responsibility when I asked him about his attitude toward casual sex: "If she does this, a girl will feel she has a sense of responsibility to the guy. Many men will think, 'The girl loves me, otherwise she wouldn't do this.' Men will think that this kind of relationship is very, very special. This [casual sex] would result in a kind of burdensome attachment [for the girl]." Though some women complained of men being irresponsible in sexual behavior, the mutual understanding of "responsibility" struck some other women as burdensome. A fear of being responsible to a man was a reason several women gave me for avoiding casual sex with men. As one young woman said, "I am afraid of responsibility. I don't want to be someone's girlfriend. People have too many feelings [when they have sex]." Lanping, the attractive professional introduced in chapter 6, complained to me that she wasn't meeting men she liked. Knowing that she had been sexually active before, I asked her if she sometimes just wanted a sex partner.

> I think about this, but it is so much trouble. I feel like guys think having sex is like a promise to them. They think it means that you have a certain feeling toward them. It is so much trouble really. A long-term relationship is better. A physical relationship and the mental relationship are all important. The problem with just sleeping with a guy is that guys will think that you somehow belong to them. Guys will think, "Oh, you were willing to do this with me, so it means that you have given me some promise." And guys will tell a lot of people. I really don't like to have my privacy aired in public.

There is a clear social-class symmetry to the statements of sexually active women about responsibility. Lower-status and less attractive women, like Little Chen, complained about men's lack of responsibility toward them. Higher-status, women, like Lanping, complained more about men's sense of ownership. It wasn't as much their definitions of "responsibility" that differed, however, as their status vis-à-vis the men they dated. Lower-status women struggled to obtain the respect that higher-status women took for granted, while higher-status women struggled to defend their autonomy against the proprietary attitudes of men they slept with.

Responsibility, though vague and contested, contained certain basic assumptions. Regardless of their social positions, most women expected that men would value the token of sexual intimacy, be honest, keep in touch, and allow a relationship to develop. "Responsibility" usually implied fidelity during the relationship, although not when one was the third person intruding in a previously existing relationship or when one was clearly playing around. The meaning of responsibility had clearly changed from the days when it meant a promise to marry (though not in all cases was this old meaning dropped), but it still retained the notion that sex was an especially meaningful gift of a woman to a man, which should be taken seriously, especially if it was her first time. Ironically, by giving the "gift," the woman assumed as much responsibility as

the man to whom she gave it. This perhaps explains the extraordinarily negative reaction of Johnny's young girlfriend when she lost her virginity to a
scruffy dance hall playboy in a night of drunken passion.

Therefore, responsibility could be burdensome for women also. Alternatively, when women were interested in casual relationships, they could try to
find men they thought were "safe." These included married men, bohemian
playboys, or foreigners. (Westerners, like artists, are assumed to believe in casual sex with no strings attached.) Responsibility was thus a useful term, but
one that vexed young people who were searching simultaneously for freedom
and commitment. For the minority of youth who had multiple sexual partners,
this often involved a degree of "cheating" or obfuscation, but many young
women and men I met found ways of justifying complex sex lives to themselves and friends. "Respect" and "responsibility" were flexible categories, unlike the hard-and-fast terms of chastity they replaced.

Likes, Needs, and Desires

As described in the previous chapter, Shanghai women in the 1990s
conventionally legitimated sex acts as an expression of "love" or "feelings," or
even as the "sublimation of feelings." Such "love" (and sex) could sometimes
arrive suddenly, as in the romantic notion of love at first sight, a conjunction of
feelings, circumstances, and "fate." Both men and women, however, sometimes
found other descriptions of sexual passion more convincing or useful than
"feelings" or "love." A weaker motive than "love" or "romantic feelings" was
simply "liking" someone (haogan, literally "good feeling") "Haogan" is even
more usefully ambiguous than "ganqing," implying and allowing that other
more practical motives might be involved in a relationship. I asked one
nineteen-year-old woman who had had several lovers what her conditions
were for agreeing to sleep with a man. She said, "I don't have to love someone
to have sex. I just have to have a good feeling [haogan] about them." She said she
hadn't had feelings (ganqing) for any of her lovers except for her first boyfriend.
Some of her lovers were well-off men she barely knew, but who took her on expensive dates. For her, "liking someone" was a very flexible standard, legitimating pragmatic sexual arrangements.

Whereas women seemed to prefer the romantic ambiguity of "feelings"
and "liking" to describe their sexual feelings, men sometimes employed a
consciously antiromantic discourse of sexual "needs" (xuyao), ascribing these
needs to both themselves and women. For men, the "need" motive worked
both as a self-legitimation and a dismissal of more complex emotional motives.

For instance, I asked Zhu, a frequent visitor of social dance halls, to tell me about the last woman he met at the dance hall. He said:

> She was an old cabbage leaf, a woman about forty. We danced for a while and she seemed to like me [dui wo you haogan]. When we danced the two-step, I put both my arms around her waist and she didn't resist. She put both arms around my shoulders, and I knew that she liked me. We danced some more, and I could tell that she liked it. So after the dance I asked her if she wanted to go for a walk, and we had a snack, and then we went dancing again during the late-night session. You can tell when a woman wants this. So after dancing I just asked her, "Why don't we go get a room?" And in that modest way particular to women, she went along. She didn't say anything, but she was willing. And then we went to the room and did it. The next morning it was just "Good-bye." She left me a number, but I didn't leave her a number. She really wanted to see me, but I didn't want to see her. She liked me a lot. This kind of woman, she is just out to play around—that's all she wants. Maybe her husband can't satisfy her, so she wants another man. But a woman's not going to talk about that sort of thing, so I'm just guessing. In the end, you know, I need it; she needs it. It's just a mutual need. That's all there is to it.

His rhetoric of need reduced what even in his own account was a complex emotional interaction to a simple and impersonal motive. Naturalized "need" rhetorically erases personal bonds and loyalties and simplifies motives. Women, on the other hand, typically deemphasized generic physical "needs" even in short-term relationships. Even when their own motives were uncertain, women usually emphasized men's strong feelings for them.

Older and more experienced women were more likely to describe sexual desire, rather than romantic feelings, as a motive for sex. I asked thirty-one-year-old Lan, now cohabiting with a married man, about her sexual standards: "Well, I don't think I ever really thought about it [why I have sex]. If I go to bed with a man, it is because I think it will make me feel happy [kaixin]. I have never really thought clearly about why I go to bed with men." Later she told me, "There are times when I am feeling really crazy—when I just meet a guy, and I like him. Then I will do anything with him, and I won't worry about it afterward." She then told me about a one-night stand with a married man. "I went home that night thinking, 'He was really good,' and I didn't mean he was a good man, or an interesting man, but merely that he was good in bed. He really satisfied me. I never regretted that or thought anything bad about it."

Active and Passive

Even if women felt a strong desire for casual sex, many waited for the man to define the situation for himself. Partly they worried about the reaction of the man and whether he could accept a sexually active woman. For instance, Old Guo, a forty-year-old married playboy, liked to brag about his sexual conquests within the college campus community where he grew up. He told me this story in a conversation in a college coffee shop:

> When my wife was not at home, I went to a party and wanted to find a girl that I could take home. I saw a girl who wasn't very unusual from her dress but had a certain look in her eye, and after dancing I asked her if she wanted to go out with me after the dance. She was willing. Then we walked toward my building. As we got closer to the door, I intentionally started talking about something really interesting in order to get her inside, but she came on in with no problem. Then [as we were going up the steps] I was really shocked that she started telling me what she liked sexually, with the mouth, and stuff like that. I couldn't believe it. I am married and wouldn't dare say these things. That night I didn't do anything with her. It turned me off. That girl was a student, but a wild one.

As the man described the campus community in the 1980s, just talking with a strange girl had seemed daring when he was young. Now some girls were openly making sexual demands before they even got in bed. His story also explains why women so rarely blatantly expressed their sexual desire. Men might be afraid of it. Men desired to stay in control of the progression of sexual events, a norm in which women usually colluded. Old playboys, such as Guo, wanted to feel they were "playing with" women. Men could tolerate the forwardness of older women, who were assumed to have stronger desires but also were less conventionally attractive and therefore less threatening. When an attractive, single young woman showed her sexual desire, however, she threatened the man's control of the situation, eliminating the illusion that she was the captive of his attention. (Not that some young women didn't enjoy threatening men's control, but that was a more advanced game.)

In practice, most younger women found ways of being sexually aggressive that were compatible with men's need to feel they were the active party. For instance, Aihua, a thirty-year-old single woman, told me how she seduced her married Japanese boss at her company in Shanghai. She said she invited him on a trip after she had known him six months: "I was very aggressive with him. I really liked him, so I invited him to travel with me to Suzhou, so that we would have the chance. I knew that we would do that when we got there. He also already had a mental preparation. But I was the one who arranged it." Her "arrangement," however, still left the final sexual moves up to him, as was expected in the gendered grammar of sexual action. (In the end, both his company and his wife found out, and he was transferred to another city. Aihua went on to pursue another married businessman from Britain, whom she successfully persuaded to divorce his wife and marry her. They had a house in Shanghai and a baby in 2000.)

Younger women did seem more passive. As described in the next chapter, dance was an especially important activity through which young women expressed sexual desire directly, exploiting the ambiguity of dance to send a strong message, but one that can also be readily denied. In dance halls and nightclubs, I frequently observed young women perform sexy dances with men in whom they were interested, grabbing the man tightly and wrapping both arms around his shoulders in a slow two-step or dancing in front of him with a confident sexy stare, gyrating their torsos. Expressing and evoking desire openly was more problematic for women, but women could find ways of expressing it through dance, gestures, or arranging a trip, using the ambiguity of these expressions to their advantage. As a result of their more subtle strategies, women also felt they were in a position to manipulate the desires of men.

The Games People Play
Deepening Feelings

Among single young adults, sex was no longer merely permitted but an expected part of a relationship. In the language of youth, making love (zuoai) was now a part of deepening feelings (shenhuaganqing), where "feelings" now had the connotation of a sexual relationship. Jie, a thirty-five-year-old salesman, explained the current goals of sex, based on his own experience with several girlfriends: "I was with my first girlfriend six years. Back then [in 1990] people took sex much more seriously. People's ideas weren't very open. For a long time we didn't have a sexual relationship. After seven or eight months we naturally just did this without thinking about it too much. We didn't think that we would necessarily get married. But she loved me, so she was willing."

I asked him about his current girlfriend. He said:

> My girlfriend now [1996] is nine years younger than me. We often sleep together, but she comes from a traditional family, so she doesn't dare sleep

overnight. Her parents wouldn't allow that. Of course you can have sex without sleeping over. But this gives the parents peace of mind [he laughed]. This is a real Oriental idea. The most important thing is face. You can, in fact, do what you want, but you just shouldn't let others know.

I asked him if some girls feel like they should wait until marriage.

I had one girlfriend who felt like she should wait until she got married. I told her if there was no sexual relationship, then there is no way that we can understand this relationship. If it is only one of these psychological relationships, then I can't really understand it. There is no basis. . . . When our feelings developed, then she changed her mind. I didn't have this problem with others.

I asked if men were willing to accept not having sexual relationships with their girlfriends. "The only men who are willing to accept this are those guys who feel like they just can't find another woman. So they are willing to accept this condition. These are guys who can't meet any women or who have bad conditions."

I asked under what conditions sex was possible. "We have to have a pretty good feeling [ganqing], then we will start a sexual relationship. And then through the medium of this sexual relationship, we will develop an even deeper feeling [ganqing]. Sexual relations are the means by which men and women come to a deeper relationship. That's my point of view."

Jie's expectation means not only a sexualization of courtship, but a deepening of the courtship process itself into something resembling a "trial marriage" (shihun), a term popular in media discussions in the late 1990s, reflecting a widely recognized interest in trying out a relationship more deeply before a formal commitment of marriage.[6] Such regularized premarital sexual relationships could last weeks, months, or years before marriage was seriously considered. However, they were seldom as formal as these media discussions of trial marriage suggested, and among my informants usually evolved incrementally out of dating relationships. Despite the seriousness with which Jie pursued his relationships (marrying his seventh girlfriend in 1999), his conversation also illustrates how sexual experience was associated with masculine ability and attractiveness. Men were now under pressure to collect sexual experiences, rather than to show their discipline and honesty. Jie felt secure telling his girlfriend that sex was a requirement for a relationship. Such an attitude was common among confident, attractive young men. Young women were thus under contradictory pressures. While parents still were pressuring them not to be sexually active, boyfriends were likely to expect sex as a normal part of a relationship.

Conquest

Single women and men faced somewhat conflicting sexual pressures in the 1990s. Among men, a lack of experience was mildly disgraceful. Among women, too much experience would be more disgraceful. For men, sexual conquests gained status. Women only gained status from sexual relationships with high-status men leading to marriage. Women in particular felt that to sexually "give in" to a man with lesser "conditions" and less "experience" than themselves was to lose status. For younger women, "holding out" on their boyfriends was also a statement about their "value" (shenjia) to the boyfriend, and some women therefore "held out" for a long time.

Conversely, women also pointed to the strength, or ability, of men as a motive for having sex. This is somewhat different from the simple considerations of material conditions in relationships. "Strength" included all aspects of a man that made him an attractive and a high-status sexual partner, including elements of charisma, sex appeal, and physical power that were not part of the pragmatic discourse of material conditions. I asked Lei, the successful young white-collar woman quoted at the beginning of this chapter, under what conditions she would have sex with a man:

> I haven't had sex in quite a while, so I will have to think about that. At the very least I would have to really appreciate him [xinshang ta]. Because, at least this is the way Chinese women feel, when you do that with a man, then you feel he is conquering you [zhengfu ni]. So you want to feel he is strong [qiang] in some way. You want to be able to feel he is strong in some way, such as career, or something else.

I asked the same question of another woman at the lower end of the social ladder, a twenty-five-year-old salesgirl in a state-owned store, and she replied:

> If you are talking about a sexual relationship, then I am not really a loose kind of girl. I won't just do that with any guy. I have to feel like he is stronger than me in some way, that there is something stronger in him that allows him to conquer [zhengfu] me, because for a woman there is the feeling of being conquered, so he must be stronger than me in some way, so that I feel I couldn't resist him.

This notion of sex as a kind of conquest sets up a game between men and women, but not a zero-sum game in which the one or the other necessarily must lose. These young women felt as though being "conquered" by a stronger man was not as much a loss of status as a fulfillment of a gendered sexual fantasy, which might even bring status. Such relationships could involve the serious pursuit of marriage or the playlike interactions of seduction in a dance hall. The game derived from a notion of male sexual attraction associated with recognized signs of social status and physical attraction, setting up a game of conquest in which a man must prove his "strength" in order to win her sexual assent (whether for "real" or just for "play"). For both of these young women, sex was a naturally gendered arena in which the usual norms of equality and autonomy were subordinated to the play. Lei, in particular, was very successful in her career and highly valued her autonomy, but she enjoyed the idea of conquest.

Another way this status element of the sexual game was described was in terms of vanity and competition. The following description comes from a beautiful and talented young woman, Gigi, who had lived in several Chinese cities and been the lover of many successful men. I asked her how she became involved with a handsome foreign man she dated briefly:

> I think I wanted him because it was such a feeling of satisfaction to be wanted by such a man who other people wanted, that he wanted to sleep with me instead of all those other women. Later I realized that I didn't even like him, that I was with him only because of vanity. I have had lots of [Chinese] boyfriends. I was with them because they were attractive, talented, and they loved me. I was always very satisfied that I never loved any of them. I felt that it was a good thing that I didn't love them. They loved me. I guess you could say I was motivated by vanity. Women love to feel they are chased, chosen above others, that they are loved.

Such understandings were based on conventional standards of status. However, they were more than a kind of social ecology of dating, but were a gendered game of sexual seduction and flirtation, even among steady couples. For instance, one young woman who married a Western man complained that he didn't understand the gendered grammar of conquering (zheng) and giving in (or surrender, fu) that defined sexual relations for her:

> My husband, he doesn't understand the way that Oriental women show their sweetness. Sometimes my way of showing my sweetness to him, you know kind of acting babyish and feminine, he doesn't understand it at all. He doesn't know what I'm doing. Maybe Westerners don't have the same sense of conquering [zheng] and giving in [fu] that a woman wants to feel with a man. I think that for Westerners maybe men and women act just the same with each other.

Most Shanghai men and women assumed that for men and women, sex could be a conquest. For a man, the conquest was more or less sexual, but also depended on the status of the woman. To sleep with a little country sister was not a conquest for the Shanghai dance hall playboys I interviewed, whereas, sleeping with a white collar would be a big prize. For a woman, the victory of winning over a man depended on his status, but also on the strength of his attraction to her. He must be in love with her for it to be a total victory. The market economy intensifies the game by increasing status differences, a fact often noted by my informants.

These rules of the game weren't accepted by all. In particular, the notion of sexual conquest was resisted by some women who wanted to emphasize the definition of sex as an expression of feelings and mutuality. Ailin, the white-collar woman whose story begins chapter 6, said, "One thing that I do believe is that a sexual relationship doesn't mean that a girl was conquered." For this inveterate romantic, sex retained the primary purpose of deepening the relationship. But playing one game more seriously doesn't mean completely giving up on the other. And denying others' objectives ("sexual conquest") also was a tactic for playing the game to one's own advantage. Even Ailin was unwilling to abandon the competitive sexual game entirely and enjoyed the satisfaction of "nixing" men when they had fallen for her, displaying her own attractiveness and a feminine power of refusal.

Some theorists might want to interpret games such as "conquest" as a biologically programmed routine or as an economic calculation. Neither essentialist theories of gender nor theories of economic exchange, however, explain the ways youth frame these games within a larger grammar of aesthetic, ethical, and pragmatic terms that describe the game and situationally frame a particular interaction as for "real" or just for "play." Sex was considered "serious" by most older Shanghaiese, but the notion of "conquest," of "strength," and other ludic metaphors among youth also made sex a playful competition in which men and women displayed their attractiveness and exercised their desirability on people they felt worthy of playing with. The game and its long-term consequences were separate issues judged by different standards.

Playing Around

Not all sexual relationships were premised upon "responsibility." Some were seen as play—at least by one of the partners. "Play," "fooling around," or "stirring glue" implied no responsibility. The term "play" ("*wan*" in Mandarin/"*baixiang*" in Shanghaiese) was also a frequent term for engaging in illicit sex (as in "*wannuuren*"—"playing with women"), and flirtation was also described as "*wan*." As Johan Huizinga suggests, sexual "play" most clearly refers to flirtation and illicit sexual activity, never to normative, marital sex.[7] Married friends who frequented social dance halls sometimes told me "*Wanyi-wan meiguanxi*": "It doesn't matter if you play around." Literally the sentence means "playing around has no connection [with anything]." The statement was frequently followed by the condition "just make sure it doesn't influence your family," specifying the referent of the "real life" with which play *should* have no connection. The dance hall provided a space for this (often fictive) sexual play with "no connections." The same notions, of course, could be applied to play-ing around outside of committed and routinized premarital relationships. This formulation should also serve as a warning to researchers who would measure "satisfaction" with short-term affairs by the same standards as "satisfaction" with marital. First of all, play is not about "satisfaction" but about "fun" and "experience." Second, such judgments of its psychological rewards are post hoc. Play is self-contained and ephemeral. Once it is over, its pleasures fade quickly.

Huizinga argues that sexual intercourse involves too many elements of the routine world of bodily functions and too many earnest consequences and pur-poses to be generally playful. Based on my fieldwork, I would have to agree, but only in part. Unlike the flirtations of the dance hall described in the next chap-ter, sexual intercourse is rarely purely play. Sex can be play, but it is a treacher-ous kind of play that draws heavily on categories usually meant earnestly, such as "feelings" and "fate." Put simply, the brief sexual affair is a matter of playing at love as much as playing at sex, and it is often ambiguous as to whether the activities are "real" or "play," or perhaps meant earnestly by one partner and not the other. This ambiguity makes the game of seduction and sexual play richer and more pleasurable for some, intolerably insincere and confusing for others.

I met many men who bragged about their sexual play and, predictably, far fewer women. This didn't mean that women didn't play around, but casual sex was considered less in keeping with women's romantic character. Therefore, they claimed to engage in it less often or described their play in the language of romance. (The exaggerated performances of romance easily lend themselves to play.) For both men and women, sexual playing around seemed to occur in brief periods in their lives between relationships, although for some people, playing around could constitute a long-term pattern or lifestyle. Han Ping, a thirty-year-old saleswoman, described such a period in her life to me. She had just broken up with a boyfriend with whom she was deeply in love. She said:

> After this I went out with many men trying to forget about this man and put the past behind me. I went out with men who were of a similar background to him, or a similar status. I just had casual relationships with them. I probably hurt many men. I probably made many men really confused. They probably felt, "Why are you treating me this way?" I just wanted to make myself forget this man. But I just couldn't bring myself to love them as much as I loved him. I went out with guys and just let myself go. I was trying to get rid of these feelings. This was a really stupid way of dealing with this. If you get involved with someone, and it isn't based on real feeling, then you just hurt another person, so later I won't do this.

She describes sexual play as motivated by a desire to forget a lover. Play relationships were often interpreted in this utilitarian or therapeutic fashion, but these retrospective views probably don't adequately represent the play experience. The ulterior motives may be a way of reexplaining play behavior that had only short-term goals, which now are forgotten or seem trivial.

A melodramatic story of a disappointment in a true love leading to a series of casual sexual encounters was a typical narrative of playboys and playgirls with many sexual partners. These narratives were part of the performance of feelings that made seduction emotionally engaging. Andy, a young man I often ran into at a local nightclub, was the most consummate performer of this sensitive, wounded style of storytelling, which he smoothly combined with a playful, sensual dance style. At twenty-three, he was in the midst of a string of sexual relationships when I knew him. He was proud of his sheepish, boyish look and of the number of women who had fallen for it. After being left by his "true love" eight months before, he had slept with about thirty women, he said, mostly women slightly younger or the same age as himself, more than half of whom were students at local colleges and universities. His story of his lost love seemed to be an important part of his romantic self-presentation to these women. He described the process of sexual seduction from his perspective:

> I think if two people have feelings for each other, then it is natural. Sometimes we don't love each other, just like each other. Maybe they like to listen to me and think I'm really interesting. So sometimes it will be like this. We both have this need, so we [have sex]. Girls also want sex. They are now open, so they can accept this.
>
> Of course, they are girls, so they aren't going to say this directly. Oriental girls use body language and eye expressions to let you know. I will go out and meet a girl. When it gets really late, I will say, "I really like you." Then she will start acting like my girlfriend. That means she will get close

to me, let me put my arm around her, so forth. Then later I will ask her, "Do you want to go to my place?" Sometimes you must persuade them. Oriental girls are like that. Sometimes they want to go with you, but they want you to think that they are good girls. So you have to use a few words to let them know that it is all right.

Sometimes I have my own place free. But I have a roommate, so this isn't always possible. Sometimes I go to a hotel. I will say that I know this hotel where I have good connections. I tell them [the women], "Nothing will happen if we go there. We will have this time for ourselves." Usually they will agree. When we get into the room, we will sit there and talk about ourselves, about childhood things. Once they decide to go there, they know what they want, but sometimes I just have to reassure them. I say, "We have feelings for each other, so it's okay."

I asked what the girls expect sexually. "Some girls are really crazy. They always want more. Some are really wild; they will make me really tired. If they know you well, they tell you where to touch them, what they want. They care a lot about their orgasms. They will be upset if you finish too fast."

I asked, "Do most of the girls really think that they have feelings for you?"

Most of them feel that they have feelings. . . . Sometimes it takes a few hours. Sometimes it just takes a few minutes, like love at first sight. Many girls are really attracted to me. They will say, "You aren't all that good-looking, but you really have style." Or, they will say, "You don't seem like a Chinese." For instance, the girl I am seeing now. She told me that I was "dangerous." Later she said she had told herself that she would refuse to go with me, but when I finally asked her to go home with me, she did it anyway. Later she said, "I didn't want to go with you. But I realized that if I went with you, I would experience more interesting things." I have the charm to attract people that way.

I asked, "What about yourself, after that do you really want to stay with them?"

"I am the kind of person who really needs his own time, and sometimes I will really want them to leave. [So I will get them to leave]." He said many of these women had boyfriends and were unhappy, bored, or simply not satisfied sexually. I asked how many of these girls wanted him to be their real boyfriend.

He said, "About 80 percent of them." He laughed.

One girl was with me one night and told me she wanted me to be her boyfriend. She wanted to go and break up with her boyfriend immediately. I told her not to. Many girls have told me, "I love you, but you don't have what a man needs to have to give a girl a feeling of safety." They all think I am dangerous, because that is how they met me. They don't want to have to worry about their man. They think a man with less charm, more ugly, or whatever, will give them a greater sense of safety. They won't have to worry so much.

I said, "So these girls will tell you that they love you."

He said, "Yes, they often say this, very often." He laughed with embarrassment.

> They are really moved by this [sex]. I easily make people have feelings for me. But I am not a bad boy. I am not cheating girls [pian nuuhaizi]. I am different from other guys. I don't deceive girls. When they meet me, they already know what I am like. They are really interested in me, but they know that they can't control me, to always be with me. They know that it is just temporary. Girls will often stay friends with me. They will tell me to call them and will say to me, "If you have trouble, give me a call." They will always tell me to call them. Those with boyfriends will tell me to call them also. They will say, "I will arrange a time when my boyfriend isn't around."

I asked where he finds it most easy to meet girls. "The easiest place to meet girls is the university dance hall. In the bars girls often have a defensive mentality. In the university dance hall, girls are easy. Many people go there to relax and get happy, but many people also think it is a good place to meet the opposite sex."

Finally I asked him what he did to protect himself and his partners from disease. He replied, "I always use condoms. But I am probably the only person in China who always walks around with a condom in his pocket."

Andy was, by his own account, unusual. He made fun of his former university classmates, mostly out-of-towners (waidiren) who had no sexual experience or wanted to marry a virgin. (Andy was himself an out-of-towner, but from a large coastal city.) He said his classmates also made fun of his earrings and his foreign airs. When I met Andy, he worked at various odd jobs in bars and discos, having failed out of his university. Like many young playboys, he had very little money. Women often gave him money or offered their support in other ways. Most of the young women he met had much better jobs than he or were university students with an allowance from their parents. These educated Shanghai women enjoyed the feeling of helping out a cute poor boy who needed so much attention from women, sexual and otherwise. These younger women were fascinated with the exotic lifestyle he led surrounded by foreigners speaking English, his earrings, his smooth tan skin, and, above all, his charming, disarming smile. They may have said they loved him, but I doubt many would have seriously considered marrying him, certainly not the university students with far brighter futures than his. Despite his own narrative, I think he was attractive because a relationship with him was merely playing around and would have no serious consequences. Young women sometimes wanted this, too, as he himself said.

Andy's story shows that sexual playing around was possible for young men and women, but that young women in this age group still overwhelmingly associated sex with feeling, even in play. Just as dating shades into leisure, romance shades into romantic play. The verbal expression of intense feelings had become a feature of sexual play among young people who had grown used to the ideal of sexual romance being spoken as well as acted out. Verbalizations of feeling made the affairs "deeper" and more "moving," an effect both Andy and the women wanted to achieve. His story shows the rhetoric of respect and responsibility among young men and women engaging in sexual play. Women made shows of responsibility in their offers of help and the exchange of phone numbers. He evoked the ideal of respect in his claims that he never lied to or cheated on his lovers.

On the other hand, his story also shows the duplicity of sexual play among Shanghai people in his age group. It involved a display of deep feelings and responsibility that was in fact a quick love affair with no strings attached. This was not, I believe, a case of women being "tricked" or lied to, expecting a long-term relationship when none was in the offing. These young women were attracted to him principally because he was "foreign," "dangerous," and "unable" to have a long-term relationship (because of his romantic "wound"), and thus "safe" in the sense of not requiring them to be responsible to him. On the other hand, to maintain their own show of romance and respect, they went through the motions of giving him a number, though few women college graduates would really have wished for a long-term relationship with an unemployed college dropout. Such sexual play must be interpreted as satisfying contradictory goals simultaneously, including depth of feeling, adventure, vanity, sexual pleasure, mutual respect, self-protection, autonomy, and escape from tedious relationships. For at least some Shanghai youth, romantic play is a useful "comic corrective" to the romantic moralism and ironic pragmatism of the mainstream dating culture.

Bodies Performing Pleasures

Perhaps Foucault is wrong. Perhaps modern people talk about sex so much because the talk and other forms of symbolic communication about sex are simply more interesting than the mere physical performance of "bodies and pleasures"—to cite Foucault's epigram.[8] As Gigi, a woman with wonderful and bitter stories of love and many varied sexual experiences, wryly summed up, "Sex always seems like the same progression, from kissing, to petting, then taking off the clothes and making love. Then there are these motions, which are the same old motions, natural, habitual." Despite her beauty, glamour, and dramatic lifestyle, when the "final goal" of making love was achieved, there was for her a sense of habit, letdown, or absurdity. She continued, "Of course, there is an excitement with a new person, but with the same person it gets routine." For her, the real thrill was flirtation and seduction, at which she was a widely appreciated artist.

The accepted routine of making love was changing among young Shanghaiese. Young Shanghai people were now learning about the physical performance of sex from sexological books sold in bookshops, from Hollywood movies, and from pornographic videos.[9] In particular, pornographic videos emphasized novel sexual positions including fellatio and cunnilingus.[10] One Shanghai informant told me that his friend went to Japan in the 1980s and returned telling him about oral sex he had observed in videos. Before that, the informant had never heard of oral sex. In 1990s Shanghai, in contrast, most young men and women had seen graphic sexual performances in illegally copied pornographic videos. These videos and other less graphic representations of lovemaking (including Hollywood films) formed a visual vocabulary of the sexual performance: from frantic disrobing, to acrobatic positions, athletic motions, and loud moans, and also standard body shapes and sizes.

In the new performative script, men's pleasure was more or less taken for granted, but women's pleasure was considered an accomplishment.[11] Although it was expected that the first time would be uncomfortable for women, after this initial phase of discomfort, women were supposed to enjoy sex and men were supposed to be able to please them. The importance placed on the woman's orgasm became apparent in focus group discussions of a magazine story in which a woman must "choose" between an impotent husband and a potent lover. Almost all agreed she should choose the man who satisfied her sexually, and that she should leave her husband if he could not be cured. A man had a responsibility to please the women he was involved with, specifically by providing an orgasm (*gaochao*). Of course, she could also be accused of being "frigid" if performances didn't go according to script, so the pressure to perform was not only on the man. Little Liu, the elementary schoolteacher, described the pressure of sexual performance with Hong, her first long-term boyfriend:

> Our relationship developed quite smoothly, but he was very unsatisfied with me sexually. Maybe the problem was with me. He always told me that I was a little sexually frigid. He said that! I always felt happy just to sleep with him, but I didn't think we had to do that. Maybe it is because up until now I have never had an orgasm. Maybe that's the reason. He said he didn't know if I was especially strong [*lihai*] or especially weak. He always told me that. And the fact is a lot of time I did that just to please him, to give him that kind feeling. But he was always good to me. He always did his best to give me that feeling. He always said to me that if I couldn't get that feeling, it was his fault. He said that to me. But I really didn't care so much; I don't really care so much about that thing. I feel that feelings are more important than physical needs. Maybe it is because I have never experience that sensation [of orgasm].

Other young women were more positive about their sexual performances, including a preference for particular acts. Several mentioned a preference for cunnilingus, as did Yinyin, explaining, "Men all seem to think that sex must involve putting it inside and then thrusting back and forth. I'm not sure that is the most pleasurable thing for a woman." However, many younger women, such as Little Liu, disputed the general emphasis on orgasm and other physical measures of sexual performance. Many said they expected their sex drive to increase with age, a common belief in China.[12]

Men's standards for their sexual performance were most clearly related to their ability to bring their partners to orgasm, but there were other standards of male sexual performance. For instance, I frequently heard men brag or ask one another about the duration of intercourse, the idea being that a man who could have sex for a longer period of time was considered sexually strong (*qiang*). In an extreme instance, a rich businessman bragged to me that he had intercourse with one of his lovers without pause for six hours. Another indication of sexual strength is the number of times a man can have sex in a certain period of time. This notion of strength was mentioned, for instance, by men who claimed to me that Western men were sexually "stronger" than Chinese men. According to this traditional Chinese notion, one could increase one's

sexual strength by eating certain foods and diminish it by being in poor physical condition. Men's anxiety about sexual overexertion and dispersal of their
energy could even lead them to restrict their sexual activities with women. For
instance, Little Bai told me of his recent relationship with an athletic married
woman (a bowler):

> A man can't do that too much without hurting his body. It happened to
> me this summer with that woman bowler. She wanted it so much, my
> body couldn't keep up. She didn't have a problem. A woman won't have
> any problem [having sex often]. She was always calling me up at work and
> asking me to meet her. Sometimes she would want it three times a day;
> otherwise she would hug me by the neck and wouldn't let me go. So I did
> it, but it was in the summertime, when it especially uses up your energy.
> So I got sick.

As men aged they became less secure about their sexual prowess, while women
of the same age were becoming more sexually "strong" and aggressive.

Though less pronounced than among men, single young women also had
standards of sexual strength and performance, such as talk of a particular
woman being sexually strong (qiang) or fierce (lihai). One woman informant described Mei as very "powerful" in bed because she was once a competitive
swimmer. She also mentioned another friend who was very pretty, "but I don't
think she is good in bed; she is too young." In general, however, women
seemed much less anxious about their sexual athleticism and technique than
men. The greater performance anxiety for women was being visually appealing
to a man. The rhetoric of women's sexiness was especially clear in advertisements for women's underwear, which, as in the West, were dominated by a
conventional grammar of sexual desirability (for instance, the popular Good-
Up bra in Shanghai). A new beauty industry profits from women's sexual anxieties, including breast enlargement devices and diet pills. For this reason, the
anxiety women mentioned most with a new lover was not about sexual performance, but about her own physical appearance, particularly the size of her
breasts, body fat, and other features normally concealed by clothing. The rhetoric of making love thus involved a highly gendered and reciprocal performance. To simplify, women began with a display of "sexy" beauty to which
men responded with passionate desire. Men displayed their sexual "strength,"
to which women responded with a performance of orgasmic pleasure. All these
reciprocal performances were fraught with potential for failure.

Unexpected Consequences: Pregnancy and Disease

Sexually active young people I interviewed seemed aware of the dangers of pregnancy and sexually transmitted diseases, although I was astounded how little many of them did to avoid these problems. The norm of responsibility was sometimes interpreted to mean that boyfriends would not make their girlfriends pregnant, but poor contraceptive practices often made this ideal vacuous. Condoms were easily available and widely used, but many people used methods far less effective, such as withdrawal and calculating "safe periods" based on the ovulation cycle. One twenty-two-year-old said typically, "I don't like condoms. It's like having sex with a rubber thing." She used withdrawal and said she would get an abortion if she got pregnant. Another twenty-three-year-old who preferred mutual masturbation and seldom engaged in intercourse also expressed distaste for condoms. "Right when you are feeling the strongest passion, you have to stop and prepare your 'instruments,'" she said. "That seems like it would destroy the moment." Condoms were unromantic for women for whom romance was an important frame for sexual behavior. Many men told me that pregnancy was not much of an issue because abortion was easily available, and disease was a worry only with prostitutes. Moreover, they assumed that women would deal with the problem of contraception, especially in casual affairs. Women were reluctant to buy condoms themselves. I asked one sexually active young woman if men cared about the problem of pregnancy. She said, "No, they don't really care. It's easy now to take a pill and have an abortion. All you need is money. You don't even have to let your parents know about it." One twenty-seven-year-old woman informant bought her own condoms and carried them with her on dates, but she also became pregnant when she and her boyfriend had sex during a "safe period." (She said that no other woman she knew carried her own condoms.) Many young people I knew practiced unprotected sex during "safe periods," and incidences of premarital pregnancy were correspondingly quite high among my informants, as among the sexually active unmarried population as a whole.[13]

Almost all such pregnancies ended in abortion, since an unmarried woman having a child would have been in violation of state regulations, involving far too much trouble for most Shanghai women to even consider the possibility. Doctors in the state medical establishment told me in personal communications that well over half of all abortions in Shanghai were now performed for unmarried women.[14] According to my informants, the experience of abortion had become much less traumatic for women in the 1990s than in the 1980s.

The women I spoke with who had abortions in the mid-1990s described hospital staff in Shanghai as polite, though mechanically efficient and providing little information about birth control. Unlike the early 1980s, there was no moral or political preaching to unmarried women having abortions, and no reporting of abortions to work units or schools. In the mid-1990s abortions only cost forty to a hundred yuan at state hospitals, a cost boyfriends usually were expected to bear. (The newer pharmaceutically induced abortion procedures cost several hundred yuan.) Moreover, because of state support of abortion as part of family planning, there were few public doubts about the morality of abortion. Still, the physical and emotional discomforts of abortions were usually far greater than what these women had imagined beforehand. Since women didn't typically share these experiences with anyone but their boyfriends and a few female peers, younger men and women often assumed abortion was an unproblematic and easy procedure. For men, it became merely a problem of extra expense and for the more "responsible" boyfriends, a few hours at the hospital accompanying their girlfriends.

Awareness of sexually transmitted disease also seemed to be increasing in the 1990s as more people were in fact being infected.[15] One close informant, a thirty-five-year-old man, contracted gonorrhea from a woman he met at a dance hall (she turned out to have been an occasional prostitute). His friend— also thirty-five years old—quite proudly told me that he had "never even seen a condom." Both claimed that condoms would ruin their experience of sex. Even a man selling condoms at a sex store told me he wouldn't use one, saying that catching an STD was a question of bad fate, like getting cancer. These two informants did change their behavior after the one contracted gonorrhea, they said. They now avoided younger unmarried women at the dance hall who looked like prostitutes in favor of married women who they felt were less likely to be infected with disease. Many men reported avoiding prostitutes out of fear of contracting disease, but most men seemed to feel they could distinguish between women who were likely to be "clean" (disease free) and those who were "dirty" based on their behavior and social position. (Professional prostitutes in Shanghai generally did insist on condoms, I was told by a former madam, but some men refused, sometimes bargaining over the price.) Younger men seemed more accepting of condoms than middle-aged men, but condom use was not a universal norm among youth. Andy said he always used them, but he also described his behavior as unusual. Confirming this young man's assessment, another group of sexually active men in their early twenties bragged to me that they never used condoms. One said with seeming pride, "I wouldn't even know what to do with one." They assumed the women they were dating were "clean" because they were likable and "respectable." Disease was associated with a separate world of commercial sex. To the detriment of youth, these health issues were considered largely separately from the games they constructed around premarital sex, whether "romance," "conquest," or "play."

The Dialectics of Premarital Sexual Culture

The meanings of premarital sex change in a dialectic process with both internal and external influences. When "sex" is redefined as an "expression of feelings" or "respect" as "mutual consent," then other aspects of the sexual game shift accordingly. Each redefinition changes the conventionalized game as a whole, which never achieves a stable definition. The external dialectic between sexual culture and the larger market culture also induces changes. The market introduces new mediated criteria for sexual performances (as it does for romantic performances), accentuating performance anxieties within the relationship while increasing the accepted repertoire of behaviors. More significantly, the market economy creates differences in social class that accentuate distinctions within status-driven games such as sexual "conquest." These inequalities also mean that less affluent women may simply demand material compensation as a token of responsibility. Given that sexual play takes place in a world of commercialized leisure interactions, it is also not surprising that games of sexual play and seduction can easily become simple paid performances. But commercial leisure also means that these performances are more successfully walled off from the outside world, and hence become more playful, as discussed in the next chapter.

9 白相

PLAY
Dance and Sex

Dance Hall Play

One night in a cheap Shanghai discotheque, I asked a couple of young women I met on the dance floor if they felt they could make friends with the guys in the discotheque. They said, "Only play friends." I said, "What about a boyfriend?" They laughed. "No, they know how to play *too* well!" Later in the evening I asked some young men in the disco the same question about the young women, and they replied with the same expression: "They know how to play too well." Social activity in the dance hall is defined from the start as play, not serious long-term behavior. The triviality of relationships is thus insured, although many relationships are in practice redefined later as "real," perhaps even "fated" (*youyuanfen*). In Shanghai the word most commonly used for leisure activity is "play" (*baixiang/wan*). A conversation in a bar illustrates a further association of the idea of play with sexual fun. A man whom I had talked with for hours over beers teased me as he was leaving, "You can say we talked well [*tandehao*] together, but you can't say we've played well [*wandehao*]—because we got no girls."

Shanghai was always known for play, as a "playground for adventurers," a city of "playboys," and for having an "attitude of playing with life."[1] Beginning in the 1920s the dance hall has been the prototypical scene for imagined sexual adventures in Shanghai.[2] They are the most popular leisure venue among Shanghai youth. After karaoke, dance halls were the largest culture and entertainment industry in Shanghai in terms of revenues, with around 45 million yuan of income in 1996.[3] According to counts by the Ministry of Culture, the number of commercial dance halls in Shanghai rose from 52 in 1985, to 310 in 1990, to 1,347 in 1996.[4] A visit can cost as little as one yuan for a cheap   291 social dance hall in the afternoon, and as much as a hundred yuan for the current hottest nightspot. Unlike karaoke halls, dance halls in Shanghai are seldom places for business negotiations, but instead places of personal leisure, including a great many outdoor venues (particularly public parks) and noncommercial venues (particularly schools) not listed in the figures above. Unlike many karaoke rooms (often really "hostess clubs"), dance halls are not generally organized around prostitution, although prostitutes sometimes solicit customers there.[5]

Dance halls are often described as "*luan*" (literally "chaotic"), connoting vice, violence, and promiscuous sex. There are derogatory names for many dance hall characters. Married or divorced middle-aged women who go to dance halls too often are jocularly denigrated as "old cabbage leaves" (*laocaipi*, tough old women waiting to be picked up) and older men put down as "old gourds" or "old tortoises" (*laobengua, laowugui*, or dirty old men). Young women who fish for money from "big moneys" are known as "fishing girls" (*diaomazi*). Young dance hall men are dismissed as "dandies" (*kaizi*) or "playboys" (*baixiangren*). In general, people who dance too often are suspected of having a sexual motive, "looking for a direction" (*zhaofangxiang*). Almost no one describes dancing as a way to meet a real boyfriend or girlfriend. "I only come here for fun," many say. Such claims should not be taken completely at face value. Many women told me they had no intention of meeting men dancing, but they were quite willing to meet me, for instance. The dance hall is a culturally ambiguous place, and its ambiguity has many uses. Serious social roles are suppressed in dance hall interactions. Spouses, fiancés, fiancées, boyfriends, and girlfriends usually aren't mentioned. Even if people make friends, they often exchange only names and beeper numbers. People may alter their identities.[6] Participants interact with strangers with an assumed intimacy, touching, joking, whispering in the ear, and pretending feelings that aren't "real." "Fun" (*haowande*) people avoided talking about serious topics altogether.

"Dancing is a particular and particularly perfect form of playing," writes Johan Huizinga. "It is not that dancing has something of play in it or about it, rather that it is an integral part of play: the relationship is one of direct participation, almost of essential identity."[7] The opposite of play isn't seriousness but goal-oriented work and earnest routine.[8] Victor Turner points out that sexuality, like other areas of social life, has been bifurcated into the "work" of procreation and child rearing and the liminoid "fun" of nonprocreative sex. In the context of Shanghai's industrial society, dance hall play is a prototypical liminoid activity: a "proto-structural, anti-structural, creative activity outside of work."[9] It is through the framing of sexual interactions as "play" that commercial dance halls are especially nurturing of new forms of sexual interaction and display. But, as Turner indicates, leisure play mirrors the serious life outside. Youth in dance halls develop new genres of sexual play that reflect different orientations to the "real world." The sexual display of the disco, for example, is very much a culture of showing off (zuoxiu), a culture of self-promotion for youth oriented toward an imagined global marketplace.[10] Sexualized images of foreigners and foreign commodities are especially prominent in Shanghai discotheques. Rather than seeing this appropriation of the sexualized West as a self-marginalization, Shanghai youth understand themselves as participants in a global youth culture, consumers and contributors to a global flow of exoticized sexualized images that Marta Savigliano calls the "world economy of passion."[11] However, some Shanghai youth are able to participate more fully than others. Commercial dance halls are segmented by age, price, and genre of dance. Different types of dance halls, therefore, mark different positions in the local market economy and in an imagined global sexual culture.[12]

By "creating a virtual world of time and space,"[13] dance allows a playful self-presentation outside the obligations of everyday life. The dance hall deliberately distorts everyday appearances. The darkness in social dance halls creates anonymity and diminishes flaws in appearance. The sour-faced forty-year-old elevator operator becomes a mysterious "girl" (xiaoguniang).[14] In the giant "disco plaza," pulsing strobes add an intensity and fluidity to the clumsy, shuffling dance steps of white-collar workers. Dance halls distort the visual and aural space around the individual, creating intimacy, fragmenting social interactions, and making overt sexual display and play acceptable and ritualistic, as if performed by someone else. Describing how she kissed a man she barely knew while dancing with him, one young twenty-one-year-old woman laughed and said, "I don't know what happens to me. I just get dizzy and excited when I dance. I guess I have to control myself." As with many people in the dance hall, the sexual atmosphere of the music and dance colluded with her passion. The embarrassment she experienced in recounting this experience reflects the ironic distance between this play role and the everyday world of Chinese courtship in which deep kissing usually signifies a meaningful relationship. Finally, dance is not merely a means to achieve sexual ends: it itself is an expression of sex and gender.[15] Angela McRobbie, for instance, points out how women's dance involves a less goal-oriented sexuality than that described in studies of male youth, "a displaced, shared and nebulous eroticism rather than a straightforwardly romantic, heavily heterosexual 'goal-oriented' drive."[16] Sexual but ambiguous, women's dance performances say things that words won't or can't say.

For nearly three years, from 1993 to 1996 and again in shorter visits in 1999 and 2000, I frequented discos and social dance halls in all price categories in Shanghai, interacting with and carrying out formal interviews with staff and customers.[17] One reason for the lack of good ethnographies of youth subcultures is the practical difficulty of studying nightlife interactions. Other arts are more accessible to study by virtue of there being a concrete text, image, score, or artifact to study.[18] Geoff Mungham, writing on British dance halls in the 1960s, lists several practical difficulties that I also encountered: noise that almost eliminates conversation, ambiguous and elliptical communication, the groupiness of dance hall youth, and sexual jealousy and violence directed at the researcher.[19] He doesn't mention the ethnographer's own social involvement in the scene, and those wicked little chimeras of sexual desire we all too often excise from our finished written accounts, but whose inclusion tells much about our path to understanding and about the nature of sexual interactions in the places we study. None of these are easy issues for the researcher. Over time, however, I grew to enjoy these places, met many regulars, and got to know a side of Shanghai life not recognizable in the earnest claims of most sociology.

The Development of the Dance Hall Market in Shanghai

Western-style dance halls opened in Shanghai in the 1920s and proliferated throughout the 1930s, becoming popular with all classes of Shanghaiese. Dance halls were associated with prostitution, taxi dancing, and other disreputable activities.[20] Even after the Communist takeover, state-controlled work units and labor unions continued to organize dance parties during the 1950s, and dancing was reportedly a popular activity of high-level Party cadres. Nevertheless, social dancing was banned in Shanghai as a "bourgeois" tendency during the anti-rightist campaigns of the late 1950s. One contemporary newspaper article explains the problem of sexual behavior in dance halls as a problem of worker discipline: "A portion of young factory workers has indulged in this pleasure to the extent of degrading themselves. This undesirable tendency fostering moral degeneration and slackness in discipline is growing and has directly affected community life and production."[21] After a hiatus of only twenty years, Western-style ballroom dancing reappeared in Shanghai in the late 1970s. During the initial uncertain phases of dancing's political rehabilitation, many older people taught younger people how to dance at home. Home dance parties in the late 1970s and early 1980s included "lights-out dance parties" in which couples groped in the darkness, leading to arrest and administrative detention for some people judged to be engaging in "indecent behavior." Other parties were more sedate. A male informant who frequented these early private parties described how they changed:

> One important difference from later was that people in those days always came with their girlfriends or wives and danced with them or maybe danced with friends. In any case, the party wasn't meant as a place to meet people of the opposite sex. It wasn't a pickup opportunity. Later on, as dancing developed, the practice changed, and men began to think that when they went dancing, they wouldn't bring their girlfriend, just so they would have a chance to dance with other women.

Public dances at neighborhood cultural centers began in 1981, and the first commercial social dance halls opened in 1984. One man recalled that tickets ranged from .4 to 1.2 yuan, not especially cheap on his apprentice salary of 38 yuan a month. Beginning in the mid-1980s, the dance program usually included a half hour of disco dancing, but most dancing consisted of traditional partnered steps: four-step, three-step, fast waltz, and jitterbug. Men asked women to dance, and it was considered rude to refuse an offer. Zhu, a low-corner man in his late thirties, remembered these early dance events as an easy opportunity to "pick up girls," describing young women then as "naive" about men's sexual intentions:

> Girls then were different. They were so simple; if you took them out for a coffee, they really believed you liked them, and then they would easily like you. And you could easily win them over. Girls now they have watched so many television programs and they know how complicated [sexual] feelings can be, so they don't care if you buy them a cup of coffee. They are not moved. They are only thinking about getting away.

A woman friend of the same generation agreed. She said that dance hall playboys could easily bully young women with little social and sexual experience into dancing and then into other activities, including cases of coercing them into sexual intercourse. She had a friend who became pregnant after what she described as unwanted sex with a man she met in a dance hall. According to many informants, young women became both more wary and more choosy during the 1990s, but not more conservative. Women began to feel free to reject offers of dances from men, a change in practice my low-corner male informants complained about but that women saw as a necessary improvement.

Women and men implicitly recognized that dance was a sexual as well as social interaction, involving sexual appraisal and a right of refusal.

Dancing in Shanghai in the mid-1980s was an activity far less differentiated by age, dancing styles, and income level than it is now. People of all ages and classes danced the same dance steps at the same public social dance halls. The first specialized discotheques didn't open until the late eighties and were initially located in hotels restricted to foreigners. The biggest change in the consumer dance culture came in the early 1990s with the advent of expensive modern "disco plazas" (Casablanca, JJ's, Galaxy, New York New York, and Time) built to international standards and open to well-off Shanghai youth as well as foreigners. Much as in the West in the 1970s, the disco in Shanghai replaced the local social dance hall as the most fashionable meeting place for youth, a place for youth to experience a cosmopolitan modernity.[22] By 1996 Shanghai boasted of at least ten such multilevel disco plazas, mostly in high-corner West Shanghai and charging thirty to a hundred yuan for admission. The remaining eighty to one hundred discos were smaller local youth dance halls scattered throughout the city, charging five to thirty yuan for admission. While social dance halls and neighborhood discos tended to be managed and owned by local entrepreneurs or state-owned enterprises, the metropolitan discos were often owned by outsiders. In 1996 the three biggest and most popular discos in Shanghai were owned by Hong Kong investors, representing the pinnacle of the nightlife scene, and were investments of 5 to 10 million yuan each. In January 1999 Japanese music producer Komuro Tetsuya captured the top spot with Rojam, a state-of-the-art complex with separate dance spaces for techno and hip-hop and occasional guest performances by some of the world's top DJs. After paying thirty-five yuan for admission and a drink,[23] the customer at Rojam in 2000 glided down a draped tunnel featuring gargoyles and a pricey Japanese flower arrangement, emerging suddenly into a cavernous vista of delightful gyrating bodies in tiny tank tops (*diaodaishan*) and short skirts, polo shirts and baggy shorts, bouncing to the racing techno beat. Two bars served cocktails to youth (mostly eighteen to twenty-five), who seemed to drink much more alcohol than youth in dance clubs did a few years before. Visiting dance troupes, drawings for prizes, and laser light shows entertained the crowds of up to a thousand until the taxis waiting outside took them home at the new compulsory closing time of 2 A.M.

In the mid-1990s bars and clubs catering to a rapidly expanding resident population of Westerners and Japanese opened up in high-corner West Shanghai.[24] As the clientele grew larger and more local, a new genre of dance clubs, sometimes locally called the "disco pub," evolved out of this mixed bar scene. By 2000 a strip of "no-cover" dance clubs on Maoming Road became a mini-nightlife district for expats and local youth attracted to this exotic scene.[25] These clubs supported a new class of nightlife celebrities such as Coco, Kika (Mian Mian), DJ Chris Lee, and Snow (a self-made nightlife entrepreneur from rural Anhui). Cultural entrepreneurs such as Coco not only were paid performers in the fashionable nightlife scene, but were earning commissions to attract the "right people" to new clubs. For these celebrities, nightlife cache became a form of "subcultural capital" that relied upon a contrast with a more accessible, younger, and popular "mainstream" disco culture.[26]

At the other end of the market were still the roughly one thousand social dance halls, the largest of which were in low-corner districts, frequented mostly by middle-aged patrons, but also attracting local youth unable to afford the newer trendier dance venues. (Older people preferred social dance regardless of class.) By the mid-1990s social dance was a downwardly mobile form of leisure, losing its classy (once politically stigmatizing) "bourgeois" label, and becoming largely a working-class pursuit identified as more "Chinese" than discos and bars.[27] Shanghai's largest social dance halls were open all day, with two-hour sessions starting at nine in the morning and finishing with a midnight session ending about 1 A.M. Morning-session tickets were priced cheaply at one to five yuan for retirees and laid-off workers. Evening prices ranged from five to fifteen yuan. The most popular dance halls in my district had between a hundred to five hundred visitors at every session of the day, seven days a week. With five or ten times the number of separate venues, the social dance hall market was clearly larger than that of the discos and clubs, but for youth it was a less popular type of venue. The low end of the dance market also included many cheap neighborhood discos frequented by local teens.

By 2000 Shanghai's nightlife worlds no longer seemed connected. Some young people knew the larger disco plazas but were ignorant of the increasingly cosmopolitan club scene. Similarly, many Shanghaiese patrons of the fashionable disco pubs were now unaware of the existence of social dance halls with thousands of visitors every night. Many fashionable youth couldn't even dance the partnered steps danced in social dance halls (as could trendy youth a few years before). Within a very short time, Shanghai's dance scene had become a divided society of multiple and increasingly separate subcultures, reflecting little of the common urban culture taken for granted only a decade before.

Dance Hall Sexual Subcultures

The dance hall illustrates how the consumer market economy has produced a proliferation of social contexts for sexual interaction. While dance halls
have much in common in their definition as "play spaces," different genres of
dance halls also represent different classes of customers, different dancing cultures, different sexual styles, and ultimately different relations to the market
economy. Each form of dance hall sociability thus is a distinct "text" for experiencing a sexualized relationship to an imagined social world.[28] The following
discussion is organized around different types of dance halls.

Waiting for the "Heavenly King"

One night in the spring of 1996, I visited the Time Disco Plaza on
Huaihai Road in the heart of high-corner Shanghai. Time was still one of the
top nightspots in Shanghai, charging sixty-five yuan for admission on a weekend night, when about six hundred people would visit. The popularity could
be judged from the long lines of taxis waiting to take customers home and the
numerous pimps who blocked the entranceway, offering to take male customers to meet girls, usually in expensive karaoke parlors. I had recently received some free passes from a friend, Zheng, a bouncer at Time, who I had met
at my local low-corner weightlifting gym. That night I arrived fairly early,
around 9 P.M. and bought a beer for twenty yuan. After talking for some time
with some fishing girls, the manager (a middle-aged Shanghaiese woman), and
a few Beijing businessmen who were planning to reopen the famous JJ's Disco,
I stood alone on the railing above the dance floor hoping—like many customers in the disco—that something interesting would happen. Suddenly
Zheng walked up to me and told me portentously, "Liu Dehua is supposed to
be coming tonight." Liu Dehua is the most heavenly of Hong Kong's "Four
Heavenly Kings," Hong Kong's four most famous male pop star idols who were
immensely popular in Shanghai. The news of his possible arrival sent the disco's
small security detail into a frenzy of excited preparation. So I decided to wait
for this rare, celestial visitation.

In the meantime I made my rounds on the dance floor below. I met two
young businesswomen who were friends of the Beijing men planning to reopen JJ's Disco (now called Yang Yang). Then I met four cheerful female college
students sitting near them, all in their second year, but in different institutions.
The college women happily danced with me together on the edge of the large
dance floor. Such casual group dancing was common, sometimes leading to

conversation. One student was intent on practicing her English with me. The others told me promoterishly, "She is a university student." That compliment made the young woman even more eager to display her English skills. The students said they didn't get out too often to this sort of place, a typical comment from students. Two of them said their parents would be angry if they went home late (although it was after midnight when they finally left). While I was listening to the college girls speak English, a more mature young woman in a leather miniskirt, a leather jacket, and a silk lace chemise started paying attention to me. She was definitely more interesting than my English class with the college students. When she came over, I turned to dance with her, itself a usefully ambiguous act that can be interpreted as intentional or accidental depending on the reaction of the potential dance partner. Ambiguous or not, the college girls were annoyed, and perhaps jealous, that I stopped my conversation with them, but I began dancing with the leather-clad woman, who looked to be in her late twenties.

She enjoyed showing off. She liked to plant her legs apart and put her arms above her head, gyrating her hips seductively and swinging her long hair, a kind of dance known locally as *saowu* (hot dancing). The movement opened up her leather jacket, revealing the full view of her flowing torso. Then she stopped, as though embarrassed, and continued dancing in the shuffling incoherent manner common among the less adept dancers, like myself. It was a self-conscious but sexy performance. Taking a break, she introduced me to her company colleagues sitting at a nearby table, a man and two other women, all office workers and typical customers at Time. They said they often came out together after working long hours, as a way of relaxing. It wasn't clear if they were married or single, dating one another, or simply friends. They seemed amused by their colleague's antics and encouraged her to dance with me. It was getting close to midnight, and the Time DJ played several slow pop songs as a kind of romantic intermission between loud fast techno sessions, a common practice in Shanghai discos. I danced a slow two-step with the leather-clad woman for several dances. The musky, leather potion of the slow dance seemed too serious somehow for the chrome, neon, and glitz of the disco. Many Shanghai trendy youth claimed they didn't like these intimate schmaltzy dances, which they don't consider "cool" enough, but in practice slow dances seemed quite popular. The darkened floor was full of embracing couples. The woman said she liked karaoke and suggested I go with her singing karaoke. She gave me her number and told me I could call her. Being "unavailable," I couldn't do that, but I made the usual polite excuses and said good-bye to her and her friends.

Old Liu, the Heavenly King, had still not appeared this night, and it was midnight. The DJs put on a colorful show of lights and sound. Two miniskirted dancers rode up and down in an open-air elevator as a skinny orange-haired Malaysian woman DJ in a tank top counted down in English, "Three, two, one, Shanghai, are you ready?!" The trendy twenty-somethings howled and hooted, and the roof of the discotheque slowly opened to the dull rusty lid of the Shanghai sky drizzling rain down upon them. Everyone screamed out into the midnight air. The ritual, which occurred every night, defined Time in its brief heyday as the hot center of Shanghai's nightlife, a short-lived status, which had begun to fade by the time of my visit that night. Later that week I saw Zheng again at the gym. He told me I had left too early. That same night the star of the American TV series Growing Pains had appeared in the disco. This wasn't a Heavenly King but still a visitation from the ethereal realm of televised fame.

As for myself, being a Western man made me a novelty and an object of interest in the disco, almost always a good thing in the nightlife world. On another visit to Time, the dance floor was dominated by five young Russian women. "They are really poor," the manager told me that night, "they don't even have enough money to put their coats up [in the cloakroom for ten yuan]." She gave them free passes. As though on a dare, the local young men would dance up to them to participate in their sensuous version of the Macarena, a dance that reached Shanghai a few months after its brief burst of popularity in the United States. For Shanghai youth in the early and mid-1990s, foreigners were part of the sexualized music, glamorous decor, and exotic atmosphere they consumed at the discotheque.[29] Dancing with a "foreigner" (Westerner) was a novelty and thrill. Therefore, foreigners were often given free passes, or let in for free, as were fashionable and pretty young women. The Russians got in on both counts.

More than two years later, I returned to Time with Johnny, a young man who had once performed there as a dance leader.[30] Time was no longer on the map of the most fashionable places, and the manager had converted most of the dance floor into a restaurant, letting the disco largely serve as a form of after-dinner entertainment, including an expanded dance show. This night the show included a boyishly pretty young man who danced a hot sexy dance in a pair of tight red shorts and a stomach-revealing T-shirt, his pelvis suggestively cavorting above the heads of the dancers on the floor below. Johnny said the young man was homosexual (tongxinglian), but when I spoke with him, he was shy to talk to me about his sexual orientation. While he danced on the steel grate above the dance floor, someone in the audience—I couldn't tell whom—

kept a red laser pointer light directed on his crotch, which he vigorously displayed in his leg-sprawling dance. Beside me on the dance floor, two fashionably dressed female medical students laughed with apparent pleasure, but they said they liked watching the women dancers more. In general, most people spent their time in discos watching and waiting, hoping to see something exciting and sexy. It was the most passive of Shanghai's dance subcultures, a cross between viewing and participation suitable for the occasional consumption of a broad range of working youth.[31]

Shanghai's large discotheques in 1996 were a place where youth could watch or take part in a glamorous cosmopolitan modernity that was usually available only on television. Perhaps one could even see a star, or at least a foreigner. Everyone could watch sexy shows with miniskirted performers. Daring men and women could flirt with foreigners, still a glamorous novelty in Shanghai. Some performed themselves, climbing on a stage above the dance floor, showing off a halter top, a pair of good legs, or some fast dance moves. The disco was a place that normalized—actually glorified—sexual voyeurism and display. Young women who would have been careful not to show themselves as "loose" in daily life could dance with wild pelvic thrusts or snuggle up to a stranger in a slow two-step. Even the presence of colleagues and friends didn't matter; all was dismissed as dance and play. Even the serious sexual pass or attempt at getting a date could be forgotten as a passing silliness. The scene, occasionally with the help of alcohol, served as erasure.

"T.D.K.": A College Education in Gender

When I first arrived in Shanghai as a foreign student in 1993, the world of the commercial disco seemed far removed from student life. Among Chinese university students, only "student nobles," usually local Shanghai students with extra-large allowances, dared go to these expensive and disreputable places, such as JJ's. Students in the early 1990s socialized largely among themselves and danced at college dances (less so by 2000). College dances represented the legitimate extreme of dance hall culture, the most socially segregated and least commercially oriented of Shanghai's youth dance venues. The atmosphere at school dances recalled the high school dances I attended in the United States: a mediocre sound system, faculty monitors, and a large barren gymnasium full of anxious young people, equally shy and eager to meet the opposite sex. Social dances (slow and ballroom partnered dances) occupied about two-thirds of the program, disco dances, one-third.[32]

College and university dances were popular with students and recent college graduates, including recently arrived graduates from out-of-town. Shanghai youth who didn't identify with the college life didn't frequent these places. Some college dance halls limited dances to their own students. A few didn't allow foreign students to attend (to prevent Chinese students from dating foreigners, who rarely expressed interest in such dance halls anyway). But even less restrictive college dance halls open to the general public were perceived as more orderly than commercial dance halls. Social homogeneity, school policing, and policies of exclusion conferred legitimacy on the college dance hall. Although college dances started up in 1981, student dancing still wasn't accepted by everyone. One grandparent expressed his horror that the first class his grandson attended at Fudan University was a crash course in dance steps organized by the student committee. The father of the student, who related the story to me, said that the older generation still considered dance a "dirty" (xia-liu) behavior. In fact, faculty counselors monitored college dances, controlling even the types of music played.

College dance halls were often the means by which "good students," a socially recognized character type, entered the world of dating and sexual interaction. Under extreme time pressure to prepare for college entrance exams, successful entrants into college were less likely than others of their age to have previously dated. For many, college was the first opportunity to relax, have fun, and date. Students classified one another by three categories designated by the initials "T.D.K.," for "TOEFL," "Dance," and "Kiss." "TOEFL" students were those who continued studying hard in order to achieve entrance into a U.S. graduate program.[33] "Dance" students were those who went to the dance hall to find a boyfriend or girlfriend. "Kiss" students were those who already had one.

In contrast with the commercial dance hall, the college dance hall was considered a legitimate marriage market or dating market by many students. Some young women I interviewed at a vocational college said that they went to dances at a nearby prestigious university to meet men from that university. One admitted that in her conversations with men there she changed the name of her college to that of a similar-sounding more prestigious university. Such deceptions are one reason other students view even the college dance halls with suspicion. However, most first-year students I spoke with went to the dances anyway. As with commercial dance halls, the sexual potential of the college dance hall was also its attraction.

College dances stood out for the mix of regional backgrounds of the participants, many of whom were from outside Shanghai. For out-of-town (waidi) students, who were often poorer, more conservative, and less knowledgeable of the nightlife than Shanghai students, the college dance hall was often their only experience of nightlife. Even at the college dance, Shanghai students were at the top of the social hierarchy, while students from poor and remote provinces were at the bottom. Animosity between Shanghai students and out-of-towners sometimes ran very deep. Shanghai students privately complained that out-of-town women students were poorly dressed and the men ill-mannered. Out-of-town students complained that the Shanghai students were snobs. Standing on the sidelines of the dancing action at one dance, a man from Hangzhou (an economically well-off tourist destination near Shanghai) complained that "90 percent" of the women refused to dance with him that night. "Shanghai people look down on outsiders, even people from Hangzhou," he complained. Even as a foreign outsider, I noticed the reluctance of out-of-town women dance partners to disclose their home places, seemingly concerned that I also might look down on them. One out-of-town female student speaking in a student focus group said she was reluctant to talk with people she danced with out of fear they would ask where she was from: "Sometimes when you answer these questions [about where you are from], you can feel the person's stereotypes and prejudices, so it makes you feel even worse." One Shanghai playboy I interviewed took advantage of this prejudice by making up a little song about how "girls from X province are so pretty," changing the name of the province to fit each partner. He claimed many women were impressed by his positive "appreciation" of their "old home."

For both Shanghaiese and out-of-town students, the college dance was a chance to assume adult roles and relax from the pressures and boredom of student life. Clothing displayed students' aspirations for adult life. Most young men wore jackets and ties and many young women wore business suits, appropriating the dress of the business-oriented society they aspired to. Other women still donned the long pleated skirts Chinese female students have worn for years, emphasizing an innocent, ladylike (shunuu) image frequently associated with the protected world of college life in China. In group interviews at local colleges, most male students claimed to prefer this "ladylike" look to the sexy miniskirts worn by some women or casual jeans worn by others. More adventurous men—especially Shanghai men—sported jeans and more contemporary dress, trying to impress the opposite sex with a sense of ironic urban cool missing among most students. The mix of dress indicates different social backgrounds and the changing meaning of the university, from a place of relative social isolation to a springboard into the market economy for which one can't start practicing too early.

The continued dominance of partnered social dance says much about gender interactions in the college dance hall. Many young people showed more interest in partnered dancing than in nonpartnered disco dancing. When a disco tune was played in one college dance, I overheard one young man say, "Not another disco tune!" "He wants to ask a girl to dance," a friend explained. The partnered dance is generally preferred by both men and women because it involves a chance to meet and embrace the opposite sex, although some also expressed an interest in partnered dance because of the additional skill and expertise it involves. In any case, the conventions of social dance confer clear gender roles on the partners. The man asks, and the woman accepts or refuses. The man leads and the woman follows. Despite its popularity, this interaction was also the site of much animosity between young men and women (a problem also in commercial dance halls). Women accused men of rudeness in the way they asked for a dance, often casually throwing out an arm without a direct glance or a polite word. Men accused women of being overly picky about accepting an offer to dance, such as refusing to dance with out-of-town students. Men felt cheated by these arrangements more than women, complaining more about rejection than women complained about waiting to be asked.

Young women were aware of the contradictions between the highly scripted roles on the dance floor and the ideology of gender equality espoused by the socialist education system. Women most typically resisted (or avoided) the embarrassment of waiting to be asked by dancing with other women. (Men occasionally danced together for similar reasons.) Others preferred dancing disco, "avoiding the problem of the dance partner," as one female focus group participant put it. "A group of women students can dance disco with each other," another explained. Only very rarely did women ask men to dance. On two occasions women students asked me to dance, assuming that as a Westerner I might not find such behavior offensive. On each occasion the young woman asked if I would be offended to be asked for a dance, adding that "Chinese men wouldn't accept a woman asking them." Their actions, however, indicated a desire to break these gendered rules—and practice their English. One recent college graduate said that when she was at university, she and her roommates complained among themselves about the norm of men asking women to dance. They chose one representative to break the rule by asking a man to dance, which she also did by asking a foreign man to dance.[34] Despite men's and women's displeasure with the strict gender codes, most college men and women endured the embarrassments of waiting and refusal rather than the even greater embarrassments of violating the gendered norms of dance. These interactions could be gratifying or demoralizing depending on the evening. One young woman explained the ego gratification of being popular at the dance. "I always wore glasses in high school and felt I was really ugly. When I went to college, I got contact lenses and I went to the dance every weekend my first year. It was the first time I felt I was attractive." While women must wait to be chosen to dance, their chances were improved by being slightly outnumbered by men.[35]

For most students, the college dance was a place to meet dates or simply a chance to embrace a dance partner in a close hug. Men tried out a panoply of compliments to increase women's interest, one young woman said. "One guy tried making a pass by saying, 'I've never danced with a woman whose waist is as comfortable as yours.'" In a focus group interview, young women said they preferred not to talk while dancing to avoid giving men their names or other personal information. Yet when I actually observed the dances, there was rampant conversation all around, and most young women happily told me their names. Mistrust was the ideology of dance, but curious interaction was the practice. For some students, it was a chance to find casual sex partners. One college student said that he and his friends tested women's availability by embracing them tightly in the dance. If the young woman didn't complain, then they would continue dancing. He bragged that he could tell if a woman was willing to have sex by how comfortable she was dancing closely with him. Conversation was optional, he said. "I don't say anything at all to them unless I am trying to pick them up," he explained. "What's the point?" A recent woman graduate explained a typical dating process at the popular university dance hall she frequented:

> If a boy and a girl are interested in each other, they will continue to dance together for several dances. Then the boy may invite the girl for coffee or a drink at the "salon," where they can talk. Later they may walk out together in the campus. Sometimes they will kiss. If they come with friends, that will be the end of it. They will leave with their friends and say goodbye.

She said that some men wanted to move faster: one college man tried to take her back to his empty dorm room after meeting her at a dance. Still, one-night stands and quick sexual pickups seemed to be rare at college dance halls. Students were restrained by the familiarity of the situation and the chance they might encounter one another on campus. For many sexually inexperienced students, intimacies such as kissing typically signified the beginnings of a boyfriend-girlfriend relationship and were not taken lightly among classmates. Compared with commercial dance halls, college dance halls were the least likely place for anonymous sexual play, although larger, less restricted university dance venues could be more "chaotic" in that sense.

The college social dance was a schooling in gender and sexual roles for young college students, who were largely removed from the dangers and pleasures of the outside sexual marketplace. The college dance also shows the salience of regional ethnicity in courtship in Shanghai, expressed sometimes in strong words and actions. It was a place where young Chinese were socialized into a gender-specific regime of sexual interactions, monitored by conservative administrators. Because of the social segregation and high level of social control, the college dance hall was the exception to the general assumption that dance halls aren't acceptable places to begin a relationship.

From "Floor Rolling" to "Head Shaking"

In 1995 I visited a small neighborhood discotheque near a second university where I was a visiting student, also in low-corner Shanghai. A Taiwanese classmate, an avid dancer who told me about Happy Disco, described it as a "fourth- or fifth-rate" establishment, his lowest category being sixth-rate. Few university students visited Happy, he said. University regulations prohibited visiting commercial dance establishments, and most students considered the place socially beneath them. Also, they might have been afraid of trouble with local youth, a realistic consideration.

I first visited Happy with a mixed-sex group of Chinese and American friends. We found it in a largely working-class neighborhood, above a cinema in a shabby local cultural center now leased out to private entrepreneurs. Entrance was ten yuan for men and two yuan for women. The pricing gimmick seemed to work, because there were slightly more women than men in the club, most under the age of twenty-one, and some merely fifteen or sixteen. Women also got a free cup of tea, which cost four yuan for men. The first thing our female companion noticed was the smell of cheap perfume, probably worn by the young girls. Or maybe it was sprayed out by the management to obscure the stale odor of mildew and cigarette smoke that pervaded the small dance club. Many youth lounged in the dingy wood-paneled foyer, chain-smoking and joking with their friends. One sullen girl of fifteen said she never danced but came just to have a place to smoke away from her parents. Some of the young men at Happy looked, acted, and smelled drunk. As in most local Shanghai dance halls, few people drank alcohol inside, though some people drank over dinner before they arrived. The interior of the dance hall was dark, the toilets filthy and broken, and the floors stained.

Most were children of working-class parents from the neighborhood, almost none on a college track. On weekend nights more working youth came, slightly older and with more money. Most of the teenage regulars were poor, and their dress showed it. The teenage boy regulars at Happy wore tired-looking leisure suits, with open collars and a silk scarf tightly wrapped around their necks. The open-collared suit was a popular style among working-class disco youth that year, seemingly out of touch with international styles. A few had short-cropped hair, but most had long oily locks combed off to one side. Few girls wore the sexy short skirts prevalent in the fancy discos. Several of the teenage girls I saw on my first visit wore jeans with tight sweaters. Lingling, a seventeen-year-old girl who danced well and talked to me and my friends, wore purplish jeans that she had unraveled at the bottom, leaving a long frazzled edge. She held up her leg to show us her work, saying she had done it herself. Some girls wore knee-length black skirts. All used lipstick.

The sexual culture of local dance halls like Happy is a bit difficult to describe. On the surface, it is an extension of neighborhood youth culture, and thus not sexy at all. Many neighborhood youth seemed to know one another too well to take seriously the possibility of a sexual relationship. Still, sex was a frequent topic of joking, and when an outsider entered, there might be speculation about them as a potential romantic partner or sexual rival. I was sometimes treated as the latter during my half dozen visits. Occasionally taunts of "foreigner" carried a violent, provocative edge, and I had to keep my head low and move on past the apparent offenders. During slow dances at the Happy, youth often seemed embarrassed to ask one another to dance. Girls more frequently danced with girls, and boys with boys. They all seemed to know the social dance steps, however, and when my Shanghaiese girlfriend came with me, young men asked her to dance. Outside women seemed to be fair game. Local girls told me they preferred dancing disco and didn't like partnered dances.

On my first visit to Happy, I talked to one teenage boy who danced particularly well. He wore jeans and a jacket with a white shirt unbuttoned low down his chest. When I asked him about his work, he didn't want to reply. Then he said he was a professional dancer but was out of work. He danced every day at Happy and other neighborhood discos. I asked him if he brought a girlfriend to these dances. He said he always came alone. "It is really easy to meet girls at dances; I don't need to bring girls." Pointing to a local girl sitting beside him, he said, "If she were my girlfriend and I brought her here, I wouldn't be able to meet other girls." She scowled at him and slapped his leg, not wanting to be mentioned even as an example of his girlfriend. Like most young women I spoke with, she claimed to despise these poor local male youth.

Despite these expressions of mutual aversion, youth at local discos often dated one another, at least in a casual, ambiguous fashion that allowed them to keep looking for better opportunities outside the community. Youth in Happy and other neighborhood discos more easily interacted with one another than in the larger metropolitan discos. Social networks were dense, and more sexual relationships probably were formed in the neighborhood disco than in larger places like Time in which many people participated purely as spectators. In most neighborhood discos, there were always some very young couples making out vigorously in back corners, some of which seemed designed for this purpose, with plush occluded sofas and no lighting. I don't remember seeing this kind of behavior in Happy, however, perhaps because it was too small, too public, and particularly violent.

The style of dance that received the most recognition in Happy as in other neighborhood discos in the mid-1990s was break dancing (zhanwu). Break dancing in Shanghai was a heavily masculine form of gender display. As an increasingly large circle of spectators formed around them, young men hurled themselves upon the floor, spun and flipped about, legs and arms flailing, a display of skill, physical power, and social daring. Young women typically stood in the circle of spectators watching these performances, urging the men on with applause and admiration. Most young women found the sprawled-legged, floor-spinning action unfeminine, and only a tiny minority of participants were women. Lingling with the tattered jeans was an exceptional female participant. In this male-dominated culture, however, she performed her break-dance routines alone, rather than in the competitive circles with the boys. Pleased with our attention, she performed in front of our table at the Happy the first time we visited. After we praised her technique, she told us that she had been to many of the bigger discos and hoped to work as a dance leader. She said she learned from foreign videos, just imitating them. She said, "Actually you guys [meaning we foreigners] should be able to dance better than us." Clearly, this wasn't true, we replied.

In contrast to the cosmopolitan discos, the neighborhood disco generally was a male-dominated space. This break-dance culture fit well within the masculine peer culture of low-corner Shanghai boys, who admired physical prowess, male competition, and group solidarity. The young men who aspired to be dance leaders typically excelled at break dancing. This kind of performance, however, was losing its popularity by 1995. The youth at Happy were behind the times. Johnny disparaged this old group as the "floor-rolling tribe" (*gundizu*). The newest dance crazes, Johnny said in 1996, were forms of dancing he called "*saowu*" (hot dancing), vaguely Latin dances involving a sensual motion of the hips that he said women performed to better effect than men. Other male dance leaders whom I knew from a different neighborhood disco disparaged this new kind of dance performance as just "wiggling the butt." But, like Johnny, they insisted that it was popular and men also did it. Break dancing was now for "idiots" (*caobao*), they said. In any case, break dancing worked best in the local dance halls that a group of young men could dominate spatially and socially. The voluptuous *saowu*, however, would seem out of place in front of the neighborhood crowd and was something for the anonymous gaze of the large metropolitan discotheque.

Young men proudly described themselves as "local snake heads" (*ditoushe*) who would protect their space from intruders. The first night I went to Happy, there was such a fight. A young man accidentally bumped another man while dancing, and the other guy hit him back hard. According to friends who had a better view, the men assaulted each other with chairs. In a short time three young men, looking battered, were escorted out by the older men working at the club, one swearing to wait outside until the other parties in the fight came out. Fights broke out on many occasions when I visited local dance halls, mostly in response to casual insults or arguments about a girlfriend. Fighting, like "floor rolling," is a highly choreographed form of male gender display. As Huizinga notes, play often contains a strong element of conflict,[36] and most dance hall fighting can be considered a form of play because the issues men fight over are almost always described as conventional transgressions of male honor like stepping on a foot or looking at someone the wrong way. Even the participants frequently dismiss these insults as trivial after the fight. Like a dance, the fight is scripted and contained by the environment of the dance hall. The participants briefly flail at one another, and the bouncers separate them and toss them out, almost always inflicting more damage and causing more ruckus than the fight itself. The bouncers are an integral part of the fight routine, providing closure and safety and also a surrogate object of verbal abuse. As with dance hall flirtations, in most brief encounters everyone can go home and declare himself a winner. However, not all dance hall fights end harmlessly or victoriously. My one experience as the protagonist of a dance hall brawl provided insight into this common dance hall ritual. After a party in honor of my impending marriage, a large group of Chinese and foreign men took me to a fancy dance club frequented by minor Hong Kong gangster types. Properly intoxicated, I managed to insult a crew-cut Hong Konger, who theatrically tried out his kick boxing while I was being dragged away by the bouncers. Little Bai uselessly staggered out after me, vowing to call up a group of his Riverside Alley buddies (a conventional promise, soon forgotten). Emboldened by the attentions of the bouncers, I hurled a series of invectives about Hong Kongers in my bad Shanghaiese, much to the amusement of the Shanghaiese bouncers, who deposited me on the street with enough bruises to show off for a week. Even my Chinese mother-in-law seemed amused at my unusual show of masculine foolishness.

In such a subculture, young women find their own movements, particularly their associations with other men, restricted by their male peers. Women seem to have the greater incentive to prefer the relative anonymity and civility of the metropolitan discos, as many of them do. Later that first night at the Happy, when we were sitting in the smoking lobby chatting with the regulars, a father came in trying to find his daughter who hadn't come home that day. One girl said she must have gone to another dance club. He replied that she didn't have any money with her. Someone said, perhaps with a note of sarcasm, "Oh, she will find someone to pay for her ticket." Eventually her father left. Lingling said that the daughter he was looking for often didn't return home. She hung out at larger discotheques like Time where she fished tips from men. Many young women in the local dance hall community (and some young men) were tempted by commercial sex opportunities they encountered in larger clubs, including fishing, hostessing, and prostitution, activities through which they could earn several thousand yuan a month in the mid-1990s.[37]

When we left Happy that night in 1995, many people said good-bye. The manager told us to come again, and the old man who worked there told us to "come back every day." Lingling, the young break dancer, came out of the discotheque to see us off. Again, as foreigners, we were a novelty in the small dance hall. When I returned to Shanghai in 1999, Happy was closed. In search for the same type of scene, I went to a neighborhood disco nearer my own home in low-corner Yangpu called Buff. While Happy was described as a fourth- or fifth-rate disco, Buff was solidly third-rate, perhaps second-rate. It had a newer sound system, a full bar, and an elaborate mural of the Chinese myth "Pangu Opening the Heavens" covering one wall. Its thirty-yuan admission charge was probably priced too high for many teenagers, but I found a large group of sixteen- and seventeen-year-olds lounging about in the lobby. Girls got in free as long as they purchased a drink, and the boys often finagled free passes from friends working in the club, a typical pattern in neighborhood discos. The demographics of this group resembled those at Happy. One eighteen-year-old girl with red-dyed hair brought her puppy that night. She said she came every night. She didn't have work, and she was lonely. She said matter-of-factly that she was being kept (*bao*) by a single young man, but her patron (*baozhu*) didn't visit her often because he had a girlfriend.

By 1999 and 2000, I noticed changes in the neighborhood disco scene. The youth at Buff in 1999 sported fashion elements that I recognized immediately from the pages of Japanese style manuals I saw youth perusing in Shanghai: punky orange hair, platform boots, little black party dresses, pigtails shooting out sideways under cute knit hats, the stocking caps of Tokyo rappers, thick-rimmed glasses, and glitter eye shadow. Tokyo style was the chief model for Shanghai youth, though Hong Kong, Korean, and U.S. influences were also evident. Local fashions also appeared, such as the *dudou* (stomach apron), a traditional undergarment popularly worn in discos in the summer of 2000 as a sexy backless top.

A more startling change, also widely evident in other dance venues in 1999 and 2000, was the blatant appearance of a youth drug culture of "head-shaking pills" (*yaotouwan*, the local term for MDMA, or "ecstasy"), named for the energetic "head-shaking dance" (*yaotouwu*). One newspaper article associated this "head-shaking culture" with the imported idea of "rave dance," but I never heard youth use this term,[38] nor did any of them seem to see "head shaking" as "foreign." The pills cost two hundred or three hundred yuan each, Johnny said (others quoted lower prices). He also said that some youth sniffed solvents. The girl with the puppy said teenagers at Buff drank cough syrup because it was cheaper. "After drinking that, you feel good shaking your head for an hour," she told me. Many (probably most) "head shakers" didn't take any drugs at all, but imitated its effects through the head-shaking dance, conspicuously embracing an image of deviance and illegality. The dance, which consisted of planting oneself firmly and swinging the head mechanically back and forth, was not particularly suggestive of gender or sexuality, and many teenage girls seemed to like it just for that reason. It projected an image of self-contained "cool" and a seeming rejection of the gendered sociability of the local dance hall. Of course, it also attracted attention, without which it would have been a pointless gesture.

Though not strictly local dance halls, some second-rate discos became known as "head-shaking bars" (*yaotouba*), of which there were about fifty in Shanghai in 1999.[39] Because head-shaking pills are supposed to be most effective at high temperatures, head-shaking bars often didn't use air conditioners, creating a sweaty atmosphere in which young men removed their shirts and women wore only tank tops (dangerously risking dehydration[40]). Steamy, crowded head-shaking bars allowed easy displays of sexual affection, and pills lowered inhibitions, but the head-shaking dance itself seemed to distract from sexual interests and interactions. Music was mostly techno and trance. One young woman I interviewed in 2000 raved about the atmosphere of these clubs (many already shut down by the police by the time of our conversation): "These places were such great fun. Everyone there really let themselves go. I took one of these head-shaking pills, and I kept shaking my head for four hours. I didn't even want to stop when I went to the bathroom." She said that her neck hurt for four days after one night of head shaking. When I visited one of the few remaining head-shaking clubs in 2000, only about 20 percent of the clients seemed to be high. A full-figured DJ dancing in an orange bikini shouted, "Shake it! Shake it!" (*Yao ah! Yao ah!*)—revving up the techno beat. The most determined shakers crouched forward in a circle and shook their heads in a coordinated frenzy that seemed intended to persuade others they were on drugs. Girls created a whirlwind of flying hair, slapping other dancers in the face, an ambiguous message of flirtation, aggression, and self-absorption. Those who didn't actually take pills could "shake" for a few minutes. The truly "high" shook for hours, sometimes grabbing a rail or chair for support, their heads bobbing rapidly and their free arm flailing. (Bouncers sometimes moved them to a dark corner, so they would attract less attention from plainclothes police.) The widespread popularity of head-shaking pills (along with prostitution) was a major reason for a nationwide clampdown on nightclubs in August 2000, in which 30 percent of Shanghai's dance clubs, bars, and karaoke clubs were closed.[41]

The youth culture of the neighborhood disco represented a contradictory but complementary mix of escapist pastimes (such as head shaking, break dancing, and fishing) and situations from which you were trying to escape (age, gender, and economic status). Most youth were unsatisfied with the sexual and social options in their neighborhood circles. They wanted out of their own small clubs and into more glamorous forms of consumption, such as the metropolitan discos and disco pubs. In particular, youth seemed to fear a decline into the socially and economically marginal lifestyles of the adults in their neighborhoods, the sort of people who frequented the social dance clubs I will describe next.

"Stirring Glue" at the Social Dance Hall

One night in 1999 Little Bai and Little Zhu, old low-corner friends, took me to a social dance hall in Hongkou called Pony. Zhu was short and pudgy; Bai, tall, athletic, and somewhat bookish in his horn-rimmed glasses. Zhu divorced his wife after she had an affair with another man (though he stilled lived with her and his son, sleeping in the same bed). His mother took daily care of their son, while he lived off a 3,000-yuan monthly rent from a street-front property his family owned, spending his days at mah-jongg tables and occasionally dancing. Bai, a swing-shift worker at a local brewery and never married, was an accomplished dancer. He found time in his schedule several times a week to visit a social dance hall. When he worked second shift, he visited the early afternoon session. When he worked night shift, he danced in the morning or at night before work. I was a blond foreigner, Little Liu in Chinese, an odd character in the low-corner dance hall.

Although not his usual haunt, Bai said he heard Pony had a good atmosphere, meaning (for him) many younger women (though not necessarily single). We found its obscure entrance between several small shops by following the large number of people entering. It was relatively small for a popular place (perhaps two hundred customers) and cheap, only five yuan, compared to eight for Come Again, Bai's most regular haunt in Yangpu. The floor arrangement was standard, a large dance floor, a stage for a band, tables tightly arranged around the floor, occluded and more private booths along the walls. Although no one probably noticed in the dark and smoke, the rafters along the back wall were decorated with images of Santa Claus and other Christmas regalia, perhaps the forgotten remnants of a theme party but also a common decoration in cheap bars and discos in Shanghai. Santa Claus has become a kind of patron saint of cheap nightlife, a romantic Western version of the Chinese God of Fortune who decorates the walls of a similar class of local restaurants.

The crowd was the usual middle-aged married crowd of men in suits and ties, women in formal skirts and pantsuits. Most people came in groups with coworkers, neighbors, or other friends they met dancing; men and women were present in roughly equal numbers, leaving spouses at home or at other activities.[42] "No one comes with their husband or wife," Bai and others had told me many times. In fact, I met very, very few married couples together at low-corner social dance halls. Although people seldom mentioned the point, there also were many divorced people and a good many working-class men of Bai's age who had never married. Dancing was a way Bai evaded the difficult issue of long-term relationships while pursuing short-term liaisons. As another River-side Alley friend told me: "Little Bai has a problem with women. The whole time we have known each other, he has never had a normal girlfriend the same age as himself. He criticizes me for wanting a little country sister, but he isn't being realistic. He is almost forty. How is he going to find some young [Shang-hai] maiden at his age?" That night at Pony there were a few conspicuously young women about twenty years old, maybe little country sisters, Bai specu-lated. I told Bai he could try dancing with them. He replied that he never tried to pick up these girls. "I don't like to fool with country [waidi] girls. If you get one pregnant, then you will have real trouble. With the old cabbage leaves [mar-ried women] that is not a possibility."[43]

We found a table quickly. Foreigners never visited social dance halls, so I was a conspicuous target of jokes when I entered any new place ("Look, a foreigner comes here to pick up Shanghai girls" was a typical taunt, not that anyone sus-pected I could actually understand it). We poured our tea water out of a Ther-mos and began to look around us. The tables were too close together, Bai com-plained, with almost no space to walk between them to find a dance partner. Come Again was bigger, easier to move around. Luckily, a group of three friendly people (including a good-looking young woman) at the table beside us offered conversation and a free dance partner. The man was a former para-trooper in the PLA, now an office worker of some sort, about forty years old. He was married but said his wife didn't like dancing. He met the two women he was with at a dance hall in Xujiahui in high-corner Shanghai, near where both of them worked in sales at a department store. They were all happy to meet a foreign person writing about Shanghai. The older of the two women sat inti-mately close to the paratrooper and danced primarily with him. They seemed to be lovers (pingtou). There was an unwritten rule of not asking other men's "dates" to dance, though who was dating and who was merely together in a group was not always clear. The younger woman, Little Li, was free, however, and Bai and I took turns dancing with her. Zhu scarcely danced, sulking over his recent gambling losses.

About thirty, Little Li was tall, with very long straight hair and a red plaid miniskirt with black transparent stockings. Her low-cut blouse exposed her strikingly white skin—"like tofu," Bai said with a grin. Bai danced the fast dances that actually required skill, while I danced only the slow three-steps and two-steps. Li said she was glad that I couldn't dance well because that proved I didn't come to such places often—something to be denied even by the most regular dancers. "It doesn't matter that you don't know how to dance. What matters is that you can have some success in your career," she added solicitously. "I never thought I would come here and meet someone from a foreign land," she added later.

As in the neighborhood discos, there were some perceptible changes in the atmosphere of social dancing since the mid-1990s. The most palpable was the sexualization of the slow dances and the darkening of the lights, contravening city regulations against lights-out dancing. Shanghai social dance clubs, which I had been visiting since 1995, had always had a session of slow melodies (the symphonic Liangzhu was a favorite) during which the lights were turned down and couples danced a slow two-step. Now at the Pony—and the scene was no different at a half dozen other low-corner social dance halls I visited in 1999 and 2000—the lights were almost completely extinguished on all the slow four-step and two-step dances. On the outer edge of the floor, about half the couples danced a real four-step, illuminated only by the glow of the exit signs and the flare of cigarette lighters. The others huddled in the crowded middle of the floor, shifting about slowly. Most were hugging each other tightly, a few kissing. Some were bent over nearly backward, the woman's arms wrapped tightly around the man with her face buried on his shoulder. Some men's hands roamed over their partner's body. Though some women refused to dance such dances with strangers, these slow two-steps—also jokingly called "bone rollers" (yaoguwu) or "love stickers" (tieqingwu)—were the most popular of all dances. As Bai's jocular lover Little Su (introduced below) told me, "People like it like that. The closer the better, the darker the better; they would be happiest if they could slip their things right in the hole." There were also ways of signaling sexual interest in more subtle ways during these dances. The most popular was continuing to hold a partner's hand after the dance was over, or simply by holding a partner closely. Both men and women gave these signals.

Like many people who were not regulars—or pretending not to be—Little Li expressed shock at the surrounding scene on the dance floor (along with some small signs of eagerness in participating in it). Taking the stance of outsider, she whispered viciously during the slow dance about the quality of the low-corner clientele dancing around us:

> This dance hall, I will never come to again. It's chaotic! There are all kinds of people here. The quality of people here is very low. You don't know what kind of people they are. And they turn the lights down. This is not even really dancing, people just hugging each other, like a lights-out party. This is a typical low-corner (xiazhijiao) place.

The main problem was the quality of the air, she said. Everyone smoked, the ventilation was terrible, and she had a serious heart problem that made the smoke particularly bad for her. She told me that she sometimes visited a dance hall in high-corner Xujiahui associated with a woman's fitness club. "It is a much nicer place," she said. "You can see who is there, and men can move around and ask you to dance." It costs twenty-eight yuan, much more than the Pony. She said she learned dancing in the college dance hall, but they had done none of this hugging dancing. While we danced, she made suggestive conversation about places people go for dates: "not too expensive, like these little Hong Kong restaurants, and then they go for bowling or dancing or go to a tea house to talk."

After the slow dancing, the crowd was shaken up with a half hour of contemporary techno/pop and Latin dancing (salsa and cha-cha), also a standard part of the social dance session. During this session the youngest dancers typically took the center stage. That night the two young women who Bai thought were little country sisters danced a sexy leg-tangling Lambada with each other, gaining the attention of an unusually persistent "old cucumber," who tried to break in and dance with them. Regardless of the dance venue, young women often performed their most conspicuously sexy dances with other women. The most popular were Latin dances. Group line dances also were popular, particularly a version of the cha-cha danced together. At the larger Come Again dance hall, there was a floor show of disco dancing during this fast-dance intermission, frequently including an employee waving a giant American flag.[44]

We left soon after the disco session, said good-bye to our new acquaintances, and then discussed who they really were. Li had told me that she lived with her mother, and when I told Bai this, he said that meant she is divorced. When I said she gave us her friend's beeper number, Zhu said that was a sure sign she was married. I told him I thought she was single because of her heart ailment. Zhu replied, "Bullshit, look at her age; she is a little cabbage leaf." That is what dance hall men called young married women trying to be picked up in the dance hall. Older married women were called "old cabbage leaves," the kind left to be picked up for free on the market floor. Old married men are called "old cucumbers"—which refers to their poor-quality "household furniture [jiaju, penis]," Little Su said with her usual directness. Later that night Bai told me about this recent dance hall lover, Little Su:

> Last time I went dancing at Come Again, I met an old cabbage leaf. She immediately grabbed me really close to her. She pressed her big tits right up

against me, and I could tell she really wanted to get close to me. The problem with this woman is that she is really fat. But later when I was dancing the two-step with her, I picked her up off the floor. She said I was really strong. I told her, "You haven't felt my real strength yet."

He said he took her back to his friend's house in Riverside Alley. Bai said he liked her because she gave him a "feeling of accomplishment" when they were having sex:

> [When we are having sex,] she yells out, "Oh, I'm really happy, I'm really happy." She won't stop yelling. I was at my friend's house, and he has neighbors, so I was worried that they would hear, but she didn't care. I put a sweater on her face and she kept yelling. Finally, my friend on the top bunk put his head down and told us to be quiet, but she didn't pay any attention. He had another old cabbage leaf up on the top bunk. . . . This woman is a big idiot [dacaobao], but she is really straightforward. She is honest about what she wants.

The story seemed more credible after I met Little Su herself, who at forty-three was actually eight years older than Little Bai. A short muscular woman, she blamed her hard life (and her irreverent, ribald humor) on eleven years as a sent-down youth in Yunnan Province near the Burmese border. Like many other sent-down girls, she married there and then divorced her husband in order to be able to return to Shanghai. She had once owned a beauty parlor, but one of the girls working for her injured the eyeball of a customer while tattooing her eyebrows. Little Su was sued and was still paying off the judgment. After that incident she divorced her second husband because he had a mistress. He still slept on the enclosed balcony of their small apartment, but "he doesn't bother me," she said. "Nobody controls me." Her mother lives with her and helps take care of her son, who was already working. Little Su made a living through odd jobs and small trading ventures.

Her frankness and sharp wit prompted me to meet up with her at Come Again several times in 1999 and 2000, despite her bear-hugging dance style and constant entreaties for me to find her a "foreigner or Japanese" to marry. ("Don't worry if he is a bit old or not too good-looking, as long as he has some money. It doesn't matter. Don't worry if he is eighty years old. I will make him die happy—in bed," she joked.) Bai didn't mind me spending time with Su, dismissing her as a "big fool" and "old cabbage leaf." Dancing at the Come Again dance hall, she also dismissed Bai, saying he was too skinny, "all bones, nothing to grab on to," a statement she reinforced with a big squeeze while we were dancing. In fact, she liked Bai a great deal and wondered out loud why he didn't call her. Su said she only danced with younger men, "When these old cucumbers ask me to dance, I never accept. I give them a big goose egg [*chibaiban*, 'eat a white card' (from mah-jongg)]." She saw nothing wrong with sleeping with any man for whom she had feelings, thought sex was important for happiness, and said she enjoyed kissing and hugging with all of her male "friends." But, she said, she couldn't imagine having sex with a man just for money: "I'm cold, he is hot, what kind of thing is that?" Little Su had a sharp tongue for the members of her low-corner community who aroused her contempt—that is, most of them, especially women, whom she divided into two groups:

> A lot of young girls, they are really just trading their looks for money. They are just cheating men out of their money. I tell my son, "Don't let yourself be cheated by these girls." . . . As for those who are a little older already, these married Shanghai women, they are greedy for a little enjoyment; they want a man to buy them some little thing or take them out to dinner. They are so happy when a man gives them some little thing, or when a man gives them two crisp banknotes [two hundred RMB]. They will be really happy. . . . They all start with being a little greedy, or just having a greedy mouth [*zuibachan*] [i.e., enjoying eating out].

Su also complained about how others gossiped about her: "One woman told her male friend that I am not clean, that I have a disease. . . . I never do that kind of thing." When I asked what she meant, she explained that she never took money for sex, repeating the dance hall wisdom that sexual diseases come from prostitution, but also revealing others' suspicions of her own motives. (When I saw Su in 2000, she said she was working in a factory. Bai, who no longer dated her, suspected she also worked as a casual prostitute at Come Again, where she sat near the door with a group of rough, older women known for their sexual availability, though not for their attractiveness.)

Su articulated what was for me the sharpest change in the social dance hall scene during the years I visited: an increasingly crass and clear rhetoric of sexual desirability and material exchange, especially prevalent among those dance hall regulars at the lower end of the social status hierarchy. Some dancers still described their dance hall relationships in terms of the comradeliness and companionship that characterized the work-unit culture out of which it developed,[45] but it seems that this egalitarian salaried-class culture was rapidly dissipating into a rhetoric of unequal exchanges and mercenary motives. This rhetoric of mercenary sexual motives also seems related to an apparent increase in prostitution in this social world. In 1995 few prostitutes frequented social dance halls, but in the increasingly difficult labor market of 1999, some young prostitute women turned their attention to this market.[46] The other change, which my informants also pointed out, is the increasingly desperate economic straits of older women, particularly the female factory workers of low-corner Shanghai, who were losing their jobs at a greater rate than others in Shanghai. Many needed and expected favors from their dance hall lovers. Finally, there was a change in the general discourse of dance hall relationships—influenced, of course, by these practices—in which people evaluated sexual relationships in a crass discourse of motives. Dance hall regulars could lay out a virtual chart of monetary and sexual compensation. Bai told me his standards, which seemed representative of these low-corner regulars:

> Whether they will ask for money depends on your conditions. If you are young—if you are about the same age as them—then they can't ask for money. They want it, you want it, you are the same. If you are an old ugly guy or you don't know how to talk them up, then maybe they won't be so interested in you. Then they will ask you for money. This is a way of balancing things, of achieving equality. Age matters. Looks matter. Your ability to talk [koucai] also matters. The money balances it out.

Or as Little Su put it more concisely, "Little cabbage sprouts, you have to spend money; old cabbage leaves, you have to spend less; the old cabbage stalks, you can get for free." If a woman really liked a man, then direct cash pay would have seemed crass, though noncash gifts and treats were expected and cherished.

Although some people fell in love with their dance hall lovers, in the eyes of friends and onlookers, such dance hall relationships were not "serious." Such relationships were just "stirring glue" (daojianghu, fooling around) regardless of the serious feelings they might involve. For instance, after we left Li and her friends at Pony, I told Zhu that I probably should not have taken her beeper number. She seemed to be looking for a serious boyfriend, I thought. He replied, "What does that matter? With people you meet in the dance hall, you are just 'stirring glue.'" I had heard the expression "stirring glue" many times in the dance hall to refer to sexual affairs that were just "fooling around," "cheating," going nowhere. In this case, Zhu explained, "What I mean by 'stirring glue,' you can ask her to give you her phone number, but you don't have to give her yours, and then if you want to call, you can. If you don't, you don't have to. You do what you want." "Stirring glue" means getting advantage through sly pretense, cheating your way out of some small pleasures, while avoiding responsibility or proper compensation. When I asked a young woman what she meant by "stirring glue," she replied, "Today he is playing with you. Tomorrow he is playing with another. He doesn't have a true heart." In addition to justifying one's own playing around or condemning the cheating of others, the subcultural ethos of "stirring glue" allowed everyone to lower their expectations of what they would get out of relationships in the dance hall. Young women still looking for boyfriends knew they probably would not find a good one here, thus justifying an evening's fun with an unlikely partner or a profitable date with an older man. Men like Bai, looking for a girlfriend with difficulty (as he always said he was), could justify dating older, married, and conventionally unattractive women. Married couples could justify adulterous affairs as just "fooling around." Even the casual visitors could "stir glue" with a stranger in a slow two-step in the middle of the dark dance floor, engaging in harmless physical "exercise," which required no explanation.

Real Love

To an overseas visitor, the disco pub would be the least surprising—or most familiar—of these dance venues. That is no accident. Most of these new clubs were imitations of similar places in New York, Tokyo, or Hong Kong, run by managers with experience overseas, catering to a cosmopolitan crowd. Yet these clubs were no longer artless imitations of the West like Shanghai's older discos. They incorporated into their decor "Shanghai" elements that appealed to foreigners and white-collar Shanghaiese, both eager to consume the city's "decadent" past. In comparison to the disco plazas, the club crowd was older, more foreign, and started much later at night, sometimes beginning at midnight and continuing until five in the morning.[47] One such club I visited had the improbable name of Real Love (Zhen'ai). With an entrance price of fifty yuan, this was not the ritziest of Shanghai's nightclubs, nor the most expensive, certainly not the most popular with the foreign crowd, but it was one of a few large clubs that did big business throughout 1999 and 2000.

Entering the first time in 1999, I found a tasteful Orientalist interior of luxuriant vermilion columns, red paper lamps and soft red booths, and Chinese-style windows and shades. This was no longer the glass, chrome, and marble of the modern Shanghai disco plaza, trying to be anything but Chinese. At 10 P.M., when I entered, I met teenagers, white-collar workers, and couples on dates sitting at the tables by the dance floor. I spoke with two teenage girls whose orange hair, dowager hats, and ponytails made them look very Japanese. They told me the names of several Japanese pop stars they admired. They were seventeen years old, in their last year of high school. One of them received a thousand yuan a month from her father, who was a pilot. They both had boyfriends, one a waiter and the other a student in Japan. "You can never be sure about a boyfriend," one of them replied to my questions. "I might meet another." She added, "We are good girls." I'm not sure what she meant, but I heard this often, and it sometimes seemed a hint at rather opposite possibilities.

Sometime around midnight there was a half hour of slow dancing. The lights were not as dark as the social dance hall, but there was no need. These people were young and wanted to be seen. A big Western man and a small Chinese woman kissed heavily on the dance floor. Two women caressed one another in a close embrace, one of them with her eyes closed, entranced. They must be lovers, I thought; this was not a usual dance position for heterosexual women. Two tall and elegant Chinese men danced similarly close together, arms around one another. Certainly they were lovers. Anyway, Chinese dances always involved same-sex couples dancing together, so no one would be shocked, and the scene certainly attracted no attention here.

Around 1 A.M. the crowd was changing. The young people and dating couples were going home. Coming in were older men, people getting off work from other jobs in nightlife establishments, women who look liked prostitutes—or who wanted to look like prostitutes—people getting drunk at the bar, many foreigners, several boys with yellow hair, and a big round guy with a big face and a ponytail pushing his way through the crowd like he owned the place. No one really knew who anyone was, and not knowing added excitement. By this time the dance floor was packed and hot. A woman danced up to a male stranger and brushed with her breasts against his chest, smiling, then backing off with a little laugh. Men and women met easily, moving in on each other in the crush of the dance. No longer were only young women dancing together in a blatantly provocative style, but more men and women were doing dirty dances together. Some big foreign men hogged the floor space with their lunging moves. They still thought they were the center of attention, but not as many people were noticing. The music at Real Love was insipid disco pop and techno, with a surprising amount of Chinese pop thrown in and covered with a drum and bass beat, including the theme song of a television ad that seemed to be the most popular song with the local crowd, loudly singing along.

In my several visits to Real Love in 1999 and 2000, I noted changes from the old disco styles of past years, the most important of which might be called a change in "emotional style." One French manager at a new Shanghai disco in

1994 complained to me that the local customers were "like tourists," that they "never smiled" and "don't seem to be having fun, just watching other people." By 1999, in comparison, the younger customers at Real Love seemed more certain of their own performances and more playful. Women dancers in tank tops communicated to their friends with their hands above their heads, flinging their hair and emitting high-pitched whoops, smiling and laughing. Wearing a black leather miniskirt, red lipstick, and frowning all evening was no longer enough. Being a wacky girl with orange-tinted hair and funky-colored glasses was much better: "sexy" and "cool." It seemed that the style of emotional cool at Shanghai's young dance locales had changed in tone from a standoffish "cold cool" to a more self-confident "hot cool," even friendliness. An aficionado of the older diffident style of cool, Mian Mian bemoaned this change: "Everyone has learned to be fake. I go to YY's [the trendiest club in 1999] and it's 'Oh, how are you, I'm wonderful. Nice to see you. Kiss. Kiss.' It's all fake now, and that's good. That's the way a city should be, but I liked the old way better." Although I share Mian Mian's skepticism about these affectations, I see this variation in emotional styles[48] also as emotional rhetoric, a way of telling spectators, "I am having fun; this place belongs to me."

Another apparent change over the decade was the status of foreigners in this exclusive nightlife scene. When most of the first large discotheques opened, foreigners were let in for free. By 2000 that practice was largely passé. Several of my informants mentioned that foreigners were no longer the models of style and behavior they used to be. Shanghai clubs now had local fashion leaders, some foreign, some Chinese. As Coco said to me: "Local people now know how to have fun themselves. It used to be they wanted to watch the foreigners to know how to have fun. The foreigners are now like everyone else. If you come to my place, that's good, but I am not going to beg you to come." This is not to say that foreigners—especially Western European and North American men—no longer had it good in Shanghai's sexual marketplace. The entire disco pub scene developed out of the bars frequented by foreign students and businesspeople, the "expats" as they call themselves. The English-dependent expat social scene overlapped with the exclusive clubs frequented by white-collar Shanghaiese, many of whom worked for foreign companies. English-language nightlife publications served both audiences, including personal ads for people seeking international dates. Many single young foreign men had strings of Chinese women lovers, a habit many participants attributed to the city itself. Surprised at her own constant stream of one-night affairs (with men of unspecified nationality), one British woman wrote in a letter to a local bilingual magazine:

Shanghai is the city where sack races take on a whole new meaning. I find it hard to explain but a "cosmopolitan swingers utopia" are the 3 words that come to mind. The city is sooo weird. Everything is kosher, everything goes, nothing seems to be taboo or forbidden other than being in a totally monogamous relationship.[49]

The once private and seemingly transgressive world of international dating in China, largely shrouded from public scrutiny before the expat club scene developed, now found a public institutional locus rather closely resembling the crassly material sexual marketplace of the social dance hall. By that I only mean that as such relationships became part of Shanghai's public sexual culture, they were also "recognized" with the same cynical vision applied to everyone else in Shanghai, even by the foreign barflies themselves. Like the low-corner social dance hall, the high-corner club scene has come to have its own cast of imaginary characters, those negative definitions of normalcy and decency as recognizable to insiders as the old cabbage leaves and old cucumbers of the social dance hall. They include, in my "insider's" view: the old married businessman (always a "German" in the sanctimonious talk of Americans) clutching a poisonous young prostitute from the interior of China; the drunken "China-hand" professional deluded about his fading youth, dancing in the grip of a marriage-eager, aging Shanghai party girl; finally, the clean-scrubbed exchange student "fresh off the boat," out for a night on the town with his equally clean-scrubbed Shanghai student girlfriend, he "clueless," she eager to "experience life" (foreign boyfriend, English, travel, U.S. graduate school, sex). Then there is the brash expat woman jealously draped around her expat mate, her exposed cleavage glowering down at the local competition. As awful as they sound when applied to ourselves, such stereotypes are the coarse everyday tools of humor and self-righteous gossip, foils for our own stories and deflections for our transgressions.

As for local Shanghai participants in the club scene, many expressed the typical outsider's view that Chinese women who danced with and flirted with foreign men sought two things: money or a ticket abroad. But others saw these relationships more complexly, or in this context, more playfully. In the 1990s sexually "playing with foreigners" became fashionable among some Shanghai women nightclubbers. One Shanghai woman who frequented the bars explained her curiosity: "I don't want anything from them, but I just want to play with a foreigner. I have never played with one before, and I think it must be interesting. Who says that only men can play with women? I can play with men too." For Shanghai women, playing with foreigners was not only more exotic and chic, but implied less responsibility than playing with a Chinese man. I saw far fewer Chinese men dancing with Western women, consistent with the pattern of cross-national courtship outside the clubs.[50] Only well-off Shanghai male professionals generally had access to single expat women (a small group to begin with), and these men had far easier options among local women. In Shanghai clubs foreigners were mainly an object for women's sexual fantasies, their showing off (including English-language ability), and their tentative explorations of "international love." More generally, the club scene, while marked off by its expense as an upper-class subculture, showed an increased tolerance for all sorts of sexual relationships, including gay and lesbian relationships, international relationships, and commercial sex exchanges. In the clubs on Maoming Road, Shanghaiese Internet entrepreneurs with Harvard MBAs regularly shared a dance floor with prostitutes marking foreign johns. The exotic atmosphere of mixed sexual possibilities was part of the club scene's attraction.

"Playing with Life"

Dancing was not for everyone, of course. Many Shanghaiese never went. Many people who did go did not engage in any of the "deeper" forms of sexual play I have described. These dance hall worlds can be described as sexual subcultures within a larger set of nightlife subcultures. These subcultures were increasingly separate and unequal. Though rarely exclusionary in any overt way,[51] they have become class cultures, marked through the spatial grammar of the city: for example, the low-corner social dance hall and the high-corner expat club. Within each subculture there were also social hierarchies of admired and denigrated people, marked through prototypical characters. The dance, music, and sexual interactions in each type of venue also differed, as I have described above.

Given the difficult circumstances of some participants, one might skeptically ask if what people are doing in dance halls is really so playful. Some people were financially desperate; others were bored and disenchanted. Others were determined to make some money out of their dance hall play. But I think play is still the best label for these interactions (and the one local people use). People may not always play well or very convincingly, but when they go to the dance hall, they are intentionally exiting a world of earnest everyday activity for one of silly, focused rituals—waving your hands in the air at no one, feet in a rhythmic flow, mouthing the words of a love song to a stranger. Even the disco fishing girl was playing—though in an impure sense. Although she has goals beyond the immediate play, she still must play well and convincingly in order to draw anyone into her game. Most prostitutes and fishing girls I met made a big show of enjoying themselves, an advertisement but also a self-affirmation.

Not only the well-off and content played, but even more so the marginal and desperate. Some people found in the dance hall an alternate world in which popularity and "face" were achieved that were not available in the real world. Little Bai was that way. He charmed women on the dance floor more than he ever could as a brewery worker in the "real world." The fashionable hotel workers and public relations girls who frequented discos and clubs similarly attained a status as glamorous divas unavailable in everyday life. Despite his greater income and status, the expat barfly was not much different. "I rule this city!" he exulted as he attracted the curiosity of another local woman. He didn't rule it, though, and was often excluded from its ordinary social interactions as well as its circles of power. For many dance hall regulars, the addiction of dance hall sexual play lay in this temporary affirmation of status and attractiveness.

In these descriptions I too much emphasize the cynics' view of dance hall play, rather than the more positive, ephemeral, even addictive pleasures of play itself. It is difficult to describe the subjective "flow" of dance, the thrill of self-display, the emotional effervescence of the crowd, the perfumey sweetness of the two-step, and the wicked repartee of flirtation. For those things I caution against a post hoc sober analysis. Play has its own rewards, only recognized in experience and not easily retained in memory. But "real-world" cynicism also makes play possible. It is the ironic framing of the dance hall as a play space that makes sexual interactions "merely play," "stirring glue," or "just dance." It sometimes happens that such play relations develop into something "real" or even succeed as long-term relations. Some people do go to the dance hall actually "looking for a direction," but, here again, it is also the playfulness of the dance hall interaction that lightens the risk of failure and makes exploration and seduction possible. The supposed triviality of dance hall play is its most successful ruse. It is what allows, for instance, a young woman to communicate sexual desire and desirability through dance without "meaning anything"—without revealing her hand. It is what allows married men and women to dance intimately with strangers without admitting to infidelity. The relationship of the nightlife to day life is ironic. Because people in dance halls are regarded as "unreliable," there is no need to be "responsible" for one's sexual play. "We were just playing around" is the normal epitaph of the dance hall love affair and now part of the sexual repertoire of many Shanghai youth.

Playfulness, like romance and irony, is an acquired competency and an emotional rhetoric for dealing with the fluid sexual interactions in the new market society. It is also a way of experiencing the social world. Dance hall sexual play resembles the romantic irony of the magazine story (or the gossip) in that both are an entry into Shanghai's public sexual culture, and an aestheticization, or fictionalization, of its moral contradictions and gendered tensions. But they bring us into this world from very different positions. The "true story" magazine narrator grudgingly accepts the necessary compromises of a morally ironic world, assuming the position of the virtuous survivor, the "little person," the neighborhood gossip. The dance hall player eagerly celebrates these contradictions from the inside, enjoying them as materials for tricks and games. As the poet Friedrich Schiller wrote, "Among all the conditions of man, it is exactly play and only play which makes him complete and at the same time reveals his dual nature."[52] The "dual nature" Schiller refers to is the tension between freedom and necessity in all human endeavors, a tension explored dourly in romantic irony, more whimsically in play.[53] With its fixed rules and the element of pretense, sexual play gives fundamental expression to this conflict between individual freedom and external social necessity. Alienation, material necessity, and gender expectations are not denied through such games, but given full expression in playing with their positions and boundaries. The poor youth who successfully portrays a playboy temporarily assumes power in the sexual economy of the dance hall, allowing him to poke fun at respectable white collars he knows have an easier time in the world outside. Play thus has a critical potential and a fundamentally social nature, a finding of freedom and creativity in interactions with others rather than through individual activities.[54] At its best it is mutually liberating; at its worst, mean-spirited, though usually trivial. Dance hall play makes life freer in contemporary Shanghai, or at least, as Kundera might put it, "lighter."[55] Not everyone plays, and not everyone plays equally. But especially for the young and light of heart, reform-era Shanghai provided spaces both for falling in love and for fooling around.

METHODOLOGICAL
APPENDIX

Putting Together a Story

Ironically, historians of sexuality often are able to produce more vivid descriptions of sexual cultures out of the dead matter of archival materials, than sociologists out of the living matter of interviews and personal observations. In my view, the explanatory and narrative thinness of much sociological writing on sexuality lies in its failure to reconstruct the local vocabularies through which people interact and construct personal sexual meanings. The instinct of the properly trained sociologist is to "control" for local context. In writing this book, I strove to represent Shanghai's sexual culture dramatistically, laying out a full grammar of story elements rather than focusing on a narrow range of behaviors and institutions usually associated with "sex" or "sexuality." Since the diversity of informants makes a full reconstruction of their various life worlds impossible, I focus on the most basic shared building blocks of Shanghai sexual culture. In designing this study, I was inspired by the historiographic use of multiple types of data. In order to make my story empirically accountable, however, I limited the scope of data collection to particular subsets of the media, the nightlife, neighborhoods, and activities of Shanghai youth. In this appendix I describe each type of data I used to construct this partial grammar of Shanghai's sexual culture.

Personal and Ethnographic Interviews

The methods for conducting an ethnographic study are similar to those of learning a language: prolonged contact and interaction with a subset of native speakers and cultural "texts" from whom the complexities of the language can be learned. Of course, the assumption is that the teachers one has chosen speak a language common to other members of society, and one must take account of dialects that vary across social groups. In its essence, however, ethnography is not a sampling procedure, but a process of learning a cultural and social grammar from informants. I began "learning" Shanghai's sexual culture in 1993. I spent a little over three of the next seven years in Shanghai: eight months in 1993, two years from **327**

1994 to 1996, and another half year in short visits since then. During this time in Shanghai, I continuously conducted unstructured life history interviews, ethnographic interviews, and informal ethnographic observations and conversations. By unstructured life history interviews, I mean that I invited informants to sit down; I prompted discussion with a series of open-ended questions; I recorded the conversation, or took running notes, and afterward transcribed the interview. Most of these interviews simply began with the "first love" and ended with the most recent, though no formal procedure dominated the flow of conversation. Personal life history interviews usually ran on for two to five hours, sometimes spread out over more than one meeting. It is difficult for me to count the number of life history interviews I conducted. If only the longer, more successful interviews are considered, there are roughly seventy-five individual "cases," with women somewhat outnumbering men. Occasionally I interviewed strangers I met in a bar or tea shop, but most were introduced by other informants. I conducted interviews in Mandarin Chinese, which young Shanghai people use in daily life along with local dialects (mostly Shanghaiese but also Subei dialect). Some group conversations were in the Shanghai dialect, which I understood less perfectly. If I had trouble with Shanghaiese expressions, I asked my interlocutors to explain them in Mandarin.

I also conducted ethnographic interviews with individuals who described to me their social lives, their schools, their magazine publishing company, or the nightclub we were in. Quantifying ethnographic interviews is pointless because some "interviews" lasted twenty minutes; others went on week after week for years. I have about a dozen very close Shanghaiese friends who helped me and continue to help me with my research, also dozens more less intimate friends who invited me to participate together in the public sexual culture of Shanghai: dancing in a disco, lecturing at a local library, speaking on a television talk show, or just chatting with their friends. These long-term informants are the guiding lights of ethnographic research, but a brief argument with a stranger may also provide the sudden critical insight. Over these years at least a thousand casual conversations contributed to this research. I can thus consider my interview data in terms of increasing quantitative orders of magnitude, quantitatively approximately 20 close informants, 75 life history interviews, 100 ethnographic interviews, and 1,000 informal conversations. In terms of their qualitative importance, however, these four types of interview data weigh about the same.

More important than numbers is the composition of my various circles of informants and interviewees. The two largest circles are represented metonymically in chapter 2 by Little Bai and Bei. I met Little Bai in 1995 in a cheap social dance club near my home. I met Bei through contacts within a marketing firm in 1995. Bai gradually introduced me to a great many low-corner friends, more men than women, and slightly older than the group I usually met in other circumstances. (Bai's friends were mostly my own age. I was born in 1964.) Although Bai was by no means my only conduit into the working-class sexual culture of the surrounding neighborhood, he was one of my earliest and longest-term informants. Later I often ventured out to these dance clubs with other friends, some Bai introduced to me, others I had met myself. In contrast, Bei was not my first entrée into the white-collar subculture, which came in late 1994 through teaching English at several foreign firms in Shanghai. Some of these professionals and office workers became long-term friends and informants. In contrast to Bai's group, this white-collar circle was proportionately more female.

Given the topic of my research, my own sexual status greatly influenced the formation of both circles of informants.[1] Many white-collar Shanghai women seemed to enjoy discussing their personal lives with an educated American male friend. My constant discussions of sexual and romantic matters seemed more off-putting to white-collar Shanghai men, who might have sensed a sexual competition, or perhaps simple boredom. Working-class men, on the other hand, typically saw me as participating in a different sexual marketplace to which they had no access. They enjoyed the novelty of my companionship. Working-class women perhaps saw me as "out of their league," or perhaps sexually threatening, and generally were more standoffish. I interviewed many white-collar men and working-class women, but my own public sexual identity as a heterosexual foreign male meant that my closest friends in Shanghai were high-status women and low-status men, the groups who have the most reason to be discontent in Shanghai's hypergamous sexual culture. Their relative marginalization also may have made some of them more willing to see a foreigner as a confidant. Generally, being a male, aged twenty-nine to thirty-seven for the period of this research, may have given me a different perspective on gendered sexual interactions than that of the female researcher: seeing a more flirtatious side of heterosexual women and a more "macho" style of male self-presentation when women were absent.

Other groups I interviewed included magazine editors (discussed below) and fiction writers, including a dozen members of Shanghai's small literary establishment, only a few of whom make it into this book. Mian Mian was my closest friend who also was a writer, and I mostly knew her as a fellow nightlife junkie and a confidante for my own romantic tribulations. (For that, she called me her "big idiot," dahuobao.) I also socialized with and conducted interviews among a group of Shanghai elementary schoolteachers I met in 1995 during a semester teaching English to children in an after-school class. As a generally less sexually active group, they provided a more "conservative" perspective on Shanghai's dating culture. Equally important was my contact with my wife's family, including nearly daily conversations with my mother-in-law, who consciously sought to help me with my research, arranging interviews with former colleagues and collecting newspaper clippings. I also got to know my wife's friends, her college classmates, and her colleagues at the Shanghai office of a prestigious U.S. business firm. Finally, I never use the real names of informants except for public figures who want the publicity. Occasionally I change details such as an occupation or a country of origin to further protect an identity.

Participant Observation

I was an inveterate participant in Shanghai's nightlife, visiting some type of club or disco two to four times a week during most of my stay. My choice of nightlife establishments was more sociological than personal. Although not much of a dancer, I mostly attended dance clubs. As with my larger ethnographic project, I focused on dance clubs at all levels of prestige, from the cheapest low-corner social dance hall to the most expensive discos and expatriate bars. In addition to participant observation, I interviewed the owners or managers of the clubs I regularly visited, as well as many customers. Of course, I also danced, as best I could, and used these dances, especially slow dances in the social dance clubs, as a time to converse with female informants. I usually spoke with men off the dance floor. As a self-conscious researcher, I told those I extensively questioned that I was writing a book about the clubs I visited. As an observer and participant, this was not always possible or practical. As a writer, my principle ethical concern is with protecting the privacy of people I met or observed regardless of their knowledge of my writing. Otherwise, in my view, the ethics of personal interactions in the nightlife are no different for the researcher than for anyone else, including basic courtesy and respect for the autonomy and dignity of others.[2]

In addition to providing life history "interviewees," the groups of informants described above also formed the context of my "participant observation" in Shanghai's sexual culture, meaning that we "hung out" together, met one another's friends, and shared stories. Most of them know my love life as well as I know theirs. We also changed one another's lives to some degree. Several of my white-collar informants dated or married foreign men in my circle. In general, this white-collar circle included a disproportionate number of women involved in "international" relationships. I have tried to take account of this special circumstance in my ethnography. One reason that I conducted focus group interviews (discussed below) is to have a "normative discourse" against which to compare the idiosyncratic stories of informants. (Despite their unusual plots, the vocabulary and rhetoric of their stories were not unusual.)

Beyond the dance clubs and friendship circles, my participation in Shanghai life as a husband, as a son-in-law, as a student, as a teacher, as a television viewer, and as an academic all provided insights into Shanghai's sexual culture, which are represented in this book. I must admit, however, that the nightlife and its culture of sexual play take a larger place in my account than they would in the accounts of others. On the other hand, commercial sex and hostess bars, in which I did not participate for ethical and financial reasons, take up a far smaller place in my account than they might have, especially given my emphasis on the "money motive" in Shanghai's culture.

Magazine Stories

Chapter 4 is based primarily on an analysis of articles on the topics of love, marital relations, dating relations, and sex from the Shanghai magazine *Young Generation*. However, my preparations for this chapter were far broader, reading articles

Table A.1. *Youth Generation* articles on love and sex by genre and year of publication.

	'79–80	'83	'88	'95–96	'00
Reports/Educational Articles					
Overseas/Historic Reports	9	2	1	2	4
Social Issue Reports	6	1	7	12	11
Instructive/Educative Articles	2	2	1	0	7
Essays					
Moral Instruction Essays	6	1			
Love Essays			5	6	4
"True Stories"					
Moral Exemplar Stories	9	2	1	1	3
Social Melodramas	3	8	7	16	15
Love Stories	3	6	9	16	12
Reader's Letters					
Reader's Letters	8	13	12	11	11

from five different magazines (*Young Generation, Family, Golden Age, Culture and Life,* and *Girlfriend*). I read available editions of these magazines from four years: 1979–80, 1983, 1988, and 1995–96. (*Girlfriend* was only available beginning in 1995. *Golden Age* and *Family* were available from 1983.) From these editions I selected all articles that were about sexual love, marriage, courtship, and sexuality—a total of 504 articles. An assistant summarized the principle narratives from all articles in English to allow for easy qualitative comparisons of narrative structure. To supplement this initial study, I also read the 2000 editions of *Young Generation* and *Girlfriend*. In order to understand the production of these magazines, I interviewed thirty-five magazine editors and writers, including chief editors and midlevel editors from all these magazines. I also used magazine articles as stimuli to discussion in twelve focus group interviews about sexual norms, revealing to some extent how readers react to these articles. The following table shows the distribution of articles from *Young Generation* for each of the five sampled years subdivided into genres. The genres are ad hoc but intuitive categories based on a conventional understanding of the magazine article deemed reasonable by a small group of informants in Shanghai. This division into genres should not obscure the important fact that almost all articles in the sample used "true stories" of real people as examples.

As stated in chapter 4, most articles fell into the genre of the "true story," which I have divided here into three subgenres: "love stories" focusing on the emotions of two individuals; "social melodramas" focusing on the social problem exemplified by a case; "moral exemplar stories" describing the love life of a historical figure or model youth. Second most common were reports about sexual phenomena in society, such as sexual promiscuity, extramarital affairs, homosexuality (very rare), and less controversial topics. In fact, this genre showed substantial change over the period of the study. The 1979–80 and 1983 social reports were more opinionated and propagandistic. Reports from 1995–96 and 2000 were much more likely to involve interviews with more examples and data.

All of these magazines were much broader in focus than U.S. magazines. Self-described youth magazines, *Young Generation, Girlfriend,* and *Golden Age* covered any problems editors consider relevant to youth (ages eighteen to thirty-five). *Family* covered everything editors considered relevant to families. *Culture and Life,* popular in the early 1980s, was even more broadly conceived and became too much of a hodgepodge even for the Chinese market. It stopped publishing in 1999. Magazine article topics are best conveyed through examples. Following are examples of articles from the most recent (summer and fall 2000) editions of *Young Generation* (YG) and *Girlfriend* (G), including some titles not about love or sex. First, some articles describe the conditions youth face in the market economy:

"'Do It Yourself': Changing Your Career on Your Own" (YG 2000, no. 9, 14–16)
"The ABC's of Packaging Yourself for an Interview" (YG 2000, no. 9, 6–7)
"Women Talent Managers in Shanghai" (YG 2000, no. 4, 33–35)
"The Career Sutra" (YG 2000, no. 6, 14–15)
"Questions to Ask Yourself before Accepting a Job Offer" (YG 2000, no. 6, 58)
"Making Money on the Internet" (YG 2000, no. 7, 4–7)

In the still strong tradition of magazine melodrama, described in chapter 4, many articles deal with the sexual dangers peculiar to the new market economy.

"How Can Private Entrepreneurs Deal with the Problems of Sexual Passion?" (YG 2000, no. 4, 16–18) (a survey of the numerous love affairs and bad marriages of private entrepreneurs)
"A Female Teacher Jumps into the Sea of the Market Economy" (YG 2000, no. 8, 22–25) (A woman must avoid the temptation to become a mistress.)
"The Extramarital Loves of a 'Strong Woman'" (YG 2000, no. 7, 60–63) (a female entrepreneur's love affairs)
"The Experience of Being the 'Third Person'" (YG 2000, no. 8, 11–12) (A young male employee becomes the paid lover of a rich female boss.)
"The Terrible Outcome of a Passionate Love" (YG 2000, no. 8, 26–28) (A married man falls deeply in love with a former student who is now a wealthy female entrepreneur, only to discover he is only one lover among many.)
"The Diary of a 'Bird in a Golden Cage'" (YG 2000, no. 4, 58–61) (A secretary becomes the "kept woman" of her boss.)
"Investigating a Mysterious Ad for 'Male Escorts'" (YG 2000, no. 4, 20–21) (a scam for swindling money from young men)
"Gambling with International Marriage" (YG 2000, no. 4, 30–31) (A fake marriage proves disastrous.)
"A Beauty Loses Her Way" (YG 2000, no. 8, 34–35) (A beautiful woman swindles money from big moneys.)

Many stories and articles deal with the conditions of choice in an increasingly free and fluid dating culture:

"What Do Men Want Today?" (*YG* 2000, no. 8, 4–5) (still beauty, but the "inner beauty" of educated women can win a man's heart)

"Falling in Love with the People You Serve" (*YG* 2000, no. 8, 8–9)

"Is It Okay to Marry a Girlfriend Six Years Older?" (*YG* 2000, no. 6, 34–35)

"Beauty Is My Capital" (*YG* 2000, no. 1, 33)

"Who Will They Give Their Embroidered Ball To?" (*YG* 2000, no. 1, 62–63) (the difficulties women managers have finding a suitable partner)

"Men Don't Like Perfect Women" (*G* 2000, no. 7, 52)

"A Plain Woman and a Handsome Man" (*YG* 2000, no. 8, 62–64)

"Two Love Affairs of a Woman Director" (*YG* 2000, no. 6, 22–25) (Love is a growth experience.)

"The Feeling of First Love" (*YG* 2000, no. 6, 44–47) (nostalgic reminiscence)

"Love Him and Keep a Distance from Him" (*G* 2000, no. 8, 61) (keep some emotional distance in dating)

"The Same Love Doesn't Come around Twice" (*YG* 2000, no. 6, 38–39) (One can't look for the same qualities in a new lover that one liked in the first.)

"Does a Girl's Jealousy Mean that She Loves Me?" (*YG* 2000, no. 8, 42)

"Just Passing through: Feelings beyond Love" (*G* 2000, no. 9, 12–16) (describes brief romantic moments between strangers)

"No More Love Contracts" (*G* 2000, no. 9, 44–45) (College students decide there is still "true love," but it may not lead to a permanent relationship.)

Then there is the occasional discussion of the problem of premarital sex:

"I Am Modern, but I Am Pure" (*YG* 2000, no. 7, 44–45) (lives with boyfriend she truly loves)

"Sexual Civilization on the College Campus" (*YG* 2000, no. 6, 62–63) (survey)

"The Worries of Unmarried Mothers" (*YG* 2000, no. 7, 26–29) (cautionary tales)

Finally, articles discuss youth's uncertainties about marriage and fears of family life:

"What Will Marriage Be Like in the New Century?" (*YG* 2000, no. 1, 20–21)

"In the 21st Century, Will We Marry?" (*YG* 2000, no. 1, 4–7)

"Giving Birth: The End of Youth" (*G* 2000, no. 8, 52–53)

"Life without Men: An Investigation of Single Women and Women Living Alone" (*YG* 2000, no. 8, 12–13) (Most are lonely.)

"Not Afraid of Being Single" (*G* 2000, no. 8, 15–21)

Discussion Groups (Focus Groups)

While I use the conventional term "focus group" in the text, the Chinese term "zuotanhui" best translates as a "discussion group," sounding rather more dignified, less focused, and less commercially oriented than the English term. I used group interviews for several reasons. First, for the purpose of studying language, focus groups provide the most reliable material, because they were recorded most thoroughly and exclude the researcher (myself, a foreign man with good Mandarin but poor spoken Shanghaiese). Shanghai women moderators could easily switch to the Shanghai dialect with less-educated informants. These discussion groups produced lively conversation. Although the context differs from conversations in everyday life, the contents of conversations were similar to those I heard between casual acquaintances at work, school, and other situations. Second, focus groups have inherent advantages over individual interviews, originally pointed out by Robert Merton.[3] Focus groups prompt ordinary people to speak who might not be willing to participate in a one-on-one interview. Less-inhibited members tend to speak first and encourage the others to speak out. Focus groups widen the range of responses, allowing the interviewer to discover a wider variety of definitions of the situation. Most important for this project, group interviews have the advantage of activating forgotten details. In particular, focus groups proved useful in reconstructing the conventions of dating in the early reform era.

I conducted three sets of focus group interviews. In writing, however, I relied mostly upon a set of eleven focus group interviews conducted under the auspices of the Shanghai Academy of Social Sciences (SASS) in 1996 with help from an SASS-affiliated market research firm. The participants in the SASS groups were chosen by professional interviewers from the market research firm in door-to-door visits in local neighborhoods. Geographically, the sample was centered in Luwan District (near SASS offices) and was segmented by gender and age group, to facilitate conversation through social homogeneity.[4] An attempt was made to further segregate the participants by education level (college vs. no college) and was largely successful, although some mixing seems to have occurred. Crossing these three dimensions—gender, two ages (20–25 and 35–40), and two education levels—produced eight groups. Two groups of respondents aged 25–30 (men and women) and an eleventh group of older men were added. (Group 11 made up for an insufficient turnout in group 7.) Participants in the SASS groups were provided with gifts or cash and refreshments. Most participants enjoyed the conversation and were willing to talk well beyond the two-hour suggested time period. The SASS interviews were conducted by two Chinese women moderators in their early twenties and a separate note taker, who recorded and transcribed the interviews.

Before I organized interviews at SASS, I personally conducted a set of eight group interviews among students at a major four-year university and six group interviews with students (including two groups of young faculty) at a smaller two-year college in Shanghai in 1995 and 1996. Both schools draw students from all over China. I moderated all the student interviews with the help of Chinese collaborators and note takers. The size of each group ranged from four to twelve participants. In the student interviews, I experimented with different formats. Most, but not all, of the college interviews were segregated by sex. I found it even more important to segregate Shanghai students from out-of-town students because of the social tensions between these two groups and their rather different attitudes toward sexual matters. Most of the interviews at the four-year university were organized by choosing students randomly from dorm rooms. Some other groups were roommates or classmates. Although these student interviews provided valuable background information, I relied upon them less as examples in the book than upon the SASS interviews because the SASS interviews were more accurately transcribed and because SASS interview participants were Shanghaiese from a wider range of backgrounds.

All of the SASS informants were asked to fill out a form providing basic personal information (not including their level of education, which was a selection criterion for setting up the groups). They were asked their age, occupation, income in yuan, how many times they dated before marriage, and whether they had experienced premarital sex.[5] Younger respondents were only asked if they had ever dated (lianai). Names, as with other interviewees, are pseudonyms.

Focus Group Interviewees Cited in the Text
Focus Group 1
Female, all unmarried, mostly college educated

Cheng	21, sales representative, 800 RMB a month, no lianai, no premarital sex
Shen	20, secretary, 1,500 RMB, no answer, no premarital sex
Luo	24, teacher, 800 RMB, yes lianai, no premarital sex
Qing	21, between jobs, no income, yes lianai, no premarital sex
Zen	22, teacher, 800 RMB, no lianai, no premarital sex
Cui	22, secretary, 1,200 RMB, yes lianai, yes premarital sex
Xuan	24, customs clearer, 1,000 RMB, yes lianai, no premarital sex

Focus Group 2
Male, all unmarried, mostly college educated

Wan	23, graphic designer, 2,000 RMB, yes lianai, no premarital sex
Ni	20, office worker, 1,000 RMB, yes lianai, no premarital sex
Han	22, unemployed, no income, yes lianai, yes premarital sex
Feng	21, office worker, 700 RMB, yes lianai, yes premarital sex
Peng	21, office worker, no answer, no answer, no answer

Focus Group 3
Female, all unmarried, mostly no college

Guan	23, clerical worker, 2,000 RMB, yes lianai, no premarital sex
Zhung	23, illegible answer, 1,500 RMB, yes lianai, no premarital sex

Shang   22, secretary, 1,300 RMB, yes *lianai*, no premarital sex
Du   23, teacher, 800 RMB, no *lianai*, no premarital sex
Da   23, executive assistant, 1,400 RMB, yes *lianai*, no premarital sex
Pu   24, bookkeeper, 1,200 RMB, yes *lianai*, no premarital sex
Meng   24, office worker, 3,000 RMB, yes *lianai*, no premarital sex
Xi   25, medical specialist, 2,000 RMB, yes *lianai*, no premarital sex

Focus Group 4

Male, all unmarried, mostly no college

Hao   22, driver, 750 RMB, yes *lianai*, yes premarital sex
Wei   23, advertising sales, 2,500 RMB, yes *lianai*, no premarital sex
Fang   22, sales, 1,500 RMB, yes *lianai*, no premarital sex
He   22, office worker, 1,500 RMB, yes *lianai*, no premarital sex
Hua   25, account representative, 2,000 RMB, yes *lianai*, yes premarital sex
Ji   23, office worker, 1,500 RMB, yes *lianai*, no premarital sex

Focus Group 5

Female, all married, mostly no college

Ming   37, factory worker, 350 RMB, one time *lianai*, no premarital sex
Nong   35, factory worker, 800 RMB, one time *lianai*, no premarital sex
Ping   38, bookkeeper, 2,000 RMB, two times *lianai*, no premarital sex
Sang   38, factory worker, 850 RMB, no *lianai*, no premarital sex
Shi   38, bank teller, 1,500 RMB, no answer, no answer
Si   31, retail sales, 600 RMB, no answer, no answer
Sui   39, factory worker, 800 RMB, one time *lianai*, no premarital sex
Dong   34, factory worker, 800 RMB, two times *lianai*, no premarital sex
Xiang   29, retail sales, 1,500 RMB, two times *lianai*, yes premarital sex

Focus Group 6

Male, all married, mostly no college

Song   33, driver, 1,000 RMB, two times *lianai*, yes premarital sex
Yuan   34, technician, 1,000 RMB, four times *lianai*, yes premarital sex
Yan   32, factory worker, 3,600 RMB, five times *lianai*, yes premarital sex

Focus Group 7

Male, two married, college educated

Xiao   36, art editor, 700 RMB, five times *lianai*, yes premarital sex
Xie   29, sales manager, 3,000 RMB, two times *lianai*, yes premarital sex

Focus Group 8

Female, all married, mostly college educated

Xin   32, office worker, 600 RMB, one time *lianai*, no premarital sex

Yao   38, quality-control officer, 690 RMB, two times *lianai*, no premarital sex

Ye   36, factory worker, 2,000 RMB, one time *lianai*, no premarital sex

Yi   38, bookkeeper, 600 RMB, one time *lianai*, no premarital sex

Zhan   33, office worker, 1,800 RMB, two times *lianai*, no premarital sex

Zhong   34, personnel office, 1,000 RMB, no answer, no answer

Focus Group 9

Male; unmarried except Zhao and Qian, who are married; not segregated by education

Zu   27, air-conditioning, 1,500 RMB, four times *lianai*, yes premarital sex

Wang   25, project manager, 3,000 RMB, three to four times *lianai*, yes premarital sex

Huang   27, section chief, 2,000 RMB, two times *lianai*, yes premarital sex

Zhao   30, private entrepreneur, 20,000 RMB, no *lianai*, yes premarital sex

Qian   32, customer representative, 1,000 RMB, countless times *lianai*, yes premarital sex

Sun   25, sales, 2,000 RMB, three times *lianai*, no premarital sex

Li   26, retail sales, 1,000 RMB, three times *lianai*, yes premarital sex

Liu   no data

Focus Group 10

Female; unmarried except Lu, who is married; not segregated by education

Zhang   25, administrative assistant, 1,000 RMB, one time *lianai*, no premarital sex

Wu   25, customer service representative, 1,000 RMB, three times *lianai*, yes premarital sex

Lu   30, factory worker, 800 RMB, no *lianai*, no premarital sex

Chen   25, office worker, 2,700 RMB, three times *lianai*, yes premarital sex

Pang   25, technician, 1,200 RMB, three times *lianai*, yes premarital sex

Hu   25, office worker, 1,600 RMB, no *lianai*, no premarital sex

Focus Group 11

Male, all married, mostly no college

Deng   39, factory worker, 700 RMB, three times *lianai*, yes premarital sex

Jiang   38, cadre, 1,000 RMB, three to four times *lianai*, no premarital sex

Jin   37, unemployed, no income, one time *lianai*, no premarital sex

Quan   37, office worker, 800 RMB, one time *lianai*, no premarital sex

Hong   35, driver, 800 RMB, five times *lianai*, no premarital sex

Cai   39, factory worker, 1,000 RMB, one time *lianai*, no premarital sex

Questions Used in Focus Group Interviews

SASS conversations, and most student group conversations, were prompted by providing each participant with a set of magazine articles about love, sex, and marriage used to stimulate conversation. Most had read the articles before arriving. Conversations centered on their own experiences and ideas rather than the contents of articles. Topics ranged from group to group but included:

Dating Practices

Who initiates a date and how? (Describe how recent date was initiated.)
What goals to men and women have in dating? If not marriage, then what?
Is it okay to date more than one person?
When is it okay to break up? (Describe recent breakups.)
What do family/friends say about dating?
Who pays? Do you ever "go dutch"?
What activities do you engage in?

Ideal Mate

Describe your ideal mate. What is important: economics, education, looks?

Development of Relationships

How do you get started as friends?
Are you looking for a marriage partner?
How do you express love?
When do you start telling friends and family about it?
When do you decide to get married?

Romantic Love

What is it? How do you express it?
Is romantic love more important for men or women?
Who do you talk to about your love problems?

Sexual Norms

Do many people have sex before marriage? Live together?
Why do/don't people have sex?
Do women want sex as much as men?
Does sex before marriage destroy love? Add to love?
In premarital sex, will women be "hurt"?
Is there pressure from men for sex/resistance from women?
Where do you learn about sex?
What does your family say about sex?
Do friends talk about sex?
What kinds of sexual behavior are illegal or against social norms?

Has anyone in your (school/work unit) gotten into trouble because of their sexual behavior?

Shanghai versus Waidi (Out of Town)

What are your attitudes toward relationships with out-of-town people?

Marriage and Extramarital Sex

Is "marriage the graveyard of love"?
Do people "love the new and forget the old"?
When men have money, is it bad for women?

Attitude toward Change

How is society changing with regard to sex?

NOTES

Introduction

1. Cf. Rofel 1999; Liu 2000.

2. Glaser and Strauss 1967.

3. Killick 1995, 78–79.

4. Wei 1987, 266.

5. Unless otherwise noted, the statistics in this section are from the 1999 *Statistical Year-book of Shanghai* (Beijing: China Statistical Publishing House, 1999), which reports figures from 1998 and previous years.

6. Peter McGill, "Shanghai Too Now Nurses Hangover from a Giant Property Bubble," *Asahi Evening News*, June 5, 1999.

7. Opposite-sex massage is officially illegal in Shanghai, but thousands of "beauty parlors" staffed by young migrant women workers (also called "little country sisters" [*wailai-mei*]) provide this service, with additional sexual services sometimes provided off-premises.

8. *Izakaya* are Japanese taverns. Bubble-tea (*paomohongcha*) is a milky sweet iced tea drink. These shops became popular in Taiwan in the early 1990s, reaching Shanghai in 1996, where they became popular dating venues.

9. Cochran 1999; Lu 1999b; Chan 1999.

10. For example, Chen 1998; Dai 1999; Wu 1998. There is also a great boom in historical Shanghai studies among Chinese and Western scholars, mostly focusing on the Republican era, for example, Yeh 1992; Fan 1994; Yang 1994; Hershatter 1997; Lee 1999; Lu 1999a. Link 1981; Sergeant 1990; Shih 1996; Yuan 1994; Zhang 1996.

11. Hershatter 1997, 331.

12. Beijing remains home to China's literary and artistic avant-garde and "underground" rock music culture. Shanghai seems to lead in more conventional areas of consumer culture: fashion, restaurants, and discotheques. Hong Kong and Taiwan lead Chinese tastes in film and pop music. For that matter, Japan, the United States, Europe, and even Korea have distinct areas of cultural influence on Chinese youth culture.

13. Various models of this one-city, ethnographic approach to sexual culture include Chauncey (1994) for New York; Wolf (1998) for San Francisco; Bailey (1999) for Lawrence, Kansas; Hershatter (1997) for Shanghai; and Jankowiak (1993) for Huhot in Inner Mongolia.

14. I borrow the term "sexual culture" (*xingwenhua*) from Chinese scholars who use the

term to emphasize the cultural specificity of Chinese sexual practices (Liu Dalin et al. 1997). I like the connotation of cultural constructionism.

15. I use the term "youth" (*qingnian*) in the Chinese sense to refer to people eighteen to thirty-five, generally connoting the unmarried. My primary focus is on singles in their twenties.

16. Honig and Hershatter 1988; Li and Wang 1992; Jankowiak 1993; Pan 1995; Evans 1997; Dikotter 1998; Li 1998; Erwin 2000; Gillette 2000; Chou 2000.

17. Jankowiak (1999) criticizes a tendency of Western scholars to study Chinese sexuality only through the experiences of Chinese women.

18. Burke 1945.

19. Burke 1945; 1950; 1989. Gusfield provides an organized introduction to Burke's thought for social scientists. He also points out what I also see as the relevant distinction between Erving Goffman's dramaturgical approach to culture and Burke's dramatistic approach: "Burke's central preoccupation is the analysis of language, Goffman's preoccupation is the actor. For Burke the play's the thing. For Goffman it is the actor" (Gusfield 1989, 37). For me, also, "the play is the thing" in reconstructing a sexual culture.

20. Gusfield 1989, 6.

21. Burke 1945, 5.

22. Gusfield 1989, 17.

23. For example, Plummer 1995; Theophrastus 1953; Huizinga 1950; Ben-Ze'ev 1994; McRobbie 1994; Bech 1998; Stearns 1994.

24. See Longmore (1998) and DeLamater and Hyde (1998) for a discussion of this tradition and distinctions from competing paradigms.

25. Buss 1998; Jankowiak 1995.

26. Burke 1989, 268; Wess 1996, 1–38.

27. Sprecher 1998, 40.

28. Rival, Slater, and Miller 1998.

29. Turner 1982.

30. Douglas 1966; Rose 1999.

31. Seigel 1999, 296; Giddens 1992.

32. Goffman 1959.

33. De Certeau 1984, xx.

34. Bakhtin 1981, 280.

35. McGee 1999, 71.

36. Farrell 1999; Charland 1999.

37. Burke 1950, 50.

38. Swidler 1986.

39. Plummer 1995; 1996; Thompson 1995.

40. Charland 1999, 468.

41. McGee 1999, 69.

42. White 1973, 25; Thompson 1995.

43. Burke 1945, 402.

44. Charland 1999, 470.

45. Bakhtin 1981; Rose 1999.

46. Plummer 1996, 45.

47. Liu 2000, 80.

48. Ong 1999; Dutton 1998.

49. Chou 2000.

50. Foucault 1978.

51. Erwin (2000) shows how Shanghai telephone hot lines work as disciplinary technologies.

52. De Certeau 1984, xv.

53. Giddens 1992.

54. Giddens 1992, 176–77.

55. Coward 1984; Ewen 1988; Tomlinson 1990; Wernick 1991.

56. Marcuse 1955; Deleuze and Guattari 1983.

57. For example, Altman 2001; Farrer 1999.

58. Ong 1999; Erwin 1999; Kelsky 1996.

59. Guthrie 2000.

60. The per capita average annual incomes of Shanghai urban residents quadrupled in the 1990s (from 2,182 yuan in 1990 to 8,773 yuan in 1998), which even with 20 percent inflation rates for the early years of the decade, still means more than a doubling in real income. At the same time, the gap between the lowest household incomes, defined as the cut-off for the first decile, and the highest household incomes, defined as the cutoff for the tenth decile, widened from a ratio of 2.5 in 1990 to 4.0 in 1998 (1999 *Statistical Yearbook of Shanghai*).

61. Nee 1996; Bian 1994; Tang and Parish 2000.

62. Liang 1997.

63. The areas of the old Western concessions in Shanghai are often called "high corner" (*shangzhijiao*), while the factory districts and largely working-class districts of North and East Shanghai are called "low corner" (*xiazhijiao*). See chapter 2 for a more detailed discussion.

64. Frazier 2000.

65. Davis 2000.

66. Farrer 1999; 2000.

67. Zha 1995.

68. Tang and Parish 2000.

69. Foucault 1978, 18.

70. Swidler 1986.

71. Evans 1997, 84.

72. Xu and Ye 1999; Beck and Beck-Gernsheim 1995, 32.

73. Oppenheimer 1988.

74. Collier 1997; Beck and Beck-Gernsheim 1995; Illouz 1998; Bailey 1988.

75. Collier 1997, 6.

76. Beck and Beck-Gernsheim 1995.

77. Parish and Busse 2000; Parish and Farrer 2000.

78. Bai Zhi, "In the 21st Century, Will We Marry?" *Young Generation*, January 2000, 4–7.

79. Zhong 2000.

80. Yang 1992.

81. Illouz 1998, 176.

82. Simmel 1971; 1984.

83. Farrer 2000.

84. "*Baixiang*" is Shanghai dialect for "play." I transcribe all Shanghaiese words in Mandarin pinyin.

85. Simmel 1971, 129.

86. Wang Yuru, "Sexual Civilization on the College Campus," *Young Generation*, June 2000, 62–63.

87. In a 1994 nationwide Gallup poll that asked all those interviewed about their personal philosophy of life, "Work hard and get rich" was by far the most common response, given by 68 percent of all those interviewed. In the 1997 poll, a slightly lower 56 percent chose this description, while about one Chinese in four (23 percent) opted for the compensatory alternative of "don't think about money or fame, just lead a life that suits your own tastes"—up from just 11 percent in 1994. Expression of a preference for following one's own tastes irrespective of wealth or fame roughly doubled during those three years among urban and rural Chinese (urban: 1994—21 percent, 1997—38 percent; rural: 1994—7 percent, 1997—13 percent). In both rural and urban sectors, approval of this alternative attitude to pursuing wealth has become particularly common among younger adults (rural aged 18 to 29: 18 percent; urban aged 18 to 29: 47 percent). None of the other options accounted for more than a small fraction of responses, with "never think of yourself, give everything in service to society" being the least frequently selected at just 3 percent nationally ("Gallup Special Reports: 1997 Survey: The People's Republic of China Consumer Attitudes and Lifestyle Trends" [Gallup Organization, 2000]).

88. Burke 1989, 167–70.

89. Yang 1994.

90. Hershatter (1994, 171) and Evans (1997, 176) discuss the general use of the prostitute as a representative of the aspirations and dangers associated with the market economy.

91. Rorty 1989, 73.

92. Farrell 1995, 41.

93. Burke writes, "A comic frame of motives, as here conceived, would not only avoid the sentimental denial of material factors in human acts. It would also avoid the cynical brutality that comes when such sensitivity is outraged" (Burke 1989, 261).

94. Japp 1983, 52; Schiller 1967, 130.

95. Japp 1983, 58. Uwe Japp describes this kind of irony about life as world irony (*Weltironie*), the perceived contradiction between ideal and reality, expectations and outcomes.

96. Schiller 1967, 138. For Friedrich Schiller, aesthetic freedom lies in the productive tension between ideal striving and material reality, or duty and fate.

97. Berlant and Warner 1998.

98. Gusfield 1989, 27.

Chapter 1

1. One yuan renminbi (RMB) was about twelve cents U.S. for the central period covered by this study (1993–96). For many locally produced commodities and services (e.g., fresh vegetables, a bowl of noodles, a haircut), one yuan had the purchasing power of about one dollar for a comparable commodity or service in the United States, while high-tech or luxury products typically were priced at or higher than U.S. levels.

2. H. Evans 1995; Dikotter 1995, 1998.

3. Foucault 1978, 97.

4. Foucault (1973) begins his book *The Order of Things* with Borges's description of a "Chinese" zoological taxonomy that violates all the orderly conceptual boundaries of modern scientific reason.

5. Burke 1945.

6. Plummer 1995; Thompson 1995; Weeks and Holland 1996; McRobbie 1984; 1994; Taylor 1994; Ben-Ben-Ze'ev 1994; Bech 1998.

7. de Certeau 1984, xix.

8. These first three quotes are from focus group interviews I conducted. The final quote is from an ethnographic interview. See the appendix for a discussion of how the interviews were conducted and for a list of participants. All names are pseudonyms.

9. Bailey 1999, 2.

10. Touraine 1990, 121.

11. Sergeant 1990.

12. "KTV" is short for "karaoke television," a term that appeared in Taiwan in the 1980s to describe clubs where one could rent a room to sing karaoke privately. The term seems to have been borrowed from "MTV," "movie television" clubs where one could watch a rented video in a private cubicle.

13. Burke 1954, 49.

14. Translated by William Crawford in Link (1981, 240–60).

15. Engels 1978.

16. Yuan 1994; Lee 2001.

17. Xu 1996, 401.

18. This came to my attention in a 1994 interview with a popular call-in host on the radio program *Qiaoqiaohua*. She justified a tolerant attitude toward extramarital affairs with the statement "I think that feelings (*ganqing*) can never be wrong." In another interview Liu Xuyuan, a male author of popular sexual advice books, related this tolerant attitude to Engels's idea that love is the only moral basis for sexual relationships.

19. Both Mian Mian and Wei Hui are pen names. Wei Hui's real name is Zhou Weihui. Mian Mian prefers to use her pen name publicly.

20. "Teizoku poruno ka, xinjinrei bungaku ka" (Crude porn or new humanity literature?), *Asahi Shimbun*, May 4, 2000, 4; Sheila Melvin, "A Book Battle to Make the Critics Blush," *International Herald Tribune*, June 20, 2000; Melinda Liu and Kevin Platt, "China's e-Rebels," *Newsweek*, October 2, 2000. Mian Mian personally told me about dumping a beer on Wei Hui's head in front of a Shanghai bar.

21. Barmé 1993; 1999, 179–200.

22. Mian Mian rather suddenly married a British expatriate in 2000 and moved, at least briefly, to rural Cornwall.

23. John Pomfret, "Letter from China: The Coveted Stamp of Disapproval," *Washington Post Foreign Service*, June 27, 2000.

24. Mu 1996; Liu 1997; Lee 1999.

25. Mian 1997; 2000.

26. Mian 1997. Translations are my own.

27. Wei 1999. Translations are my own.

28. Ibid., 98, 129, 207.

29. Ibid., 86.

30. Ibid., 212.

31. Ibid., 148.

32. Kelsky (1996) describes Japanese women's sexual consumption of foreign men as a reflexive critique of Japanese men. While similar arguments are being made about *Shanghai Baby*, I do not read Wei's work as a studied critique of Chinese men. For Wei's CoCo, foreign men are simply "good to think with" (and fuck with), tools for sexual fantasy and self-definition.

33. White-collar women are ambiguous figures in Wei Hui's fiction. On the one hand, as Yinghong Li points out, Wei Hui uses CoCo's voice to make fun of white collars' philistine pretensions to subcultural sophistication (Li 2001). At the same time, the sexually liberated

artist heroine represents the white-collar fantasy of sophisticated consumption, sexual freedom, and financial independence.

34. De Certeau describes this spatial rhetoric of exaggeration and elision as a combination synecdoche and asyndeton that transforms mythologized urban spaces into "enlarged singularities and separate islands" (1984, 101).

35. Wei 1999, 73. When I spoke with YY's Hong Kong owner in 2000, he was furious that his real name was used in the novel and that his club was described as a place where prostitutes do business. In fact, YY's did not have a reputation for prostitution (unlike some other nearby bars).

36. "I want to tell people that freedom is great, but that it can also be dangerous," Mian Mian says in an interview with Gary Jones for the *Observer* ("China Syndrome," reprinted in the *Japan Times*, June 3, 1999).

37. Craig Smith, "Sex, Lust, Drugs: Her Novel's Too Much for China," *New York Times*, May 11, 2000.

38. Plummer 1996.

39. She was most likely referring to Lin Bai and Chen Ran, since Mian Mian and Wei Hui were not yet publishing.

40. Honig and Hershatter 1988, Evans 1997.

41. Plummer 1996.

42. An 1999.

43. After *Absolute Secrets*, An Dun published another collection of true stories titled Huijia (Returning home), which describes people "returning to the family," a response in her words to the "sexual imbalance" (liangxingshiheng) described in *Absolute Secrets*.

44. Gamson 1998, 19.

45. "An Dun, Ni shi shei?" (Who is An Dun?), *Shenjiangfuwudaobao*, March 10, 1999.

46. *That's Shanghai*, July 2000, 78.

47. Burke 1945.

48. Dutton 1998, 193.

49. Zhang 1996.

50. Bech 1998; de Certeau 1984, 101.

51. Chan 1999.

52. Such commercial stands offer a plethora of sexual remedies and sex toys, including vibrators with handles shaped like the animals of the Chinese zodiac. In 1996 there were already 517 such specialty shops and 3,778 counters marketing sexual hygiene products in China (Xinhua, January 2, 1996).

53. Yao Zhilong, "The Ups and Downs of the Great World: In Search of Shanghai's Old Entertainment Places," *Meizhouwenyijiemu*, March 27, 1997; also described in Sergeant (1990, 250–51).

54. Hershatter describes how Shanghai's celebrity courtesans were important fashion leaders in the city in the first few decades of the twentieth century. The "flower contests" ended in 1920 when the foreign-run Municipal Council began closing brothels (1997, 168).

55. Caesars is featured in the popular Japanese travel book *Kojinryokochugoku* (Individual travel: China) (Tokyo: Shobunsha, 2000).

56. Unable to pay the high commercial rents on Nanjing Boulevard, Liu's museum closed in 2001 after three years of business. Business at the museum suffered because it was not allowed to post a sign on Nanjing Road, supposedly because advertising regulations prohibit the word "sex" in public signs. It was planning to move to a new suburban location.

Ching-Ching Ni, "The Curtain Falls on a Racy Past: Deserted Sex Museum Looks for a Better Home," *International Herald Tribune* (Tokyo Edition), June 9–10, 2000.

57. Ian Johnson of the *Baltimore Sun*.

58. "Fashionable Woman," *Young Generation*, April 1996, 22.

59. Swanson 1995; Waara 1999.

60. Wilson 1991; 1995.

61. Simmel 1969; Bech 1998, 220.

62. These are all comments I heard in conversations in which people described their thoughts and reactions to such relationships.

63. The Chinese novelist Mao Dun famously describes such a scene in the novel *Midnight* (1979, 13–14).

64. The statue disappeared in the summer of 2000, reportedly stolen. A number of new statues commemorating Shanghai's nuclear family, including the bronze shopping family at the end of the Nanjing Road pedestrian mall, appeared in nearby green areas.

65. Suttles 1984.

66. Waara 1999; Shih 1996.

67. Burke 1989, 258–59.

68. Link 1981; Zhang 1996; Yeh 1992; Hershatter 1997; Lee 1999.

69. Shih 1996.

70. For instance, "The Changing Fashions of the 'Shanghai Girl,'" *Young Generation*, January 2000, 12–15.

71. "Fashionable Woman," *Young Generation*, April 1996, 22.

72. Rose 1999.

73. "Shanghai: China's Urban Soul, 1999, the Illusionary City that Belongs to the World," *Time* 154 (no. 12), September 27, 1999.

74. This is from an item on the "Sample Survey Data of Women's Status in Contemporary China," Chinese Academy of Social Sciences, 1992. It surveyed people of all ages, and the results thus contrast starkly with surveys conducted only among youth (see chapter 7).

75. Suttles 1984.

76. Weeks and Holland 1996, 6.

77. Quite a few of my Shanghai friends used an "English name" in social interactions with casual friends, especially in the nightlife world. In cases where informants usually used an English name in the social interactions in which I encountered them, I give them an English pseudonym.

78. Dance leaders (*lingwu*) are employed by dance club owners to dance on stages, sometimes as a formal performance, but more typically to generate a more sexually charged atmosphere through their provocative dances and clothing and to stimulate others to dance.

79. Johnny is Catholic. His story is presented in greater detail in chapters 5 and 8. Chapter 8 discusses the issue of "responsibility" in premarital sex.

80. Whyte 1943; Peiss 1986; 1989.

81. Sewell 1999, 49.

82. Gusfield 1989, 17.

Chapter 2

1. Bauman 1998.

2. Studies of urban sexual geography tend to focus on commercial districts and boulevard sexual cultures, as in my discussion of Nanjing Road in the previous chapter (cf. Wilson 1995; Swanson 1995; Bech 1998).

3. "Gongyuan, luuhuadidai de shangfengbaisu xingwei wuran shehuifengqi" (Immoral behavior in parks and green areas pollutes the social climate), no author or attribution, 1983.

4. Community policing teams (lianfangdui) were groups of neighborhood men led by police officers who policed the parks and other public spaces. One of their principal preoccupations was to monitor "public morality" in parks and other wooded areas ("greenery areas") during the summer months.

5. The former editor of *Young Generation* told me in an interview that the magazine also published an influential article criticizing these abuses.

6. About one-third of all hair salons in Shanghai were shut down in the summer of 2000 for providing illegal sexual services. However, opposite-sex massage remained available in many places.

7. Wank (1998) describes more generally this dependent relationship between Chinese state authorities and entrepreneurs.

8. Soja 1996.

9. Dutton 1998, 42.

10. Shaw 1996; Gaubatz 1995.

11. Stacey 1983; Dutton 1998, 45.

12. Shaw 1996.

13. Kwok 1981; Ma 1981.

14. Ning and Yan 1995.

15. Lu 1999a.

16. Frazier 2000.

17. Suttles 1984.

18. Burke 1945, 3.

19. Fischer 1982.

20. Wirth 1938; Suttles 1968; Sennett, 1970.

21. Lu 1999b.

22. 1999 *Statistical Yearbook of Shanghai*. The proportion of population still living in such dwellings is not provided, and because of higher densities is considerably greater than 17 percent.

23. Lu 1995.

24. Murphey 1974; Ma 1981.

25. Ning and Yan 1995.

26. Taubman 1994.

27. 1999 *Statistical Yearbook of Shanghai*. Such per capita housing figures don't account for up to 3 million migrant workers now living in the city. Most of these laborers live in crowded dormitories at construction sites or in the market stalls where they work. Moreover, during the late 1990s, much of the overpriced new housing remained unsold and empty. Actual household densities for most Shanghai families may not have changed as much as these figures indicate.

28. Suttles 1968, 90–92.

29. 1999 *Statistical Yearbook of Shanghai*.

30. Sennett 1970.

31. Frazier 2000.

32. Frazier 2000.

33. Fischer (1982) describes a similar pattern among young urban residents in the United States.

34. Honig 1992; Lu 1995. Despite a decreased emphasis on such ethnic or home-place distinctions in contemporary life, Subei people still experience discrimination, particularly in the courtship and sexual interactions that are the focus of this book.

35. Low corner does not have agreed-upon boundaries and is used to describe a type of neighborhood within a larger area as well as the larger area in which such shanty areas were located. Because of its famous shanty districts, for instance, Yangpu is usually described as "low corner" despite its high concentration of company housing. On the other hand, Nan-shi District, which was on the southern fringe of the international settlements, shares the social and demographic history of these other low-corner districts (Henriot and Zu'an 1999), but my informants generally associated "low corner" with the contiguous northeastern districts of the city.

36. Shortly before the demolition in September 2000, the daily newspaper ran an article celebrating how "Poor Street" had finally been supplied with an adequate electric supply ("Good-bye to the Era of Electricity Shortages: A Meter for Each Family in 'Poor Street,'" *Xinminwanbao*, August 22, 2000). The article failed to mention that most of the homes in the area had been demolished and the residents removed. Little Bai said there had never been enough electricity to run an air conditioner.

37. Bailey 1999.

38. In the fall of 2000, Little Bai moved into a new apartment in Pudong. He says he has trouble getting used to apartment life. "It is stifling, always staying inside that one place." He doesn't know any of the people there and doubts he will easily get to know them. Most people from the neighborhood moved to Pudong, where they are scattered over a wide area. "When we get together, people are particularly happy to see each other," he said. Bai said that he now has a regular "girlfriend," a woman from Wenzhou who owns a hair salon in Shanghai. She is married, but her husband lives in Wenzhou.

39. There was some ambiguity in her story at this point, and it seems she may have had another lover before her fiancé.

40. Taylor 1994; Sabini and Silver 1982; Collins 1994.

41. Ben-Ze'ev 1994, 19; Morreall 1994.

42. Code 1994.

43. Collins 1994, 113.

44. Farrer (forthcoming).

45. My earliest stay was spring 1995; my most recent was summer 2000. Altogether I have stayed there two years.

46. Lu (1999b) describes the density and diversity of Republican-era Shanghai alleyways, suggesting that close exposure to such diverse lives contributes to a peculiar Shanghai-style (*haipai*) mentality of pragmatism and irony. I tend to agree with this judgment, but the historical context of the 1990s work-unit housing is very different, its social heterogeneity emerging out of the process of market reform, especially the widening of income differences.

47. Though the ages of these women ranged from twenty to forty, my mother-in-law, like most Shanghaiese, would find the term "girl" (*nuuhai/xiaoguniang*) more natural and polite than "woman" or "female."

48. Cf. Wolf 1972.

49. It might be the case that the mothers of sons would focus more exclusively on stories of young men, and that the predominance of stories I heard about daughters was influenced by the fact that my mother-in-law had only daughters.

50. De Sousa 1994, 32.

51. Ayim 1994, 95.

52. Code 1994, 100.

Chapter 3

1. Simmel, 1969; Goffman 1959.

2. Zhang 1996; Yang 1992.

3. These reputations were not unrelated. According to Hershatter (1997), Shanghai's celebrity courtesans were important fashion leaders in the city in the first few decades of the twentieth century. In many ways the Shanghai celebrity courtesan was a prototype of the commercialized sex symbol starlets and supermodels of the late twentieth century.

4. "Survey Seeks True Image of Husbands," *Shanghai Star*, May 9, 1995.

5. Long 1999, 15. The book reprints an essay she published in a Shanghai paper followed by a series of reader letters defending and attacking these common typifications of Shanghai men.

6. "What's the Taste of Stolen Love: An Interview with a Woman," *Young Generation*, September 2000, 17.

7. Yang 1992, 517.

8. Xu 1996, 397–98.

9. In the 1997 Chinese movie *Temptress Moon* situated in Shanghai in the 1920s, the country servant boy Duan Wu spends several days in Shanghai observing the sexual machinations of men and women around him. In an epiphany, which marks the turning point of the film, he declares to his coldhearted mistress (played by Gong Li): "Shanghai is a battle between men and women, and I want to win."

10. Park 1969 [1906].

11. Plummer 1996, 41.

12. Wuthnow (1987) encourages the empirical study of collective representations. Lakoff (1987) describes the centrality of prototypes, including stereotypes, in reasoning.

13. MacIntyre 1981, 28.

14. Burke 1989, 280–81.

15. Theophrastus 1953.

16. Goffman 1959.

17. Parsons 1968 [1937].

18. McMahon 1995.

19. Yeh 1992; Lu 2000.

20. Frye 1976, 56.

21. Suttles 1984.

22. Fan 1994.

23. Redfield and Singer 1969, 212.

24. Yang 1992.

25. Wu Yiqin personal communication.

26. Suttles 1984.

27. Fan 1994.

28. According to the 1990 census, 66,500—27.9 percent of the national total (Yang 1992, 477).

29. Fan 1994.

30. Wakeman and Yeh 1992.

31. Hershatter 1997, 390; Xu 1996, 391.

32. Burke 1945, 59–61.

33. Herschatter 1992.

34. Shih 1996.

35. Bailey 1984, 1999.

36. Kipnis 1998.

37. Ullman 1997, 136.

38. Kon (1993) describes the prominence of prostitution in the popular discourse of postsocialist Russia.

39. Burke 1989, 170.

40. In Chinese: *Piaoliangdenurenkaolaoban, youbenshidenanrenbushangban, bunanbunudefansanban.*

41. If we were to look further, at low-corner Shanghai humor, for instance, we would also find particular characters that correspond to the local social divisions highlighted in the last chapter, especially the distinctions between high corner and low corner, or between Ningbo and Subei Shanghaiese.

42. According to Xu (1996, 387), the term "foreigner third party" (*yangren disanzhe*) is used to describe the common figure of the foreign man involved with a Chinese married woman.

43. Zhong 2000.

44. Focus groups provide excellent transcripts of conversational language. See methodological appendix for more detailed descriptions of participants and methods.

45. This use of the example of the polygynous man to justify the extramarital affairs of women is also described in Xu (1996, 399). Such appeals to a "single standard" of sexual behavior for men and women were very common in conversations among Shanghai youth.

46. The February 1995 television series *Yanghangli de zhongguoxiaojie* (Chinese misses in foreign firms) represents an early example of the popular interest in white-collar women workers in Shanghai, following the careers of three young women and their romantic relations with their foreign bosses (reviews in *Xinminwanbao*, February 26, 1995; also Farrer 1998, 130–35).

As foreign firms "localized" their staff in Shanghai in the late 1990s, greater distinctions among white collars appeared, and popular attention shifted to the truly high-earning professionals in foreign firms. At the time of these focus group discussions in 1996, most Shanghaiese were just becoming aware of the professional and salary distinctions in foreign firms, and all women in foreign firms seemed to be secretaries, partly a reflection of their young age.

47. This program is described briefly in chapter 5.

48. McMahon 1995.

49. She also calls herself Kika, from the eponymous Pedro Almodóvar film about a cyborg femme fatale.

50. "Shanghai: China's Urban Soul, 1999, the Illusionary City that Belongs to the World," *Time* 154 (no. 12), September 27, 1999.

51. Wei 1999, 100–1, 71–72.

52. Chou argues that "potato queen" and "rice queen" emerged in Hong Kong in the 1970s to describe men with racialized sexual orientations. Based on his interviews with men involved in cross-national relationships, Chou argues that gendered stereotypes of the feminized Chinese and the masculinized white male still exist, but that in actual interpersonal relationships these categories are highly contested, as they are by Coco (Chou 2000, 199).

53. For instance, in the increasingly popular trips to Thailand and border areas of Burma, transvestite shows (*renyao biaoyan*) are a must-see for the Shanghai tourist. The sex

tourism of Pattaya near Bangkok has two theaters specializing in these shows, one sung in English, the other in Chinese. When I stepped into the Chinese theater, I saw a transvestite performer singing Chinese revolutionary songs to an audience of vacationing Chinese cadres.

54. For Burke, the scapegoat, the victim, is essential to order in society. Rhetorically, the materialistic Shanghai girl and the big money are victims, outcasts from the normative world of the small family life, whose rhetorical sacrifice defends social order.

55. Described in chapter 9, the "old cabbage leaf" is the middle-aged woman whose sexual capital (her looks) is exhausted and who is as "worthless" as a cabbage leaf left on the market floor. This term also is an example of character slang particular, at least in frequency of use, to low-corner Shanghai.

56. The term "gongxinxiaofei" (salaried-class level of expense) is often used in advertisements for family-style restaurants and entertainments, including the social dance halls I studied. It also is used by popular magazine editors to define their target audience. Many people describe themselves as members of the salaried class.

57. According to a survey by Shanghai's Youth Daily, most Shanghai youth prefer residing alone with their spouse after marriage (65 percent). Incidentally, most prefer the currently impossible ideal of having a boy and a girl (56 percent), but of the remainder, slightly more prefer having a lone daughter (17 percent), to having a lone son (16 percent), evidence of the high status of daughters in the city (Qingnianbao, April 4, 1995).

58. Parish and Farrer 2000.

59. From the standpoint of youth facing the labor market, little remains of socialism. Jobs are found in a free job market, not assigned. Wages are increasingly disparate across professions. Gender discrimination in hiring is increasing. Job security cannot be assumed. Housing is no longer provided by work units, and medical benefits may be lacking. (Tang and Parish 2000).

60. See Dutton (1998) for a good discussion of this floating population centered in Beijing.

61. Rose 1999, 231.

Chapter 4

1. Such magazine "true stories" are a variety of jishiwenxue, or journalistic literature, also published in book form (Xu 1996). I take the term from the very similar U.S. magazine genre of the early twentieth century.

2. Griswold 1987; 1989.

3. Editors I interviewed at Democracy and Law and Family made similar and equally plausible claims to being the first to initiate these discussions of love and sex in the Chinese media. Some editors gave credit to literary representations, especially Zhang Jie's "Love Must Not Be Forgotten," for beginning the public dialogue on love and sex.

4. 1999 Statistical Yearbook of Shanghai. Similar magazines were published in Shanghai before the Communist takeover in 1949. The Shanghai magazine Life Weekly promoted free-choice marriage and the nuclear family in the 1920s (Yeh 1992). The Good Companion (Liangyou) promoted fashion and popular culture. After 1949 Chinese Woman and Chinese Youth, the official publications of the women's federation and youth league, monopolized marriage, family, and youth topics.

5. McCracken 1993; McRobbie 1991; Winship 1987; Gallego Ayala 1990.

6. Honig and Herschatter 1988; Evans 1997; Kunz 1996.

7. For example, Wehrfritz 1996. In a personal conversation, Wehrfritz told me that it

was necessary to use a familiar narrative of revolution to emphasize the dramatic nature of this social change to U.S. readers.

8. Honig and Herschatter point out the cautionary nature of these stories. Young women are told how to be attractive to men and simultaneously warned against the disaster of losing their virginity (1988, 59). Women are encouraged to date but are warned through "cautionary tales" of the dangers of male sexual predators (63). Single women who intrude into marriages are singled out for criticism (222). Evans (1997) similarly describes and critiques the construction of an anxious female sexuality in popular Chinese media.

9. Brooks 1976.

10. Xu 1996, 405.

11. Burke 1945, 514.

12. Frye 1957; 1976.

13. Ci 1994.

14. Evans 1997, 94.

15. Most of *Young Generation's* older competitors have experienced similar declines because of the explosion in the number of competitors. *Young Generation's* steep decline also reflects a poor distribution network outside of Shanghai. Even in 2000, however, it remained popular in Shanghai.

16. The international inroads into Shanghai most prominently include the mainland China edition of *Elle* (Hachette, France), copublished with a Chinese publisher (Kunz 1996). With a national circulation of over 250,000, this magazine had already surpassed the most popular Chinese fashion magazine *Shanghai Fashion* within Shanghai (Shanghai circulation 50,000; national circulation 1 million).

17. Guangzhou and Beijing editors naturally objected to any Shanghai assertions of cultural leadership in China. The most popular and trendy magazine in the mid-1990s, *Girlfriend*, was published in the provincial city of Xian. In any case, the Chinese publishing industry had no exclusive national center of the stature of New York.

18. A *Young Generation* readers' survey found that readers were 59 percent female. Over half have a high school education, 26 percent with college or junior college degrees. Seventy-nine percent purchase the magazine at newsstands. Only 13 percent subscribe. The pass-along readership is very high, with 33 percent of copies read by more than eight people (*Young Generation*, July 2000, 9). The head of the Chinese periodical association, and editor of *Gushihui*, told me that rural villagers account for only a small fraction of magazine sales, even for his popular story magazine.

19. Frye 1957.

20. For a sociological treatment of the genres of romance and irony in U.S. political discourse, see Jacobs and Smith (1997).

21. White 1973, 25.

22. Rorty 1989, 73; Burke 1989, 261.

23. Farrell 1995, 41.

24. These are summaries of two stories that appeared in Shanghai's most popular youth magazine *Young Generation*. The first appeared in 1980 (no. 10) and the second in 1996 (no. 4).

25. Frye 1957, 186.

26. Essays from this period frequently use literary figures in the construction of an ideal moral universe. "Love Is Noble" (*YG* 1980, no. 3) uses the character Paul from Gorky's short story "How Steel Is Made" to illustrate an ideal lover: faithful to one's lover, idealistic (dedicated to the socialist cause), and noble (looks beyond physical handicaps). The essay

also quotes extensively from Engels. Other essays of this nature quote from Lenin and Marx and stories about the private lives of famous Western and Chinese thinkers and political figures, for instance, how Marx's daughters chose husbands (*YG* 1980, no. 3) and how Beethoven dealt with a failed love affair (*YG* 1980, no. 3). The biographies of Marx and Engels are used as legitimations for pursuing romantic love, though their revolutionary philosophy is largely ignored.

27. During the Cultural Revolution, youth were encouraged to put the revolutionary cause ahead of all others and give first consideration to the political views and class sentiments when choosing a partner. Young people were nonetheless encouraged to find their own partners and resist marriages arranged by parents (Lu 1969).

28. Evans 1997, 98.

29. "Bigamy Returns to Shanghai" (Hunwaihun zai Shanghai sihuifuran) *Jiefangribao*, April 1, 1995. In 1997 the women's federation of China issued a report criticizing the rise in bigamy and concubinage in China, describing those likely to engage in this practice as the wealthiest men in society (*Chicago Tribune*, April 2, 1997).

30. See Zha (1995) and Barmé (1993). Also Melinda Liu, "China without Illusions: A New Generation Loses Faith in the Ideals of the Past," *Newsweek*, June 7, 1999; Terry McCarthy, "Lost Generation," *Newsweek*, October 23, 2000.

31. Xu 1996, 388.

32. See, for instance, the discussion of "Love Must Not Be Forgotten" in chapter 1 and the famous case of Yu Luojin, which appeared in the popular magazine *Democracy and Law* (Minzhuyufazhi) in 1981.

33. Although the stories might read like cautionary tales to Westerners, it was clear from interviews with editors in Shanghai and other cities that they wanted to portray a more sympathetic and understanding attitude toward extramarital affairs.

34. Unlike most forms of nonmarital heterosexual behavior (e.g., extramarital and premarital sex) that have received extensive, often sympathetic, and ultimately legitimating treatments in "true story" reportage, gay and lesbian sexuality is seldom represented in these articles, and then only as a psychological ailment or bizarre sensation. Xu argues that such fictional treatments will eventually normalize homosexual relationships in the same way (1996, 398). But there are obstacles to this in the media, I believe. Magazine editors I interviewed said that positive portrayals of homosexual behavior would not be allowed by censors, so they usually avoided the topic.

35. Japp 1983, 52–59.

36. The narrative is doubly ironic in that a period of relatively strong social controls on dating and socialist propaganda against individualism is now reconstructed as an era of true romantic feeling.

37. Schudson 1984.

38. Griswold 1987; 1989.

39. Zhao (1998) describes a similar dynamic in other journalistic branches.

40. Many of the consequences of the economic reforms of Deng Xiaoping were genuinely unpopular, especially rising inflation but also increasing disparities in wealth. These disparities were identified with many of the sexual social problems that emerged in this era, including prostitution, mistresses, and materially minded marriage choices. See Tang and Parish (2000) for a discussion of the increasing unpopularity of reform in the late 1980s.

41. McRobbie 1990; 1991.

42. I also believe that it is the revolutionary romantic idealism of the post–Cultural Revolution generation of editors that sets off mainland Chinese magazines and other print

media from the less activist positions in magazine and newspaper sexual culture in 1980s and early 1990s Taiwan (Farrer 1995).

Chapter 5

1. In a "hypergamous" marriage market, high-status women have the greatest difficulties. According to sociologist Xu Anqi, who was a consultant for the program, when the program first started, women wishing to participate outnumbered men by thirty to one. By 2000 the ratio of female to male applicants was three to one.

2. Oppenheimer 1988.

3. In 1998, 144,800 people married for the first time in Shanghai, 59,200 people divorced, and 26,700 remarried (1999 Statistical Yearbook of Shanghai).

4. Chen Xiaopei, "Xinrenlei: lianai zoupianfeng," Shenghuozhoukan, August 4, 2000, W7. "New humanity" is a Japanese loan word, originally used to describe the first generation of Japanese youth who grew up in the affluence of postwar Japan.

5. Bailey 1988; Rothman 1987; Peiss 1986; 1989; Illouz 1997; Modell 1983.

6. The 1980s seem to have been a period of transition all over China. In his research on the provincial Chinese city of Huhot in the 1980s, Jankowiak describes a shift from what he calls "formal dating" to "informal dating," similar to the changes I describe here (1993).

7. "Shanghai qingnian lianai diaocha" (Qingnianbao, April 4, 1995).

8. Based on reports of a survey, the China News Service reported that 60 percent of Shanghai high school students were "talking love" (dating) in 1991, a high estimate in my view ("Sexual Problems Out in the Open," Reuters, December 4, 1992). A survey of college students studying in Shanghai found that 61 out of 190 were dating. These students gave an average age of 18 for their first dating experiences, compared to 14.69 for American students. Based on my interviews, good students who enter university typically begin dating somewhat later than poor students (Tang and Zuo 2000).

9. Illouz 1997, 46.

10. Movies, ice cream, and park entrance fees were all a few cents each in 1980, very cheap, even when low incomes are considered.

11. Zhuang and Gu (1990) make a similar point for Taiwanese dating culture.

12. Li and Wang 1992; Chou 2000, 102.

13. 1999 Statistical Yearbook of Shanghai.

14. Anyone aiming to impress a date in Shanghai in the late 1990s had to spend at least a hundred yuan and as much as a thousand. Dating expenses are difficult to judge, since the most expensive items might be gifts purchased before or during the date. Teenagers might meet at the cheapest local dance hall and share a soda for as little as ten yuan. Married men and women who patronized social dance halls also were likely to engage in similarly inexpensive forms of consumption (usually with their dance partners, not their spouses). Teenagers and those already married were outside of the marriage market and had less pressure to impress others.

15. Zhuang and Gu argue that the Chinese style of love lacks the idea of breaking up, so breaking up is seen as a failure and is especially painful (1990, 14).

16. According to a survey of youth (under age thirty) by Shanghai's Youth Daily, 44 percent of respondents had had two to four romantic relationships (lianaijingli), and 5 percent had five or more such relationships. Forty-three percent had had only one romantic relationship (Qingnianbao, April 4, 1995).

17. Married women face a heavy double burden of work and household chores (Parish

and Farrer 2000). When I asked married women in focus groups what they found "romantic," I was surprised by how many found "time alone" the most romantic idea.

18. Dutton 1998, 281; de Certeau 1984, xv.

19. Exceptions include conservative state organizations such as elementary schools, where young teachers told me that premarital cohabitation would be frowned upon by their colleagues and could not be mentioned to principals.

20. Whyte and Parish 1984; Xu and Whyte 1990.

21. The expression comes from *Fortress Besieged*, a 1947 novel about the comical and unsatisfactory love lives of a group of Shanghai intellectuals during World War II (Qian 1979,[1947]). "Marriage is the tomb of love" also dates from this period. The contemporary popularity of these jokes points to the recycling of discourse from the Republican era, often unawares (though not the case of this famous novel). According to a survey of youth (under thirty) by Shanghai's *Youth Daily*, 58 percent of respondents have some degree of fear of "life inside the fortress" of marriage, showing the contemporary relevance of the metaphor (*Qingnianbao*, April 4, 1995).

22. A reverse imitation also occurs in which marriage borrows from the culture of dating and romance. In Shanghai some richer married couples were beginning to observe birthdays and anniversaries with dates without their child and other family members, a form of dating after marriage that is still rare in China but perhaps increasing.

Chapter 6

1. This seemed to be a popular piece of sexual rhetoric among late-marrying youth in Shanghai, that for a young woman, not having sex was a "waste of youth."

2. Jankowiak 1995.

3. Hyde and DeLamater (1997, 338) point out that romantic love involves two components: physiological arousal and cognitive labeling of the feeling. While I do not doubt that romantic passion has a physiological element, my research focuses on these culturally variable "cognitive labels."

4. Lindholm 1998, 258.

5. Beck and Beck-Gernsheim 1995.

6. Collier 1997, 75.

7. For instance, Evans (1998) and Jamieson (1999) argue against Giddens's naive ideal of "pure intimacy."

8. Luhmann 1986.

9. Illouz's historical argument bears some resemblance to the one I make in chapter 4; however, the grounding in disparate historical materials makes our actual stories quite different. The "romance" of love and modernity I describe in early 1980s magazine fiction is far more a political comedy that attempts to ground a humanistic conception of romantic feelings in a quest for "modernization" guided by the Party-state. The "irony" I describe in that chapter is a recognition of the incompatibility of this socialist romantic vision with the social inequality, individualism, and money orientation of the emerging market society.

10. Illouz 1997; 1998.

11. See methodological appendix for a discussion of how I conducted personal and group interviews, used as data here.

12. Yu 1997.

13. Lee 2001.

14. Burke 1989, 172.

15. In the 1980s there was such a shortage of housing that simply having one's own

room was sometimes a difficult condition to achieve. By the late 1990s better-off couples expected their own apartment.

16. Xu 1996, 403.

17. Romantic feeling also was the main moral justification for extramarital affairs in Shanghai. Other important elements in the moral rhetoric of extramarital affairs were "friendship" (with the lover) and "responsibility" (to the family and spouse). Secondary, but also important, were notions of "fate" (bringing the lovers together), monetary compensation (to a younger lover) and "human nature" (the natural pursuit of sexual novelty). Unmarried youth also displayed very tolerant attitudes toward extramarital affection (*hunwailian*) (Farrer 2001).

18. Such simple stories were told by older informants. In a study of Chinese rural villagers, Potter (1988) argues that such statements of "good feelings" have nothing to do with emotions but refer to generally agreeable circumstances for marriage. This might have been true earlier in Shanghai, though I am skeptical. In the case of contemporary Shanghai, I would argue that the emotional element of *ganqing* is evident even in these simple stories.

19. Gu and Gu 1990b.

20. Yu 1997.

21. Luhmann 1986.

22. Potter 1988, 198.

23. The verb "love" (*ai*) was seldom used in the Shanghaiese dialect. Shanghaiese focus group participants agreed that the expression "I like you" (*wo huanxi ni*) was much more comfortable and common than "I love you" (*wo ai ni*).

24. Except for some intellectuals, people who grew up in the Maoist era showed little interest or awareness of romantic themes from pre-1949 Shanghai culture.

25. Frye 1976, 56.

26. Illouz 1997; 1998.

27. The Chinese characters used to transliterate "romance" as "*langman*" (literally "wave" and "overflow") connote the unrestrained, overflowing nature of romantic feeling (Erwin 2001).

28. Qiong Yao is a prolific Taiwanese author of romance novels. She is read almost universally by Shanghai schoolgirls, and some give her singular credit for popularizing ideals of melodramatic romantic performances among schoolgirls. See Grace's story below for a second reference.

29. Schiller argues that an aesthetic approach to life entails a playful approach: "Mit dem Angenehmen, mit dem Guten, mit dem Vollkommenen ist es dem Menschen *nur* ernst, aber mit der Schoenheit spielt er." (With the comfortable, the good and the perfect, man is *merely* earnest, but with beauty, he plays" [my translation].) (Schiller 1967, 130).

30. Grace, like several other Shanghai friends, preferred using her English name, which her Shanghaiese friends also used when discussing her with me. Probably my foreigner status influenced this usage.

31. According to Burke (1945, 514), the narrator in "romantic irony" uses a cast of negative characters as foils to express a morally superior attitude toward a philistine society. It thus lacks the humility of true irony. By Burke's definition, Grace's story, with its self-ironic reflections, is closer to "true irony" than most stories I describe below.

32. White 1973, 9–10.

33. For character irony (*Charakterironie*), see Japp (1983, 49). For practical irony (*praktische Ironie*), see Japp (ibid., 63).

34. Plummer 1995, 26.

35. Hollway 1996, 96.

36. The melodramatic narratives of these men remind me most of the narratives of two women prostitutes I interviewed. These prostitutes described themselves as cheated by men, becoming "victims" who then became "bad girls." Thompson (1995) discusses how such melodramatic narratives can be destructive for young women, denying their own agency in constructing their lives. For adult men, these narratives legitimate an emotional detachment in sexual relationships.

37. Illouz 1997, 293.

38. Stearns (1994) describes "cool" as an "emotional style"; I prefer "emotional rhetoric" because of the social communication and persuasion involved in the forms of self-expression I am describing.

39. Shanghai cultural critics point out that once strictly gendered emotional styles are now appropriated by the opposite sex. For instance, a newspaper article, "Zuo, zuo nan" ("Acting up male style," *Shenjiangfuwudaobao*, March 3, 1999), describes a male appropriation of a feminine form of temperamental flirting, "acting up" (*zuo*), which was previously considered a feminine practice (acting angry, pouting, etc.). Another article describes "cool" (*ku*) as a once exclusively male pose of emotional distance and reserve, now copied by women ("Cool, Do You Dare Not to Care?" *Haishangwentan*, March 1999).

40. Illouz 1998.

Chapter 7

1. Lei Feng was a PLA soldier held up as a model of patriotism and revolutionary fervor during a time when urban elites were accused of a lack of revolutionary spirit (Spence 1990, 597). Xu Hu was a 1995 model worker who was widely praised in the media for doing repairs on neighbors homes for free, displaying the virtue of not being concerned about profit, during a time when urban elites were accused of money worship.

2. According to a survey of 2,580 never-married women undergoing the required premarital medical exam in Shanghai (from August 1995 to July 1996), 69.3 percent had engaged in premarital sexual intercourse. (Gao, Yu, and Yuan 1997). Pan (1995) finds even higher percentages in Beijing in 1992, but it is unclear if people undergoing such exams consider themselves to be engaging in premarital sex. In the Shanghai study, of the 1,789 sexually experienced women, 48.6 percent had first experienced sex within the twelve months previous to the exam.

3. Honig and Hershatter 1988; Zha and Geng 1992; Pan 1993; Kaufman, Poston, Hirschl, and Stycos 1996; Evans 1997.

4. A 1991 sample survey of 2,190 college students at sixteen Shanghai campuses shows that 80 percent of male students and 60 percent of female students approved of sex before marriage if there is "mutual agreement and love." However, only 41 percent of male students and 48 percent of female students could accept that their future spouse will have had sexual relations with another person before them, the more critical question in China. Forty-five percent of female students and 51 percent of male students could accept extramarital sex, a typical finding in China (cf. Pan 1995 and Liu et al. 1997). With an upper limit of age twenty-two, 17 percent of female and 19 percent of male students reported sexual intercourse. Seventy-five percent of female students and 56 percent of male students reported sexual petting. Nine percent of female and 8 percent of male students reported homosexual behavior. Twenty-four percent of female students and 52 percent of male students reported masturbation. (About half of these students were from outside Shanghai, according to the researcher, Fan 1993.) A 1995 youth league survey of a broader segment of Shanghai youth,

including many already married, found slightly lower levels of support for premarital sex (*Qingnianbao*, April 4, 1995).

5. Reiss 1960.

6. Wouters 1998; Foucault 1978.

7. Gagnon and Simon 1973; Weeks 1985; Plummer 1995; Thompson 1995.

8. Burke 1950, 50.

9. Swidler 1986.

10. Tang and Zuo 2000; DeLamater and MacCorquodale 1979, 176.

11. DeLamater and MacCorquodale 1979, 232.

12. Plummer 1996; Weeks 1998; Wolf 1998.

13. Formal engagement (*dinghun*) was and remains rare in Shanghai, so these agreements were open to interpretation and easily devolved into the current norm of feelings as a criterion for premarital sex.

14. Holland 1996.

15. This older discourse—pure spiritual love versus impure physical love—is implied in the comment of Zen above, who opposes premarital sex in order to maintain "the purity of love." It was very common in early reform-era magazine articles.

16. Hochschilds 1979; Stearns 1994.

17. Wolf 1998.

18. Xue 2000, 160. In Shanghai the term is pronounced "*lasan.*"

19. "The Most Dangerous Age," *Young Generation*, June 1980.

20. Xue 2000, p.293.

21. As Evans points out, premarital sex was associated in 1950s magazine articles with "'dirt,' the only way out of which was to 'crawl'" (Evans 1997, 99), a metaphor of "filth" that was also found in early reform-era media representations.

22. The sexual connotations of the white-collar woman were especially evident in discussions with working-class men, but also in television programs such as *Chinese Misses in Foreign Firms*. The strong woman, or sexual female boss or entrepreneur, is sometimes characterized as "unfeminine" or sexless. However, she is also characterized by her sexual tactics. In Shanghai there was a popular expression that described this idea: "Behind every successful man there stands a woman, but behind every successful woman there are many men." The idea being that she has slept her way into her position.

23. The exception to this concern with motives rather than physical symbolism is the renewed discourse of "filth" applied to prostitutes, who are now seen as carriers of sexual diseases and are sometimes described as "unclean."

24. Thompson 1995.

25. DeLamater and MacCorquodale (1979, 232) describe the importance of close friends in defining sexual norms among U.S. teens.

26. Kelsky 1996.

27. Evans 1997, 103.

28. Ge Liming, "Feifatongjuu mianmianguan" (All about illegal cohabitation), *Xinminwanbao*, August 8, 2000, 7.

29. In the mid-1990s some Chinese cities, notably Wuhan, imposed fines on couples at premarital medical checkups who were found to have engaged in premarital sex. The pros and cons of such policies were debated in more liberal state-controlled newspapers, with most comments indicating that such policies were illegal and should be stopped. Wuhan officials reacted by denying that checkups were meant to enforce chastity, and that they were meant only to insure health ("Wuhan: chunuumojiancha yufenghua" [Reactions to Wuhan's

hymen checks], *Nanfangzaobao*, May 10, 1996; "Wuhan hunjian yulunhuaran" [The outcry over Wuhan's premarital checkup], *Beijingqingnianbao*, May 22, 1996).

30. Evans 1997, 99–100.

31. One new magazine, *Renzhichu*, published by the Guangdong Ministry for Family Planning and dedicated to sexual matters, did run some practical articles on premarital sex.

32. Yan Lijun and Yang Meijian, "The Telescope of the Girls' Dorm Room," *Renzhichu*, August 2000, 23.

Chapter 8

1. Burke 1945.

2. Charland 1999, 470.

3. Levine 1985.

4. See Harvey and Shalom (1997) for a review of the broad literature on language and desire.

5. The typical advice of magazine articles to a woman was if a man wanted sex "as an expression of love," she should demand "respect" (abstinence) from him as an expression of a truer love.

6. Li 1998; Li 1999.

7. Huizinga 1950.

8. Foucault 1978.

9. Pan (1993) reports that in a 1989 sample of Beijing college students, 34 percent had seen video pornography and 50.5 percent hoped to see it.

10. People wanting to act on such representations must overcome strong cultural inhibitions, however. For instance, both men and women informants described to me a feeling that the female genitalia are "dirty" as an inhibition against performing or accepting cunnilingus.

11. Hyde and DeLamater (1997, 292–93) argue that a performance ethic in adolescent sexual relations leads to increased variety in sexual practices. The idea of sex as a performance following a script is elaborated in Gagnon and Simon (1973), and the notion of orgasm as a disputed achievement is discussed in Duncombe and Marsden (1996).

12. Jankowiak 1993.

13. According to a survey of unmarried women, 39.9 percent of sexually experienced women had been pregnant or were currently pregnant, and of these pregnancies, 89.5 percent had ended in abortion. Also, 77.4 percent of women who became pregnant said they used no contraception, and 20.7 percent said that contraception failed. In general among these women with sexual experience, 17.6 percent said they used oral contraceptives, 43.6 percent used condoms, 14.4 percent used the method of calculating the "safe period," and 24.4 percent used withdrawal or "outside ejaculation." The survey shows that education and income have a strong positive effect on the use of contraception. Only 22 percent of those surveyed used contraception, mostly condoms, during first sex (Gao, Yu, and Yuan 1996).

14. Other than these verbal estimates, I don't have statistics from the late 1990s. In the late 1980s about one-quarter of all abortions in Shanghai were for unmarried women, a total of 15,593 abortions, double the number for unmarried women in 1982. The rates for 1988 were 56 per 1,000 women for unmarried women aged 15–19, 159 per 1,000 for unmarried women aged 20–24, and 94 per 1,000 for unmarried women aged 25–29 (Wu et al. 1992).

15. According to official statistics, rates of sexually transmitted diseases in the mid-

1990s were increasing rapidly (273 percent for herpes to 122 percent for syphilis) ("Woguo xingbing uiqing xingshiyanling," *Xinminwanbao*, November 26, 1995). Reports of sexually transmitted disease increased nationally from 1,000 per year in 1983 to over 300,000 per year in 1994, including about 80,000 cases of gonorrhea (Kang 1996). A study of STD patients in Shanghai found that less than 5 percent used condoms. Sixty-seven percent of male patients and 16 percent of female STD patients admitted to having at least one commercial sex encounter (Zhao, Qian, Miao, and Yu 1996). These statistics indicate that most men were contracting STDs from commercial sex, while women were likely contracting STDs from their regular partners who visited prostitutes.

Chapter 9

1. Zhang 1996, 22.

2. Lee 1999, 23–29.

3. Given the higher cost of karaoke, it seems likely that dance halls have far more business on a person-visit basis (*1997 Statistical Yearbook of Shanghai*).

4. The colloquial term "dance hall" (*wuting*), including discotheques, social dance halls, nightclubs, and song-and-dance halls.

5. Shanghai dance halls also involve very little organized taxi dancing, an illegal practice common in small-town dance halls I visited.

6. Some students changed the names of the colleges they attended. Some people made up a better-sounding profession. Some married people pretended to be single. Some poor men borrowed cell phones from friends to look like big moneys.

7. Huizinga 1950, 164–65.

8. Ibid., 44.

9. Turner 1982, 33.

10. Farrer 2000.

11. Savigliano 1992.

12. Farrer 1999.

13. Hanna 1988, 14.

14. My middle-aged male acquaintances typically described the women they found interesting, including those nearly forty years old, as "*xiaoguniang*" (girls).

15. Frith and McRobbie 1990; Hanna 1988; Rust 1969; Dyer 1990; Polhemus 1993.

16. McRobbie 1984, 134.

17. Refer to the appendix for a brief discussion of this issue.

18. Ward 1993.

19. Mungham 1976.

20. Lee 1999, 23–29.

21. "Evil Tendency Noted in Social Dance Parties in Shanghai," *Survey of the Chinese Mainland Press* 1441, January 2, 1957; originally *Shanghaiwenhuibao*, November 28, 1956. Thanks to Maris Gillette for bringing this article to my attention.

22. Walsh 1993.

23. As with many other areas of consumer culture, Shanghai dance hall admissions experienced significant deflation in the late 1990s.

24. Small privately run bars for foreigners first appeared near hotels in the mid-1980s, notably the Angel, Napoleon, and Manhattan near the Hilton. The first discotheque for foreigners opened in the Jinjiang Hotel in 1988. Judy's, the first expat nightclub with dancing, appeared only in 1993. DD's, which opened in 1995, is often credited as the first real "club," playing "underground house" music imported from New York.

25. Several Maoming Road clubs were closed in a nationwide August 2000 police action against vice and drugs. About fifteen foreigners were arrested for cavorting with prostitutes in one bar on nearby Julu Road, and its license was permanently revoked.

26. Thornton 1996.

27. There were also a few more expensive social dance venues in high-corner Shanghai, but they were not considered fashionable by any of my young informants nor of much interest to low-corner working-class informants.

28. Geertz 1973.

29. Farrer 1999.

30. "Dance leader" (lingwu) is the term Shanghaiese use to describe dancers who are paid to perform in discos, ostensibly to "lead" the dancing of customers. In recent years dance leaders have taken on more of the role of professional performers in these often very sexualized spectacles. There are more women dance leaders than men, but most clubs had both.

31. Time closed in 1999. According to Johnny, before it closed Time had become a "head-shaking club," where dealers (not the management) sold "head-shaking pills" (ecstasy) in a back room. As business slowed, a former Hong Kong associate at the club took some of the young men, including Johnny, to work in an underground "duck shop" (a duck is a male prostitute, a pun on the "pheasant," the female prostitute). There the young men entertained well-off women and an occasional gay friend of the Hong Kong boss. This club was also raided and closed.

32. The term "disco" (disike) is used in China to describe all forms of fast nonpartnered dancing including the artless jumping about that most youth (and the author) engaged in.

33. Short for "Test of English as a Foreign Language," a usual requirement for U.S. graduate admission.

34. Some women may be seeking more than a dance with foreigners. In 1996 one woman asked me to dance and then told me that she was "very open" and suggested we "make friends."

35. In 1995 there were forty-five institutions of higher education in Shanghai with a total enrollment of 144,082 students, of which 38.1 percent were women, explaining the general tendency for men to outnumber women at these dances (1996 Statistical Yearbook of Shanghai). Most colleges held dances on a weekly or even daily basis.

36. Huizinga 1950, 31, 42.

37. Fishing (informally asking for tips in discos) and working as K-jie (a formal job accompanying men in private karaoke rooms) were similar in that the work didn't require sexual intercourse, although some women did engage in sex with customers. Johnny, himself a dance hall hustler, claimed that the income for young women engaged in these activities dropped in Shanghai during the late 1990s, possibly a result of the bad labor market during the Asian financial crisis. Shanghai girls also were facing increased competition from out-of-town women willing to work for less.

38. "Ruiwu: zhunlingdianchuji" (Rave dance: the attack begins at midnight), Shenjiangfuwudaobao, March 24, 1999.

39. "Shencheng dixia yaotouba caifangji" (An investigative report into Shanghai's underground head-shaking bars), Xinminzhoukan, July 31, 2000, 21–25.

40. John Cloud and Nisid Hajari, "The Lure of Ecstasy," Time Magazine, November 13, 2000, 42–48.

41. Xinhua, "China Shuts Pubs in Vice Crackdown," Asahi Evening News, January 29, 2000, 5.

42. Most were between thirty and fifty. Younger single women usually went to discos. Young married women with small children (and fresher marriages) were also less likely to dance. Because of the one-child policy, many women had light child-care responsibilities by their mid-thirties. Grandparents provided easy baby-sitting. Many married women also reported leaving their children with their husbands while dancing. The legitimate daytime excuse for regular social dancing was "exercise." From my interviews, it seemed that a significant number of married dance hall regulars had spouses who were mah-jongg addicts and therefore didn't care where their partners spent their evenings (cf. Farrer 2000).

43. Neither Bai nor Zhu had ever used a condom.

44. This was before the U.S. bombing of the Chinese embassy in Yugoslavia in April 1999, after which I doubt the U.S. flag would have been waved. I don't recall seeing the stars and stripes at Come Again in 2000.

45. Farrer 2000.

46. According to some informants, there was also less work in more lucrative commercial sex and entertainment venues such as karaoke parlors in 1999. In the informal practices of prostitution in the social dance hall, prices for sex depended on many subjective factors. One man told me that older men paid 300 yuan, while younger men paid as little as 100. Others mentioned paying 150 yuan regardless of age. Professional prostitutes who picked up clients in fancy discotheques could expect ten times as much (or roughly 1,000 yuan), but prices seemed to be falling here also.

47. New regulations after the police actions in August 2000 mandate a 2 A.M. closing time for all nightlife establishments.

48. Stearns 1994.

49. "Cosmopolitan Swingers Utopia?" MetroZine, August 1, 2000, 12.

50. Around three thousand foreign-Chinese marriages were registered each year in the late 1990s (about 3 percent of total marriages), with 90 percent involving a Chinese female marrying a foreign male (1999 Statistical Yearbook of Shanghai). According to the municipal registrar who processes international marriages, the most common marriages were between Japanese and Chinese, followed by Chinese and Americans, many of whom were Chinese American males and local women.

51. For instance, almost no club in Shanghai turns away paying customers or allows a bouncer to choose among customers waiting at the door. Clubs exclude principally through price. Working-class venues exclude through intimidation by local men.

52. "Dass unter allen Zustaenden des Menschen gerade das Spiel und nur das Spiel es ist, was ihn vollstaendig macht und seine doppelte Natur auf einmal entfaltet" (Schiller 1967, 129; the translation is mine).

53. For Schiller, human freedom arises in the tension between form and substance, material reality and ideal strivings, duty and fate. (ibid., 138).

54. Winter 1995.

55. Milan Kundera, The Unbearable Lightness of Being (New York: Harper, 1984).

Methodological Appendix

1. Markowitz (1999), Chao (1999), Salamone (1999), and Poewe (1999) argue for the necessity of recognizing one's own sexual persona in ethnographic fieldwork about sexual issues.

2. Lunsing (1999) argues for a similar ethical position. See Markowitz and Ashkenazi (1999) and Kulick and Wilson (1995) for detailed discussions of the personal and ethical issues of sexuality in fieldwork.

3. Merton, Fiske and Kendall 1990 [1956], 142–47.

4. See Morgan (1997) for a discussion of focus group research design.

5. In general, the younger people reported a lower level of sexual experience than seems typical from survey data. Some might not have wanted to admit sexual experience on these forms, which were not anonymous vis-à-vis the moderators who collected them. Except for one private entrepreneur, incomes also are low and more homogenous than would be the case in 2000.

BIBLIOGRAPHY

1999 Statistical Yearbook of Shanghai. 1999. Beijing: China Statistical Publishing.

Altman, Dennis. 2001. *Global Sex.* Chicago: University of Chicago Press.

An Dun. 1999. *Juedui insi: Dangdai zhongguoren qinggan koushu jilu* (Absolute secrets: contemporary Chinese talk about love). Beijing: Xinshijichubanshe.

Ayim, Maryann. 1994. "Knowledge through the Grapevine: Gossip as Inquiry." In *Good Gossip,* edited by Robert F. Goodman and Aaron Ben-Ze'ev, 85–99. Lawrence: University Press of Kansas.

Bailey, Beth. 1988. *From Front Porch to Back Seat: Courtship in Twentieth-Century America.* Baltimore: Johns Hopkins University Press.

———. 1999. *Sex in the Heartland.* Cambridge: Harvard University Press.

Bakhtin, Mikhail M. 1981. "Discourse in the Novel." In *The Dialogic Imagination: Four Essays by M. M. Bakhtin,* edited by Michael Holquist, 257–422. Austin: University of Texas Press.

Barmé, Geremie R. 1993. "Soft Porn, Packaged Dissent and Nationalism: Notes on Chinese Culture in the 1990's." *Current History* 93.

———. 1999. *In the Red: On Contemporary Chinese Culture.* New York: Columbia University Press.

Bauman, Zygmunt. 1998. "On Postmodern Uses of Sex." *Theory, Culture and Society* 15 (nos. 3–4): 19–34.

Bech, Henning. 1998. "Citysex: Representing Sex in Public." *Theory, Culture and Society* 15 (nos. 3–4): 215–42.

Beck, Ulrich, and Elisabeth Beck-Gernsheim. 1995. *The Normal Chaos of Love,* translated by Mark Ritter and Jane Wiebel. Cambridge, Eng.: Polity Press.

Beck-Gernsheim, Elisabeth. 1998. "On the Way to a Post-Familial Family—From a Community of Need to Elective Affinities." *Theory, Culture and Society* 15 (nos. 3–4): 53–72.

Bell, Daniel. 1976. *The Cultural Contradictions of Capitalism.* New York: Basic Books.

Ben-Ze'ev, Aaron. 1994. "The Vindication of Gossip." In *Good Gossip,* edited by Robert F. Goodman and Aaron Ben-Ze'ev, 11–24. Lawrence: University Press of Kansas.

Berlant, Lauren, and Warner. 1998. "Sex in Public." *Critical Theory* 24 (no. 2): 547–66.

Berman, Marshall. 1982. *The Experience of Modernity: All that Is Solid Melts into Air.* New York: Simon and Schuster.

Bian, Yanjie. 1994. *Work and Inequality in Urban China.* Albany: State University of New York Press.

Brock, Bernard. 1995. "Evolution of Kenneth Burke's Criticism and Philosophy of Language." In *Kenneth Burke and Contemporary European Thought: Rhetoric in Transition*, edited by Bernard L. Brock, 1–33. Tuscaloosa: University of Alabama Press.

Brooks, Peter. 1976. *The Melodramatic Imagination: Balzac, Henry James, Melodrama, and the Mode of Excess*. New Haven: Yale University Press.

Burke, Kenneth. 1945. *A Grammar of Motives*. Berkeley: University of California Press.

———. 1950. *A Rhetoric of Motives*. Berkeley: University of California Press.

———. 1954. *Permanence and Change*. 2nd ed. Indianapolis: Bobbs Merrill.

———. 1989. *Kenneth Burke: On Symbols and Society*, edited by Joseph R. Gusfield. Chicago: University of Chicago Press.

Buss, David M. 1998. "Sexual Strategies Theory: Historical Origins and Current Status." *Journal of Sex Research* 35 (no. 1): 19–31.

Chan, Wellington K. K. 1999. "Selling Goods and Promoting a New Commercial Culture: The Four Premier Department Stores on Nanjing Road, 1917–1937." In *Inventing Nanjing Road: Commercial Culture in Shanghai, 1900–1945*, edited by Sherman Cochran, 19–36. Ithaca, N.Y.: Cornell University Press.

Chao, C. Antonia. 1999. "Performing like a P'o and Acting like a Big Sister: Reculturating into the Indigenous Lesbian Circle in Taiwan." In *Sex, Sexuality and the Anthropologist*, edited by Fran Markowitz and Michael Ashkenazi, 128–44. Urbana: University of Illinois Press.

Charland, Maurice. 1999. "Rehabilitating Rhetoric: Confronting Blindspots in Discourse and Social Theory." In *Beyond the Cultural Turn: New Directions in the Study of Society and Culture*, edited by Victoria E. Bonnell and Lynn Hunt, 464–74. Berkeley: University of California Press.

Chauncey, George. 1994. *Gay New York: Gender, Urban Culture and the Making of the Gay Male World*. New York: Basic Books.

Chen Danyan. 1998. *Shanghaide fenghuaxueyue* (Shanghai memorabilia). Beijing: Zuojiachubanshe.

Chou, Wah-shan. 2000. *Tongzhi: Politics of Same-Sex Eroticism in Chinese Societies*. London: Haworth Press.

Ci, Jiwei. 1994. *Dialectic of the Chinese Revolution: From Utopianism to Hedonism*. Stanford: Stanford University Press.

Cochran, Sherman. 1999. "Commercial Culture in Shanghai, 1900–1945: Imported or Invented? Cut Short or Sustained?" In *Inventing Nanjing Road: Commercial Culture in Shanghai, 1900–1945*, edited by Sherman Cochran, 3–18. Ithaca: Cornell University Press.

Code, Lorraine. 1994. "Gossip or in Praise of Chaos." In *Good Gossip*, edited by Robert F. Goodman and Aaron Ben-Ze'ev, 100–5. Lawrence: University Press of Kansas.

Collier, Jane Fishburne. 1997. *From Duty to Desire: Remaking Families in a Spanish Village*. Princeton: Princeton University Press.

Collins, Louise. 1994. "Gossip: A Feminist Defense." In *Good Gossip*, edited by Robert F. Goodman and Aaron Ben-Ze'ev, 106–16. Lawrence: University Press of Kansas.

Coward, Rosalind. 1984. *Female Desires: How They Are Sought, Bought, Sold and Packaged*. London: Paladin.

Cressey, Paul G. 1932. *The Taxi-Dance Hall: A Sociological Study of Commercialized Recreation and City Life*. Chicago: University of Chicago Press.

D'Emilio, John, and Estelle B. Freedman. 1988. *Intimate Matters: A History of Sexuality in America*. New York: HarperCollins.

Dai Yunyun. 1999. *Shanghai xiaojie* (Shanghai girl). Shanghai: Shanghaihuabaochubanshe.

Davis, Deborah. 1995. "Introduction: Urban China." In *Urban Spaces in Contemporary China: The Potential for Autonomy and Community in Post-Mao China*, edited by Deborah Davis, Richard Kraus, Barry Naughton, and Elizabeth J. Perry, 1–22. New York: Woodrow Wilson Center Press and Cambridge University Press.

———. 2000. "Introduction: A Revolution in Consumption." In *The Consumer Revolution in Urban China*, edited by Deborah Davis, 1–24. Berkeley: University of California Press.

de Certeau, Michael. 1984. *The Practice of Everyday Life*. Berkeley: University of California Press.

de Sousa, Ronald. 1994. "In Praise of Gossip: Indiscretion as a Saintly Virtue." In *Good Gossip*, edited by Robert F. Goodman and Aaron Ben-Ze'ev, 25–33. Lawrence: University Press of Kansas.

DeLamater, John D., and Janet Shibley Hyde. 1998. "Essentialism vs. Social Constructionism in the Study of Human Sexuality." *Journal of Sex Research* 35 (no. 1): 10–18.

DeLamater, John, and Patricia MacCorquodale. 1979. *Premarital Sexuality: Attitudes, Relationships, Behavior*. Madison: University of Wisconsin Press.

Deleuze, Giles, and Felix Guattari. 1983. *Anti-Oedipus: Capitalism and Schizophrenia*, translated by Robert Hurley, Mark Seem, and Helen R. Lane. Minneapolis: University of Minnesota Press.

Dikotter, Frank. 1995. *Sex, Culture, and Modernity in China: Medical Science and the Construction of Sexual Identities in the Early Republican Period*. Honolulu: University of Hawaii Press.

———. 1998. *Imperfect Conceptions: Medical Knowledge, Birth Defects, and Eugenics in China*. New York: Columbia University Press.

Douglas, Mary. 1966. *Purity and Danger: An Analysis of the Concepts of Pollution and Taboo*. New York: Ark.

Duncombe, Jean, and Dean Marsden. 1996. "Whose Orgasm Is This Anyway? 'Sex Work' in Long-Term Heterosexual Couple Relationships." In *Sexual Cultures: Communities, Values and Intimacy*, edited by Jeffrey Weeks and Janet Holland, 220–38. New York: St. Martin's Press.

Dutton, Michael. 1998. *Streetlife China*. Cambridge: Cambridge University Press.

Dyer, Richard. 1990. "In Defense of Disco." In *On Record: Rock, Pop, and the Written Word*, edited by Simon Frith and Andrew Goodwin, 410–18. New York: Pantheon.

Ehrenreich, Barbara, Elizabeth Hess, and Gloria Jacobs. 1986. *Re-making Love: The Feminization of Sex*. New York: Doubleday.

Engels, Friedrich. 1978. "The Origin of Family Private Property and the State." In *The Marx-Engels Reader*. 2nd ed., edited by Robert C. Tucker, 734–59. New York: Norton Press.

Erwin, Kathleen. 1999. "White Women, Male Desires: A Televisual Fantasy of the Transnational Chinese Family." In *Spaces of Their Own: Women's Public Sphere in Transnational China*, edited by Mayfair Mei-hui Yang, 232–60. Minneapolis: University of Minnesota Press.

———. 2000. "Heart-to-Heart, Phone-to-Phone: Family Values, Sexuality, and the Politics of Shanghai's Advice Hotlines." In *The Consumer Revolution in Urban China*, edited by Deborah Davis, 145–70. Berkeley: University of California Press.

———. 2001. "Consuming Desires: The Meanings of Romance in Post-Socialist China." Paper presented at the Association for Asian Studies Annual Meeting in Chicago.

Evans, Harriet. 1997. *Women and Sexuality in China: Female Sexuality and Gender since 1949*. New York: Continuum.

Evans, Mary. 1998. "'Falling in Love with Love Is Falling for Make-Believe': Ideologies of Romance in Post-Enlightenment Culture." *Theory, Culture and Society* 15 (nos. 3–4): 265–76.

Ewen, Stuart. 1988. *All Consuming Images: The Politics of Style in Contemporary Culture*. New York: Basic Books.

Fan Minsheng. 1993. "Dangdai daxueshengde xingxingwei yu xingguannian" (Sexual attitudes and behavior among contemporary university students). *Dazhongyixue* (June): 23–25.

Fan Weiguo. 1994. "Immigrant Society in Shanghai and the Development of the Shanghai School (Haipai) Culture during the Late Qing Dynasty." In *SASS PAPERS*, no. 5, 331–55. Shanghai: Shanghai Academy of Social Sciences.

Farrell, Thomas. 1995. "Comic History Meets Tragic History: Burke and Habermas on the Drama of Human Relations." In *Kenneth Burke and Contemporary European Thought: Rhetoric in Transition*, edited by Bernard L. Brock, 34–75. Tuscaloosa: University of Alabama Press.

———. 1999. "Knowledge, Consensus and Rhetorical Theory." In *Contemporary Rhetorical Theory: A Reader*, edited by John L. Lucaites, Celeste M. Condit, and Sally Caudill, 140–52. New York: Guilford Press.

Farrer, James. 1995. "A Sexual Opening in Taiwan: Narratives of Sexual Change in Taiwan Popular Magazines." Master's thesis. Chicago, University of Chicago.

———. 1998. "'Opening Up': Sex and the Market in Shanghai." Ph.D. diss. University of Chicago.

———. 1999. "Disco 'Super-Culture': Consuming Foreign Sex in the Chinese Disco." *Sexualities* 2 (no. 2, May): 147–66.

———. 2000. "Dancing through the Market Transition: Discotheque and Dance Hall Sociability in Shanghai." In *The Consumer Revolution in Urban China*, edited by Deborah Davis, 226–49. Berkeley: University of California Press.

———. 2001. "The Discourse of Extramarital Love in Shanghai." Paper presented at the Fifth Annual Asian Studies Conference Japan, Tokyo.

———. Forthcoming. "Idle Talk: Neighborhood Gossip as a Medium of Social Communication in Reform Era Shanghai." In *Social Networks in China: Institutions, Culture and the Changing Nature of Guanxi*, edited by Thomas Gold, Doug Guthrie, and David Wank. New York: Cambridge University Press.

Fass, Paula. 1977. *The Damned and the Beautiful: American Youth in the 1920's*. New York: Oxford University Press.

Fischer, Claude S. 1982. *To Dwell among Friends: Personal Networks in Town and City*. Chicago: University of Chicago Press.

Foucault, Michel. 1973. *The Order of Things: The Archeology of the Human Sciences*. New York: Random House.

———. 1978. *The History of Sexuality: An Introduction*. New York: Random House.

———. 1979. *Discipline and Punish: The Birth of the Prison*. New York: Vintage.

Frazier, David. 2000. "Inventing Oasis: Luxury Housing Advertisements and Reconfiguring Domestic Space in Shanghai." In *The Consumer Revolution in Urban China*, edited by Deborah Davis, 25–53. Berkeley: University of California Press.

Frith, Simon, and Angela McRobbie. 1990. "Rock and Sexuality." In *On Record: Rock, Pop, and the Written Word*, edited by Simon Frith and Andrew Goodwin. New York: Pantheon.

Frye, Northrop. 1957. *Anatomy of Criticism*. Princeton: Princeton University Press.

———. 1976. *The Secular Scripture: A Study of the Structure of Romance*. Cambridge: Harvard University Press.

Gagnon, John H., and William Simon. 1973. *Sexual Conduct: The Social Sources of Human Sexuality*. Chicago: Aldine.

Gallego Ayala, Juana. 1990. *Mujeres de papel: De Hola! a Vogue: La Prensa feminina en la actualidad.* Barcelona: Icaria.

Gamson, Joshua. 1998. *Freaks Talk Back: Tabloid Talk Shows and Sexual Nonconformity.* Chicago: University of Chicago Press.

Gao Ersheng, Yu Shaowen, Yuan Wei. 1996. "Shanghaishi weihun nuuqingnian biyun fangfa yingyong zhuangkuang jiqi yinxiang yinsu fenxi" (An analysis of the contraceptive behavior of unmarried Shanghai women). *1996 Shanghai xingxue yantaohui lunwenhuibian.* Shanghai: Shanghaishi xingjiaoyu xiehui.

Gaubatz, Piper Rae. 1995. "Urban Transformation in Post-Mao China: Impacts of the Reform Era on China's Urban Form." In *Urban Spaces in Contemporary China: The Potential for Autonomy and Community in Post-Mao China,* edited by Deborah Davis, Richard Kraus, Barry Naughton, and Elizabeth J. Perry, 28–60. New York: Woodrow Wilson Center Press and Cambridge University Press.

Geertz, Clifford. 1973. "Deep Play: Notes on a Balinese Cockfight." *The Interpretation of Cultures.* New York: Basic Books.

Giddens, Anthony. 1992. *The Transformation of Intimacy: Sexuality, Love and Eroticism in Modern Societies.* Stanford: Stanford University Press.

Gillette, Maris. 2000. "What's in a Dress? Brides in the Hui Quarter of Xi'an." In *The Consumer Revolution in Urban China,* edited by Deborah Davis, 80–106. Berkeley: University of California Press.

Glaser, Barney, and Anselm Strauss. 1967. *The Discovery of Grounded Theory.* Chicago: Aldine.

Goffman, Erving. 1959. *The Presentation of Self in Everyday Life.* New York: Anchor Books.

Griswold, Wendy. 1987. "A Methodological Framework for the Study of Culture." *Sociological Methodology* 17: 1–35.

———. 1989. "Formulaic Fiction: The Author as Agent of Elective Affinity." *Comparative Social Research* 2.

Gu Yawen and Gu Yujun. 1990a. "Aiqing jianhuodan" (Love shopping list). In *Zhongguoren de hunlianguan* (Chinese concepts of marriage and love), edited by Gu Yujun, 21–24. Taipei: Zhanglaoshichubanshe.

———. 1990b. "Bizhe yan, quan kao yuan" (Close your eyes and rely on Fate). In *Zhongguoren de hunlianguan* (Chinese concepts of marriage and love), edited by Gu Yujun, 42–44. Taipei: Zhanglaoshichubanshe.

Gusfield, Joseph R. 1989. "Introduction." In *Kenneth Burke: On Symbols and Society,* edited by Joseph R. Gusfield, 1–52. Chicago: University of Chicago Press.

Guthrie, Douglas. 2000. *Dragon in a Three-Piece Suit: Foreign Investment, Rational Bureaucracies and Market Reform in China.* Princeton: Princeton University Press.

Hanna, Judith Lynne. 1988. *Dance, Sex, and Gender: Signs of Identity, Dominance, Defiance, and Desire.* Chicago: University of Chicago Press.

Hannerz, Ulf. 1992. *Cultural Complexity: Studies in the Social Organization of Meaning.* New York: Columbia University Press.

Harvey, Keith, and Celia Shalom. 1997. "Introduction." In *Language and Desire: Encoding Sex, Romance and Intimacy,* edited by Keith Harvey and Celia Shalom, 1–20. London: Routledge.

Hebdidge, Dick. 1979. *Subculture: The Meaning of Style.* New York: New Directions.

Henriot, Christian, and Zheng Zu'an. 1999. *Atlas de Shanghai: Espaces et representations de 1849 à nos jours.* Paris: CNRS Editions.

Hershatter, Gail. 1992. "Regulating Sex in Shanghai: The Reform of Prostitution in 1920 and 1951." In *Shanghai Sojourners,* edited by Frederic Wakeman Jr. and Wen-hsin Yeh, 147–86. Berkeley: University of California Press.

————. 1994. "Modernizing Sex, Sexing Modernity: Prostitution in Early Twentieth-Century Shanghai." In *Engendering China:Women, Culture and the State*, edited by Christina K. Gilmartin, Gail Hershatter, Lisa Rofel and Tyrene White, 147–74. Cambridge: Harvard University Press.

————. 1997. *Dangerous Pleasures: Prostitution and Modernity in Twentieth-Century Shanghai*. Berkeley: University of California Press.

Hochschild, Arlie R. 1979. "Emotion Work, Feeling Rules and Social Structure." *American Journal of Sociology* 85: 551–75.

Holland, Janet. 1996. "Reputations: Journeying into Gendered Power Relations." In *Sexual Cultures: Communities,Values and Intimacy*, edited by Jeffrey Weeks and Janet Holland. New York: St. Martin's Press.

Hollway, Wendy. 1996 [1984]. "Gender Difference and the Production of Subjectivity." In *Feminism and Sexuality:A Reader*, edited by Stevi Jackson and Sue Scott, 84–100. Edinburgh: Edinburgh University Press.

Honig, Emily. 1992. "Migrant Culture in Shanghai: In Search of Subei Identity." In *Shanghai Sojourners*, edited by Frederic Wakeman Jr. and Wen-hsin Yeh, 239–65. Berkeley: University of California Press.

Honig, Emily, and Gail Hershatter. 1988. *PersonalVoices: ChineseWomen in the 1980's*. Stanford: Stanford University Press.

Hu, Hsien Chin. 1944. "The Chinese Concept of 'Face.'" *American Anthropology* 46: 45–64.

Huizinga, Johan. 1950. *Homo Ludens:A Study of the Play Element in Culture*. Boston: Beacon Press.

Hyde, Janet Shibley, and John DeLamater. 1997. *Understanding Human Sexuality*. Boston: McGraw Hill.

Illouz, Eva. 1997. *Consuming the Romantic Utopia: Love and the Cultural Contradictions of Capitalism*. Berkeley: University of California Press.

————. 1998. "The Lost Innocence of Love: Romance as a Postmodern Condition." *Theory, Culture and Society* 15 (nos. 3–4): 161–86.

Jacobs, Ronald N., and Philip Smith. 1997. "Romance, Irony and Solidarity." *Sociological Theory* 15 (no. 1): 60–80.

Jamieson, Lynn. 1999. "Intimacy Transformed? A Critical Look at the 'Pure Relationship.'" *Sociology* 33 (no. 3): 477–94.

Jankowiak, William R. 1993. *Sex, Death and Hierarchy in a Chinese City:An Anthropological Account*. New York: Columbia University Press.

————. 1995. "Introduction." In *Romantic Passion:A Universal Experience?*, edited by William Jankowiak. New York: Columbia University Press.

————. 1999. "Chinese Women, Gender and Sexuality: A Critical Review of Recent Studies." *Bulletin of Concerned Asian Scholars* 31 (no. 1): 31–47.

Japp, Uwe. 1983. *Theorie der Ironie*. Frankfurt: Vittorio Klosterman.

Kang Laiyi. 1996. "Zhongguo Aizibing liuxingde quushi jiqi fangzhi duice tantao" (A discussion of AIDS in China, its prevalence and countermeasures). *1996 Shanghai xingxue yantaohui lunwenhuibian*. Shanghai: Shanghaishi xingjiaoyu xiehui.

Kaufman, Gayle, Dudley L. Poston Jr., Thomas A. Hirschl, and J. Mayone Stycos. 1996. "Teenage Sexual Attitudes in China." *Social Biology* 43 (nos. 3–4): 141–54.

Kelsky, Karen. 1996. "Flirting with the Foreign: Interracial Sex in Japan's International Age." In *Global/Local: Cultural Production and the Transnational Imaginary*, edited by Rob Wilson and Wimal Dissanayake, 173–92. Durham, N.C.: Duke University Press.

Killick, Andrew P. 1995. "The Penetrating Intellect: On Being White, Straight, and Male in

Korea." In *Taboo: Sex, Identity and Erotic Subjectivity in Anthropological Fieldwork*, edited by Don Kulick and Margaret Wilson, 76–106. New York: Routledge.

Kipnis, Laura. 1998. "Adultery." *Critical Theory* 24 (no 2): 289–327.

Kon, Igor. 1993. "Sexuality and Culture." In *Sex and Russian Society*, edited by Igor Kon and James Riordan, 15–44. Bloomington: University of Indiana Press.

Kulick, Don, and Margaret Wilson, eds. 1995. *Taboo: Sex, Identity and Erotic Subjectivity in Anthropological Fieldwork*. New York: Routledge.

Kunz, Jean Lock. 1996. "From Maoism to ELLE: the Impact of Political Ideology on Fashion Trends in China." *International Sociology* 11 (no. 3): 317–35.

Kwok, R. Yin-Wang. 1981. "Trends of Urban Planning and Development in China." In *Urban Development in Modern China*, edited by Laurence J. C. Ma and Edward W. Hanten, 147–93. Boulder, Colo.: Westview Press.

Lakoff, George. 1987. *Women, Fire, and Dangerous Things: What Categories Reveal about the Mind*. Chicago: University of Chicago Press.

Lee, Haiyan. 2001. "The Republic of Virtue: Freedom, Ethics and the Education of Love in the Post-May Fourth Era." Paper presented at the 2001 Association for Asian Studies Annual Meeting in Chicago.

Lee, Leo Ou-fan. 1999. *Shanghai Modern: The Flower of a New Urban Culture in China, 1930–1945*. Cambridge: Harvard University Press.

Levine, Donald N. 1985. *The Flight from Ambiguity*. Chicago: University of Chicago Press.

Li Yinhe. 1998. *Zhongguonuuxingde ganqing yu xing* (Love and sexuality of Chinese women). Beijing: Jinrizhongguochubanshe.

Li Yinhe and Wang Xiaobo. 1992. *Tamen de shijie: Zhongguo nantongxinglian qunluo toushi* (Their world: a look at Chinese male homosexual groups). Taiyuan: Shanxirenminchubanshe.

Li Yinghong. 2001. "Shanghai Re-Narrativised: Weihui's Blank Fiction and the Commodification of Desire." Paper presented at the Fifth Annual Asian Studies Conference Japan, Tokyo.

Li Zechun. 1999. *Zhongguo shihun xianxiang diaocha* (An investigation of trial marriage in China). Beijing: Zhongguoshehuichubanshe.

Liang Xiaosheng. 1997. *Zhongguoshehui gejiecengfenxi* (An analysis of Chinese social classes). Beijing: Jingjiribaochubanshe.

Lindholm, Charles. 1998. "Love and Structure." *Theory, Culture and Society* 15 (nos. 3–4): 243–64.

Link, E. Perry. 1981. *Mandarin Ducks and Butterflies: Popular Fiction in Early Twentieth-Century Chinese Cities*. Berkeley: University of California Press.

Liu, Dalin, Nan Lun Ng, Li Ping Zhou, and Erwin J. Haeberle. 1997. *Sexual Behavior in Modern China: Report on the Nationwide Survey of 20,000 Men and Women*. New York: Continuum.

Liu Na'ou. 1997. *Liu Na'ou xiaoshuo quanpian* (The collected stories of Liu Na'ou). Shanghai: Xuelinchubanshe.

Liu, Xin. 2000. *In One's Own Shadow: An Ethnographic Account of the Condition of Post-Reform Rural China*. Berkeley: University of California Press.

Long Yintai. 1999. *A, Shanghainanren* (Oh, Shanghai man!). Shanghai: Xuelinchubanshe.

Longmore, Monica. 1998. "Symbolic Interactionism and the Study of Sexuality Status." *Journal of Sex Research* 35 (no. 1): 44–57.

Lu, Hanchao. 1995. "Creating Urban Outcasts: Shantytowns in Shanghai, 1920–1950." *Journal of Urban History* 21 (no. 5): 563–96.

———. 1999a. *Beyond the Neon Lights: Everyday Shanghai in the Early Twentieth Century*. Berkeley: University of California Press.

————. 1999b. "'The Seventy-two Tenants': Residence and Commerce in Shanghai's *Shiku-men* Houses." In *Inventing Nanjing Road: Commercial Culture in Shanghai, 1900–1945*, edited by Sherman Cochran, 133–86. Ithaca, N.Y.: Cornell University Press.

Lu, Hanlong. 2000. "To Be Privately Comfortable in an Egalitarian Society: A Study of Chinese Urban Consumer Culture." In *The Consumer Revolution in Urban China*, edited by Deborah Davis, 124–44. Berkeley: University of California Press.

Lu Yang. 1969. "The Correct Handling of Love, Marriage, and Family Problems." *Chinese Sociology and Anthropology* 1 (no. 3): 7–59.

Luhmann, Niklas. 1986. *Love as Passion: The Codification of Intimacy.* Cambridge: Harvard University Press.

Lull, James. 1991. *China Turned On: Television Reform and Resistance.* New York: Routledge.

Lunsing, Wim. 1999. "Life on Mars: Love and Sex in Fieldwork on Sexuality and Gender in Urban Japan." In *Sex, Sexuality and the Anthropologist*, edited by Fran Markowitz and Michael Ashkenazi, 175–96. Urbana: University of Illinois Press.

Ma, Laurence J. C. 1981. "Urban Housing Supply in the People's Republic of China." In *Urban Development in Modern China*, edited by Laurence J. C. Ma and Edward W. Hanten. Boulder, Colo.: Westview Press.

MacIntyre, Alisdair. 1981. *After Virtue: A Study in Moral Theory.* Notre Dame: University of Notre Dame Press.

Madsen, Richard. 1995. *China and the American Dream: A Moral Inquiry.* Berkeley: University of California Press.

Mao Dun. 1979 [1933]. *Midnight.* 2nd ed., translated by Teh Chien-yu. Beijing: Beijing Foreign Language Press.

Marcuse, Herbert. 1955. *Eros and Civilization: A Philosophical Inquiry into Freud.* Boston: Beacon Press.

Markowitz, Fran. 1999. "Sexing the Anthropologist: Implications for Ethnography." In *Sex, Sexuality and the Anthropologist*, edited by Fran Markowitz and Michael Ashkenazi. Urbana: University of Illinois Press.

Markowitz, Fran, and Michael Ashkenazi, eds. 1999. *Sex, Sexuality and the Anthropologist.* Urbana: University of Illinois Press.

McCracken, Ellen. 1993. *Decoding Women's Magazines.* New York: St. Martin's Press.

McGee, Michael Calvin. 1999. "Text, Context and the Fragmentation of Contemporary Culture." In *Contemporary Rhetorical Theory: A Reader*, edited by John L. Lucaites, Celeste M. Condit, and Sally Caudill, 65–78. New York: Guilford Press.

McMahon, Keith. 1995. *Misers, Shrews, and Polygamists.* Durham, N.C.: Duke University Press.

McRobbie, Angela. 1984. "Dance and Social Fantasy." In *Gender and Generation*, edited by Angela McRobbie and Mica Nava. London: Macmillan.

————. 1990. "Settling Accounts with Subcultures: A Feminist Critique." In *On Record: Rock, Pop, and the Written Word*, edited by Simon Frith and Andrew Goodwin. New York: Pantheon.

————. 1991. *Feminism and Youth Culture: From Jackie to Just Seventeen.* Boston: Unwin Hyman.

————. 1994. "Shut Up and Dance: Youth Culture and Changing Modes of Femininity." *Postmodernism and Popular Culture.* New York: Routledge.

Merton, Robert K., Marjorie Fiske, and Patricia L. Kendall. 1990 [1956]. *The Focused Interview: A Manual of Problems and Procedures.* 2nd ed. New York: Free Press.

Mian Mian. 1997. *La La La.* Hong Kong: Xianggangxinshijichubanshe.

————. 2000. *Tang* (Candy). Beijing: Zhongguoxijuchubanshe.

Mills, C. Wright. 1940. "Situated Actions and Vocabularies of Motive." *American Sociological Review* 5 (December): 55–61.

Modell, John. 1983. "Dating Becomes the Way of American Youth." In *Essays on the Family and Historical Change*, edited by Leslie Moch. College Station: Texas A&M University Press.

Modleski, Tania. 1982. *Loving with a Vengeance: Mass-Produced Fantasies for Women*. New York: Routledge.

Morgan, David L. 1997. *Focus Groups as Qualitative Research*. 2nd ed. Thousand Oaks, Calif.: Sage.

Morreall, John. 1994. "Gossip and Humor." In *Good Gossip*, edited by Robert F. Goodman and Aaron Ben-Ze'ev, 156–64. Lawrence: University Press of Kansas.

Mu Shiying. 1996. *Mu Shiying xiaoshuoquanji* (The collected stories of Mu Shiying). Beijing: Zhongguowenlianchubanshe.

Mungham, Geoff. 1976. "Youth in Pursuit of Itself." In *Working Class Youth Culture*, edited by Geoff Mungham and Geoff Peterson, 182–204. London: Routledge.

Murphey, Rhodes. 1974. "The Treaty Ports and China's Modernization." In *The Chinese City between Two Worlds*, edited by Mark Elvin and G. William Skinner, 17–72. Stanford: Stanford University Press.

Nee, Victor. 1996. "The Emergence of a Market Society: Changing Mechanisms of Stratification in China." *American Journal of Sociology* 101 (no. 4): 908–49.

Ning, Yuemin, and Zhongmin Yan. 1995. "The Changing Industrial and Spatial Structure in Shanghai." *Urban Geography* 16 (no. 7): 577–94.

Ong, Aihwa. 1999. *Flexible Citizenship: The Cultural Logics of Transnationality*. Durham, N.C.: Duke University Press.

Oppenheimer, Valerie Kincade. 1988. "A Theory of Marriage Timing." *American Journal of Sociology* 94 (no. 3): 563–91.

Pan Suiming. 1993. "A Sex Revolution in Current China." *Journal of Psychology and Human Sexuality* 6 (no. 2): 1–14.

———. 1995. *Zhongguo xingxianzhuang* (The state of sexuality in China). Beijing: Guangmingribao chubanshe.

Pan Xiangli. 1999. "Ku: ni gan bu gan buzaihu?" (Cool: do you dare not care?). *Haishangwentan* (March).

Parish, William, and Sarah Busse. 2000. "Gender and Work." In *Chinese Urban Life under Reform: The Changing Social Contract*, edited by Wenfang Tang and William L. Parish, 209–31. Cambridge: Cambridge University Press.

Parish, William, and James Farrer. 2000. "Gender and Family." In *Chinese Urban Life under Reform: The Changing Social Contract*, edited by Wenfang Tang and William L. Parish, 232–72. Cambridge: Cambridge University Press.

Park, Robert. 1969 [1906]. "The City: Suggestions for the Investigation of Human Behavior in the Urban Environment." In *Classic Essays on the Culture of Cities*, edited by Richard Sennett, 91–130. Englewood Cliffs, N.J.: Prentice-Hall.

Parsons, Talcott. 1968 [1937]. *The Structure of Social Action*. Vols. 1, 2. New York: Free Press.

Peiss, Kathy. 1986. *Cheap Amusements: Working Women and Leisure in Turn-of-the-Century New York*. Philadelphia: Temple University Press.

———. 1989. "'Charity Girls' and City Pleasures: Historical Notes on Working-Class Sexuality, 1880–1920." In *Passion and Power: Sexuality in History*, edited by Kathy Peiss and Christina Simmons, 57–69. Philadelphia: Temple University Press.

Plummer, Kenneth. 1995. *Telling Sexual Stories: Power, Change and Social Worlds*. London: Routledge.

———. 1996. "Intimate Citizenship and the Culture of Sexual Story Telling." In *Sexual Cultures: Communities, Values and Intimacy*, edited by Jeffrey Weeks and Janet Holland, 34–52. New York: St. Martin's Press.

Poewe, Karla. 1999. "Afterword: No Hiding Place: Reflections on the Confessions of

Manda Cesara." In *Sex, Sexuality and the Anthropologist*, edited by Fran Markowitz and Michael Ashkenazi, 197–206. Urbana: University of Illinois Press.

Polhemus, Ted. 1993. "Dance, Gender and Culture." In *Dance, Gender and Culture*, edited by Helen Thomas. New York: St. Martin's Press.

Post, Robert. 1994. "The Legal Regulation of Gossip: Backyard Chatter and the Mass Media." In *Good Gossip*, edited by Robert F. Goodman and Aaron Ben-Ze'ev, 65–71. Lawrence: University Press of Kansas.

Potter, Sulamith Heins. 1988. "The Cultural Construction of Emotion in Rural Chinese Social Life." *Ethos* 16 (no. 2): 181–208.

Qian Zhongshu. 1979 [1947]. *Fortress Besieged*, translated by Jeanne Kelly and Nathan K Mao. Bloomington: Indiana University Press.

———. 1980 [1947]. *Weicheng* (Fortressed besieged). Beijing: Renminwenxuechubanshe.

Radway, Janice A. 1984. *Reading the Romance: Women, Patriarchy and Popular Literature*. Chapel Hill: University of North Carolina Press.

Redfield, Robert, and Milton Singer. 1969. "The Cultural Role of Cities." In *Classic Essays on the Culture of Cities*, edited by Richard Sennett, 206–20. Englewood Cliffs, N.J.: Prentice-Hall.

Reiss, Ira L. 1960. *Premarital Sexual Standards in America*. New York: Macmillan.

Rich, Adrienne. 1996 [1980]. "Compulsory Heterosexuality and Lesbian Existence." In *Feminism and Sexuality: A Reader*, edited by Stevi Jackson and Sue Scott, 130–43. Edinburgh: Edinburgh University Press.

Rival, Laura, Don Slater, and Daniel Miller. 1998. "Sex and Sociality: Comparative Ethnographies of Sexual Objectification." *Theory, Culture and Society* 15 (nos. 3–4): 295–322.

Rofel, Lisa. 1999. *Other Modernities: Gendered Yearnings in China after Socialism*. Berkeley: University of California Press.

Rorty, Richard. 1989. *Contingency, Solidarity and Irony*. Cambridge: Cambridge University Press.

Rose, Sonya O. 1999. "Cultural Analysis and Moral Discourses: Episodes, Continuities, and Transformations." In *Beyond the Cultural Turn: New Directions in the Study of Society and Culture*, edited by Victoria E. Bonnell and Lynn Hunt, 217–40. Berkeley: University of California Press.

Rothman, Ellen. 1987. *Hands and Hearts: A History of Courtship in America*. Cambridge: Harvard University Press.

Ruan, Fang Fu. 1992. *Sex in China: Studies in Sexology in Chinese Culture*. New York: Plenum.

Rust, Frances. 1969. *Dance in Society: An Analysis of the Relationship between the Social Dance and Society in England from the Middle Ages to the Present Day*. London: Routledge.

Sabini, John, and Maury Silver. 1982. *Moralities of Everyday Life*. New York: Oxford University Press.

Salamone, Frank A. 1999. "'Oh, There You Are!' Sex and the Heterosexual Anthropologist." In *Sex, Sexuality and the Anthropologist*, edited by Fran Markowitz and Michael Ashkenazi, 57–74. Urbana: University of Illinois Press.

Savigliano, Marta E. 1992. "Tango in Japan and the World Economy of Passion." In *Re-made in Japan: Everyday Life and Consumer Taste in a Changing Society*, edited by Joseph J. Tobin, 235–51. New Haven: Yale University Press.

Schell, Orville. 1988. *Discos and Democracy: China in the Throes of Reform*. New York: Pantheon.

Schiller, Friedrich. 1967. *Friedrich Schiller Ueber die Aesthetische Erziehung des Menschen*. Munich: Wilhelm Fink Verlag.

Schudson, Michael. 1984. *Advertising: The Uneasy Persuasion*. New York: Basic Books.

Seigel, Jerold. 1999. "Problematizing the Self." In *Beyond the Cultural Turn: New Directions in the*

Study of Society and Culture, edited by Victoria E. Bonnell and Lynn Hunt, 281–314. Berkeley: University of California Press.

Sennett, Richard. 1970. *The Uses of Disorder: Personal Identity and City Life*. New York: W. W. Norton.

Sergeant, Harriet. 1990. *Shanghai: Collision Point of Cultures 1918–1939*. New York: Crown.

Sewell, William H., Jr. 1999. "The Concept(s) of Culture." In *Beyond the Cultural Turn: New Directions in the Study of Society and Culture*, edited by Victoria E. Bonnell and Lynn Hunt, 35–61. Berkeley: University of California Press.

Shaw, Victor N. 1996. *Social Control in China: A Study in Chinese Work-Units*. Westport, Conn.: Praeger.

Shih, Shu-mei. 1996. "Gender, Race and Semicolonialism: Liu Na'ou's Urban Shanghai Landscape." *Journal of Asian Studies* 55 (no. 4): 934–56.

Simmel, Georg. 1969. "The Metropolis and Mental Life." In *Classic Essays on the Culture of Cities*, edited by Richard Sennett, 47–60. Englewood Cliffs, N.J.: Prentice-Hall.

———. 1971. "Sociability." In *Georg Simmel on Individuality and Social Forms*, edited by Donald N. Levine, 127–40. Chicago: University of Chicago Press.

———. 1984. "Flirtation." In *Georg Simmel: On Women, Sexuality, and Love*, edited by Guy Oakes, 133–52. New Haven: Yale University Press.

Smith, Michael. 1979. *The City and Social Theory*. New York: St. Martin's Press.

Soja, Edward W. 1996. *Thirdspace: Journeys to Los Angeles and Other Real-and-Imagined Places*. London: Blackwell.

Spence, Jonathan D. 1990. *In Search of Modern China*. New York: Norton.

Sprecher, Susan. 1998. "Social Exchange Theories and Sexuality." *Journal of Sex Research* 35 (no. 1): 32–43.

Stacey, Judith. 1983. *Patriarchy and Socialist Revolution in China*. Berkeley: University of California Press.

Stearns, Peter N. 1994. *American Cool: Constructing a Twentieth-Century Emotional Style*. New York: New York University Press.

Suttles, Gerald D. 1968. *The Social Order of the Slum: Ethnicity and Territory in the Inner City*. Chicago: University of Chicago Press.

———. 1984. "The Cumulative Texture of Local Urban Culture." *American Journal of Sociology* 90 (no. 2): 283–304.

Swanson, Gillian. 1995. "'Drunk with the Glitter': Consuming Spaces and Sexual Geographies." In *Postmodern Cities and Spaces*, edited by Sophie Watson and Katherine Gibson, 80–98. London: Blackwell.

Swidler, Ann. 1986. "Culture in Action: Symbols and Strategies." *American Sociological Review* 51: 273–86.

Tang, Wenfang, and William L. Parish. 2000. *Chinese Urban Life under Reform: The Changing Social Contract*. Cambridge: Cambridge University Press.

Tang, Shengming, and Zuo Jiping. 2000. "Dating Attitudes and Behaviors of American and Chinese College Students." *Social Science Journal* 37 (no. 1): 67–78.

Taubman, Wolfgang. 1994. "Shanghai: Chinas Wirtschaft Metropole." In *Megastädte in der Dritten Welt*, edited by Erdmann Gormsen and Andreas Thimm, 45–72. Mainz: Universität Mainz.

Taylor, Gabriele. 1994. "Gossip as Moral Talk." In *Good Gossip*, edited by Robert F. Goodman and Aaron Ben-Ze'ev, 134–46. Lawrence: University Press of Kansas.

Theophrastes. 1953. *The Characters of Theophrastus*, translated and edited by J. M. Edmonds. Cambridge: Harvard University Press.

Thompson, Sarah. 1995. *Going All the Way: Teenage Girls' Tales of Sex, Romance and Pregnancy*. New York: Hill and Wang.

Thornton, Sarah. 1996. *Club Cultures: Music, Media and Subcultural Capital*. Hanover, Conn.: Wesleyan University Press.

Tomlinson, Alan, ed. 1990. *Consumption, Identity and Style: Marketing, Meanings and the Packaging of Pleasure*. London: Routledge.

Touraine, Alain. 1990. "The Idea of Revolution." In *Global Culture: Nationalism, Globalization and Modernity*, edited by Mike Featherstone, 121–42. London: Sage.

Turner, Victor. 1982. *From Ritual to Theater: The Human Seriousness of Play*. New York: Performing Arts Journal Publications.

Ullman, Sharon R. 1997. *Sex Seen: The Emergence of Modern Sexuality in America*. Berkeley: University of California Press.

Waara, Carrie. 1999. "Invention, Industry, Art: The Commercialization of Culture in Republican Art Magazines." In *Inventing Nanjing Road: Commercial Culture in Shanghai, 1900–1945*, edited by Sherman Cochran, 61–90. Ithaca, N.Y.: Cornell University Press.

Wakeman, Frederic, and Wen-hsin Yeh. 1992. "Introduction." In *Shanghai Sojourners*, edited by Frederic Wakeman Jr. and Wen-hsin Yeh. Berkeley: University of California Press.

Walsh, David. 1993 "'Saturday Night Fever': An Ethnography of Disco Dancing." In *Dance, Gender and Culture*, edited by Helen Thomas. New York: St. Martin's Press.

Wank, David. 1998. *Commodifying Communism: Markets, Trust and Politics in a South China City*. Cambridge: Cambridge University Press.

Ward, Andrew H. 1993. "Dancing in the Dark: Rationalism and the Neglect of Social Dance." In *Dance, Gender and Culture*, edited by Helen Thomas. New York: St. Martin's Press.

Weber, Max. 1976. *The Protestant Ethic and the Spirit of Capitalism*, translated by Talcott Parsons. New York: Scribner.

Weeks, Jeffrey. 1985. *Sexuality and Its Discontents*. London: Routledge.

———. 1998. "The Sexual Citizen." *Theory, Culture and Society* 15 (nos. 3–4): 35–52.

Weeks, Jeffrey, and Janet Holland. 1996. "Introduction." In *Sexual Cultures: Communities, Values and Intimacy*, edited by Jeffrey Weeks and Janet Holland, 1–16. New York: St. Martin's Press.

Wehrfritz, George. 1996. "China's Sexual Revolution: Whisper it Softly—There's More to Life than Economics." *Newsweek* (International Edition), April 15, 1996.

Wei Hui. 1999. *Shanghai baobei* (Shanghai baby). Shenyang: Chunfengwenyichubanshe.

Wei, Betty Peh-T'i. 1987. *Shanghai: Crucible of Modern China*. New York: Oxford University Press.

Wernick, Andrew. 1991. *Promotional Culture: Advertising, Ideology and Symbolic Expression*. London: Sage.

Wess, Robert. 1996. *Kenneth Burke: Rhetoric, Subjectivity, Postmodernism*. New York: Cambridge University Press.

White, Hayden. 1973. *Metahistory: The Historical Imagination in Nineteenth-Century Europe*. Baltimore: Johns Hopkins University Press.

Whyte, Martin King, and William L. Parish. 1984. *Urban Life in Contemporary China*. Chicago: University of Chicago Press.

Whyte, William Foote. 1943. *Street Corner Society: The Social Order of an Italian Slum*. Chicago: University of Chicago Press.

Williams, Rosalind. 1991. "The Dreamworld of Mass Consumption." In *Rethinking Popular*

Culture, edited by Chandra Mukerji and Michael Schudson, 198–236. Berkeley: University of California Press.

Willis, Paul. 1984. *Learning to Labor: How Working Class Kids Get Working Class Jobs.* New York: Columbia University Press.

Wilson, Elizabeth. 1985. *Adorned in Dreams: Fashion and Modernity.* Berkeley: University of California Press.

———. 1991. *The Sphinx in the City: Urban Life, the Control of Disorder, and Women.* Berkeley: University of California Press.

———. 1995. "The Invisible Flâneur." In *Postmodern Cities and Spaces*, edited by Sophie Watson and Katherine Gibson, 59–79. London: Blackwell.

Winship, Janice. 1987. *Inside Women's Magazines.* New York: Pandora.

Winter, Scarlett Christiana. 1995. *Spielformen der Lebenswelt.* Muenchen: Wilhelm Fink Verlag.

Wirth, Louis. 1938. "Urbanism as a Way of Life." *American Journal of Sociology* 44 (July).

Wolf, Margery. 1972. *Women and the Family in Rural Taiwan.* Stanford: Stanford University Press.

Wolf, Naomi. 1998. *Promiscuities: The Secret Struggle for Womanhood.* New York: Fawcett Columbine.

Wouters, Cas. 1987. "Developments in the Behavioural Codes between the Sexes: The Formalization of Informalization in the Netherlands 1930–85." *Theory, Culture and Society* 4 (nos. 2–3): 405–28.

———. 1998. "Balancing Sex and Love in the 1960's Sexual Revolution." *Theory, Culture and Society* 15 (nos. 3–4): 187–214.

Wu Liang. 1998. *Lao Shanghai: Yishi de shiguang* (Old Shanghai: a time long past). Nanjing: Jiangsumeishuchubanshe.

Wu, Z. C., E. S. Gao, X. Y. Ku, S. Y. Lu, M. J. Wang, W. C. Hong, and L. P. Chow. 1992. "Induced Abortion among Unmarried Women in Shanghai, China." *International Family Planning Perspectives* 18: 51.

Wuthnow, Robert. 1987. *Meaning and Moral Order.* Berkeley: University of California.

Wuthnow, Robert, and Marsha Witten. 1988. "New Directions in the Sociology of Culture." *Annual Review of Sociology* 14: 49–67.

Xu Anqi and Ye Wenzheng. 1999. *Zhongguo hunyin zhiliang yanjiu* (Studies on the Chinese marital quality). Beijing: Zhongguoshehuikexuechubanshe.

Xu, Xiaohe, and Martin K. Whyte. 1990. "Love Matches and Arranged Marriages: A Chinese Replication." *Journal of Marriage and the Family* 52: 709–22.

Xu Xiaoqun. 1996. "The Discourse of Love, Marriage and Sexuality in Post-Mao China: A Reading of the Journalistic Literature on Women." *Positions* 4 (no. 2): 381–414.

Xue Liyong. 2000. *Shanghaixianhua* (Shanghai sayings). Shanghai: Shanghaishehuikexueyuanchubanshe.

Yang Dongping. 1992. *Chengshijifeng: Beijing he Shanghai de wenhua jingshen* (City fashions: the cultural spirits of Beijing and Shanghai). Beijing: Dongfangchubanshe.

Yang, Mayfair Mei-hui. 1994. *Gifts, Favors and Banquets: The Art of Social Relationships in China.* Ithaca: Cornell University Press.

———. 1999. "From Gender Erasure to Gender Difference: State Feminism, Consumer Sexuality and Women's Public Sphere in China." In *Spaces of Their Own: Women's Public Sphere in Transnational China*, edited by Mayfair Mei-hui Yang, 35–67. Minneapolis: University of Minnesota Press.

Yeh, Wen-hsin. 1992. "Progressive Journalism and Shanghai's Petty Urbanites: Zuo Taofen and the Shenghuo Enterprise, 1926–1945." In *Shanghai Sojourners*, edited by Frederic Wakeman Jr. and Wen-hsin Yeh, 186–238. Berkeley: University of California Press.

Yu, Anthony C. 1997. *Re-reading the Stone: Desire and the Making of Fiction in* Dream of the Red Chamber. Princeton: Princeton University Press.

Yuan Jin. 1994. "Awakening and Escaping: Love Fiction in the Early Days of the Republic of China." In *SASS Papers*, no. 5, 230–49. Shanghai: Shanghai Academy of Social Sciences.

Zha Bo, and Geng Wenxiu. 1992. "Sexuality in Urban China." *Australian Journal of Chinese Affairs* (no. 28): 1–20.

Zha, Jianying. 1995. *China Pop: How Soap Operas, Tabloids, and Bestsellers Are Transforming a Culture.* New York: New Press.

Zhang, Yingjin. 1996. *The City in Modern Chinese Literature and Film: Configurations of Space, Time, and Gender.* Stanford: Stanford University Press.

Zhao, Yuezhi. 1998. *Media, Market and Democracy in China: Between the Party Line and the Bottom Line.* Urbana: University of Illinois Press.

Zhao Pengfei, Qian Hanzu, Miao Mingmei, Yu Hong. 1996. "STD bingren de shehuixinli xingweixue" (A study of STD patients' psychosocial behavior). *1996 Shanghai xingxue yantaohui lunwenhuibian.* Shanghai: Shanghaishi xingjiaoyu xiehui.

Zhong, Xueping. 2000. *Masculinity Besieged? Issues of Modernity and Male Subjectivity in Chinese Literature of the Late Twentieth Century.* Durham, N.C.: Duke University Press.

Zhuang Huiqiu and Gu Yujun. 1990. "Wei jiehun er lianai" (Love for the sake of marriage). In *Zhongguoren de hunlianguan* (Chinese concepts of marriage and love), edited by Gu Yujun, 42–44. Taipei: Zhanglaoshichubanshe.

INDEX